"Eight years after its original publication, *Transforming Body Image*—a book which has influenced countless clinicians—is still required reading. Filled with ideas, it remains an essential source for body image therapy."
— Susan C. Wooley, Ph.D., co-editor
Eating Disorders: A Feminist Perspective

"Marcia's gentle guidance has been instrumental in helping my clients get to the root of their feelings about their bodies. *Transforming Body Image* is indeed transformational as it empowers women to stop battling their bodies, heal the wounds from within and celebrate a life of unlimited choices inside a body they can happily claim as their own."
— Gail Johnston, author
If I Know I Should Be Exercising,
Why Aren't I? A Guide For Women

"*Transforming Body Image* offers clarity, wisdom and caring guidance for women struggling with concerns about weight and body image. (And who isn't?) Full of practical imagery exercises, it offers much food for thought and action. A wonderful resource for professionals working on these issues with individuals or groups."
— Pat Lyons, R.N., M.A., co-author
Great Shape: The First Fitness Guide
for Large Women

Testimonials from readers of
Transforming Body Image
and participants in
Transforming Body Image Workshops
upon which the book is based:

"I had been totally conditioned to believe that I had to change my body on the outside before I could feel good about myself. *Transforming Body Image* taught me that I needed to learn to love myself first, and to change my internal images before any external changes could happen."

"*Transforming Body Image* freed me from the tyranny of hatred for my body. I have a history of eating disorders. For a time I was anorexic, and later became bulimic...I didn't start losing weight for about a year after I did the program. First I stopped dieting, then eventually I stopped binging also. I have a general attitude of gentleness toward myself which gives me a much greater sense of peace."

"I know that my body will never be a thin body...but I can still be really comfortable with it at whatever weight my body settles at. I'm eating in a way that supports me, and my body will find its way to a comfortable weight. I value myself as I am. My sense of myself is not tied up with how I look, so any weight my body is comfortable at will be fine with me."

"I have recently read *Transforming Body Image*. The material in the book is invaluable. Thank you—from the bottom of my personal and professional hearts."

"It will help me help my patients feel better about themselves. The work can be applied to both males and females. I feel men could benefit more than perhaps they think they would."

"The visualizations were an excellent source of information for me, about me. They also helped me break through some resistance that had been impeding my progress for years. Seeing more clearly how I have mistreated my body has already started me treating myself differently."

"I am teaching a course for women on this topic and have greatly enjoyed using this book. My thanks and congratulations to Marcia Hutchinson for such a fine work.

"I will be forever grateful that our paths have crossed. I have continued to listen to the tapes and know I am healing each time I make that investment in myself."

"I am a dance/movement therapist working primarily with eating disordered patients...Your book has been invaluable in my work. The exercises are extremely powerful, and have been tools of transformation for several of my patients. I truly feel that your work is helping to open the way to finding what our culture seems to have lost, the connection with our bodies which is really the connection with the very roots of our being."

"I applaud your book. Your text is clear, powerful, and sensitive."

Transforming Body Image

Learning to Love the Body You Have

by
Marcia Germaine
Hutchinson, Ed.D.

THE CROSSING PRESS / Freedom, California 95019

The exercises in this book are designed to elicit deep psychological material. Anyone who has a history of psychiatric disorder or emotional instability, or who is currently using major tranquilizers or anti-depressant medication is advised to consult a qualified mental health professional before doing these exercises.

Cover illustration by Carole Odell
Cover design by William Houston
Text design by Martha J. Waters and Betsy Bayley
Typesetting by Martha J. Waters
Printed in the U.S.A.

Library of Congress Cataloging-in-Publication Data

Hutchinson, Marcia Germaine.
 Transforming body image.

 1. Body image. 2. Self-acceptance. 3. Reducing--
Psychological aspects. I. Title.
BF 697.5.B63H87 1985 158'.1 85-17524
ISBN 0-89594-173-2
ISBN 0-89594-172-4 (pbk.)

Dedicated to the many women who had the courage to trust me and my method, the courage to dive into deep, unknown waters. If you saw yourselves as I see you, you would know what beauty is. Without you there would be no book.

In the scenery of spring
there is nothing superior
nothing inferior;
flowering branches
are by nature
some short
some long.

Zen Proverb

Acknowledgments

A book is the culmination of a long chain of events, and thanks are due to many people. My long-time friend, Donna Mildvan, suggested that my doctoral dissertation needed to become a book. A friend, Marilyn Taylor, led me to Kathleen Spivack, my relentlessly positive literary guide, who cheer-led me through a year of writer's anxiety, sharing the secrets of the Viennese along the way. Carole Odell, my dear friend, graced the book jacket with her intelligent, sensitive, and beautiful artwork that captures so well the essence of this material. I'd like to acknowledge Andrea Fleck Clardy. And finally, Elaine Goldman Gill, my editor, whose warmth, humanity, and profound commitment to this project came through in every red editorial squiggle.

I have drawn intellectual inspiration from Moshe Feldenkrais, Fritz Perls, Roberto Assagioli, Win Wenger, Robert Masters, and Jean Houston.

My dog, Lina, has been my faithful companion throughout. Snuggled calmingly nearby while I typed endlessly, she was a constant reminder of peace, ease, and simplicity.

Most of all I want to thank my husband, Bill Hutchinson. He held down the fort and kept the home fires burning (literally) while I was lost in thought and/or deadlines. His patience, understanding, and emotional support provided a holding environment in which I could create.

Thank you all.

Contents

INTRODUCTION

My own struggle with my body stretches back into early childhood. It was clear to me that my body was not quite right: it was too large, too chunky, too muscular. It could never be sufficiently petite and delicate to be considered feminine and beautiful by the standards that prevailed during the forties and fifties when I was growing up. I have a body that is sturdy and robust even at its thinnest. It's the kind of body that exceeds the height-weight tables even when there isn't an ounce of extra fat on it. It's the kind of body whose unique proportions do not easily adapt to ready-to-wear clothing. And finally, it is the kind of body that gains weight at the sight of food and loses weight and keeps it off only with the greatest hardship and constant deprivation.

My body image, the way I see and feel about my body, has been my greatest personal stumbling block. I was obsessed with my body and its awfulness, its deviation from what was socially acceptable and from my own ideals. No area of my life escaped the ravages of my obsession. I spent most of my 43 years letting my body's imperfections taint my sense of the real person living inside. I used to look at my body and forget that inside there lived a kind, intelligent, and valuable human being — me.

I am struck and saddened by how much power I have given to others to shape my behavior and the way I have felt about myself. I had the absolute conviction that others were judging me as harshly as I judged myself, as a bundle of flaws. I was shy, awkward, and withdrawn, and this made it very easy for people to ignore or reject me. I made it happen.

In group situations I really became invisible and was ignored. This hurt me a great deal because I was aware of how many opportunities I was missing: to meet interesting people, to share my knowledge, to get recognition for my abilities and personal qualities. I spent years feeling like a nobody. No one noticed me therefore I did not exist. The worse I felt, the more effectively I hid myself away. I harbored secret feelings that I was really an undiscovered treasure and that some select people with vision would recognize me. Indeed some did, but I hate to think how many did not.

Every new encounter with a woman made me feel self-conscious, intimidated, envious, and inadequate. I used to look at women who were thin and imagine how happy they were, how they had partners who loved and admired them, how they felt easy and uninhibited every time they took off their clothes or sauntered along the beach. I no longer see physical beauty as a guarantee of happiness. I no longer delude myself that if I were thin a series of wonderful and miraculous events would take place. In fact those periods of my life when I was thin (although of course I didn't believe it at the time) were in no major ways happier than any of my fat times. It was easier to find clothes that fit me, but that was all. I never felt free of the judgment of others (because I still judged my body and myself severely). I never attracted men who were interested in me or capable of carrying on a serious relationship. I met men who were interested in me for the wrong reasons, because I looked good at their side. The truth of the matter is that those men with whom I have established lasting and meaningful relationships met and accepted me when my weight was on the high side.

My own weight has run the gamut from low to high, mostly high. My genes, my constitution, and my ethnic heritage, predispose me to overweight. And the years of chronic dieting, deprivation, and overeating have deranged my metabolic system to the extent that now, even though I am a moderate and conscious eater, it is virtually impossible for me to be anything but overweight.

There is no question that it is difficult to be a heavy woman in a thin world. It has been the source of much pain for me over the years. And it has also built character. I, like most people, had unquestioningly accepted the many stereotypes about fat people and used them as weapons to torture myself for being larger than average. Frankly, I can no longer identify the me that I know with those stereotypes. I have seen little evidence of compulsive overeating in my life for many, many years. I am emotionally healthy, in control of my life. I am healthy, strong, fit, supple, and graceful. And my life includes intimacy, friendship, meaningful work, and a life style of my own design. And I'm overweight.

After much struggle, I have grown to accept my body as it is. I have come to realize that the superhuman effort it would require for me to lose and keep off my extra weight is better applied to more important (to me) projects such as writing this book. It is a choice I make.

My years of anguish around my body image drove me to therapy, innumerable diets, dance classes, silent suffering, commiserating with other women—you name it. Still I could not unravel this stubborn knot until I stumbled on an important clue.

For several years I studied the Feldenkrais Method, an ingenious body-mind, movement-oriented therapy hoping to cure a chronic back problem. One phase of the method consists of movement sequences designed to help you learn through playful, childlike discovery how your body is designed to operate. Experiencing my body in the Feldenkrais way not only helped my back immensely—it also gave me a heightened awareness and appreciation of the intelligence and functional integrity of my body. It instilled in me an attitude of playfulness and discovery about my body as well as a new sense of ease and fluidity.

At the last meeting of our Feldenkrais study group, a video camera recorded our floor movements and, with considerable trepidation, I watched the playback on the monitor. What I saw (through the distortions of my body image) was a huge lump with enormous hindquarters. I was inconsolable.

Somehow my visual impression was translated into a kinesthetic experience. My image (the one I saw on the monitor) became a feeling. I felt my body as a tree-stump: too short, too compact, too immobile, too much. At that moment I felt an intense hatred of my body. This painful experience (both the image that I saw and the image that I felt) made me question how women get locked into distortions about their bodies and, more important, it directed me to find ways that might *alter* a woman's relationship to her body so that she could accept it.

Several things became clear. My body image had very little to do with my physical body. In fact they were quite separate. It was possible for me to look lovely from an objective point of view and yet feel fat and ugly. And the reverse was also true. Image and reality are separate and distinct phenomena when there is a distorted body image.

I realized that my body image was a special kind of *image,* a product of my imagination. I had a strong hunch that it could therefore be altered by using my imagination in a controlled and directed manner. Five years ago I used my doctoral dissertation* as an opportunity to explore the problem of body image hoping to find a creative solution.

* Sankowsky, M.H. (aka M. Hutchinson) "The effect of a treatment based on the use of guided visuo-kinesthetic imagery on the alteration of negative body-cathexis in women." Unpublished doctoral dissertation. Boston University, 1981.

I set up a controlled experiment using a group of women who identified themselves as having negative body images. After administering tests of body image (I asked each woman to rate her feelings about different aspects of her body and her self) and interviewing all the women, I randomly divided them into two comparable groups. I guided one group through a 7-week therapeutic process that I created, called Transforming Body Image. During the experimental workshop these women were led through a series of exercises that used their imagination as a way of learning about their body image and healing its wounds. Although they went through the workshop in a group, each woman worked independently and privately, using a journal with guiding questions to process her experience. The other group of women passed the seven weeks in their usual manner. After the workshop ended I tested and interviewed all the women again. I found that the women who had experienced the workshop were significantly changed both in their body images and their self images. A follow-up questionnaire six months later indicated that for most of the women the changes were holding and even deepening.

Since those early days I have adjusted, expanded, and refined this process in the Transforming Body Image workshop for women in the Boston area. The workshop consists of ten weekly two-hour meetings. In addition to the work with imagery and journal-keeping, the workshop now includes Feldenkrais movement work. I still use a group format in which each woman does her own inner work in the context of a supportive group. It is this process of Transforming Body Image that I offer you in this book.

Over the last five years I have felt a great satisfaction watching many women grow more contented with their bodies. Many have come to appreciate their bodies just the way they are. Others have chosen to make loving changes and refinements in their appearance. For some, a new compassion for their bodies has helped them to listen to and take care of their bodies in a way that has helped normalize their weight and health.

In the years since I began work on my body image my values have begun to move from the inside outward rather than the other way. I have really learned to love and respect and accept myself as I am. This has been a powerful and significant change in me. I am not going to tell you that the appearance of my body or your body is irrelevant. But I will say that unless you love and accept your *self,* unless you *feel* beautiful *inside,* you will not see your outer beauty, let alone believe it or enjoy it.

My own process continues. I still have bad days when I'm convinced that I'm repulsive. But most of the time I live in a state of truce—I can enjoy my body and all the ways it moves me through life. I don't delude myself into thinking that my body will be declared the new standard of beauty for the world. I don't delude myself about my body at all. I know that there is room for improvement when I'm ready, if I choose. But, more important, I know that I am much, much more than my body—my sense of my own worth is not attached to my body.

In my search for a peaceful relationship with my body I have not had the luxury of being led through one of my workshops or of being taken by the hand through a book such as this. My own peace has come from trial and error. Certainly the process of creating *Transforming Body Image* and listening to the stories of hundreds of women has deepened my understanding of what is involved in straying from and reclaiming our bodies. I have done much deep soul searching, and psychological housecleaning. I have become willing to forgive others who have hurt me and to forgive myself for not looking the way I always dreamed I should look. My work with the Feldenkrais Method has given me a feeling of ease, comfort, and grace in movement that pervades my experience of living in my body. My body feels more like a home.

Changing my body image has meant holding on to my own vision of myself even when some people sometimes reflect a different and less accepting vision back to me. Along the way I have had the help of friends who have loved me regardless of how I look. But it took a shift in my own internal perception before I could really let that in. *Feeling* lovely is more central than *looking* lovely. The inner shift precedes the outer change.

Most profound to me was my experience with the many women for whom I designed this work. Witnessing the suffering of the many truly lovely women who hate their bodies has helped me to challenge many long held assumptions about outer beauty. With each encounter my own conviction to let go of this struggle became stronger. Each interview brought home to me the futility and waste involved in hating our bodies. Throughout this book I will share with you their pains, their struggles, and their progress.

The majority of women in our culture do not accept their bodies as they are. In fact, it is a rare woman today who has a healthy body image, who is not actively doing battle with her body. Eating disorders such as anorexia nervosa, bulimia (binging-purging)—once rare and obscure conditions—have now become commonplace. They are extreme symptoms of the body/mind split so common in our culture. When the mind and body are at war, they no longer work together for the good of the whole being. The body is experienced as a foreign object or hated antagonist.

The inability to feel at home in our bodies can make life miserable on every front. We are so busy obsessing over what is wrong with us—whether it's our weight, misproportion, wrinkles, pimples, excess hair, or functional limitations—that we fail to develop our potential as human beings. If we could harness a tiny fraction of the energy and attention wasted in body hate and use it as fuel for creativity and self-development, just think how far we could travel toward our life goals.

Any movement toward self-improvement must be propelled not by disgust and self-rejection, but by a realistic acceptance of who *we already are* and a desire to be the best possible version of that reality. Any diet or regime that we impose on our bodies that is inspired by self-disgust will be punitive and our bodies will rebel and fight us at every turn. Any fitness program we undertake will make us fit only if it is done with awareness and gentleness. Only when our motives are based on love and respect, will our bodies respond as we wish them to. Only when we know and accept who we are, can we change.

The task of coming to a place of union within yourself involves a lifelong process of listening to your body, of respecting and trusting its messages. It involves letting go of the negative tapes that you chronically run in your head while at the same time giving stronger voice to the part of you that sees clearly and wants to be whole again. You will learn to accept the idiosyncrasies of your own body type and to adopt realistic and gentle goals for realizing your greatest potential. It is a process not of changing your body but of changing your *outlook*.

Isn't it about time that someone told you that your body is all right, just the way it is? Isn't it about time you picked up a book that offers you a road back to mind-body wholeness instead of some new way to "fix" yourself? *Transforming Body Image* isn't about changing your body. It's about learning to love and accept the body you already have. It's about making your body a home that you can live in.

•

How To Use This Book

This is a self-help book adapted from my workshops. It is designed so that you can proceed from step to step on your own, using the tools and guidance provided. There is a natural order to the exercises. Some can stand alone, but if you follow them in the order given you will benefit the most. Each exercise is a stepping stone to the next. Simply reading through the exercises will do something for you, but for this process to transform you, you must *do* the exercises.

These exercises are self-exploratory experiences that will enlighten you about your body image—what it is, how it has come to be the way it is, what is right for your body, how to heal the wounds and shift the attitudes that keep you from perceiving your body and yourself as beautiful, healthy, and whole.

This book is not a quick fix. You did not develop your current body image overnight—nor will you transform it overnight. For some of you the road will be one mile, for others one hundred miles. Allow yourself ten weeks or even longer to work through this book, pacing yourself so that you can assimilate the changes. It takes time to integrate such an important shift in attitude toward yourself. So please respect your own timing.

It is possible to do the work alone, but if you know other women who struggle with the same issues, it will help to go through the process with them. Your body image is delicate psychological territory. Many of the exercises may evoke strong feelings, some painful. Working with others will provide support and encouragement to persevere.

The exercises in this book rely very heavily on the positive and controlled use of the imagination—that powerhouse for healing which we all possess.

The exercises are presented so that it is possible to read each step and then go inside to do the work in your imagination. You will have a deeper and more powerful experience if you let someone else lead you through the exercises. There are several ways to do this. If you are working with a friend or a small group, you can take turns leading each other through the exercises. If you are working alone, it will help to tape the exercises from the scripts provided, pausing after each step [. . .] to allow time to work with your imagery. I have also recorded the exercises in this book on a set of cassette tapes which you can order. (See the Resource Section of the book for ordering information.)

Each exercise has a brief introduction that sets the stage. In it you will often find *seed questions* that will help you to begin thinking about issues that are relevant to the exercise that follows. Please take the time to reflect on these questions as your thoughts will facilitate the imagery that follows.

Following each exercise is a *worksheet* which contains questions to help you process your imaginal experience. The best way to use the *worksheet* is to write down the answers to these questions immediately after completing the exercise. Images like dreams are very fragile, and the longer you delay at this step, the more your imaginal experience will evaporate. The *worksheet* is a very important phase of the work, so please do not skip over it. This work is designed to use both halves of your brain. The right half does the imaging, and the left half processes the imagery through language. The two together will give you a whole-brained, integrated experience.

Finally, in *Guiding Words* I have included some words of guidance as well as verbatim experiences of some of the women who have participated in my workshops. Their stories will stimulate your associations and will illustrate important points.

Section 1
Straying From Home

I
WOMAN'S SELF/ WOMAN'S BODY

To men a man is but a mind. Who cares
What face he carries or what form he wears?
But woman's body is the woman.

Ambrose Bierce

Your Self

As a woman your body is so intimately linked with your sense of self that your body attitudes readily spill over into self attitudes. If you are dissatisfied with your self, you will most likely take it out on your body. Similarly, if you are down on your body, you will chip away at your self-esteem. In women, body-esteem and self-esteem appear to be married to each other. (In men this is not true.) Most women who devalue their bodies also devalue themselves. Or is it that most women who dislike themselves also dislike their bodies? It is a classic chicken and egg question.

As women, we are raised to see our bodies as the means to achieving control of our lives. We often forget that we are more than our bodies. We blame and punish our bodies for our failures and disappointments—we don't look at other features of our personalities and behavior that could use overhauling. It is this maligned body and the image that we have of it that we haul around, effecting all areas of our lives.

When that attractive person failed to notice us, it must have been because we were too fat or not pretty enough. It had nothing to do with the fact that we were frozen in fear. When we were passed over for that promotion at work, our body was the culprit for its failure to achieve the right professional look. We overlooked the fact that our major competitor had been busy impressing the boss with her/his ideas while we hung back.

When we relate to another person, she or he becomes a mirror that reflects back to us our own vision of ourselves. If that vision is positive and healthy, others will see and respond to that same wholesomeness. If we experience our bodies and ourselves as negative or lacking in some way, others will experience us in that light. We are incredibly powerful in shaping others' reactions to us.

•

How do your feelings about your body affect the choices you make in social situations?

•

Many of us feel shy or awkward around people. We may hide and withdraw before others have the chance to accept or reject us. And, interestingly enough, when others do seek us out, we find reasons to reject them. Like Groucho Marx, we wouldn't want to belong to any club that would admit us as a member. Many women withdraw completely from social contact. This leads to a narrow and restricted social world which in turn breeds loneliness and a sense of inadequacy that make matters worse.

It is very difficult to relate to others when we are thoroughly absorbed in our worries and obsessions about our bodies. This kind of self-absorption can distance us from others, blocking the possibility for contact and closeness and draining our energy and interest away from relating. We miss out on opportunities for genuine human connection.

If you are like the many women I have worked with, it is likely that you automatically compare yourself to other women, especially women you meet for the first time. You wonder whether you are prettier or uglier, fatter or thinner. Women who struggle with their bodies are very severe judges of themselves and often of others. The comparison is painful and senseless, breeding envy, self-doubt, and distance. You are you and they are they. Moreover, the way that you see other women may be very different from how they feel inside. I have spent years interviewing and working with women who are objectively very lovely and attractive but who see themselves as fat, ugly, ungainly, and inadequate.

Many women with poor body images withdraw from competition with other women. Taking themselves out of the running protects them from failing. It is amazing how many women use this as a rationale for remaining overweight or for not projecting the beauty or pizazz available to them. We are afraid to incur the envy of our sisters and possibly lose their friendship. But what a price to pay!

Our negative feelings about our bodies really create difficulties in our intimate relationships with either men or women. We are brainwashed to believe that we have to be beautiful or at least thin in order to be sexual or sexually desirable. Therefore many of us deny ourselves the pleasures of love and intimacy. One woman put it succinctly, "I automatically think I'm seen as fat and therefore undesirable. How could I possibly have a relationship with a man? What man would want me?" With such strong feelings of inadequacy, the fear of rejection becomes very powerful, to be avoided at any cost. We turn down invitations, stay home and eat and feel sorry for ourselves. Some of us allow ourselves to choose only dependent partners who will not reject us because they need us too much. This type of relationship is usually doomed to failure. We avoid possible sexual experiences by not allowing ourselves to flirt or provoke interest in a potential lover. Or we adopt the role of friend to that person rather than lover. In some cases it is our own sexuality that we fear, thinking it such a powerful force that we literally run away from it.

It is almost as if we walk around with signs that say, "Make sure you notice how fat and disgusting my thighs are so you can reject me." How many of us have sabotaged our love relationships by criticizing our bodies? One woman saw how she brought it on herself.

> "I make it into a huge issue and I can't believe it isn't for my partner. He tells me he loves me and that I'm very attractive to him, but I don't believe him. He's only saying that to make me feel good or because he feels sorry for me. I mistrust him and then he feels hurt. So I criticize and criticize myself and end up without any respect for myself. Eventually he starts to come around and see things my way. That finally kills the relationship."

When we feel inadequate, it is the most difficult thing in the world to expose ourselves, to make our naked bodies vulnerable to the eyes or the touch of another. But this kind of vulnerability is the essence of intimacy. Body shyness and inhibition are major blocks to sexual enjoyment. It is nearly impossible to surrender to sexual abandon while worrying that our stomach is protruding or that our partner will see us in an unflattering angle. We suppress our feelings and deny our needs. We are shy and passive. We disown our bodies.

Many of us think that we must look a certain way before we can have a lover. We strive for the time "when I'm thin enough" or "when I get my body under control." Then we will be worthy of the pleasures of intimacy. We believe that sexuality is only permissible if we're thin, beautiful, hairless or whatever.

How sad this is, all the more tragic because it represents the secret thoughts of so many women. When you stop to think of how many of our deepest and most basic needs — the need for love, companionship, and family — have as their prerequisite the ability or willingness to form an intimate attachment, then the real tragedy becomes obvious.

•

Take a moment and close your eyes. Let yourself imagine that you are at a social gathering and you have just been introduced to a person who has all the qualities that you want in a mate. What are you feeling? What tapes are going off in your head? How are you likely to behave?

Let's take this one step further. Imagine that you have been dating this person. Imagine what it will be like for you to make love to this person for the first time. How do you feel about taking off your clothes? What do you imagine your partner is noticing about you? What are your worst fantasies?

•

If our bodies/selves are cloaked in shame and insecurity then to reveal ourselves is the last thing we want to do. And yet, to get the acknowledgment most of us need, we must take the risk to express and reveal ourselves, making ourselves vulnerable. As one woman put it:

> "I can't face people the way I am. The least I can do is to take up as little space as possible. So I am very controlled and I don't express myself. There is a lot that I want to say, but I hardly ever assert myself or take any initiative. I'm shy and reticent and I hold myself back from going after what I want or what's mine. And there's some way that I just won't give myself permission to be *me* until I look more the way I think I should."

Clothing is one way of expressing ourselves, but if we don't like our bodies or feel outsized or ill-proportioned, going shopping can be a major trauma. Most ready-to-wear clothing is only ready-to-wear if you are Brooke Shields. I call this the tyranny of the fitting room, a constant reminder that we don't fit. We must change our bodies to fit into clothes, or go naked. It is little wonder then that we rarely see our wardrobes as a means of self-expression, a way of letting the world know who we really are through our choices of color, texture, and style. More often than not our clothing becomes another way of hiding.

•

What are your special ways of not projecting yourself?

•

Advancing ourselves professionally in most fields requires that we put ourselves out there in the world complete with our full intelligence, assertiveness and competitiveness — with all our power. Most of us have not been groomed for this. We had as role models mothers who either stayed home and raised families or who went to work in jobs where they did not compete with men. Without role models and with the constant pressure on us to pursue careers, many of us feel inadequate and afraid. We question our worth and tend to shift the responsibility for our success or failure onto our poor, beleaguered bodies.

One woman came out of the cloistered environment of graduate school armed with a Masters in Business Administration. It was time to face the real world. Instead of doing so, she took refuge in her assumption that because she was overweight she simply couldn't sell herself: she didn't get a job.

Some women use their body image as an excuse to stay safe and untested while others use it as a way to stay safe and unpowerful. Many women are terrified of their own power, afraid that power spells loneliness. For others their body image is a handicap that must be compensated for by extra work: "I have to be more than perfect at my job. I work harder than three people put together and I'm always exhausted."

Another woman who would have loved to go into advertising instead works at a low paying job at a small, local newspaper. She stays away from places where she has to confront media values.

Low self-confidence keeps us from taking the kind of risks that could create the lives we want and deserve. Obsessing over our shortcomings, real or imagined, drains us of energy that could better serve us as the fuel for creativity, productivity, and self-realization.

•

Pause here and reflect on the ways that you stand in your own way, preventing your aspirations from becoming realities.

Your Body

One of the main casualties in your mind-body struggle is your body itself. All bodies need proper care to maintain good physical health. Movement and exercise are important, but proper exercise requires a real caring for the body, a program of movement performed with loving sensitivity as a gift, not as a punishment for wayward flesh. I have worked with women who have never exercised because they are embarrassed to wear exercise clothing, ashamed to be seen in a class of thin women. Other women have become so out of shape that exercise is a monumental effort. Some women take a militaristic approach, putting their bodies through Herculean ordeals in the hope of losing a few pounds or eliminating the ripples on their thighs. One woman frequently binges on several gallons of ice cream and boxes of cookies and then tries to undo the damage by going for a ten-mile run followed by two hours of strenuous gymnastics — all at 5:00 a.m.!

Body shame leads to poor posture — rounded shoulders, drooping head — which is not only unattractive but unhealthy, interfering with our ability to breathe properly. We are not giving our cells, tissues, and organs the nourishment they require. Our health suffers as does our overall energy and vitality. Poor posture also results in muscular imbalances. Many women I have worked with live with pain and minor functional complaints as if they were the premises of life rather than urgent signals. A body that is accepted and loved is listened to with a sensitive ear. In that way its needs can be known and addressed and its limits respected.

Stress is now acknowledged as one of the leading causes of disease. There are many ways to reach a dangerous level of stress: you can be a corporate executive, or an air-traffic controller, or you can be at war with your body. There is some evidence that we can actually bring on illness by holding our bodies in contempt or by disowning them. It is not unusual to find cases of women who develop cancer in their hated breasts and sexual organs and have to have them removed. In one way or another we poison ourselves with our self-rejection. Some have suggested that when we deny certain parts of our bodies or write them out of our body images, we actually create a blockage in the normal flow of energy and awareness which can eventually lead to a breakdown of the body's natural abilities to heal itself.

The women in my workshops come in every weight, shape, and size, but one thing most of them share is a distorted idea about their weight and a highly charged relationship to food. At least 90% of them perceive themselves as having eating disorders when in fact only a small proportion suffer from eating disorders in the strictly clinical sense. They are for the most part suffering not from eating disorders, but from *labelling* disorders. When fully 80% of American women have eating disorders, how can we call it a disease? Surely there are many men in our culture who engage in similar or far more extraordinary eating practices without feeling the pressure to hang a label on themselves.

Eating disorders have been woman's domain ever since Eve ate the apple. Today they are reaching epidemic proportions. The same dynamic that structures eating disorders — anorexia, bulimia, and obesity — is at work in a milder but more pervasive way in those many women who struggle with the acceptability of their bodies. They are all responding to the enormous pressure on today's woman to be thin. We are living in a world where any amount of "extra" poundage on the female body is seen as an indication of character weakness, as a sign of being out of control. Any woman carrying extra flesh on her body must lack feminine self-respect. Is it any wonder that a woman's life today revolves to such a degree around the number on her scale?

Women have been told by the medical profession and the media that their normal weight, the weight that their bodies naturally gravitate toward, is too much. And yet it is natural for us to be fatter than men. Female hormones conspire against thinness. So we feel guilty, ugly, ashamed, neurotic, self-destructive, and out of control. And naturally we want to eat more to dull the pain — food is an excellent anesthetic. Or perhaps we try to diet, starve, or otherwise whip our bodies into the desired size and shape. But the regime is too rigorous, too punitive — the body will not be so easily forced to deny its natural impulse without fighting back. Compulsive overeating takes the place of stringent dieting and the feelings of fatness, guilt, and shame return. And so the cycle goes.

●

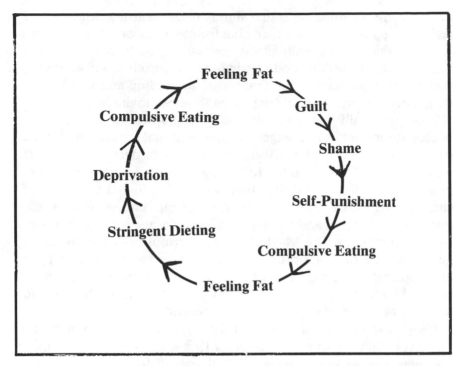

As long as women actively strive against their fleshy nature in order to fit an unnatural, external standard, how can they ever achieve a normal, healthy relationship to food?

There is a connection between eating and body image. On those days when we have been "good" and have eaten sparingly we are more likely to feel virtuous and to accept our bodies. On the other hand, when we binge we experience our bodies as swollen and engorged. Our sins are immediately visible, our guilt profound.

Time after time I hear women say, "When I feel bad, I overeat," "When I'm out of touch, I eat," "When I'm angry at myself for not controlling my eating, I punish myself by eating," "When I feel fat or bad I stuff my feelings down with food." When we are feeling bad about our bodies and ourselves we use food to soothe, punish, and numb ourselves. When we are really living in our bodies, we are far more likely to be sensitive to hunger cues and to eat appropriately in order to satisfy our needs and to stop when we are no longer hungry. When we are accepting of our bodies we are less stressed and therefore have less reason to eat to anaesthetize ourselves.

A good, healthy, positive body image is essential before we can learn how to eat and bring our weight within the proper range and keep it there. In some cases that simply means learning when we are really hungry and when we are eating for other reasons. It also means learning which foods really please and satisfy us. It may sometimes mean imposing certain food restrictions on ourselves — if we decide that a diet is necessary, our chances of succeeding and keeping the weight off are immeasurably improved if we diet lovingly.

If we are really living in our bodies and are able to accept our bodies as they are, any changes we choose to make will come from a strong base — they will be refinements, not life or death measures. If we are waiting for our bodies to be "right" before we give ourselves permission to live a full life, then we are loading the process of change with unreal expectations. We put our bodies through the rigors of deprivation and discipline and wait for the magic to happen. And it rarely does. Our knight in shining armor does not appear, a glamorous job does not drop into our laps. In fact we will really be no happier than we were before. Our outward appearance may have changed but not necessarily our body image. We will still feel fat and ungainly or whatever it was we felt beforehand.

Bodies can change much faster than body images, so we will find ourselves thin with fat body images, or firm with flabby body images. On some level we say to ourselves: "Oh, what's the use. I'm still just as awful as always. I might as well do whatever I please." So we binge or abandon our exercise program. It is absolutely crucial that we work on body image first and arrive at an accepting relationship with our bodies *before* we decide to change them.

I cannot emphasize enough how important it is to accept yourself as you are, especially if you are overweight. It is hard enough to be overweight in this culture without in addition abusing yourself. Accepting overweight is not the same thing as resigning yourself to it. In the process of learning to accept the body you have, you develop a stronger sense of yourself, with a clarity about how *you* truly want your body to be. Not what your mother wants, or your lover, or society. It will be what *you* want. If you diet to satisfy someone else, and if you have the slightest trace of rebelliousness it will come to the fore complete with anger, resentment, and the desire to sabotage your most carefully laid plans.

It is time to challenge some of the misconceptions that many of us have about overweight. Study after study has demonstrated that stereotypes of overweight people as lazy, emotionally unstable, and out of control are totally inaccurate. People who carry extra weight are just like anyone else with the same emotional ups and downs. They are no more out of control than millions of people who smoke or work too hard or drink too much or who have other ways of handling stress.

These stereotypes not only hurt fat people, they hurt anyone who thinks she has any excess fat on her body. If the scale moves up a pound, a steady stream of self-recrimination follows: "I'm out of control, I'm bad, I have no self-respect as a woman," and on and on. It is very important for us to begin challenging some of our assumptions and to realize that a pound of fat is a pound of fat and not a blight on the face of humankind.

The science and art of weight control are presently at a very primitive level of development. We really do not understand the complex problems involved in taking off weight and keeping it off. There is considerable evidence that one of the primary causes of compulsive overeating is constant dieting, and the chronic feeling of deprivation that goes with dieting. When we tip the balance in one direction and deprive our bodies of food, nature tries to restore the balance, by tipping the scale to the other extreme and making us hungrier than ever. Thus the dieting-binging-dieting cycle is born. Virtue (rigorous dieting) and vice (binging-gluttony) are natural opposites on the seesaw.

Food deprivation serves on a physiological level to lower our metabolic rate. The less dieters eat, the more slowly their bodies burn up calories, the more slowly they lose weight. And to add insult to injury, the more sluggish the metabolism, the less food it takes to put on weight. That explains the plateaus most dieters reach in the course of dieting, and the extreme difficulty in maintaining weight loss. When the weight goal is reached, it is reached in such a slow metabolic condition that the dieter must eat like a bird or exercise like a maniac in order not to undo all the hard work. Americans are fatter than ever today probably because of, not in spite of, their chronic dieting.

Scientists are discovering the individuality of every body. There is no one right way to eat, no one right way to exercise, and no one right weight. Each and every body is unique in its requirements. Some very interesting research suggests that every body has a weight range, a setpoint that is right for it. That setpoint knows nothing about what is currently in vogue. It is a stubborn and determined little mechanism with only one function, to maintain weight in the range that it considers correct.

The setpoint can be moved up or down, although it appears that it is easier to move up than down. Continued weight gain moves it up, while aerobic exercise, not dieting, can move it down, but not very easily. Recent research suggests that an aerobic program once begun, must be sustained *for life* or you will become even fatter than before. This finding emphasizes the need for very clear motives and unshakable commitment.

What this setpoint research suggests, is that those 10-15 pounds that so many women want to lose are tenacious because we are meant to have them. And all efforts to be thinner are fighting nature and nature, as you know, is no pushover—she'll fight tooth and nail to keep our weight where she thinks it belongs. For example, several rats were subjected to a surgery destroying part of their brains, causing them to eat voraciously and grow enormously fat. The scientists cut back the rats' rations to the preoperational level but instead of losing weight, the rats became even fatter than before. What happened was that the operation apparently raised the rats' setpoints. If the rats could not gain weight by eating more, they would do it by bringing their metabolic rate nearly to a halt. What this means is that our bodies have wills of their own and it is not always within the realm of conscious choice to go against this wisdom. Specifically, it means that you could probably find better and more productive ways to use your energy than to spend it in the futile struggle to lose those last 10-15 pounds.

The only procedure that will work is to become more accepting of your body as it is. From that place of peace your body should begin to find its way to its right size and form. But if that does not happen, you are still left with the harmony you have worked so hard for.

II
MAKING YOUR
IMAGINATION AN ALLY

The true nature of things, truth itself, can be revealed to us only by fantasy, which is more realistic than all the realisms.
Eugene Ionesco

About twenty years ago I discovered the joys of making pottery, especially throwing pots on the potter's wheel. Every day I would go to the studio to work at the wheel. Every day my technique improved and my enthusiasm grew. One weekend I was playing ball with a group of friends and sprained my little finger. Without the use of that finger my whole technique of throwing pots was off balance.

It would be at least four weeks before my finger would heal. My momentum in potting was so high I found myself spontaneously fantasizing the pot throwing process. I would imagine myself at the wheel, feeling the clay in my hands, imagining the position of my body needed to achieve just the right combination of pressure and timing. I experienced myself throwing perfect pots every time. From time to time I found myself doing this full-bodied imagining. I had no plan in mind. It was just something that happened spontaneously simply because I missed potting so much, and this was the closest I could get to it.

Four weeks passed, my finger healed, and I returned to the studio. To my amazement I discovered that my technique was light years ahead of what it had been before my injury! I could only attribute this dramatic improvement to my fantasizing.

This experience aroused in me a new respect for the powers of the imagination. I was an artist at that time in my life, and I already had a healthy regard for the importance of imagination for inspiration, but this was the first time I experienced imagination changing my behavior.

You can use your imagination to practice attitudes and behaviors that you wish to build into your life. You can expand your self image. If you can imagine it, you can live it.

What has this to do with body image? Body image is itself a special kind of image. When you have a negative body image, your mind's eye sees your body in a distorted manner and your mind's ear hears self talk saying your body is inadequate, ugly, and fat. You are held prisoner, controlled by your perception and sense of self. What better way to gain access to your tyrannical imagination than to turn it around by training your imagination to be your *ally* so that your body can become your home instead of a battlefield.

This training will take many forms in the course of this book. You will be using your imagination to tap into memories to find important information that you will need in order to understand and change your relationship to your body. Most therapeutic approaches rely on words to release you from your emotional binds. The use of imagery—the language of the unconscious and of feeling—is often a more efficient way to open locked doors to forgotten feelings and experiences. And the process is gentle: it nudges you softly—it never bulldozes its way.

All children naturally have rich and active imaginations. Most of our education has trained us to put aside the imaginal realm in favor of the rational, thinking mind. If you are an artist or a highly creative person, your imagination is probably still alive and well, but in most adults the imagination is rusty. Imaginal training will allow you to reclaim one of the most powerful resources that is at your disposal for changing your life.

The language of imagination is images. Images are pictures, sounds, feelings, tastes, and smells that you construct rather than experience directly through your senses.

•

For a moment, lift your eyes off this page and look carefully at any object near you. . . What you are doing right now is Perceiving *that object with your eyes. Now close your eyes and recreate this same object by imagining it. You can do the same thing with all of your senses although most people have one or two imaginal senses that are far easier to control than others. Try silently conversing with a friend and listening with your imaginal ears. . . imagine the feel of satin. . . the taste of lemon. . . the smell of vanilla.*

•

Every sense has its imaginal counterpart. For some of us these images will be clear and vivid. Others will have a hazy impression that the object is there and has certain characteristics. With practice your images will become clearer and more vivid and therefore more powerful.

When I ask you to imagine a sea shell or to imagine yourself walking up stairs, the process is called *guided imaging*. You are constructing very specific images. But if instead I ask you to imagine walking up stairs and entering a room where you have never been before and experiencing what is in the room, this process includes elements of *spontaneous imaging* where you simply allow images to pop into your mind as you would in a daydream. If I directed you to change the color of the room's walls and to move objects around, that would be *controlled imaging*.

As you work your way through this book you will be called upon to play with many different forms of imaging. At times your involvement will be active and dynamic while at other times it will be passive and receptive. Soon your imagination will become a true ally that you can use as a tool to help yourself not only in changing your body image but in changing many other aspects of your life as well.

Travelling in the realm of imagination is intrinsically healing because it demands a certain level of relaxation. Exploring your own flow of images allows you to glimpse what issues are pressing for further attention. Working through your emotional blocks on an imaginal level can relieve symptoms and produce personality and attitude changes. Your imagination is a piece of psychological space where you can monitor the rumblings of your subconscious mind. It is also a theater in which to rehearse behavior. If you can imagine something, you can do it.

Deeply felt imaginal experiences can change the contours of your feeling and your sense of self. Why is this? Because images are *real*. I know you have been taught that what happens in your imagination is the opposite of reality. But when you imagine something *vividly* using as many of your imaginal senses as you can muster, you are creating a *real* psychological event. You will have an example of this later when you do the exercise called *The Imaginal Body*. But for now, let's try something.

•

Imagine that you are perched on the ledge of a window twenty-three stories above street level. . . Look down at the street and see people and cars that look like ants. . . Your stomach is in your throat. . . You don't dare to move because you are balanced so

precariously that any false move might send you plummeting to a
sure and messy death. Take a few minutes to imagine this and do it as
vividly as you can, monitoring any changes that take place in your
body and emotional state.

•

Those of you who really let yourself do this exercise probably noticed that your heart was racing, fast and furiously, your breathing became shallow and perhaps your palms began to sweat — all physical signs of panic and terror. What you did was to create a genuine psycho-physical event simply by using your imagination. Can you still say that your images are not real? In a less dramatic but no less real way than our high-rise adventure, every time you imagine yourself walking upstairs your nervous system triggers movement and motor activity, however subtle, in the same muscle groups involved in walking up stairs. Your stair-walking, neuro-muscular pattern is responding even though there is no observable movement from the outside.

The same is true if you engage in an imaginary confrontation with someone with whom you have unfinished emotional business. If you do it vividly, using your full-bodied imagination, you will be setting off the same reactions in your psyche and nervous system that you would in a real confrontation. Such an encounter can perform two healing functions. It can serve as a rehearsal that can move you closer to a face-to-face encounter with that person so that you can clear up your unfinished business. It can function also at a much subtler level. Sometimes it is not possible to talk directly to that person. Perhaps she or he is no longer in your life, or such an encounter would be much too risky. Full-bodied imaging can convince your subconscious mind that a "real" confrontation has taken place and a shift in your perspective can result.

In other words, we can do profound psychological rearranging without leaving the safety of our inner space. Using images in this way can heal old psychological wounds that are standing in your way. That is what this process is all about: clearing away the emotional and attitudinal debris that keeps you engaged in battle with your body, that keeps you from a clear perception of who you are, or your body image. You can make use of your power and reclaim your body.

Section 2
Tools for Transformation

III
KNOWING
WHAT YOU WANT

*Before you begin a thing remind yourself that difficulties and
delays quite impossible to foresee are ahead. . . You can only
see one thing clearly and that is your goal. Form a mental
vision of that and cling to it through thick and thin.*

Kathleen Norris

This work is about making important choices: how you choose to
feel about your body; what kind of body you choose to have; how
you choose to talk to your body and to yourself about your body;
what you choose to take in from outside sources; what you choose
not to take in. Perhaps you are not accustomed to seeing these as
choices but as givens. Looked at closely, they are simply ideas that
you have swallowed whole: you haven't spit out those pieces that are
indigestible—having nothing to do with you.

Now is the time to become clear about what it is *you choose* for
yourself in your relationship with your body. These choices will then
become your goals. With your sights set, any obstacles along the way
can be more easily overcome.

EXERCISE 1
Making Choices

Part 1
1. Sit comfortably, close your eyes and relax.
2. Tune in to your experience of being in your body right now. How
are you *feeling* in your body right now?. . . How are you talking to
yourself about your body right now?
3. Write down the words and phrases that came up for you.

4. Try each one on for size by saying each of them aloud in a way that acknowledges that this is how you feel in and about your body right now, *e.g.,* "I am heavy and sluggish," "I am tight," etc. After saying each one, pause and reflect on your feeling response to each statement.

5. Acknowledge to yourself that this is the point from which you are embarking on the journey toward wholeness.

Part 2

1. Close your eyes and relax again.

2. Now go into your imagination and discover how you really would *like* to *feel* in and about your body. Do not think of how you would like to look, but how you would like to feel, say light and easy.

3. Write down the words and phrases that came up for you.

4. Try each one on for size, first by letting yourself really feel each quality, then by saying each word or phrase aloud in a way that takes ownership of the feeling as if it were already true for you, for example, "I can move with a feeling of lightness and ease," etc.

5. Assemble these feelings into a *set of choices* that you wish to make true for yourself as you live your life in your body.

6. Enter this *set of choices* on the Statement of Intent that follows.

Worksheet
Statement of Intent

Transforming Body Image is a process of awakening to my own beauty, a beauty as unique as I am.

I, _____, am in process of changing my relation to my body.

This is what I choose for myself:

1.

2.

3.

4.

5.

And I deserve it.

Guiding Words

Please make a copy of the Statement of Intent and mount it on your wall in a prominent place so that it will jog your memory about what it is you want for yourself and your body. After all, you are doing this work so that you will one day be able to feel the way you choose about your body. You may find as you progress through these exercises that you become even clearer about these choices. When that happens, feel free to add, delete, or refine any of the chosen qualities that you have written on your Statement of Intent.

I want to underline one idea because it is extremely important for your transformation: your *feelings* in and about your body are what really count here, not the way your body *looks* from the outside. Focusing on the outer form of your body makes you an *object* to yourself. It takes you outside of your body. (I am not saying that the outer form of your body is irrelevant. What I am saying is that the outer form of your body can be lovely, but unless your inner feelings support that experience of loveliness you will be blind to it.)

•

Here are some ways to use your *set of choices:*
1. Create out of it a Feeling Meditation—let yourself feel all of these qualities using all of your imaginal senses. Do this for several minutes first thing in the morning and last thing at night. This will help you stay in touch with your goals.
2. Do your Feeling Meditation for a minute or two before and after doing any of the exercises in this book.
3. Do your Feeling Meditation any time you wish to feel clear and positive in and about your body.

IV
TRAINING YOUR IMAGINAL MUSCLES

As a child your imagination was the liveliest part of your mental equipment but, unless you are a veteran daydreamer or are actively involved in some artistic or creative work, your imagination has probably grown rusty.

Working with the imagination requires a very special mental state combining relaxation with alertness. Deep relaxation allows you to be receptive to the spontaneous images that freely come and go. Images are delicate creations — the quieter and more relaxed you are, the more sensitive you can be to the images your imagination presents to you. However, you should have some degree of alertness so that you can exercise control over your imagery. You will be asked at times to be open and receptive and at other times to manipulate your images. Before you begin an exercise, find a quiet place where you will not be interrupted.

Because we are all different we have our favorite ways of relaxing. Perhaps you have already found one that works for you. If not, hopefully one of these will appeal to you. In general when doing the exercises please sit in a chair or on the floor. You want to find a way to be comfortable enough to relax, but not so comfortable that you will fall asleep.

EXERCISE 2
Learning To Relax

RELAXXXXXXX
1. Stretch your body like a cat just awakening from a nap. . . And then sit comfortably so that your body is well supported. . .
2. Breathe naturally for 5 cycles of inbreath/outbreath. While you are breathing, scan your body for any areas that are uncomfortable and in need of rearranging. . .

3. Turn your attention back to your breathing. Watch your breath go in and out—don't try to change it, simply watch your breath breathe itself. . .

4. Breathe in and mentally say the word "Relax" as you exhale. . . Repeat this cycle for five minutes or until you feel relaxed.

Cleansing Breath Relaxation*

1. Turn your attention back to your breathing and watch your breath go in and out—don't try to change it, simply watch your breath breathe itself. . .

2. Now imagine that you have a nose on the bottom of both feet. . . Picture and feel the air coming in through the bottoms of your feet as you inhale. . . With each inhalation, pull the air up all the way from your feet—through your ankles, legs, and body, through your lungs and exhale through your mouth. Do this several times. . .

3. As you breathe in, actually feel the pull of drawing the air through the cells and tissues of your body. . . Imagine debris, ashes, or dried leaves swirling up with each breath—debris representing any emotional or physical distraction in the form of tension, fear, discomfort, etc. . . . They are being swept up and released from your cells and tissues with every deep exhalation. . . See it leaving your body in clouds. . . Experience this with all your senses and continue for several minutes.

4. Now try breathing in from some other part of your body that catches your attention, pulling the air in through the cells and tissues of that part of your body, sweeping up noise and releasing it from your body as you exhale. . .

5. Continue this cleansing breath, drawing the air in through any part of your body in which you find "noise" that impedes your total relaxation.

---

* Adapted from "Noise-Removal Breathing" from Win and Susan Wenger's *Your Limitless Inventing Machine*. Gaithersburg, MD: Psychogenics Press, 1979.

Some Image Relaxations

Candle in the Sun
1. Stretch your body like a cat just awakening from a nap. . . Then sit comfortably so that your body is well supported.
2. Breathe naturally for 5 cycles of inbreath/outbreath and while you are breathing scan your body for any areas that are uncomfortable and in need of rearranging. . .
3. Turn your attention back to your breathing and begin to watch your breath go in and out — don't try to change it, simply watch your breath breathe itself. . .
4. Imagine that you are a candle sitting in a hot, sunny window. . . As the rays of sunshine beat down on you, *feel* yourself begin to melt. . . Imagine that your concerns and tensions are dropping away as the droplets of wax roll down the side of the candle. . . *feel* yourself melting into a state of soft, deep relaxation. . . Let go and give in to the warmth of the sun and the inevitability of your melting as you release all mental and bodily tension and sink into a state of soft, deep relaxation.

Cloud Ride
1. Stretch your body like a cat just awakening from a nap. Then sit comfortably so that your body is well supported. . .
2. Breathe naturally for 5 cycles of inbreath/outbreath and while you are breathing scan your body for any areas that are uncomfortable and in need of rearranging. . .
3. Turn your attention back to your breathing and watch your breath go in and out — don't try to change it, simply watch your breath breathe itself. . .
4. Imagine a beautiful clear blue sky with several puffy, white clouds floating along with the air currents. . . Hop aboard a cloud and let yourself float along totally supported by the soft and enveloping cloud. . . You have nothing to do now but relax, float, and enjoy the ride.

•

The more you practice these relaxation sequences the easier they will be for you to do. Find one sequence that you like and stick with it. Now you are ready to flex your imaginal muscles and reclaim that powerhouse, your imagination.

Whatever you can see with your eyes you can "see" with your imaginal eyes. This also holds true for all your other senses. You have imaginal ears that "hear" the sounds in your inner environment, and an imaginal body that "feels" sensations and experiences feeling states on an emotional level. We will exercise most of the imaginal senses, but three will predominate: seeing, hearing, and feeling/touching. The more vividly you can use your imagination—that is, the more present you are in your fantasy and the sharper your imaginal senses are—the more powerful will be your experience and the deeper your transformation. Full-bodied imagining will be your ticket to body-mind health.

EXERCISE 3
Sensory Remembering

1. Please sit comfortably, close your eyes and relax.
2. Imagine yourself in some room or interior space that is very familiar, perhaps your bedroom or your kitchen. . . .
3. Look around you, carefully noticing details of shape and color. Perhaps you will see it all at once, or part by part. . . Look up at the ceiling and down at the floor. Notice the rugs, the arrangement of furniture and objects. . . How many doors and windows are there in the room?. . . What color are the walls and furnishings?. . . See if you can change the color of the walls and certain objects in the room. . .
4. Listen carefully a moment and notice what sounds are characteristic of this space. . . Perhaps it is the sound of traffic outside the window, or footsteps in the hallway, or the hum of the refrigerator. Take a moment to tune in with your imaginal ears. . .
5. Walk around the room and experience fully the sensations in your body as you move—notice the pressure of your feet against the floor, the sound that your feet are making, the feel of the air on your skin. . .

6. As you move through the room reach out with your imaginal hands and touch the objects in the room—the walls, woodwork, fabrics—all the surfaces and textures. . . Now move some of these objects around. . .

7. With your imaginal nose sniff the air and notice the smells in the air. . .

8. Let the image of the room go. . . See an imaginary curtain close on that scene. Rest a moment in the dark. . .

9. And now the curtain opens on a recent scene in which you had some very pleasant physical experience with good physical sensations such as eating a delicious meal, dancing, receiving a wonderfully sensuous massage, or making love. Take a moment to choose this scene and recreate it. . . Now experience moving into this scene until you can *feel* the sensations as if they were happening to you right now. . . Enjoy the pleasurable sensations noticing also the sights, sounds, smells, or tastes attached to this experience. . .

10. Prepare yourself to leave your imaginal space/time and to return to this place and time.

Worksheet

1. Were you able to do this exercise? If not, what difficulties did you have?

2. Describe some of your most vivid images in the present tense as if they were happening to you right now.

3. Which of your imaginal senses are the most vivid?

4. Which are the least vivid?

5. Comments.

Guiding Words

Most people find that they are far more facile with some imaginal senses than they are with others. Keep practicing until you feel comfortable at least with your imaginal eyes, ears and touch/feeling sense. Imaginal smell and taste are less important to this process.

Don't expect your imaginal senses to be as vivid as your real senses. It is the rare individual whose imagination produces truly clear and life-like images. Many people, myself included, cannot actually see or hear distinct images but "know" that the images are there.

When doing such quiet inner work, it is not uncommon for your attention to wander or for you even to fall asleep. The more at home you become with this way of working, the easier it will be for you to keep your attention focused. If you do fall asleep, ask yourself whether you are too relaxed or genuinely in need of rest. Perhaps falling asleep in the middle of these exercises may be a signal that there is something in the process you would rather avoid. Try to be honest. No matter what the reason is, do the sequence again until you can stay awake throughout.

It is not necessary to be a perfectionist about your imagining. Just keep practicing Sensory Remembering and the next exercise until you have confidence in your own imaginal agility. By the end of this book imaging will be second nature to you.

In the next exercise I will be asking you to do some things which may seem silly. They will tone your imaginal muscles and bring you closer to being a full-bodied imager, one who uses all of her senses in the imaging. The more of yourself you bring to this work, the more powerful your changes will be.

Your body image exists on many levels: neurological, mental, and emotional. The part of your body image that you are about to experience involves your nervous system or, more specifically, your kinesthetic sense. It is your brain and nervous system that are ultimately responsible for your kinesthetic sense, that sense which lets you know how to move your body, where your body is in space, and where your body parts are in relation to one another. It also lets you feel sensations and responses in your body. It is your felt sense; without it you would not be able to move or function in the physical world.

Exercising your imaginal body means exercising your nervous system. When you move an imaginal limb you trigger the same nerve pathways as you do when you move a real limb. This next exercise is central to changing your body image.

EXERCISE 4
The Imaginal Body

1. Please stand up and find a space where you will have room to spread your arms later. Close your eyes so that you can turn your attention inward. Notice how your body feels as you stand. . . Notice the alignment of your body. . . The feeling of your feet meeting the floor. . . Your sense of being grounded. . . Notice your body in relation to space. . . Notice the extent to which you feel you are in your body. . . Remember how you are now as a reference point for later.

2. Turn your attention to your head and neck. Move your chin toward your chest and back again. Repeat this several times, up and down, until you grasp the sensations involved in doing this act. . . Memorize these feelings. Now do the same movement with your *imaginal* head and neck. In your imagination move your chin toward your chest and back, trying to do it as vividly as you did with your real head and neck. Do this several times. If you need to refresh your memory, do the movement again with your real body. (Don't be surprised if you feel tiny muscular contractions as you exercise your imaginal body. You are activating your nervous system merely through the *intention* of moving it.)

3. Alternate the movement between your real head and neck and your imaginal head and neck, several times. . . Let go of this movement.

4. Now raise both real arms to shoulder height, out to the sides. Slowly lower and raise them several times until you can grasp and memorize the sensations involved in this movement. . . Do the same movement now with your imaginal arms trying to do it just as vividly. . .

5. Alternate between your real and imaginal arms several times, first raising and lowering the one and then the other, refreshing your memory if you need to. . .

6. Now you will really need to concentrate. Raise your real right arm and your imaginal left arm *at the same time.* Lower them. Then reverse it and raise your real left arm and your imaginal right arm. Lower them and reverse it again. Repeat this several times. . . Lower both arms. (Don't worry if this is confusing. Take your time and realize that you are asking your brain and nervous system to stretch and expand. Keep trying. To make it easier, with your eyes closed,

slowly raise your real right arm, and then hold it there. In your imagination raise your left arm. Now bring them both down to your side simultaneously. As the process becomes easier, gradually collapse the time element until you are raising your real right arm and your imaginal left arm together.)

7. Now raise your real right arm and imaginal left arm and bring them together in front of you. Clap them together several times. . . Reverse your arms and clap them again several times. . . Lower your arms, rest a moment and center yourself. . .

8. Begin to walk forward four or five steps. . . Reverse direction and walk backwards. . . Repeat this several times. . . Now walk forward and back with your imaginal body, several times. . .

10. Walk forward with your real body while you walk backwards with your imaginal body. . . Then reverse it so that you are walking forward with your imaginal body while your real body walks backward. . . Repeat this sequence several times.

11. Rest a moment and note the feelings in your body.

12. Make a space—a radius of several feet in front of you. Now with your real body jump into that space in front of you. Jump back. Do the same thing with your imaginal body, forward and back. Now with the real body. Real body again. Imaginal body forward and back. Now with the real body. Real body again. Imaginal body, forward and back. Finally, jump forward with your imaginal body and stay there. Then, jumping as high as you can, jump with your real body *into* your imaginal body.

13. Stand quietly for a moment and compare what you are feeling now in your body to what you felt in the beginning of this exercise. And now walk around naturally and experience your body in motion.

Worksheet

1. Were you able to do this exercise? If not, describe your difficulties.
2. Describe your experience of doing this exercise as if it were happening to you right now. Include any surprises, discoveries, insights, etc.
3. How are you feeling in and about your body right now?
4. Comments.

Guiding Words

Those of us who are locked in struggle with our bodies tend to have a weak or undeveloped kinesthetic sense. It is difficult to be kinesthetically grounded in our bodies when we are disconnected from them. So please don't be discouraged if this exercise is difficult for you. It demands considerable concentration.

One woman, Francine, wrote:

> "I had difficulty in feeling my real body as it moved; therefore I had difficulty in feeling my imaginal body move. The kinesthetic sense is something I lack. . . . Because it was hard for me—I met with more resistance. Yet, I am excited because I feel this kinesthetic sense of myself is in large part what makes me feel so unreal and alienated from my body."

This is a very important point. Your kinesthetic and visual senses are the two most important senses needed to change your body image.

This exercise can be confusing. Should you concentrate on your left side or your right? On your real or your imaginal body? Obviously, it is very difficult, if not impossible, to be in two places at the same time. That is the beauty of this exercise. To do all that it asks, you must be acting from your center, not the left or right, real or imaginal. This explains Annette's response, typical of so many who have done this process:

> "I am exhilarated by actually jumping into my own body. It feels good to be *in* my body. I enjoy walking around and experiencing the sensations. Before I began I experienced my body as being like a rock, heavy and lifeless. Afterwards I felt I was alive inside my body. I have a sense of being attuned—in my body. It's a feeling of integration and wholeness."

V

GETTING TO KNOW YOUR BODY IMAGE

As conscious human beings we possess the unique capacity to see ourselves, to stand back and judge. We are the only creatures on earth who can be *objects* to ourselves. When we look at ourselves in the mirror we are both subject and object, perceiver and perceived. Out of our perceptions and experience of ourselves we have constructed a self image. And out of our perceptions and experience of our bodies we have constructed a body image.

Your body image is a very subtle and complex aspect of yourself, that piece of psychological space where your body and mind come together. It is dynamic and changeable. Elements of it are different from one day to the next; yet it is also stable. You probably have notions about your body that have been fixed for many years. It is conscious. At times you are painfully aware of your experience in your body. But it is also unconscious—you do not have to stop and think about how to move your legs to walk. You have many beliefs about your body that motivate your behavior but which are not available to your conscious mind.

Your body image is not the same as your physical body. It is the way *you* see and experience your body, not necessarily how the world sees it—although how others experience your body can be very strongly influenced by the verbal and non-verbal messages you communicate about and through your body. Body sensations and your knowledge of where your body parts are in relation to each other and in relation to space contribute to your body image.

Your body image is experienced on a visual level, how you see your body; a kinesthetic level, your felt sense of being in your body; and an auditory level, how you think about and talk to yourself about your body. You will probably find that one or two of these levels need more rearranging. Perhaps you *feel* comfortable in your body, but thinking about how you look to others depresses you. Or it could be the other way around. Maybe you *look* fine to yourself, but you catch yourself *saying* horrible things to yourself about your body.

Your body image encompasses your ideas, feelings, attitudes, and values about your body. Every time you see yourself in the mirror or catch a fleeting glance reflected in a store window, every time you look directly at areas of your body, what you see is colored by your body image.

EXERCISE 5
Body Scanning

This exercise is a way of mapping your subjective, felt experience of your body, as well as the relationship of body parts to each other and to the environment. It is also a way of mapping the emotional life of your body. The exercise is divided into two parts. It is up to you whether you choose to do them in one go or two. I will be asking you questions to which there are no right answers. The answers should come from your internal experience rather than from your ideas. It is a special and very important kind of knowing. The more times that you do this exercise, the better you will get to know your body and body image. Areas that are uncharted territories will become more clearly defined, less subject to distortion. As your kinesthetic sense develops you will function more fully in everything you do.

NOTE: Please read each step and then close your eyes and go inside yourself for your answers.

Part 1

1. Lie down directly on the floor with your legs uncrossed, arms down by your sides. Notice how you are feeling in your body. . . Begin to pay attention to your breathing, simply noticing how this happens for you. Don't try to change anything, but rather trust that, after all these years, your breath knows how to breathe itself. Just allow yourself to breathe naturally and notice. . .

— What parts of your body move when you breathe?
— In what order are they moving?
— Are you breathing through your mouth or through your nose?

— Are you inhaling all the way, or is there some restriction that prevents you from taking a full in-breath?

— When you exhale, do you empty your lungs completely?

— Follow your breath and use it as a means to getting to know the inner areas of your body.

2. Try to sense how much of the surface of your body is present in your awareness. Scan your surface to discover which areas of your body's surface are clear and which are vague or missing entirely from your awareness. . .

3. Bring your attention now to the way that your body is lying on the floor.

— How are you feeling on the floor? Light? Heavy? Free? Constricted? How is it for you right now?

— Sense the contact that your back makes with the floor. Is it the same on the right as it is on the left?

— Notice those places where you are feeling pressure. . . Move your awareness from your heels to your head, noticing those parts of your body where you accept the support of the floor and therefore feel contact or pressure. . .

— Notice where in your body there is no contact with the floor: In your mind's eye imagine the size and shape of the spaces between your neck and the floor; the tips of your shoulders and the floor; between your shoulder blades; the small of your back; your knees, ankles, and wrists.

— With your hand (disturbing the way you are lying on the floor as little as possible) explore the spaces behind your neck, and the small of your back to see if they are as you sensed them to be. . .

4. Turn your attention to experience your body as a whole.

— If the ceiling were to be lowered right now, which part of your body would it touch first? Your breasts? Your nose? Your tummy? Your toes?

— How wide are you? Internally sense the width of your body, finding where you are widest. Where are you narrowest?

— Discover those places where you carry the most and least flesh.

5. Relying on your internal sense and not your memory, sense the width of your head. . . Then represent that width holding both hands directly over your face. Gently lower your hands to your face and check the accuracy of your sensing.

6. Try to sense the width of your hips. . . Represent that distance with both of your hands, holding them just over your hips. Lower them carefully, disturbing their relationship as little as possible, and

once again check the accuracy of your sensing against the true width of your hips.

7. Now experience your body as an integrated whole. . . Say to yourself the following, inserting your own name:

"This is my body. This is where I, _____, live." Feel the impact of these words on you. Say it again.

Worksheet

1. How is your body feeling right now? Has it changed merely from paying attention to it?

2. Describe your experience as if it were happening right now (including any reactions, surprises, questions, and feelings aroused by the process).

3. What areas of your body image are clearest and which are faint or missing?

4. Are your assessments of size and shape accurate or distorted?

5. Note any difficulties you had in doing this exercise.

6. Comments.

Part 2

1. Lie down, relax and notice how you are feeling in your body right now. . .

2. Scan your body to discover where you store emotions. To locate an emotion it is often helpful to imagine a situation where you felt that emotion and then to notice where in your body you experience that feeling.

— Where in your body does your anger reside?
— Where in your body does your love reside?
— Where in your body does your guilt reside?
— Where in your body does your shame reside?
— Where in your body does your fear reside?
— Where in your body does your mother reside?
— Where in your body does your father reside?
— Where in your body does your joy reside?

3. Scan your body for any other areas that hold some emotional charge or where you feel blocked or stuck. See if you can discover what messages these areas hold for you. Take each one in turn and ask yourself what each area would say if it could speak. See how you want to respond to each one. . .

4. Now experience your body as an integrated whole. Say to yourself the following, inserting your own name:

"This is my body. This is where I, _____, live." Feel the impact of these words on you. Say it again.

Worksheet

1. How is your body feeling right now?
2. Describe your experience as if it were happening right now (including any reactions, surprises, questions, and feelings aroused by the process).
3. Draw a map of your body locating areas where you found emotions or blockages.
4. What messages did your body have for you?
5. Note any difficulties you had in doing this exercise.
6. Comments.

Guiding Words

Body scanning is a way of becoming kinesthetically grounded.

It can change the way you experience your body from an amorphous blur to a clear image. This clarity is needed for a healthy mind-body relationship. Body scanning is also a first step in opening communication with your body, providing information about needs, blockages, and emotional states.

I recommend that you do this exercise several times. Each repetition will enrich your vocabulary of kinesthetic experience, reducing the potential for your distorting body image as well as making your emotions more available to you.

Francine learned a great deal about her body image and herself:

"I am surprised how dominant the upper half of my body seems, especially my face and shoulders. When the ceiling comes down it touches my nose first. From the waist down, my body drifts away but looms large in my mind. I am surprised (and laugh) when I measure the size of my hips — they are much smaller than I imagined. They feel good to me. My hands linger on them with more acceptance. I am more accurate with the sense of the size of my head and facial features though I underestimate the fullness of my lips. I feel that I purse my lips a lot with disgust and restraint and that my lips have therefore shrunk. When I ask what messages my body parts have for me, my back feels pain and says, 'Please don't overload me.' My right ovary is also in pain and says, 'I'm aching. I'm part of your femaleness. Have you forgotten me? I am part of your link to life, to cycles, to birth and death.' My throat is blocked and says, 'I want to cry. I want to shout. I want to sing. Please don't throttle me. I want to express myself.' My abdominal/genital area says, 'Please don't hate me, I'm not bad.' My breasts are numb and they say, 'I wish I were a little girl again.'"

Francine's story makes it easy to see how feelings and ideas about our bodies can create distortion in our body images. It also shows how much rich and important information is available to us if we take the time to attend to our bodies' messages. Often feelings that we refuse to acknowledge or express will be readable in our body, so that the more in touch with our body we become, the more we can be in touch with our feelings. Identifying body feelings takes practice, so be patient if the first attempt yields only sketchy clues.

Body Scanning asks you to do a very special kind of attending to your body, a quiet, fine-tuned, mindful attention full of noticing and empty of judgment. Practicing makes it possible for you to carry this non-judgmental attention into your daily interactions with your body and with everything else in your life as well.

For most women, the visual level of the body image experience is the most distorted and prone to judgment. When we look into a mirror, we do not necessarily see what is there. Instead we probably see an image laden with past associations, feelings, criticisms, unrealized aspirations, and many other things that have little or nothing to do with what the mirror presents to us.

We have very little opportunity to see ourselves as we really are. The mirror image is reversed and usually posed. The camera freezes us into static postures and adds weight to our frames. We can see certain parts of our bodies directly by looking down at our torsos and limbs, but we see them distorted by foreshortening.

We form distorted judgments of what we look like and over time these judgments become unconscious and habitual. By making these feelings and judgments conscious and explicit, we can confront them and change them.

_____ EXERCISE 6 _____
Imaginary Mind-Mirror

1. Sit comfortably, close your eyes and relax.
2. In your imagination, go where there is a full length, three-way mirror. Stand in front of the mirror, fully clothed, and look at yourself from all angles. Study the image in the mirror very carefully and as objectively as you can. Pretend that you are seeing you for the first time. See if you can look at yourself with an attitude of discovery.
3. If you were seeing this person in the mirror for the first time, what messages would you receive from looking at her?
   — What can you tell about this person from the way she holds herself?
   — What can you tell about this person from the expression on her face?
   — What can you tell about this person from the way she dresses?
   — How does this person in the mirror appear to feel about herself and her body?
4. In your imagination, take off your clothes. Look at your naked body in the mirror with the same sense of discovery.
   — Is there any shift in the way you are holding yourself?
   — What feelings come up for you as you look at your naked body?
   — Do you feel pleased? Ashamed? Vulnerable? What?
   — What judgments do you form as you look at your naked body?
5. What areas of your body do you focus on? What areas do you avoid or gloss over?
6. What do you like about your body? What do you dislike?
7. Take a closer look at your imaginal reflection from the front and, as you observe each part of your body, notice carefully the feelings, judgments and any other bits of self-analysis that come up for you.

Acknowledge them and see if you can let them go and move on.
- How do you feel about your face and head? Notice your hair, eyes, nose, mouth, neck, and skin.
- How do you feel about your body skin? Notice its color, texture, and tone.
- How do you feel about your torso? Notice your shoulders, breasts, waist, belly, hips, and genitals.
- How do you feel about your arms and hands? Your legs and feet?
- How do you feel about the lines and curves of your body?

8. Turn around and notice how your body looks from the side. Notice your judgments and ask yourself how attached you are to them.
- Notice your posture: the way your head sits on your neck, the curve of your back.
- Notice the line of your buttocks where it meets your waist, and again where it meets your thighs.
- Notice the curve of your belly and the shape of your breasts.
- Notice the shape of your legs.

9. Now turn so that you can see the imaginal rear view of your body.
- Notice the way you are standing.
- Notice what parts are clear to you and what parts are vague.
- How do you feel about what you are seeing?

10. Turn and face yourself. Look into your reflection, and acknowledge to yourself: "This is my body. This is where I, _____, live."

Worksheet

1. What are you feeling right now? How are you feeling about your body?
2. Describe your experience of looking at your reflection as if it were happening right now (include observations, surprises, feelings, judgments, and impressions).
3. What self judgments are you willing to relinquish?
4. What self judgments are difficult to relinquish?
5. Note any difficulties you had in doing this exercise.
6. Comments.

Guiding Words

Chances are that your first attempts at this exercise yielded negative material. If you had only positive feelings about your body, you wouldn't be reading this book. It is this negative material that you must ferret out so that you see clearly what you do to yourself most of the time.

Barbara had a very active judge.

> "I see the things I don't like but don't spend much time and energy looking and thinking about the body parts I do like. Sometimes in the mirror I feel my body is screaming out 'ugly' because I can't keep my body in sync with my ideal mental image of how I should look. I sometimes come closer, but some small imperfection yells out, 'I'm here,' so that I, as well as everyone else, can see it plainly as a blemish."

We are fiercely committed to seeing ourselves in a negative light and making certain that everyone else does also. Peggy's vigilant judge was always quick to "overcrowd (her) good feelings with negative statements." It became clear to her that she was heavily invested in maintaining a negative body image to reaffirm her position that she was an unlovable, unacceptable failure.

Looking at herself in this careful way, Kathryn realized something important.

> "At first I felt nothing. Then I began to really look at myself, the curves, texture, contour, lines of the past. . . I began to feel that my denial of my body was a way to continue the denial of myself. . . that an affirmation of my body was an affirmation of myself. As long as I could hold on to a negation of my body, refuse to value and appreciate its beauty and goodness, it was easy to negate myself, continue the self-hatred, self-pity, and self-denial that filled my life, distorting my relationship with myself and others. I am beginning to see and feel quite clearly that I am my body and to love my body is to love myself."

It may make you squirm to see what you do to yourself. Growth usually requires some degree of discomfort before you are ready to let go of self-defeating attitudes and behaviors. This exercise is the beginning of a long process of identifying the many voices that live inside you. Right now your inner critics outnumber and outvoice your inner fans. This balance will begin to shift as you become willing to confront and even to silence your judges.

The next exercise will help you reach even more deeply into your subconscious mind. As you go through this sequence, see if you can be open to whatever images appear spontaneously. Try not to force the images. They may be surprising or confusing but are probably accurate expressions of your inner reality. Above all, try to trust your own process. Your subconscious mind will present you with no more and no less than you are ready to deal with.

EXERCISE 7
Opening Doors

1. Sit comfortably, close your eyes and relax.
2. Experience yourself walking outdoors. It's a lovely day. Notice the color of the sky. . . The temperature of the air against your skin. . . Feel the ground under your feet and your body in motion. . . Pay attention to any sights, sounds, and fragrances that emerge along the way. . .
3. Off in the distance you notice a building. As you approach it at closer range, you see that it is a house. Keep walking until you are standing in front of the house. . .
4. Walk around the house so that you can see it from all angles. . . Notice what the house looks like, the condition of the exterior, size, shape, color, architectural style and any other details. . .
5. Notice how the house relates to its surroundings. . . Is it landscaped? Does it have a garden? Are there other buildings nearby?
6. How do you feel about this house? Do you like it? Do you like its style and the statement it makes from the outside? What don't you like about it?

Worksheet

1. Describe yourself in the present tense the way you described the house: for example, "I am large and stately," "I am well built but in need of paint," "I am small and unpretentious in the middle of the forest," etc.
2. In what ways does your house image fit or not fit your body image or your sense of yourself?
3. What are your feelings about this house?

•

7. Return to your image of the house and walk up to the front door. Place your hand on the doorknob and think of opening the door and stepping over the threshold into yourself. . . What feelings come up for you?. . . Acknowledge them and then open the door.

8. Walk into the house and spend several minutes exploring the interior, letting your images come as freely and spontaneously as possible, without judgment or forcing. Stay in touch with your feelings as you explore. . .

9. Look around the house until you find a hallway with doors on both sides. . . Begin to walk down the hall until you find a door with the words, "Body Room" written on it. . . Place your hand on the knob and once again contact and acknowledge your feelings as you anticipate opening the door and entering the room. . .

10. Open the door and enter your "Body Room." Using all your imaginal senses, let your images of the interior of the room come as freely as possible without judging or forcing them. Spend several minutes in your "Body Room" exploring its contents, all the while staying in touch with whatever feelings come up for you. . .

11. Choose one object or quality or aspect of the room that especially attracts your attention. Go up to it and ask it: "What message do you have for me about my relationship with my body?" Now identify with the object—really become it—and respond to the question as if you were speaking *as* the object. . . Return to yourself. . . Thank the object for its help.

12. Repeat step No. 11 with any other objects or aspects of the room that feel attractive or significant to you.

Worksheet

1. Reflect on each object until you understand its meaning in relation to the way you experience your body:

    a. How are you (or your body) like this object? What part of you does it represent?

    b. What associations do you have with this object?

    c. How would you translate the message the object had for you into an understanding of the work you need to do with your body image?

•

13. Return to your image of the "Body Room" and stand back so you can survey it as a whole. . . Reflect on how you would like this room to be. What changes would you like to make in the room?. . . Take a few minutes and carry out these changes using all your imaginal senses as vividly as possible as if in a speeded up film. . .

14. Now prepare to leave your "Body Room." Take one last look and turn to leave, closing the door behind you, knowing that this is a door that you can open any time you wish to have a symbolic reading of your relationship with your body.

Worksheet

1. What have you learned about your body image from doing this exercise?

2. What sense do you make out of the images you chose? What do they have to teach you?

3. Describe your feelings upon opening doors. Do they have any relationship to your feelings about doing this work on body image?

4. How would you translate the changes you made in the room into changes you want to make in your relationship with your body?

5. Note any difficulties you had in doing this exercise.

6. Comments.

Guiding Words

A house is often thought of as an archetypal symbol of the self and the body. Opening symbolic doors can give accurate and sometimes surprising information about the self/body image. A symbol is able to burrow under the surface without arousing the same degree of resistance as a direct approach. Working symbolically can be a very powerful way of bringing what is hidden or partially hidden about ourselves into the open.

In *Opening Doors* you have tapped into information regarding the way you present yourself on the outside, how you experience yourself inside, and what is going on in your body image. Our inner symbolism is very fluid. If you do this exercise several times (and I recommend that you do), the symbolism will probably change. These different images do not cancel each other out—they add up to a richer understanding of this very subtle and complex piece of inner space, your body image.

It is often striking how accurately this exercise can reveal conflicts. Patricia saw her house as a

> "castle, cold, large, and empty. I am surrounded by water, and a small, treacherous bridge leads to the iron gates. Vines entangle the house and there are tall, green trees all around the back. The sign says, 'Beware—Do Not Enter'. . . This perfectly describes how I think and feel about myself lately."

Patricia *is* difficult to see and dangerous to approach. Her inner experience is of space, cold and empty.

It is not unusual to have an exterior and interior that convey very different qualities. Allison's house was a

> "large, urban apartment building, neat, orderly, but cold, except that each apartment is warm, cozy, and safe. . . I think I project myself as being large, self-assured and solid like the apartment building. And the way I relate to people is sometimes detached and impersonal. However, inside the various apartments there are a lot of feelings."

I suggested that Allison have a dialogue between the cold outside and the warm inside so that she could see what she was trying to accomplish by maintaining such an exterior. This is a useful technique when dealing with contradictions in imagery. Allison't image is also revealing of the way she detaches herself from her feelings by compartmentalizing them in separate apartments.

The way you feel just before opening doors to your imagery often relates to the way you are approaching this work. In a sense, beginning this work is like walking across a threshold into yourself. Some of you will open doors with gusto and excited anticipation, while others will feel some mixture of willingness, apprehension, fear, resistance, and open refusal. Whatever you experience is fine. Simply acknowledge that this is where you stand and try to decide where you choose to go from there.

The interior of your "Body Room" holds questions and answers for you about your current relationship with your body. This rich information may be couched in obscure symbols or may be blatantly obvious. It is valuable for you to come to your own interpretations of the images you have chosen. By using the technique of identifying with your images you can begin to understand them from the inside, within the context of your own set of meanings.

It is not unusual to find the "Body Room" dark or empty. An empty room is not devoid of information. Sometimes it holds the key to knowing what is *missing* in your relationship with your body, or in your knowledge of this relationship. Sometimes it means simply that it is premature for you to receive certain information. Even a dark or empty room has structural features, walls, doors, floors, etc., that can be felt, that might hold messages if you seek them. Occasionally darkness or emptiness is a signal that something will emerge from the darkness if you hold steady. Margie saw a

> "dark room with a faint glimmer of light. The image becomes slightly brighter and the light is revealed as a candle burning. It is a room with a fireplace and an overstuffed sofa with large, comfortable-looking pillows. The candle is slowly getting brighter. The fireplace looks warm and inviting (although not lit). The couch looks comfortable and safe and warm. The walls have tapestries and the room is full of different textures. However, there are no windows or plants or any living things. There is no sunlight. I have to put in windows (to see out and be seen) and many plants so the sunlight will stream in and give the room an energy and life that have been missing. The fireplace should be lit and the candle allowed to burn out naturally. I feel that in spite of fears and anxieties I do have hope."

The changes Margie wanted to make in her room give glimpses into some of the changes she needs to make in her life.

Symbolism is a very personal matter. It is not uncommon to open the "Body Room" door and see parts of the body. Occasionally we choose very literal images. But although they are literal, their meaning varies with the individual. The body parts that Beth saw represented a traumatic experience she had during surgery. She was no longer able to feel the integrity of her body. Vicki, who works in an auto parts store, saw her body parts neatly lined up on shelves. For her this symbolized the way she saw her body as a commodity.

A window is not necessarily a window. For Margie, a window was a way of making contact with the outside world and of bringing in energy. Windows can also be ways of shedding light (awareness) on the darkness. Joanne had a room where the window had no glass. She felt overwhelmed by stimuli from the outside.

Please find the meaning of your symbols by asking them to speak. You and only you know why you choose certain images, and what they are trying to tell you about yourself. Sometimes these messages are vague, requiring persistence in order to understand them. It is sometimes helpful to take some extra time and engage your images in dialogue to try to bring out more information. Your persistence will reward you with valuable material that might take years to find on an analyst's couch.

VI
CULTURAL
ROOTS

Your body image has been formed out of every experience you have ever had: the way your parents related to and touched your body as a baby and a growing child; what you have learned from your role models about what it is like to live in and value a body; the acceptance and rejection you have felt from your peers; every negative and positive piece of feedback you and your body have ever received from people whose opinions count to you; and the ways you have perceived your body to fit or not fit the cultural image.

Each of us has both familial and cultural roots which interact to shape us into the people we are. The culture in which we live has shaped our parents' values which in turn influenced the choices they made in childrearing which in turn effect the values we develop. On the other hand, those features in our upbringing that were unique to our particular families created in each of us a ready and fertile soil for some cultural seeds to flourish. It is not possible to understand how we have arrived at the relationship we have with our bodies without also understanding the culture in which we have developed.

We live in a culture that places a very high premium on physical appearance. If this is true for the culture as a whole, it is doubly true for women who have been brought up believing that their chief, perhaps their only role in life, is as ornament, wife, and mother. Although the Women's Movement has made strides in broadening the choices available, the majority of women today still believe they must be attractive enough to snare a man who will provide the ticket for the unfolding of their biological and social destiny. Conforming to the current image of beauty guarantees fulfillment and seals a woman's fate. For most of us the myth dies hard.

Men in our culture are traditionally raised to be powerful, physically agile, and successful. The male self-image hinges primarily on how well he measures up to these requirements. While some men especially when young worry over the size of their genitals and their physical strength, the concern about body adequacy is finally less important than success in the world. With other ways of validating themselves, men can maintain their self image intact even in the face of serious physical flaws. The quest for physical perfection remains woman's domain.

What is beauty? How do we know if we are attractive? Somewhere there is an ideal image which women use as a yardstick. We live in a time when for the first time in human history the media are powerful forces in shaping our thoughts, values, ideals, and aspirations. Although films and fashion magazines have been influencing the cultural norm for many years, it is only since television that the media have gained the power to manipulate our lives. The majority of people in our society under the age of 35 have been raised by TV, the electronic babysitter, and much of what we believe and have come to know about the world we have learned from this surrogate parent.

Today's woman is constantly told by media images how she measures up or fails to measure up to the unreal, restrictive, elusive, and ephemeral esthetic standard. And as Deborah Hutton said in *Vogue Complete Beauty,* "The greatest misfortune [is] to be born out of one's era, with features appropriate for some undiscovered style, but hopelessly inappropriate for the one of the day."

The media communicates its messages through images which tyrannize our fleshy, flawed, embodied realities. No matter how much we try to control or diet or deodorize our bodies, we cannot hope to match the illusion on the screen or the printed page.

As women, we are especially vulnerable to the media message. We are rewarded for directing our attention toward others and for looking outside ourselves for guidance. We are encouraged to be passive and receptive. We tend to look to others for cues about who we are, what we should be, and how we should value ourselves. First it was our parents, then our peers, then our partners, and then most pervasively the media.

•

Stop a moment and reflect on what your ideal of female beauty is. What image are you carrying around in your mind's eye? See if you can discover where your ideal came from. Consider how you measure up to it, and whether it is even remotely within your grasp to measure up to it, given your natural resources.

•

Our culture has an obsession with thinness. Fat is seen as Public Enemy Number One and dieting has become the national way of life. It has not always been this way. Throughout most of our history, an extra padding of flesh has always had both survival and esthetic values for women. In those days thinness in women was considered an aberration to be pitied. What has happened to change this?

The shift can be traced back to the 1920s. Those were the days of the flapper, the beginning of women's emancipation, when the emerging desire for equality with men manifested itself in a change in clothing and in bodies. Gone was the accentuation of curves. Gone was the extra padding. Gone in fact was anything that advertised a woman's womanliness. Breast, hips, curves, and flesh came to be seen as impediments to equality with men, to be done away with or at least hidden.

Physicians also have promoted thinness as a way to health. In 1959 a major medical study advocated a major downward adjustment of the height-weight table. People of normal weight woke up to discover that they had been declared overweight by ten to fifteen pounds practically overnight! As a result, a national mania for thinness sprang up, bringing with it a giant diet and fitness industry. A new breed of women was born whose major career was to lose that last ten to fifteen pounds.

Surely the trend toward health and fitness has had many positive consequences, encouraging people to eat healthier foods and to exercise more. However, a new kind of tyranny has emerged, to be eternally young, fit, and lean whatever the price.

Caught between equally powerful media messages at one moment extolling the virtues of slenderness and at the next tempting us with images of forbidden morsels, we are locked in a double bind. Damned if we do and damned if we don't. And the bulimic who gorges herself to the point of bursting and then sticks her finger down her throat to eliminate the traces of her excesses is a living manifestation of this bind. Bulimia is an ingenious, albeit dangerous and painful, solution to an impossible dilemma. Is it any wonder that our bodies have become the battlefield for our conflicting drives?

Data from several recent medical studies conflict with the finding of the 1959 study. They suggest that some extra flesh can actually extend life and improve health and resistance to disease. Whether it is healthier to be plump or to be lean, it is probably more dangerous to our health to yo-yo up and down in weight than to remain stably overweight.

We must begin to question some of the notions about weight and health that have shaped cultural values and have pressured many of us into going against the dictates of our bodies. We must also begin to question where to draw the line between what is normal and what is overweight. The height-weight tables have recently returned to their pre-1959 level, thereby sanctioning at least medically the return of a healthy coating of flesh to the body. How long it will take to reverse the general insanity about weight remains to be seen.

Feminism has helped to change our cultural values over the last twenty years. The challenging voice of the Women's Movement tells us not to minimize ourselves, but to be more, to be larger, to be more powerful, to expand our horizons. However, for some women this opportunity is felt as pressure, bringing with it a new sense of inadequacy. They must perform in a realm for which they have been ill-prepared. And since a woman's sense of adequacy or inadequacy often translates into the adequacy or inadequacy of her body, it is the body that is often blamed for her success or failure. For other women, the move out into the world of competition with men is often experienced as a threat both to men and to the women themselves. If a woman becomes too powerful she fears alienating people and finding herself alone. It is my sense that women respond to some internal (and externally-supported) quota about how much space they are allowed to take up. The more power a woman is permitted, the more she is required (by herself and society) to make her body smaller, less important, less threatening.

Living in a time of rapidly changing roles and contradictory and confusing demands—eat/don't eat; be more/be less—it should come as little surprise that woman's body has become a confused battlefield rather than a home. Enlightened feminism has not guaranteed immunity to this mind-body malaise.

It is necessary to dredge up the past so that we can understand the influences at work in us. If we know what excess baggage we are carrying and even where we picked that baggage up, we are in a better position to let the baggage go and move on with our lives.

VII
MUCKRAKING

Our families act as agents and mouthpieces for spreading cultural values. They raise and socialize us according to prevailing standards, but each family has its own special handwriting that makes each of our histories unique. What we learn from our families sets the stage for further learning about ourselves. If our families have given us a positive sense of our bodies and our selves either through their own example or through their behavior toward us, we will be more receptive to similar messages from the outside world. Similarly, if we have learned to experience ourselves negatively in the family, we will be rich and receptive soil in which the negative seeds of cultural values can take root. We will tend to process any information from the outside through selective filters that support what we already "know" about ourselves, and to reject any messages that conflict with that "knowledge."

The following exercises deal with material of a very sensitive nature. You will uncover memories of important people and incidents that have played a powerful role in the development of your body image.

As you undoubtedly know, your relationship with your body is an emotionally loaded subject. Some of the material you uncover may be difficult or painful. If you experience discomfort, I want to encourage you to keep looking at this material. Your subconscious mind will present you only with images and memories that *you are ready to see* and deal with.

Trust yourself and your own process and remember that whatever you uncover in any of these exercises you have *survived already*. It is time to reexperience these memories so that you can *learn* from them and *deal* with them using all your resources. If at any time the going gets too rough, you can choose to step away from the material and open your eyes until you feel ready to go back inside to do some more work.

I want to encourage you not to be afraid of the feelings that come up. The more feeling you bring to your imaginal work, the more powerful it will be in transforming you. Feelings are natural and healthy. They are your system's way of expressing and cleansing itself of old baggage that it is time for you to discard.

Since this chapter and parts of the next are designed to bring old material to the surface, your daily life and perhaps even your dreams will be affected. This is natural. There comes a point in any healing process where you will be painfully aware of your issues and yet still lack the tools for change. Be kind to yourself and be patient. Please do not skip over this very important phase of the work. If you do, you will be denying yourself an opportunity to clear the way for the kind of change that motivated you to pick up this book in the first place.

EXERCISE 8
Rolling Back the Years

1. Sit comfortably, close your eyes and relax.
2. Imagine that you are moving back in time rapidly back through the years as if each year of your life were a card in a Rolodex file. . . growing younger and younger until you stop at some point when you were a small baby. . .
3. How old are you? Look around and notice what is around you. Are you alone? If not, who is there with you? Are you feeling safe and comfortable, or do you feel vulnerable in some way? Notice what it's like to have this baby's body. Take a few minutes to experience the world through fresh and innocent eyes. . .
4. Imagine that time is beginning to move forward now. *Feel* your body growing, becoming fuller and larger and more competent as you move into childhood. At some point stop the action. . .
5. How old are you? Look down at your child's body. How do you feel in and about this body? What do you like about it? What do you not like? Move around and experience the quality of your movement and energy. . . How are you feeling in relation to the world?
6. Time is beginning to move forward now, but more slowly than before. See if you can trace the changes occurring in your body as you begin to approach puberty, letting yourself *feel* how your body is

changing and developing and in what stages. . . Notice how you are feeling about the process happening to your body. . . Move around in this body and notice how that feels. . . Become aware of how you are feeling in your adolescent body in relation to the world. . . In reaching this stage what part of childhood must you let go of and what part of adulthood must you now adopt?

7. Time is beginning to move forward again. *Feel* yourself leaving your adolescent self behind as you mature gradually into the body you now have. Take as much time as you need to let that process unfold in detail, noticing whatever changes in shape and size that your body has gone through to reach its present state. Notice what you leave behind and what you take with you into adulthood. . . Notice and experience any shifts in your feelings about your body as you gradually move into the body you have now. . .

8. Rest. Notice how it feels to be back in your present body after your journey through the years. Open your eyes when you are ready.

Worksheet

1. Describe your experience of being a baby as if it were happening right now.
2. Describe your experience of being a child as if it were happening right now.
3. Describe the process of maturing from childhood to adolescence including feelings, gains, losses, etc.
4. Describe your experience of being in an adolescent body as if it were happening right now.
5. Describe the changes your body and body image have gone through since adolescence.
6. Can you pinpoint the period in your life when you began to feel negative about your body? Describe the circumstances surrounding this shift.
7. What of importance have you learned from this exercise?
8. Indicate any difficulties you had in doing the exercise.
10. Comments.

Guiding Words

By slowing down the action and following our development it becomes possible to identify milestones where there have been significant shifts in our body attitudes. We can begin to look more closely at those turning points for information about how we lost our way. What happened? Why did our bodies become a prison rather than a home for us? When we locate the injuries we can be more accurate in directing the healing process.

For some of you perhaps the disturbance came early. Maybe when you look back on your life you will find no period when you felt at home in your body. In some families babies and young children go hungry for the comfort of touch. Early touch is very important for letting us know on a very basic level that we (and our bodies) are acceptable and lovable. The quality of that touch can communicate love and valuing or duty and devaluing. Our young bodies take in those messages, whatever they are, without the judgment necessary to put them in perspective. We simply feel and learn about ourselves and about life through these feelings.

Most of you will probably discover puberty or pre-puberty as the period in your life when your attitude toward your body went amiss. In general, those are times of intense feelings of bodily awkwardness. It is during adolescence that we begin to measure ourselves against our peers. It is a time when acceptance is most important. Do I fit in? Am I sexually attractive? What do I do with my sexual feelings? Will my peers like me? Am I O.K.?

The rapid changes that occur in our bodies during this period are stressful and often result in a confused body image even if everything in our environment is positive (an impossibility, of course). Many of us suffer loss as our fathers retreat from our budding sexuality because of their own discomfort; other young girls receive more sexual attention from their fathers and other males than they can handle. Perhaps our mothers begin to experience us as rivals, or equally detrimental, as extensions and reflections of themselves. Many girls manifest their conflicts about growing up by gaining weight, or by dieting themselves into anorexia. Both approaches have the effect of hiding the telltale signs of developing womanhood.

What we learn about ourselves and our bodies during adolescence often becomes engraved into our body images and carried over into later life.

•

Reflect on whether and how that has happened to you.

EXERCISE 9
Family Portrait

This exercise will be most enlightening if you rely on the fresh vision of your imaginal eyes for information rather than drawing from what you already think you know about your family. In order to ease memory, *Worksheet* questions are interwoven with the exercise.

1. Sit comfortably, close your eyes and relax.
2. In your imagination, go back into your past to a time when you were much younger — to a formative and impressionable time as a child or early adolescent. Create an opportunity to bring together many members of your family in one place. (Perhaps it will be a gathering that actually happened.) Include any relatives or people who were important to you in your early years.
3. Gather everyone together — including yourself — as if you were posing for a family portrait. . . Notice who is present. . . And who is missing. . . Notice how you are arranged and where you are in relation to others. . . How old are you?
4. Now step out of the picture with your consciousness, leaving your body just where it is.
5. Notice their characteristic postures. What messages — both positive and negative — are they communicating to the world with their bodies?. . .

Worksheet

1. Who is present in your portrait and how old were you at the time?
2. What were the non-verbal messages communicated to you and to the world by their bodies?
3. As role models, how have they taught you to feel about your body?

•

6. Return to your imagination. Now separate out the males as a group. Are they attractive? How are they "masculine" and "male"? How do they appear to relate to their own bodies and their sexuality?. . . Walk up to them and sense how you feel in their presence. . . What have they taught you about what it means to be a female?

Worksheet

1. What was there to learn about maleness from the males in your family?
2. What did you learn about being a woman from your experiences with these males?

•

7. Return to your imagination and, keeping your consciousness outside the image, separate out the females in your family as a group, including yourself. . . How do you feel about their bodies when you look at them?. . . Notice their body types. . . The way they carry and dress their bodies. . . How does your body measure up in comparison to their bodies?. . . What can you tell from looking at them about their feelings about their own bodies?. . . What have you learned from them about how to value and care for your own body?
8. How do they feel about being women?. . . What do they teach you about what a woman is? Or is not?. . . What can you tell about their attitudes toward their own sexuality?. . . In what ways do they project it?. . . And in what ways do they mask it?. . .

Worksheet

1. How would you characterize the women in your family as a group in regard to appearance, self presentation, and ease in their bodies?
2. Do they seem to value their bodies? How do they take care of their bodies?
3. What did you learn from them about sexuality?
4. What did these women teach you about how to feel about your own body?
5. Which women have been important role models?

•

9. Return to your imagination. Reassemble your whole family in one place. As you look at these people, what feelings come up for you?. . .

Worksheet

1. What feelings come up for you as you contemplate your family as a group?. . .
2. How have you incorporated your family into your body image?
3. Of what you have taken in, what do you wish to keep? What do you wish to discard?
4. To attain the body image you want for yourself, what kind of role model would have been helpful that was unavailable in your family?
5. Comments.

Guiding Words

One of the most important ways that our families can influence our body image is through their own body images. Our families are our primary teachers during our formative years. What they teach us by example serves as the basis for what we learn subsequently. If our parents or other significant family members negate, deny, or otherwise devalue their *own* bodies, we pick up this negative judgment from them and apply it to our own bodies.

It can be a very subtle and even insidious way of learning since it comes through non-verbal channels such as body language and behavior. It can slip into our attitudes toward the world so quietly that we may not be conscious that we have adopted our family's viewpoint.

Doing *Family Portrait* is one way to tap into information about your role models and what you have most likely internalized from them into your own body image. Another way to ferret out this information is to look through your family photo album and study what their body language—posture, expressions, clothing, relative positions—reveals to you. You can apply this same exercise to your real, in-the-flesh relatives who will unwittingly provide you with a wealth of information.

When Joan looked at her imaginal family she saw

"people with no bodies, just heads. They show no physical expression. Nobody is touching. They are devoid of affection and devoid of life. There seems to be a family standard to ignore the body. They taught me nothing—except to deny my body. I have learned to repress my sexuality and to be disconnected from it."

The women in Donna's family were all overweight and appeared ashamed of their bodies.

"They were basically hiding their womanliness and denying their sexuality as if it wasn't okay to be a woman. They taught me that if I didn't watch out, my body would spread and I'd have a weight problem. They taught me my body was to be hidden away or dieted away. They taught me to ignore my body, to pay attention to it only when it got sick—that was the only time."

Donna has had a steady stream of minor health complaints all her life. It is one of the few times she acknowledges her body. The other times come with weight gain. She lives in dread of becoming fat and has been anorexic and overweight at different times in her life. Much of the disgust she has toward her body is focused on those areas that declare her womanliness—her breasts, hips, buttocks, and thighs.

EXERCISE 10
Parental Images

Please do this exercise at least two times, once in an imagined scene with your mother and on a separate occasion with your father. You can also do the exercise with other people who were influential in your early years.

Part 1
1. Sit comfortably, close your eyes and relax.
2. Go back to a time in your life when you were young, either a child or an adolescent. Picture a familiar situation involving you and your mother or father. . . How old are you? What are you doing together?. . .

3. Look at this person and observe how you feel. . . Pay attention to any feelings or associations attached to this image. . .

4. Scan the image as if it were right in front of you; look at this person closely, noticing the details of face, body, expressions, gestures, carriage, clothes, and grooming. . .

5. What can you gather from non-verbal cues about this person's feelings about her/his own body and sexuality?

6. What do you like or dislike about this person's body?. . . What awarenesses come up for you?. . . Are your bodies alike or different? How?

7. Imagine merging with this other body and then separating. . . Which is easier for you?. . .

8. Move closer to this person, and observe carefully how you feel about your body in her/his presence? How do you feel about yourself? Do you feel accepted by this person?

9. Ask this person if she/he accepts and loves you and your body. . . What is missing for you in her/his response?

10. What do you feel that you need from this person right now? Can you ask for it?. . . What response do you get?

11. Reach out to touch this person. . . How do you feel about doing this?. . . How does this person respond?. . . Does she/he touch you back? What does the content or quality of the response communicate to you about your body and your self?. . .

12. What do you want or need to express or communicate right now to this person? Take a moment to find in yourself the feelings and words that demand expression right now. . .

13. Look at this person directly in the eye and express whatever you want to say with feeling and conviction. . .

Worksheet

1. Describe your experience with this parent in the present tense using as much detail as you can recall:

2. What sort of example did this person set for you? What do you wish to keep from what you learned from this person? What do you wish to discard?

3. What was her/his behavior toward you?

4. What do you need to express to this parent (either from the past or the present)? Is this something you are actually willing to do with your parent?

5. What is positive in your interaction with this parent?

6. Take some time to imagine what the child in you really needed from this parental figure so that your body image could have been more positive. From this information (and from question No. 5), create for yourself a *Positive Parent Image.* Consider some of the following:

- What would you have needed in the way of nurturing (feeding of food, love, support and affirmation)?
- How would you have wished this parent to express love for you? In words, touch, actions, etc.?
- How would you have needed this parent to deal with your aggression and sexuality?
- How would you have needed this parent to relate to your needs for closeness and bonding while at the same time allowing your autonomy and separateness?
- What qualities would you like this parent to have modeled for you?

7. What is negative in your interaction with this parent? From this information create for yourself a *Negative Parent Image* which you will use in Part 2.

8. Comments.

Part 2

1. Sit comfortably, close your eyes and relax.

2. Imagine that you are standing. In front and to the left of you is your *Negative Parent Image.* In front and to the right is your *Positive Parent Image.*

3. Turn toward your *Positive Parent Image* and see how much you can open yourself to the flow of positive feelings available to you from this parent. . . Let yourself receive all the affirming, nurturing, supportive feelings coming from this parent to you, allowing yourself to bathe in the love coming from this parent to you. . .

4. Notice what you can let in. . . Notice what you are blocking out. . . Notice *how* you are blocking it out. . .

5. Examine your resistance and ask yourself: What would be the risk of letting these feelings in? What would you stand to lose?

6. Now turn toward your *Negative Parent Image* and express whatever feelings you have toward that person that may be contributing to your resistance.

7. Turn once again toward your *Positive Parent Image* and repeat Steps Nos. 3 and 4.

8. Move back and forth between these two *Parent Images* until you can clear a path for taking in positive feelings or at least recognize the *clean up* work that you need to do with your *Negative Parent Figure* and the *opening up* work that you need to do in yourself. Take as much time as you need to do this work.

Worksheet

1. What is blocking your ability or willingness to accept positive feelings or information from your *Positive Parent Image?*

2. What work remains for you to do with your parents either in fantasy or in the flesh in order to improve your relationship to your body?

3. Comments.

Guiding Words

It is completely natural for us as young people to *identify* with our parents. As women, it is our mothers with whom our identification is the strongest. Many of us have been fed prophecies such as "You're going to grow up and look just like your mother!" Many of us grow up identified with our mothers. For some of us it is nearly impossible to see ourselves and our bodies in their own right as separate from our mothers'. Such was the case for Eve, a very thin woman with a fat mother and a fat body image.

> "On the beach with my mother, we are both lying on towels reading. I'm sixteen and wearing a two-piece bathing suit. I'm annoyed because she's wearing one too. I think I'm more than annoyed, I'm angry at her, and embarrassed to be near her because she looks so fat and I'm afraid of how she will reflect on me. She doesn't seem to be self-conscious. How she looked bothered me, made me concerned about how I would develop. I worried a lot about it then and I worry now."

Sometimes it is not your mother's body but what it represents that provokes an identification or in some cases a dis-identification. In her work with *Family Portrait* and *Parental Images,* Joanne came to some stunning realizations. She did *Parental Images* with her real mother and with her grandmother who had raised her. Her mother is fat and her major memories of her were warm and loving and revolved around food. For Joanne, *love* came to equal *fat*. Her grandmother, on the other hand, was a thin woman who could not provide her with emotional warmth and physical contact.

> "She never accepted me. She was critical and unbending. Her body was controlled and not very playful. I hate control, I am out of control concerning my body and what I put into it. Her body taught stiffness and control. . . I rebelled against my grandmother, saying, 'If you are in control then I am out of control.' That is exactly how I've been around food issues. When I go to my grandmother's house it's uncomfortable because if I ask for seconds she calls me a 'little pig' so I sneak food there. I feel shameful and deceitful."

Joanne's body has played out her conflicting internal images by alternately being anorexic, bulimic, and overweight.

It is common for a mother to see her daughter as an extension and reflection of herself. When she is overinvested in her daughter's bodily life, she lives vicariously through her daughter and must manage her eating and dressing habits as well as her behavior. This makes it very difficult for the daughter to feel ownership of her own body and to create an identity for herself separate from her mother.

Especially as puberty approaches, competition with our mothers and other close female models can effect body image. Julia's mother felt that she was no longer beautiful and unconsciously saw in her daughter a threat to her own self-esteem. She gave her daughter a fear of her own power and a sense of inadequacy about her body. For Bea it was her fraternal twin sister who was her major rival for parental attention. Although Bea was considered the brighter of the two, it was her sister who turned everyone's eye with her exceptional good looks. Bea had grown up with great insecurity about her own appearance. She has tenaciously clung to her "knowledge" that she is plain and always second best.

While our fathers are considerably less important to us as body role models, as the first significant male in our lives, they can have a powerful impact on how we adapt to our womanliness. Puberty often marks a shift in the father-daughter relationship. In Virginia's case, her father's own discomfort with his daughter's emerging sexuality manifested itself as a withdrawal of affection.

> "I had been Daddy's little girl. Father and I had been very close, but as I developed he pulled away and didn't know how to relate to me. I was

saddened by the loss and nurtured myself with food. Maybe even my period was slow in coming as a reaction to my fear of growing up."

Some fathers cross the line into incest, leaving traces of shame on our body images. Whether our fathers react to our burgeoning womanhood with abandonment or invasion, the lesson is that it is not safe or acceptable to be pretty and sexual.

We tend to *internalize* parental treatment (positive, critical, invasive, or denying) in a do-unto-myself-as-I-have-been-done-to manner. If you have swallowed your critical parent whole you will continue the criticism on your own.

Hopefully you were able to tap into some very important information about the source of your difficulties with your body. However, discovering what was negative or missing in your relationship with your parents does not constitute a license for open hunting. Blaming your parents for what is wrong with the way you relate to your body will not solve anything. What *will* help is understanding the roots of your attitudes and behavior so that you can begin to change.

You can also use *Parental Images* to observe your relationship with your parents in the present. You can do this simply by altering Step No. 2 of the exercise and choosing a present-day context. You may want to confront your parents in the flesh.

Most of you will begin the process of identifying what you want to discard in your body image and what you want to keep in order to make a clear statement to yourself and to the world about who *you* are as a separate individual apart from your parents.

We can find new role models for ourselves that fit our mature aspirations. We can use our imagination as a place of healing where we can give ourselves the kinds of strokes and affirmations that were not available in our real families. One way to do this is to create a regular meditation based on your interactions with your *Positive Parent Image*. This will not only help you to heal some of your old wounds and fill in the missing pieces, but will also help you to become more receptive in general to positive feedback that is available in your world.

VIII
WHO'S WRONG WITH YOUR BODY IMAGE?

This chapter and the next represent a transitional phase of *Transforming Body Image*. We will be doing a combination of three kinds of work: 1) Clarifying what you are carrying around as excess baggage; 2) Identifying some of the obstacles that block your path; and 3) Beginning to discard the baggage.

Excess baggage is any knowledge, belief, or feeling that does not really belong to you or no longer serves you. In the case of your body image, it consists of everything you have swallowed whole from your culture, your family, and other people. When you take in information or feedback from the outside and swallow it whole, you have never really evaluated it to see whether it should become part of you. Since we have been socialized to look outside of ourselves for everything, we easily adopt other people's attitudes that really are not relevant to us or sometimes endanger us.

Seed Questions

1. Make a list of the people in your life who have had a major impact on the development of your body image. These should be people in your past and present whose values have shaped your attitudes toward yourself.

EXERCISE 11
Imaginary Visitors

1. Sit comfortably, close your eyes and relax.
2. Take a few minutes to get in touch with how you see yourself, how

you feel in and about your body, and how you talk to yourself about your body—right now. . .

3. Carry out the instructions in this step with each of the people on your list, one at a time, spending as much time with each as it takes to ferret out the needed information.

- Imagine yourself standing naked.
- Imagine that this person enters the room and walks around you, looking at you from all angles.
- Carefully observe your feelings.
- Imagine what this person is noticing and thinking about your body.
- Ask this person to tell you what she/he is seeing.
- Get in touch with your body image again and notice whether and how it has been influenced by this visitor, both in this exercise and in your development.
- See if you have anything to say to this person right now. Say it with feeling and conviction.
- Stop and write down what you have taken into your body image from this person that you wish to discard.

4. Scan your body now to see where your perceptions have been influenced by others. . . For every negative judgment that you have swallowed, balance it with *two* positive statements about this part of your body. . . Take as much time as you need.

5. Study your list of excess baggage. Imagine that each observation or judgment is "food for thought." Put each bit of this food in your mouth, experience how it tastes. . . Chew it, see if you want to swallow it and make it a part of you, or see if you want to spit it out. . . Vividly imagine yourself swallowing it or spitting it out, being clear with yourself about what you are choosing to discard or to make a part of you. . . Take as much time as you need.

Worksheet

1. Think back to the positive feedback you received. How much of it are you willing to let in? How and why do you resist letting it in?
2. How have you tried to change yourself to please each person?
3. Which pieces of excess baggage seem easy to let go of?
4. Which are you unable or unwilling to let go of?
5. What would be the risk or cost to you of letting it go?
6. Comments.

Guiding Words

Hopefully, you are beginning to see the origins of some of the chronic and habitual ways you see, feel, and talk to your body. By identifying and sorting out each judgment, you begin to see that you have a choice about whether to accept it or not.

When Sharon invited her mother in:

> "Her judgments are rattled off at almost every body part. They are very familiar and powerful. 'I'm never good enough.' . . . Mother's judgments have been important ones that have stuck. I am attached to them. They keep me from enjoying myself sexually."

When Brenda did the exercise with her aunt she discovered that she associated her aunt's flamboyant, passionate, body-oriented nature with emotional instability and suffering. Her mother, on the contrary, was subdued, in control, and out of touch with her body. . . "Perhaps I'm afraid if I do become more affirming of my own body, I will be unstable and reckless like her."

All of us are bound and attached to other people by powerful feelings, positive or negative. Most of the time our feelings toward others are a blend of positive and negative. It is easy to harbor negative feelings toward someone who has hurt us. These feelings weigh us down with excess baggage and leave us vulnerable.

We cannot control everything that happens to us, but we can control how we react. We can choose to nurse our wounds and feel sorry for ourselves, spinning our wheels. Or we can choose to let go of our pain and move on with our lives.

Seed Questions

1. Think of the people in your life who have left a negative mark on your body image (*e.g.,* Mother, Slim and Perfect Aunt Josephine, the boys in your 8th grade class, etc.).
2. Arrange them in order beginning with the person who did the greatest damage to the way you feel about your body.

EXERCISE 12
Wheel of Chains

1. Sit comfortably, close your eyes and relax.

2. Experience yourself sitting quietly in a large, sun-filled space, either outdoors or indoors. . . Feel the warmth and radiance of the sun. . .

3. Mentally invite into your space those people from your past and present who have taught you to negate your own beauty. Watch them as they enter, noticing that each one is carrying a heavy chain with a loop on one end. Invite them to sit in a circle with you in the center. . .

4. When they all sit down, let yourself experience your feelings as you sit surrounded by these people. . .

5. One at a time, deal with each person in your circle according to the order you chose above.

6. See this person standing up and walking over to you. Take the looped end of the chain in your hand and place it around your body. As you do this, acknowledge that it is *you* who are binding this person to you with a chain that represents some negativity. . . Watch this person return to you with a chain that represents some negativity. . . Watch this person return again to the circle.

7. Sit quietly and let yourself remember the feelings that bind you to this person. . .

8. Turn and face the person, take a moment to gather your thoughts and then express them as clearly as you can with all the emotion that fits your words. (Remember the more feeling you can bring to the image the more healing it is.)

9. Give this person the chance to respond.

10. Thank the person.

11. Repeat Steps Nos. 6-9 with each person in your circle.

12. Look around the circle once more and check if there are any left-over negative feelings that you haven't expressed to your satisfaction. If you find any, express them now. . .

13. You are in the center of this circle bound to all of these people by chains that represent bonds of negative feelings such as pain, anger, shame, envy, and hate. Experience with all your senses the heaviness

and limitation of this kind of bondage. . . Ask yourself: "Do I want to remain bound, or do I want to let go?

14. If you wish to remain bound, acknowledge this as a decision. Stop here and pledge that you will examine this decision. If you choose to release yourself from the confines of this negativity, go on with the exercise.

15. Return to the circle. Experience yourself in the center of a ray of sunshine. . . Feel the intensity of its golden warmth melting any traces of pain in you. . . Imagine a column of light filling the interior of your body, and with each breath you take, breathe in a warmth that nurtures you and allows that inner core to grow brighter and stronger. . . With each breath allow your heart to open and your generosity of spirit to grow. . . Really *feel* your warmth and radiance. . . Take several minutes.

16. As your inner strength grows, you can allow the openness of your heart to manifest itself as feelings of forgiveness. . . Concentrate your attention on opening your heart, on letting go more and more of the negativity that binds you to these people. . .

17. Do this step for each person in your circle. Gaze at the person and as you do, breathe deeply and *feel* your inner warmth and strength increase as you direct forgiveness to this person. . . Concentrating on the feelings in your heart, say the words, "I forgive you, _____." Say it again and use the warmth in you to melt the chain that joins you, watching it transform into a delicate golden thread linking you in spirit. . .

18. Now look around you at the faces in your circle, at the glistening golden threads that join you to these people through heart and spirit instead of pain and resentment. *Feel* what this is like for you. . .

19. Turn your attention now to opening your heart to yourself, enveloping yourself in forgiveness for all the ways that you have disappointed yourself, past and the present. . . Say these words to yourself with feeling:

   "May I be happy. . . May I be free from tension, fear, worry, hate and suffering. . . May I let go of all things that bind me to pain and cause me suffering. . . May I be whole. . . May I experience my own grace. . . May I be at peace."

20. Stay quietly with these feelings as long as you can permit yourself and then gently open your eyes.

Worksheet

For each person in your circle please ask yourself:

1. How did this person cause you pain?
2. In what way(s) did this person's behavior affect your relationship to your body?
3. What feelings and statements did you need to express to this person?
4. Are you willing to let go of your grievances against this person? If not, what do you gain or accomplish for yourself by holding on to your grievances?
5. Who in your circle remains unforgiven? Are you willing to keep trying until you can dissolve the bondage? If not, why not?

Guiding Words

Joanne invited into her circle "old boyfriends, people who raped me, my father, my grandmother, lots of men, and two women I am jealous of."

> "I hate the chains. I want to break loose. I like letting out the anger and fear I've felt all these years. Some of these people go back 17 years. I can transform the chains and understand that these people are victims too. I can forgive them. The hardest one to forgive is a man who raped me when I was thirteen. I feel so much anger, but he was young then. . . I pray he has changed. The golden threads are beautiful. I wanted to bury all those people, but forgiveness feels better."

It is important to confront and express our negative feelings before we can let them go. We don't often have the opportunity to express what is in our hearts either because the risk is too great or simply because those people who have hurt us are no longer active in our lives. By using our imagination and having fantasy dialogues with them (especially when we put feeling and conviction into our words) we can safely release a great deal of emotional toxicity from our systems. An imaginary confrontation can act as a safe substitute for the real thing or can serve as a rehearsal for a real interaction.

Some of you may find that certain people in your life are difficult or impossible to forgive at first. If this happens, please do this exercise again, concentrating on that person only. You may find that you need to spend more time on the step in the exercise where you express your feelings to that person. If you have the opportunity and the risk does not feel too overwhelming, why not confront this person in the flesh, or spend some time writing about the feelings that are keeping you stuck, or writing a letter to this person that you do not send. Please make a pledge to keep working at the problem until it becomes easier to let go of these chains that bind you.

I suggested to Joanne that she do the exercise again, this time concentrating on forgiving herself. This was her experience.

> "My chains were of self-loathing and self-deprecation. I became full of glowing energy—a glowing orb of light. I said 'I forgive myself for all the pain I've caused myself.' And my other self became a glowing energy too. I was crying. I feel good that I could forgive myself and transform the chain. I feel like I have a twin that has known me all along who probably was very perplexed that I put myself through all the torture and self-destructive behavior."

When Francine did *Chains* with her mother, she got in touch with the "stubborn little girl" who was convinced that her mother hurt her on purpose because she did not love her. She found that she still wanted to nurse that hurt, because she was not yet ready to take responsibility for her own life. Because she holds on so stubbornly, she is locked in battle with her mother. Her inability to forgive her mother saddened Francine and spurred her on until she was finally successful and forgave her mother.

Forgiving those who have wronged us is not easy work, but it is crucial if we are to move on with our lives. Most of us perversely would rather hold on to our pain than let it go. We can then feel sorry for ourselves and blame all of our suffering on others. Some people live with the mistaken notion that they *are* their pain, that without it they would no longer be special. It's true that letting go of our grievances leaves a vacuum which can sometimes be perceived as a loss or a sense of emptiness. Perhaps it would help to look at this analogy. When you clean out your closet you throw away things that hold memories, but you are making room for a new wardrobe. In your emotional housecleaning you are creating a very special and fertile kind of emptiness, a fertile void, that should be embraced as an essential part of making room for new growth.

We often think that to forgive means giving up some piece of our self-respect, that somehow we lose face. This is what our pride and stubbornness tell us. Nothing could be further from the truth. In fact, it requires inner *strength,* not weakness, to forgive those who have wronged us and to move on with our lives. We lose nothing but our chains.

IX
HOLDING ON
TO WHAT?

For many of us a negative body attitude serves a defensive function: It maintains the status quo. It protects us against feeling, doing, or being something that we perceive as risky. Very often we are busy protecting ourselves from risks or losses that threatened us in the past, but are in no way dangerous to us now. Often we use our negative body attitudes so that we do not have to take responsibility for our lives as adults.

In this chapter and the next, you will begin to look at your resistance to change, the ways you are limiting yourself, and how these limitations serve you. When you have identified the function your negative attitude performs, you can begin to look around for other ways of fulfilling that function. Perhaps you will discover that many of these mechanisms do not serve you at all and you can choose to let them go.

In order to let go of these mechanisms, you will first have to identify them. Choosing to let go of these mechanisms requires a *you* who is willing to make such a choice, a *you* who, from the center of your being, chooses a life of wholeness and health.

EXERCISE 13
Cloaks of Identity*

1. Write down ten words or phrases that describe your negative feelings and attitudes about your body, *e.g.,* "I am fat," "I am ungainly," etc.
2. Choose the five that you feel closest to and write each of these on a small piece of paper.

* Adapted from Frances E. Vaughan's *Awakening Intuition*. New York: Anchor, 1979.

3. Arrange these pieces of paper in a stack with the ones that feel most essential to you on the bottom and the ones that are least essential on the top.

4. Sit comfortably with your stack of papers within easy reach. Close your eyes and relax.

5. (Please follow this two step procedure with each piece of paper.) Pick up the first piece of paper and look at the words which define your relationship to your body. Allow yourself to *experience fully* what it means to you and your life to identify yourself this way.

—How does it feel to be defined by this?

—Be aware of all the sensations, thoughts, feelings that go along with this definition of yourself.

—Acknowledge and experience in fantasy the many ramifications of this self-definition in your life (relationships, career, self-image, health, etc.).

—Experience the way in which it limits you and also the things it gives you permission to be or do.

When you have fully experienced this piece of paper turn it over and as you do imagine that you are letting go of this self identification as if you were taking off a cloak.

—Notice any shift in your body sensations and feelings.

—Who are you without this particular way of identifying yourself?

—What is it like to give it up? What do you gain? What do you lose?

—Notice whether it is easy to let it go or whether it is difficult.

—Is there anything risky about letting it go?

6. After completing these steps for all five identifications, simply be quiet and let yourself experience wordlessly how it feels to be you when you are free of them. Experience your "I AM-ness". . .

7. Meditate on this thought:

"I am the center of my identity. From here I have a sense of permanence and inner balance. From this center I affirm my identity." Take as long as you like in this step before proceeding to the next.

8. Dealing with each paper/identification, one at a time in the reverse order (*i.e.,* from most closely to least closely identified), pick each one up and imagine it as a cloak that you are putting on again.

—Experience your feelings as you take back this self identification.

—How are you feeling about this particular identity?

—Notice how your feelings and body sensations change as you take back all the identifications, one at a time.

9. Rest quietly for a moment before writing on your *Worksheet*.

Worksheet

1. Who are you without your identifications? How are you different with them?

2. Process each identification with an eye to learning what role it serves in your life and what your resistance is to letting go of each one. Try a question like, "If I let go of _____ then I will _____."

3. What feelings came up for you as you took back each identification?

4. List here any resistance to change which surfaces during this exercise.

5. For each resistance explore other ways of meeting the same needs that do not involve distorting your experience of your body.

6. Comments.

Guiding Words

I hope that this exercise has helped you to identify some of the ways that you are holding on to negative body attitudes and how these attachments serve you. Many women who have done this sequence have felt so wonderful to be relieved of their weighty cloaks that they reacted with anger and refusal when I asked them to put them all back on. I did this for several reasons. Most important, your defensive baggage has a place in your system, and it should be shed *only* when *you* are *ready* to shed it, not just because I instruct you to. Also, this exercise is an exploratory device, not a quick easy way of revamping your whole identity. Our identifications die hard, and the manner and pace at which we shed them is individual and most likely gradual. It is not my purpose to strip you of your identity and leave you naked and vulnerable. It is my purpose to lead you to a place where you can experiment with different possibilities in a safe way.

If you had a strong reaction when I asked you to take back your identifications, that is a good sign that on a very basic level you really don't want them. Yet you are still not quite ready, nor do you have all the tools necessary to let them go. But remember that feeling, remember how much you wanted to be free of all these self-imposed burdens. This memory can help you gain the courage you need to change.

If you had difficulty shedding your identifications or felt relief when you took them back, you should acknowledge the risk in letting go of your excess baggage. For you, the road may be longer. Try to respect your own process and pace.

Francine experienced considerable resistance to letting go of her attachments. She found that her clumsiness was a way of playing the clown so that people laughed with her rather than at her. By seeing herself as unfeminine she was:

> "set apart from women who are physically weak, small and unnoticed, women without stature in the world, women who are defenseless and inconsequential. . . commercialized, vulgarized objects for men. . . . They have been stripped of a woman's power, power that men fear and hate."

And her fat served as an insulation from the world.

> "It protects me from having to be a sexual human being. It allows me to exist outside the normal social order, sometimes as an outcast, sometimes as a privileged person. Sometimes it allows me to be invisible. It protects me from victimization, especially at men's hands. I was raised to be fat. My family only relates to me as a fat person."

In addition she discovered that by identifying herself as unclean she was able to maintain distance between herself and others. The pain of being unlovable was the driving force behind her creativity. Francine is using her body image as protection from sexuality, from victimization, from criticism, from the encroachment of others. She is using her body image as a political statement and a rejection of societal values, and as a way of maintaining her relationship with her family. She is using her body image to increase her sense of her separateness and specialness.

On the other hand, she could learn to maintain her individuality by being more assertive, by learning to say no with her voice instead of her body. She could channel and express her political anger by supporting a cause that challenges society's values. On a more personal level she could explore her sexuality, experiment with new ways of relating to her family, and deepen her awareness of how special she already is as a human being.

If you are not yet ready to contemplate letting go of your excess baggage, it may be that it still serves you in some way. It is up to you to discover how. You may need to do more preparatory work. Spend as much time as you need, repeating the exercises in previous chapters before going on to the next chapter.

It may be helpful for all of you to experiment with your attachments by imagining shedding them in your daily life and watching what comes up for you. By doing this, you can see how the attachment functions. It will also give you practice in letting go of it. It is your ability to move fluidly in and out of states of mind, at will, that is one of your most powerful skills in healing your mind-body relationship.

Seed Questions

1. What are some of the areas of your life where you are using your body image to restrict yourself (*e.g.,* withdrawing from social situations, making yourself invisible, sitting on your power, etc.)?
2. What are some of the ways that you use to imprison yourself (*e.g.,* negative self-talk, selective listening, comparison, etc.)?
3. What would be the benefits of feeling greater freedom in your body?
4. What would be threatening about that freedom?

EXERCISE 14
Woman in a Trap

If you dislike or struggle with your body, you are in prison. You are entrapped by the image you have of your body. You are both the *prisoner* and the *guard*. You are holding yourself prisoner. You have built the prison, your body image, out of many painful memories and negative messages from other people. You have built the prison by comparing yourself to some impossible standard which the media gave you. You have built the prison out of rejection or non-acknowledgment that took the place of needed acceptance for who you are.

Your prison is unique. You keep it strong and impenetrable by feeding yourself constantly messages of negativity and self-criticism, by selective hearing which takes in only what fits your negative self assessment, and by denying yourself the love and acceptance you deserve—*even if you have flaws.* There is no one on earth who doesn't have flaws.

1. Sit comfortably, close your eyes and relax.

2. Go inside and reflect on the very particular ways that you imprison yourself with your feelings about your body. . .

3. Get in touch with how it *feels* to imprison yourself. . .

4. See if you can find an image that symbolizes or really captures the way that you keep yourself imprisoned. Your prison can be a literal one complete with bars, or a more abstract representation. . .

5. Now step inside your image and *experience* the answers to the following questions.
   - What is your prison like?. . . What does it look like?. . . What is it made of?. . . How have you built it?
   - How do you feel being here?. . .
   - Is there a guard?. . . What is the guard like?. . .
   - What do you get out of being here?. . . Does it protect you from someone or something?. . .
   - What are other people getting from your being in prison?. . . Is your imprisonment protecting someone from you?. . . Whom are you making happy?. . . Whom are you defying?

6. Imagine what lies outside the walls of your prison. . .

7. What are the dangers and costs of being free?. . .
   - Consider what you might lose or have to give up (self-pity? sympathy? being a child? what?). . .
   - What feels risky? (fear of the unknown and unfamiliar? feeling your power and sexuality?). . .
   - What new responsibilities might you have to assume? (learn to say "no"? learn to protect yourself and regulate your boundaries? what?). . .
   - What issues might you have to confront about yourself? (stop blaming your body and start confronting what else in you needs to grow and change?). . .
   - What is the payoff for keeping yourself imprisoned?. . . What part(s) of yourself enjoy(s) being in this trap?. . .
   - Who are you if not this woman in a trap?

8. Get in touch with the you that is in prison. . . Who trapped you?. . . What qualities in you are suppressed by being imprisoned?

9. Let yourself imagine what it might be like to be free of this prison. . . What pleasures would freedom hold for you?. . .

10. Ask yourself: What do I *really* want for myself, to be free, or to be imprisoned? Let yourself sit with the question until your response is clear. . . . If your choice is to remain confined, then stop here and acknowledge your decision. Otherwise move to the next step.

11. Now spend some time fantasizing—just fantasizing, plotting, and planning at this point—how you can escape from your prison. Remember, *you* have created it and *you* know the way out better than anyone else.

Here are some suggestions:

- You can change something about yourself, the prison, or the guard. But do *not* under any circumstances destroy anything. You may *transform* but not destroy elements of your image.
- Ask your prison or guard how you can escape. Then become your prison or guard and respond. The prison or guard is a part of you that represents your negative feelings about your body. Take ownership of this aspect of yourself and the *power* that it contains. As your prison or guard, focus on helping you, the prisoner, to plot an escape.

12. Now *experience* yourself—using all your imaginal senses as vividly as you can—freeing yourself from your prison using all your cleverness. Take as long as you need to escape, and before you leave your prison, take some small momento to remember it by. . .

13. If you have difficulty escaping, come to some temporary conclusion and resolve to try this exercise again.

14. If you have successfully escaped, spend some time alternately looking back at your prison and out at the world. Stay in touch with how you are feeling. . . Are you feeling relief? Joy? Loss? Be open to whatever feelings freedom holds for you.

Worksheet

1. Describe the experience of being in your prison, including how you keep yourself there, the barriers to freedom, and any other details that feel significant.

2. In what way(s) is your prison image an apt representation of how you imprison yourself?

3. What have you learned from this exercise about your reasons for imprisoning yourself and remaining imprisoned?

4. What does your method of escape reveal about the way out of your negative body image trap?

5. Can you apply what you learned to your life (in changes in behavior, development of new skills, shifts in attitude, etc.?)

6. Where do you still feel stuck?

7. Comments.

Guiding Words

Your degree of success or failure in finding and executing an escape from your trap is a good indicator of your degree of readiness to let go of negativity surrounding your body image. Some of you will be able to escape with ease and for you the process of escaping in fantasy and feeling that process will itself be healing. Some of you will get stuck at the stage of executing your escape. In this case, it is very important for you to confront your resistance to being free. Keep asking yourself the questions that the exercise poses until you gain some insight into your blockages. If you were not able to figure out any ways of escape, it is important for you to acknowledge to yourself that you have more work to do.

For all of you I recommend repeating the exercise at least once. It is important to begin to become nimble at finding ways to escape and to give yourself many opportunities to experience the process of escaping. When you repeat the exercise, don't assume that your prison image has to be the same as it was the first time. We imprison ourselves in many ways and there are many images you can explore for insight. Be open to the wealth of your own imagery.

To represent her prison Carla chose a long, rectangular box made of rough, raspy cement that caused pain to the touch on both the inside and the outside. It was designed to keep her in and others out. Her escape involved climbing out, an experience that was difficult and painful. She persisted. To be free meant: "responsibility, adulthood, fear of failure, fear of being too hard on myself, fear of trying and not being 'good enough.' " It also brought a joy in the freedom of movement, self pride, and a willingness to move out in new directions.

In doing this exercise Carla's acknowledgment that *she* was the creator of her own trap was key in her readiness to leave it. Over a period of several weeks of living with this image, she began to find her trap increasingly uncomfortable and uninviting. As this happened, the possibility of true escape became more appealing and worth whatever risk it held for her.

The prison images we choose can be strikingly revealing, occasionally showing us more than we wish to see. Gloria, a woman in her fifties who was in a marriage of thirty years, was shocked and disturbed to find that her prison was her husband's pocket. This represented the crippling dependency that characterized their relationship. Acting and being treated like a child frustrated her. She acted out this conflict on her body, hating it and eating compulsively rather than confronting her husband and the limitations of the marriage. The shock of this recognition propelled her and her husband into psychotherapy. I give this example to show how creative the subconscious mind can be.

Each obstacle is a marker that tells you what work you still need to do. In many cases you will need to make a commitment to do whatever remedial work necessary to clear away the barriers. For some of you the next few exercises may address your needs. For others your work may require further reading, taking courses or workshops to learn needed skills, or in some cases enlisting the aid of a trained therapist who can guide you in further growth.

Exploring and clearing away your resistance to change is one of the most important aspects of *Transforming Body Image*. If you rush through this phase of the work, you will lose out in the end. It is only by clearing away obstacles that the passage along the road becomes possible. So take your time.

X
FINDING YOUR VOICE

Risk! Risk anything! Care no more for the opinions of others, for those voices. Do the hardest thing on earth for you. Act for yourself.

Katherine Mansfield

We are all overcrowded, cluttered with so many conflicting facets of our natures that it is sometimes difficult to know who we really arc. Not one of us is so simple and straightforward that we can say categorically, "This is who I am, and I am the same no matter what the situation." For example, I tend to be aloof with new people and very warm with good friends. Which is the real me? Of course they are both parts of the real me. There are many more seemingly conflicting parts of me: a part of me that needs to be close to nature and a part of me that wants the stimulation that the city offers; a part of me that needs solitude and a part of me that loves to be with people. What is remarkable is that they all manage to coexist.

We all have many subpersonalities that coexist, at times more peacefully than other times. Each represents a different facet of our being. Each has a separate voice, together forming a whole. This whole is not just a jumble of parts, but is cohesive with a center that has its own voice, wiser and kinder than the rest. In the last chapter you encountered that central identity—the woman in the trap, the *you* under all the cloaks. Your work here will be to get to know this part of you that has the ability to observe, direct, and harmonize all the many facets of your being, *at will.* You will also come to identify the other subpersonalities that figure in your struggle with your body. When a subpersonality behaves destructively and pulls you off the course *you* know you want for yourself, it becomes a *saboteur.* Each of your *saboteurs* is motivated by some positive feeling or intention—albeit twisted in its expression—that is not always apparent. By identifying your *saboteurs* and learning to recognize their voices you can pull them out of your subconscious where they can play

tricks on you and thrust them into the daylight where *you* can keep
an eye on them. Learning to let go of your *saboteurs* is not the same
thing as destroying them. Your task is to identify the positive quality
that is trying to manifest itself and to find a positive expression for it.

In this exercise you will meet four of your *saboteurs*. (There are
other voices inside you that perhaps you can discover on your own.)

1. Your *protector-saboteur* is the part of you that rationalizes, that
argues that maintaining the *status quo* is safer, that venturing out
and taking risks is dangerous. It says, "Eat and you'll feel better,"
"Don't be too beautiful, too sexy, too powerful, too successful or
you'll be alone," and so on. Your *protector-saboteur* represents your
kind, loving, nurturing qualities, but she/he is killing you with kindness.

2. Your *critic/perfectionist-saboteur* is the controlling, fault finding,
never satisfied part of you in whose eyes you will never be good
enough, thin enough, pretty enough, etc. It has the ability to analyze,
evaluate, and discriminate, but when it judges you and finds you
guilty it becomes a *saboteur*.

3. Your *rebel-saboteur* is your fighter who defies the narrow, confining rules of the *critic*. It is an angry, recalcitrant child who says, "I'll
show you." It contains your childlike energy, your assertiveness, and
your fun-loving spirit. It is trying to preserve your individuality,
often fighting for your survival but, unless its actions are channeled
constructively, it too is a *saboteur*.

4. Your *victim-saboteur* feels weak and helpless, living with chronic
feelings of guilt, defeat, depression, despair, and resignation. It feels
sorry for itself, inadequate, scared, and powerless. Its constant cry is,
"Poor me, I can't help it." It's the part of you that lets others decide
what's right for you. On the positive side, your *victim* is sensitive,
vulnerable, humble, attuned to the needs of other people. When it is
hooked on pain it becomes a *saboteur*.

EXERCISE 15
Meeting Your Saboteurs

1. Sit comfortably, close your eyes and relax.

2. Find some situation in which you feel self-accepting, comfortable, at home, pleased to be in your body. If you cannot find a real situation, make one up. Let yourself *experience* it fully: the details, your feelings, the expression on your face, the thoughts running through your mind, the sensations in your body, etc. . . .

3. This is the *you* that has chosen to do this work. This is the *you* who has been working hard and sometimes painfully to uncover important psychological material and to make room for change. This is the *you* that is moving toward health. This is the *you* that has a full appreciation and trust of yourself and your body. . . Really *experience* this central, *positive you*. . .

4. See if you can take all the positive feelings inherent in this memory and gather them all together until they flow into your dominant hand (right if right-handed, left if left-handed). Really *feel* the feelings filling up your hand. Now lock all those positive feelings in this hand. . .

5. In the course of this exercise, whenever you want to bring back the *positive you* and the feelings that figure represents, all you have to do is to squeeze this hand. Try it several times until you feel confident that you can do this.

6. Squeeze your hand and bring back the *positive you*. In a moment you will feel a tap on your shoulder. When you do, you will turn around and be face to face with your version of the *protector-saboteur*.

7. Feel the tap and turn around and meet your *protector-saboteur*. Spend some time looking at each other, getting a feel for your particular version of this *saboteur*. Give it a name that describes your sense of how it behaves. . .

8. Using a watch or a timer, give your *saboteur* exactly one minute during which it can do its thing—that special thing it does to you that takes the wind out of your sails and throws you off the course that *you* know you want for yourself. Listen as your *saboteur* speaks and notice carefully any changes in your feelings, body, posture, expression, demeanor, impulses or attitudes as you listen. Take exactly one minute.

9. Did your *saboteur* get to you? Did you buy what she/he was selling? Does your *saboteur* remind you of anyone in your life?

10. Squeeze your hand to let go of any negative feelings you adopted and to reconnect with the *positive you,* that part of you that knows that you are whole and healthy and feel good about the body you have.

11. Now give your *saboteur* exactly one more minute to tell you what she/he is doing for you and what a mess your life would be without this help. Take exactly one minute.

12. Squeeze your hand and return to the *positive you.* . . Now *become* your *saboteur,* really identify with this part of you. . . See if you can get in touch with its attitude toward you. . . See if you can discover the need that drives her/his behavior. . . See if you can connect with the power and energy that this *saboteur* embodies. . . Now return to yourself.

13. Re-establish your control by squeezing your hand, and as you look at your *saboteur,* review what you have experienced. . . See if you can discover the positive intention in your *saboteur's* behavior toward you and the basic good qualities that this part of you embodies.

14. Now verbally acknowledge your gratitude toward this part of you for its good intentions and acknowledge also that you understand what drives its behavior toward you.

15. Ask yourself if it is time to let this *saboteur* go. What would it be like to let it go? What is the payoff for holding on to it?

16. Now it is time to give the *positive you* a voice. Spend whatever time you need to explain to your *saboteur* how you wish to be treated in the future. Offer her/him suggestions about how to be more effective in dealing with you, how to retain the positive while toning down the abrasive, destructive, self-defeating elements of its behavior. (Remember that this *saboteur* represents a part of *you,* so that it is important to find some resolution for healthy coexistence. Destroying this part of you is out of the question and dangerous.)

17. Say thank you and good-bye.

18. Stop here and fill in the *worksheet,* addressing your answers to this *saboteur* before proceeding to the three remaining saboteurs.

Worksheet

Apply questions 1-4 to each *saboteur* separately.
1. Describe your *saboteur*. Include its name, its impact on you, your feelings about it, whom it reminds you of, what it says and does, its style of behaving toward you, what it is trying to accomplish for you, the needs or feelings that motivate its behavior, the power it represents, and anything else that comes up for you.
2. How was it for you to move back and forth between this *saboteur* and the *positive you?* Describe the shift in power.
3. Describe your negotiation and resolution for coexistence. Did this present any difficulties for you?
4. Comments.

•

18. Repeat Steps Nos. 6-16 in turn with the three remaining *saboteurs*.
19. Now gather all your *saboteurs,* and arrange them so that you can see each one and are in physical contact with each one. *Feel* what this is like for you. . . Look at each one in turn and reflect on your feelings about each one.
20. Imagine that a special warm beam of light slowly radiates from the sun, enveloping all of you in its light and warmth. . . *Experience* fully this *feeling* of merging and integrating, becoming one once again.

Worksheet

Some recommendations for further work with your *saboteurs:*
1. When you spot your *saboteurs* at work, talk back from the *positive you.*
2. Engage your *saboteurs* in daily conversations.
3. Write a letter to each *saboteur.*
4. Have each *saboteur* write a letter back to you.
5. Which *saboteurs* feel most central to your drama? Which will be the most difficult to tame?
6. Imagine putting all of your collective minds together to come up with some creative ideas about what the *positive you* can do to quiet the struggle and come to a working arrangement where your body becomes the victor. See if you can join forces toward the common purpose of making you feel whole.

7. Be on the lookout for other *saboteurs* that may be playing a role in your mind-body struggles. Become aware of other trips you are running on yourself, and then see if there is a pattern of behavior. Your new *saboteurs* may be offshoots, or offsplits from the four major ones.

Guiding Words

Finding and recognizing all the voices that live inside of you is extremely important work. They are always in there talking to you. They are like the cartoon devil and angel perched on your shoulder telling you whether to go left or right. Their voices are so familiar by now you may not know they are there. The work of this exercise is to sort out from your interior jumble discrete subpersonalities who are playing important roles in keeping you locked in struggle with your body and perhaps with other aspects of yourself as well. By identifying them, you will be able to spot them at work, to say "Ha! I caught you!" When you can begin to hear yourself talking in this negative, destructive manner, you have the choice of intervening and short-circuiting the pattern by talking back from your center. By understanding what motivates your *saboteur's* behavior, you have the choice to address this need without abrasive self-punishment. Barbara recognized that her *critic* was trying to get her to reach her potential. She was able to take ownership of her desire for excellence and to train her *critic* to acknowledge her positive qualities instead of focusing exclusively on her shortcomings. As she was able to tone down her *critic*, her *rebel* who defiantly overate and procrastinated now had less to rebel against. Listening to her *victim* differently she was able to get in touch with her needs for self-nurturing.

Perhaps you are feeling chopped up by this exercise. That is to be expected. Up until now you were probably not so aware of how crowded you were inside. You have always been this way. Now you have a better idea of who is in there. You may be wondering how you will maintain order, how you will ever feel whole and integrated. This is where the *positive you* comes in. *You* can get to know and understand your *saboteurs* better so that you can harmonize these disparate elements within yourself. The *positive you* knows what you want, what you need, and what is good for you. Right now, your *saboteurs have very big voices whereas the positive you* has a very small, barely audible voice. Your work, beginning now and continuing for many years to come, will be to listen to this fledgling voice. By giving stronger voice to this more central part *you* will begin to take control over your life instead of being buffeted around by this *saboteur* and that.

"But wait," you're thinking, "you said my *saboteurs* are all me." That's right. They represent roles you play, feelings you have, and very often behavior and beliefs you have swallowed whole or internalized from others. They represent more peripheral aspects of *you,* whereas the *positive you* is closer to your true self. Your true self needs a powerful voice if you are to come out whole in this world. Let's face it, the work that you do with this book is only the beginning for most of you. You live in a world that will constantly challenge whatever learning you do here. Visiting your family will be a challenge. Turning on the TV or opening a magazine will be a challenge. But challenge can be a wonderful opportunity, if you have nurtured and developed your true inner voice. It is this voice that can question values, that can talk back and challenge your *saboteurs,* your parents, your peers, the Pepsi Lite commercial on TV. You name it.

Learning to talk to yourself, with your true inner voice, in a way that nourishes you is perhaps the most valuable piece of learning you can do. You talk to yourself all the time—it may as well be good talk. Your *saboteurs* speak harshly to you and your body in ways that make you crumble or rebel. Your new voice is a voice that is full of self-trust, caring, understanding, and compassion. This is the way that you must learn to talk to your body if you ever hope to come to a place of peace within yourself.

Seed Questions

1. Make a list of the areas and parts of your body that you pick on the most. Arrange them according to how severely you treat them.
2. Which areas of your body are the neediest for love and attention?

EXERCISE 16
Body Talk

This exercise is in two parts. Please do them both in one sitting. Please do it with as many areas of your body as you can.

Part 1

1. Sit comfortably, close your eyes and relax.
2. Choose one aspect or area of your body that you victimize most with anger, judgment, neglect, or other negative feeling.
3. Bring that aspect of your body to mind or look directly at it if you can. Become aware of the feelings you generally have about it and the kinds of thoughts you typically think about it.
4. Speak directly to this part of you, expressing your thoughts and feelings without censoring what you say.
5. Now become that part of your body, identify with it, and *experience* how it must feel to be talked to this way. . . Let a response come from this body part back to you. . .

Worksheet

1. What body part did you talk to?
2. What kind of message—content, feeling tone, attitude—is this part of you typically receiving?
3. What did you learn by identifying with your body part? What was its response to you?
4. How often do you talk to your body like this?

Part 2

1. Relax again.
2. Bring your attention to this part of your body and let yourself fully *experience* this part of yourself wordlessly—simply be in communion with it. . . Notice if any images, memories, or associations appear of

their own accord as you stay in touch with this part of your body. . .
Notice any feelings that come up for you. . .
3. Ask this part of you if it has anything it wants to ask or tell you. . .
Notice your reactions. . .
4. Tell it—with feeling—all that it represents to you, and notice the
response you get. . .
5. Ask it: "How do you feel about the way I have been treating
you?". . . Notice your reaction to the response and respond to it with
feeling. . .
6. Ask it: "How do you need to be loved by me?" and "How can we
be friends?"
7. Ask it how it wants you to communicate with it in the future.
8. Ask it what else it needs from you. . . Are you willing to give
it?. . . If not, what stops you?. . .
9. Continue the dialogue until you can reach some understanding
about how to relate to each other in a way that benefits the whole of
you. Take as much time as you need.

Worksheet

1. Which part of you did you deal with?
2. What did you learn about its nature, needs, its reactions to your
behavior, the way you can love it, etc. . .?
3. Describe the resolution of your dialogue.
4. Where do you feel stuck?
5. Comments.

Guiding Words

This exercise gives you the opportunity to see more clearly how you
treat your body. Some of us deluge our bodies with toxic thoughts. It
is important to know what you are doing so you can change it. More
important, *Body Talk* lets you experience the effects of your habitual
behavior from your body's point of view. What you are doing is
opening the channels of positive, constructive communication between you and your body.

Your body is a very sensitive instrument that, if given a voice, can
teach you a great deal. First of all it can tell you how it needs to be

treated. Later, when you trust it more and have a greater willingness to listen, your body can tell you a lot about its needs, likes, and dislikes. If you will listen, your body will tell you when it is hungry, what it likes to eat, when it has had enough, what kind and how much exercise suit it best, when it is tired, when it is getting sick, when you are under stress, and much more. Your body has a wealth of useful information. But if your communication is a one-way affair, with you dumping negative thoughts on your body, then this valuable information will be lost.

Jeanne talked to her fat stomach who told her how terrible it felt to be stuffed with junk food. It said it wouldn't be fat if Jeanne would stop overeating and start paying attention to her feelings. Her stomach felt unfairly punished and suggested to Jeanne that she could change the situation only by putting the responsibility where it belonged, on herself and not on her stomach.

To create a healthy mind-body communication, you will have to develop a gentler, more compassionate way of talking to your body. It is possible to be kind to your body even if it falls short of your expectations. I used to look at my legs and say all manner of nasty things. Now I look at them and see the same legs, but I choose a different approach. I acknowledge that they will never win any beauty contests. But I see them as large, strong, and functional. They work for me — they are powerful and useful and I am grateful to them. I also see that they could be nicer if I were to lose some weight and do some spot exercises religiously. I see all that. Right now it does not feel important to me but maybe someday I will have a loving, positive reason to make changes in my legs or other aspects of my body. I can then do whatever it takes because the changes will come from a base of self-acceptance, not self-condemnation. My body and I will be working together. On the other hand, if I choose to live with my legs just as they are, that will be fine also, because I know that *I am so much more than a pair of legs! I have* a body but *I am not* a body. I am a person, and I like the person I am. I choose to be kind to me, because that is the kind of treatment I deserve.

I choose to be gentle with my body because I realize that it does a great deal of harm to treat it cruelly and judgmentally. A child who is treated this way will become a behavior problem. Speaking harshly to my legs never resulted in any positive, lasting change. It created a state of divisiveness between me and my body that could only spell trouble. It made me miserable.

Please practice *Body Talk* with all the areas of your body that you malign and carry this practice into your daily relationship with your body. Start to notice when you are speaking harshly to yourself about your body. Catch yourself. When you do, it is an opportunity to put into practice a new way of communicating. As always the choice is yours, whether to continue relating as in the past or to move into new behavior. If you do not feel ready to adopt a policy of kindness and compassion toward your body, ask yourself what it would cost to make this change, what the risk would be in letting this negative practice go. See if you can identify the assumptions that underlie your refusal. Many of us operate on the assumption that if we do not keep harassing ourselves we would go totally to pot. Nothing could be further from the truth. Harassment leads to separation and separation to further battling, It is only through peaceful collaboration that you will make your body-mind a working partnership. Keep working at this until it becomes natural and easy. It is one of the most important gifts you can give yourself.

One way to keep tabs on where you are in relation to your body is to communicate through the "mail." I recommend doing this next exercise periodically during the time that you are working with this book and afterward whenever you wish to touch base with your body.

EXERCISE 17
Express Mail

1. Write a letter to your body.
2. Let your body write a letter back to you.

Guiding Words

Here are some highlights from Carla's letters.

"Dear Body,
  I'm sorry. . . you are ruled by a woman who lives in her emotions and head and who takes out her negativism on you. If I'm worried, stressed,

overdoing it, I abuse you, overeat, smoke, don't exercise, don't floss, neglect myself. . . You're such a *good* body—healthy, strong, generally attractive. . . I don't take care of you properly. . . You are my instrument for punishing myself. You serve me so well. I am really learning how much I love you, how important you are to me.

I *make* you unattractive, I inhibit you from being your best. I'm sorry. I really do love and appreciate you. I know I often wish you were different. Really, what I am wishing is that I felt differently about the internal me, not the external you. I'm working on the internal me. Have faith in me that I will learn to love the inside me and quit abusing you. . . . Part of me loves you very much. I'm working on the other part. . . Please bear with me. . .

Always yours,
Carla"

"Dear Carla,

Hi. I know you're going through a rough time right now and I know it's getting better. Really, you get better every year. I know it's hard for you and you take it out on me. I'm strong, I can bear it. We'll make it, sweetie, really we will. We'll be working more together all the time—we already are as you accept your adult female self, your competency, your sexuality, and your vulnerability. You know you hurt me. I don't have to tell you that. But I see you trying and that's what counts. Keep working. We'll pull together! You won't be that silly, perfect ideal you had when you were 16 but I know you know you don't really want to be that. You want to be you, to like you, imperfections and all. Treat me well darlin'—I'll be my best for you. I'm really your best friend. Take care of us—all parts of us.

love,
your body"

These letters clearly reflect the progress that Carla and her body are making in their relationship, the growing affection and the deepening understanding. They both show a willingness to move toward each other for their common good. Carla had no idea that her body felt so positively about her until she received this letter.

Open yourself to your own inner voice and let it help you find your way home.

XI

EXERCISING
YOUR BODY-MIND

By this time, if you have been dutiful about doing the exercises in the last ten chapters, you are probably facile in using your imagination. Many of these exercises have required you to be flexible, to move from one imaginal state to another. This next exercise will give you some practice in learning to move from one body image to another, exploring dimensions of size, shape, density, and proportion. Your image of your body is malleable, having gone through many changes in the course of your life, and it can be altered right now at will to become something different. You are not stuck with your current experience of your body. This area is open to conscious choice. Let's play with the possibilities.

EXERCISE 18
One Pill Makes You Larger *

1. Sit comfortably, close your eyes and relax.
2. In your imagination notice that sitting right beside you is a small bottle. You reach over to pick it up and notice that it is full of pills of different colors. The label on the bottle says: "This bottle contains magic pills. Taken as prescribed, you can experience your body in a variety of sizes, shapes, substances, and even ages."
3. Reach into the bottle and take out a pink pill. Put it in your mouth. As it takes effect, you can feel your body growing heavier and heavier. It is as if a series of very heavy blankets were being laid over you, one after another. . . With each one your body grows

---

*Adapted from Robert Masters and Jean Houston, *Mind Games*. New York: Delta, 1978.

pleasantly heavier until you can't even move it. . . You have nothing to do now but to surrender your weight to the earth beneath you. . . Try lifting your arm and feel what a struggle it is to lift something as small as an arm. . . Try lifting other parts of your body. . .

4. With every bit of determination you can muster, reach your heavy arm over to the bottle and take out a green pill. . . Put it in your mouth, swallow it, and wait for it to take effect. . .

5. One by one the imaginary blankets are being lifted, and as each one is lifted you feel your body becoming lighter and lighter. . . Notice the point when you reach your normal weight and then pass it as you become lighter still. . . You are so light now that you are almost weightless. You will notice that your body has become very porous, almost without substance. You feel as if you could almost float. See what it is like to be that light. . . What do you like about this feeling?. . . What do you dislike?. . .

6. But now the pill is wearing off and gradually you feel your normal weight and substance returning. . . How does it feel to get in touch with your normal body once again?

7. Reach into the bottle once again and this time take a blue pill and swallow it. In a moment you will feel yourself growing smaller. . . Now you are four feet tall. . . Now you are three feet. . . Two feet. . . One foot. . . Stop when you reach 6" tall and look around you. . . Experience what it is like to be in the world when you are this small. . . What do you like about it? What do you dislike? But now you are starting to grow again. . . Quickly growing taller and taller. . . Stop when you reach your normal height. How do you feel?

8. Now take a red pill and swallow it. . . You are beginning to grow taller. . . Reaching six feet. . . Seven feet. . . Now you are restricted only by the height of the ceiling. . . Experience being a giant. . . Towering. . . Strong. . . How do you feel being this tall?. . . Take a moment to walk around in this body and experience your body in motion. . . What do you like about it? What do you dislike? Now you are beginning to shrink again. . . Getting smaller and smaller as you approach your normal height. Rest a moment and experience what it is like to return to your normal size. . .

9. Now reach into the bottle and take out a yellow pill. Swallow it. This pill has some very interesting properties that permit you to change whatever you want about your body. Try some of the following variations, noticing any changes in the quality of your movement, your posture and carriage, your feelings about your body, how you feel being in the world, etc. . .

— Large breasts and small hips and buttocks.
— Small breasts and large hips and buttocks.
— Petite and delicate.
— Tall and willowy.
— Muscular and athletic.
— Very thin.
— Very fat.

10. Finally, experiment with your body in any way you wish, changing and distorting any parts you wish. Explore what it would be like to live in your experimental bodies. . .

11. And now come back to your real body. Notice how you are feeling to be back in your own body.

Worksheet

1. Which body image transformations did you find easiest?
2. Which were the most difficult?
3. Recall any observations or discoveries you made while consciously distorting your body image.
4. Describe your experiences with your experiments (No. 10 above).
5. Do you have a sense of how much conscious control you have over your body image?
6. Comments.

Guiding Words

I have asked you to perform these mental gymnastics because they can teach you a great deal. This exercise can give you a sense of how much control you have over your experience of your body. If you can learn to change your body image at will, you introduce the possibility of choosing to live with a body image that is more pleasurable and healthy than the one you now have.

Your body image is not the same as your physical body. Most of the readers of this book have distorted body images that have little or nothing to do with the objective realities of their bodies. Hopefully you will come to a place where your body image is at once more comfortable and more closely aligned with reality. I am suggesting here that you can benefit right now by choosing and adopting a body image that feels comfortable to you. If you feel too short and squat, allow yourself the feeling of more height. If you feel leaden, cultivate the illusion of greater lightness. Since you are able to choose all sorts of pleasant, comfortable states in your body experience, why lock yourself into a body image that causes you pain?

Another skill you can learn from this exercise is fluidity and flexibility. The more readily and easily you can move from one mind state to another, the less stuck you will be in general. This is the kind of mental fluidity that allows negative patterns — mental, physical, or behavioral — to dissolve and change. Greta noted, "my notions of how I really look are shaken. I don't know any more how I look." It is only when we can begin to question some of our precious "knowns" that change becomes possible.

Experimentation and discovery, by increasing the range of possibilities, can also aid in dissolving dysfunctional patterns. As Marie put it:

> "It was fantastic to be able to 'play' with my body image. I could see myself in so *many* different ways, rather than the one negative image that has been implanted in my brain."

There is also important information to be gained by noticing your reactions to certain body experiences. Carol, for example, found that she was uncomfortable at any of the extremes — tiny, giant-like, etc. — because they evoked feelings of separation and alienation. She then had to confront her choice to be drab and ordinary. In general, the transformations that are hardest for you are precisely the ones you most need to do. So please play with this exercise until you are facile in all the shifts.

Finally, it is interesting to note that many, though not all, women have reported that after distorting their body images they returned to their own bodies with a surprising sense of relief and comfort. Many of the experimental bodies they thought desirable, when experienced, brought more difficulties than solutions. Home wasn't so bad after all.

EXERCISE 19
Moving Attitudes

This exercise comes in three parts. Part 1 should be done once. Parts 2 and 3 should be done daily for at least one week. It is best to make both of these sub-exercises a routine part of your day if you want to integrate the changes that you are experiencing into your life.

Part 1: Moving Attitudes
1. Stand up, close your eyes, and go into your body. . . Get in touch with the way you are feeling about it right now. . .
2. What do you imagine you are saying to the world or to any onlooker by the way you are standing?
3. Open your eyes and walk around a bit. . . What does your body say by the way it moves through space?. . . What attitudes are you projecting by the way you move?. . . What are you saying to others through your body language about how you feel about yourself?. . .
4. As you move, see if you can discover where you carry certain feelings in your movement patterns. To do this, take each feeling in turn and think of some situation where you felt this way until the feeling is present for you. See if you can incorporate it into your walk. Then observe how the feeling affects the way you move. As you move through each situation, make a mental note of which body patterns feel particularly familiar, as these are probably feelings that you habitually project with your body language. After each experiment let go of the feeling and walk normally before trying on the next feeling.
   — Any of the identifications you discovered in the *Cloaks of Identity* exercise.
   — Anger
   — Shame
   — Pride
   — Fear
   — Sadness
   — A sense of ugliness
   — A sense of inadequacy
   — Wanting to hide.
6. Once again get in touch with your body as you walk. . . See if you can identify and name the elements in your own body language.

What messages are you carrying around as you move through life?. . .

7. Now I'd like you to try on some new body attitudes as represented by the statements that follow. As you try on each statement, take a moment to let it register. Then translate it in a body posture and begin to walk around as if you believed it about yourself.

— How do you feel moving with this attitude?
— What body language accompanies this attitude?
— What do you like about it?
— What is hard to accept about it?
— What is scary about it?
— How do you imagine others would respond to you?

To clarify your experience, as you let go of each new attitude before trying on the next one, notice the changes in your feelings and your movement as you return to your normal pattern.

Statements

1. "I am perfectly all right just the way I am."
2. "I am a uniquely beautiful woman, inside and out, and I know it."
3. "I am in touch with and proud of my sexuality and my womanliness."
4. "I like myself and feel easy in my body."
5. "I am open to life and to my world."

•

8. Take as much time as you need for this step. Using what you have experienced so far as inspiration, see if you can arrive at a statement of *affirmation* that embodies the qualities and attitude which you would like to have as you move through life, a statement that your body can speak out to the world. Make it a statement of affirmation in the form "I, _____, AM. . . . . . ."

9. Make this into a *moving affirmation,* by moving around while holding your affirmation in mind. . . Let your body explore what it means to be this *you* in terms of body sensations, impulses, feelings, movement patterns, and facial expressions. . .

10. Notice your feelings about yourself. . . Your feelings in relation to your environment. . .

11. Memorize this set of feelings and allow these feelings to flow into your dominant hand (right if right-handed, left if left-handed). . . Lock the feelings in your hand. . . To reconnect with this affirmed body image, all you have to do is to squeeze your hand.

12. While walking around, shift back and forth every thirty seconds or so between your normal way of moving and feeling about yourself and your *moving affirmation.* As you shift, be especially sensitive to the *point* of shift and the differences between the two states (in terms of both body experience and self-image). . .

13. Now sit quietly and, after closing your eyes, imagine that you are asleep. Your alarm clock goes off and you awaken into your *moving affirmation,* your new, affirmed body image. Slowly, step by step, experience your day unfolding. Stay particularly in touch with your feelings, attitudes, your way of relating to other people, and theirs of relating to you. . . Notice the risks you are willing to take or not willing to take. . . What is enjoyable and what is scary about this new way of being in your body?. . . Take as long as you need to complete this process.

Worksheet

1. What are you currently saying to the world with your body?

2. What feelings and attitudes are built in to your postural and movement patterns and where in your body would you locate them (*e.g.,* shame is in my sunken chest and rounded shoulders, hiding is in my downcast eyes, etc.)?

3. What was striking or informative in your reactions to the moving attitude statements?

4. What is your *moving affirmation?*. . . How does it translate into changes in your body, attitudes, and behavior?

5. What barriers, if any, stand between you and adopting your *moving affirmation* as your own?

6. Comments.

Part 2: Mirror Affirmations

1. Every day, first thing in the morning and before bedtime at night, go to your mirror and practice your *affirmation* in the following way:
   — Face your mirror and mentally divide it into a right half and a left half.
   — Stand to the right, and look into your own eyes. With conviction say your *affirmation* to yourself.
   — Now step to the left side of the mirror.
   — Allow your reactions to your *affirmation* to surface and say them to the mirror.
   — Repeat this five times.
2. If you find it too threatening to practice your *affirmation* in the mirror, you can do it in writing until you feel ready to use your mirror. Divide your page in half, left and right. Write out your *affirmation* five times on the left side and your reactions on the right.
3. Keep track of your reactions, since they represent resistance that you will need to work on.

Part 3: Think Beautiful

1. Choose at least one 15-minute block of time each day to move your *affirmation* into your real life.
2. During that 15-minute period (which should be varied from day to day), fix your *affirmation* in your mind as you go through the paces of your daily life.
3. Notice your feelings, resistances, and the reactions of other people.

Guiding Words

Working with affirmations can be a very powerful healing device. Affirmations are antidotes to the toxic messages you feed yourself daily. This is how they work. By repeatedly feeding yourself positive, affirming thoughts, you are building a receptivity to them. Initially it may feel like a rote exercise since you won't believe the truth of your affirmation. With time and practice, belief will come more easily. It is important to speak, write and think your affirmation with feeling and conviction, *even if you do not believe it.* Each time you do, you are sending that message to your subconscious mind. Eventually you will believe it if you persevere.

Don't feel that you have to be married to the affirmation you create in your first go. It may be the perfect affirmation for you at the time—it may be only the first approximation. Be open to letting your affirmation evolve. This kind of work can be very dynamic. It is a form of deep self-exploration that you can safely do on your own.

Here are some guidelines to help the process:

1. Become very sensitive to the feedback you receive when you *think beautiful.* If you are not getting back what you think you want, perhaps you will need to rethink or refine your *moving affirmation.* As an example of this, one woman was walking down the street with "I, Joan, am a beautiful woman" and noticed she was eliciting lewd reactions from men. She discovered two things from this experience. First, her idea of being beautiful had a very seductive component. Second, she really did not want to deal with strong sexual reactions. She went back to the drawing board and experimented with other affirmations until she found one that felt right.

2. The internal reactions or resistances that your affirmation arouses in you can be used to create new affirmations. For example, if some thoughts about your unworthiness keep coming up for you, you can create an affirmation about being worthy, such as "I, Marcia, am worthy of my own appreciation." If you work with the new affirmation a while it will probably clear the way for you to accept your original affirmation, or it will inform you of further work you need to do.

3. When your affirmation becomes too easy, when it arouses no reaction at all, you should consider challenging yourself with another affirmation that can teach you something new about yourself.

4. Here is a rule that should be followed when creating affirmations. Always make it an affirmative statement. For example, "I, Marcia, am a kind and loving person," rather than "I, Marcia, am not mean and hurtful."

Please work with affirmations on a daily basis the same way you brush your teeth. Affirmations are among the best tools you can use for change. I have witnessed profound inner transformations in people who were willing to make this a regular practice in their lives. Are you willing?

Worksheet

1. Keep an ongoing list of barriers and resistance to changing your attitude that you discover doing these exercises.
2. Generate a list of affirmations that you would like to believe about yourself for use in the future.

Other Ways of Moving

Learning to feel at home in your body requires some inner psychological overhauling. It also involves kinesthetic re-education through which you can learn to experience your body differently as a moving, breathing, functioning whole.

In the workshops I lead in the Boston area, I include movement in the form of Awareness Through Movement® exercises, one part of the Feldenkrais Method®. This is a system of movement re-education and body-mind integration that has only recently been introduced in this country. I choose this kind of movement for my workshops because I believe it to be the most powerful and appropriate kind of movement experience for people who wish to feel more at home in their bodies.

The work itself — Awareness Through Movement — consists of slow, gentle movement sequences led by verbal instructions. The sequences present you with situations where you have the opportunity to learn to be *in* your body *with awareness*. There is no one right way to do each movement — you must find out what is right for your body. There is little room for comparison, competition, and self-judgment. You do not imitate a leader. You make your own discoveries guided by your own instincts. It is similar to the learning that a baby experiences as it discovers how its body is put together and functions. It is playful and fresh.

In addition to grounding you in your body, Feldenkrais work can give you the experience of having a body that moves with fluid, graceful ease. This newly found ease of movement coupled with a heightened kinesthetic awareness can lead to a far more accurate sense of your body image.

This work has been very important for me in my struggles with body image. Through it I have gained an enormous respect for the way my body functions. I have also learned to become gentle and playful in exploring my body's potential. Through changes in my body awareness I have been able to improve my posture and correct the movement patterns that had been causing chronic back pain. Most important, through my work with the Feldenkrais Method I have been able to feel that I live *in* my body with lightness, grace, suppleness, and dignity.

I am not including any examples of this method here because it is very important to have the guidance of an instructor who can communicate to you the attitude and tone of the exercises. Although there are only 200 practitioners of the method in the United States, those of you who do not live near a practitioner can experience the method on tape. This is a completely legitimate and adequate way to participate in Awareness Through Movement lessons. In the Appendix I will give directions so that you can find a practitioner nearby. I will also tell you how you can buy cassettes.

Any kind of movement is a way of learning to live in your body, but the Feldenkrais Method, the Alexander Method, Yoga, and T'ai Chi are especially useful because they are all based on moving with awareness. Dance has an expressive and artistic component that can be very helpful for some people and very trying for others. Sports, if you have the aptitude and inclination, can give you a sense of body competency and mastery.

Whatever form you choose, it is important to make a commitment to yourself to find some way of grounding yourself in your body through movement.

XII
LEARNING TO LOVE THE BODY YOU HAVE

We cannot change anything unless we accept it. Condemnation does not liberate, it oppresses.

Carl Gustav Jung

Everything we have done so far in this book is part of the healing process. First we located the psychological wounds. Then we cleaned away whatever emotional debris we could find. Now it is time to apply a soothing, healing balm—acceptance. Acceptance means acknowledging where you are and who you are. It means accepting the fact that the body you have is the body you have. It is not the same as resignation where you despairingly give in and give up. Acceptance will give you the potential to move beyond where you are. It's a paradox. To change something in ourselves we must first accept ourselves as we are.

Please imagine that you are standing on one bank of a stream. On the opposite bank is the change you want for yourself. The best way to reach the other bank is to jump across. The best way to jump is to push off from a firm solid surface, to be firmly grounded on that surface. Let us say that one bank of the stream is the reality of your body, and the opposite bank is the body image you would like to have. If all of your energy is wasted in fighting with yourself and your body and wishing it were different, you will never be grounded and energized enough to move. If you spend your time, energy, and attention in standing outside yourself and judging your present reality or in dreaming of some future time when everything will be all right, you are not being *who* you are or acknowledging *where* you are. And you will never have full access to resources. But if you can accept with compassion the body you *have*—as your home, as the place where you live, as the container for your self, flaws and all, you and your body have the potential to change. By fully being what you are—your magnificence, your power, your vulnerability, your imperfections, your conflicting voices, your struggles — you can become something else if you choose.

The two senses that play the most important roles in forming body images are sight and kinesthesia, the felt sense. They are also the most important in reforming and healing our body images.

EXERCISE 20
Mirror Breathing

This exercise is to be performed at least twice, once in your imagination and again in the flesh using a real mirror. It would be helpful to practice the *Cleansing Breath Relaxation* exercise. It will help you clear away emotional debris that blocks your perceptions.

1. Sit comfortably, close your eyes and relax.
2. Imagine that you are standing in front of a full length, three-way mirror. (If you are doing this in reality, find a mirror in a safe, warm comfortable place where you will be private.)
3. Close your imaginal eyes and slowly undress. . . How are you feeling?. . . Are you comfortable being naked?. . .
4. Take several cleansing breaths. . .
5. Keeping your imaginal eyes closed, remember back to a time in your life when you looked at someone or something that triggered feelings of love, acceptance, or awe. . . Perhaps it was a parent, a child, a lover, a pet, or a beautiful vista, or some manifestation of God. . . Whatever it was, bring it to your mind right now.
6. Let yourself see it now, and *experience* the feelings that such love, acceptance, or awe inspires in you. . . Notice especially the feeling in your eyes. . . Capture the quality of your gaze — the eyes of a lover, soft and open. . . Let the feeling flow into your dominant hand (right if right-handed, left if left-handed). . . Later when you look at yourself and squeeze your hand, you will be looking at yourself through the same eyes of love. When you look at someone or something you truly love, you do not judge or criticize them. You accept them as a beautiful whole, not as a collection of parts or flaws.

7. Please open your imaginal eyes, your loving eyes, walk to the mirror, squeeze your hand, and bathe your body in your gaze. . . Look at yourself as if you were looking at someone you love or at a beautiful sunset or a work of art. . . You *are* looking at someone lovable and beautiful—*uniquely* beautiful. . .

8. Remember if you feel resistance you can squeeze your hand and do the cleansing breath until the feeling of softness returns to your eyes.

9. Starting from the top of your head, work your way down to your toes. As you go, notice those qualities of your body that are beautiful or that you like. And acknowledge each area out loud in words, "I like the curve of my cheek," "I like the grace of my neck," "I like the full, roundness of my belly," etc. Find one part of your body right now and acknowledge it. . .

10. Find another and acknowledge it. Find five to ten more qualities of your body and acknowledge them, remembering to squeeze your hand and do the cleansing breath if you need to.

11. What else do you like about your body?. . . What do you like about the way that it functions, how it serves the purposes of your life?. . . Acknowledge these out loud. . .

12. Find something else lovable. . . Don't forget the side and rear views. . . What else about you is beautiful? Your skin? Your carriage? Your radiance? Your character that shows through in your body? The way every part of you fits together in a whole that is unique to you? The way that you move? Smile? Really *look* at yourself and find as many things about you to acknowledge out loud as you possibly can. Squeeze your hand and do the cleansing breath if you are experiencing difficulty or resistance. . .

13. Have you neglected or overlooked any part of you? If so, acknowledge it now for its own unique quality. . .

14. Once again, look at yourself with tender, loving, self-accepting eyes. And really take in the fullness of your beauty. . . Look at yourself and say, "This is me. This is my body. This is where I live." *Feel* what it is like to be loved with your own eyes. . . See how much of this feeling you are willing to bring back with you after you complete this exercise and open your eyes.

Worksheet

1. How are you feeling in and about your body right now?
2. Describe your experience in the present tense indicating whether it was done in your imagination or in the flesh. Include any feelings or obstacles that came up for you.
3. Describe your own beauty.
4. For each obstacle that came up find some antidote.
   - For every judgment find two positive counterstatements to neutralize it.
   - Take each judgment, chew on it and decide whether to swallow it or spit it out.
   - Create an affirmation to address the obstacle, *e.g.* Obstacle: "My legs are too fat to be beautiful;" Affirmation: "I, _____, can see and acknowledge my own beauty even if I do not fit the ideal."
   - If a *saboteur* is involved, engage it in dialogue and try to overcome it.
5. Comments.

Guiding Words

You were not born out of a rubber mold that came off an assembly line. You are *real, alive,* and *unique.* Your own brand of beauty is unique and has every right to be acknowledged and appreciated—*just as you are.* Through the eyes of love—your love of yourself—acknowledge and appreciate your body and your self. As you practice applying a loving gaze to your reflection in real life, it will become more natural and easier for you. Your body will respond with gratitude for your kindness and openness. The more you learn to love and accept yourself, your body will reflect that love, more and more, and will radiate a greater beauty that will permeate every aspect of your life.

Many of you will find that you have obstacles to deal with before you can fully accept your own love. Please work on these barriers using some of the suggestions in the *Worksheet.*

Toni looked at her real body in the mirror.

> "I see myself as a beautiful part of nature, a living being, unique, I see my back and thighs and ass in a new light, my belly too. I have a beautiful body—and I'm able to look at parts using the cleansing breath and see my totality rather than breaking down my body into ugly parts. I feel a sense of oneness with myself, with love for my body and eyes that gaze at myself with awe. I find new power, the power is not threatening right now. I feel peaceful. I noticed my body in a new way today doing this sequence—it's the first time I've seen *my* body—not my mother's and my sister's—or the image of the female family body that I have. I see my own curves, bulges, ins and outs, my own self."

Try not to be discouraged if your initial attempts are not positive. Growing to love yourself and your body usually comes in stages, but there has to be a true willingness to transform negativity into positivity. Contempt and hatred of your body come out of anger. As anger softens, feelings of sadness may emerge about the pain your body has had to endure. This sadness can develop into compassion, a kind and protective attitude toward your body. From compassion can grow a neutral acceptance of your body—neither positive nor negative, just a simple acceptance. Many people stop here but, if you choose, this feeling of acceptance can be nurtured into love, not a narcissistic, ego-filled love, but a deeply respectful appreciation for the body you have as an essential part of who you are.

The next exercise presents another opportunity to love your body. When I present it in my workshops I synchronize the instructions with music, Samuel Barber's "Adagio for Strings," which is deeply moving. This is such an important sequence that I recommend you make a tape of it using enough music to fill thirty to forty-five minutes in the background. Pachelbel's "Canon in D" is also appropriate music, or perhaps you have your own musical favorites that are emotionally moving.

Seed Questions

1. Find a person in your life, past or present, whom you fully trust, who cares about you. If you cannot find a real person, fabricate one.
2. Find a time in your life when you experienced love either as the giver or the receiver. It could be the love of a parent, child, animal, a sunset, or god.

3. With your real body, explore and experiment with the ways you enjoy being touched. See if you can differentiate between touches that communicate caring, healing, sensuality, sexuality, indifference, and anything else.

EXERCISE 21
Imaginal Massage

1. Lie down, close your eyes and relax.
2. Pay attention to your breathing and after taking in several complete breaths imagine that you are breathing in the smell of vanilla. Or if you like you can use a real vanilla bean or vanilla extract.
3. As you breathe in vanilla, *experience* yourself slipping into a state of deep contentment and satisfaction. Practice this for several minutes until you can do this with ease. Please use this breathing technique at any time during the exercise when you feel yourself resisting or tensing up.
4. Allow your mind to return to a time when you experienced feelings of love either as the giver or the receiver. . . (Begin music) Allow yourself to re-experience that memory as if it were happening to you right now. *See* what you saw, *hear* what you heard, *feel* what you felt. Really be in the image. Let all your senses savor this feeling of love. . .
5. *Experience* all these feelings of love centering in the area of your heart. . . *Feel* your heart alive with loving feelings. . .
6. Now become conscious of your hands. . . Become increasingly conscious of your hands. . . Put all your attention in your hands. . .
7. Now take all that loving, all those rich, warm, beautiful feelings of love, and *feel* them flowing from your heart into your hands. . . *feel* your hands filling with loving feelings, tingling and pulsating with feelings of love, acceptance, and caring. . .
8. As you breathe, breathe into your hands and *feel* the loving feelings intensify. . . See if you can keep building the intensity of this feeling with each breath. . . *Feel* the feelings of warmth intensify as you breathe even more feelings of love into your hands. . . Your hands are tingling now and beginning to glow with an aura of loving

kindness. . . Your hands are incredibly alive and vibrant now. . . *Feel* them. . . *See* them. . .

9. Your hands are now full of love, the embodiment of love. You need only to breathe naturally now to keep them filled with loving energy. They will stay vibrant now even if you shift your attention away from them. . .

10. Now please imagine that you are lying on a massage table or some other comfortable but firm surface. The room is warm and cozy. The lights are soft and low but you can still see around you. You are naked and fully comfortable. You are completely safe. Take the time you need to settle yourself comfortably in this scene. . .

11. In a moment someone whom you care about and fully trust will enter the room. . . This person is in the room now and is walking toward you. . . Look into this person's face and notice the loving, accepting expression. . . This face is full of love and the love is being directed toward you. Allow yourself to drink it in. . .

12. Now bringing your attention back once again to your hands, breathe deeply and, as you do, *feel* the feelings of loving warmth intensify once again. Your hands are vibrant, glowing, pulsating with loving energy. . .

13. Take the hands of your visitor into your own hands. *Feel* the contact. . . And as you both breathe together, *feel* the love move from your hands into their hands. *See* the radiant glow now in their hands as they vibrate and radiate with love. . .

14. Relax now and prepare yourself to surrender. . . *Feel* your body melting into the table as a candle in the sun. There is nothing for you to do but allow yourself to receive a loving, healing touch. . . Remember that you can breathe vanilla to clear the way. . .

15. Your masseur or masseuse is now annointing their hands with warm, fragrant oil. See if you can identify the fragrance. . .

16. Now you feel the warmth of these loving, radiant, caring hands as they slide tenderly along your body, covering every inch of your face and body with oil infused with love. Take some time to fully savor this experience with all your senses—the feeling of warm, slippery hands, the fragrance of the oil, the sound of breathing, the sight of loving eyes and hands that are loving *your* body, just as it is. . .

17. Now your masseur or masseuse is lovingly massaging those parts of your body that you like—those parts of your body that have received positive feelings from you. Feel what this is like for you. . .

18. As these parts of you are being massaged, *feel* some of the positive energy that they hold transferring into the loving, massaging

hands. *See* the hands glow even brighter now. . .

19. Now take as much time as you need to *experience* these loving, healing hands as they tenderly massage and caress those parts of your body that have been the seat of your shame, disappointment, and negativity. These parts of your body are being touched and handled with such love, sensitivity, and caring that they are able to melt into softness and can fully surrender and receive all the love flowing into them right now. . .

20. You can begin to feel your body coming into balance as you soak up love as a sponge does water. . . You are worthy of love. . . You deserve love. . . See how *much* love you can take in right now. . .

21. Look into the eyes of this person who loves you as you allow yourself to surrender to all the love available to you right now. . . Notice the sense of peace in your body and in your being right now. . .

22. As you look at this person you now see that they are beginning to change form. . . *See* their body being replaced by *your* body, and their face with *your* face, and their hands with *your* hands. Breathe. . . There are now two of you, a giver and a receiver. . .

23. As you *feel* your own radiant hand caressing your body and as you look into your own loving eyes, *surrender* to that part of *you* that has the wisdom, and true perception, the love and compassion—the part of *you* that *loves and accepts you just the way you are*. Spend at least ten minutes caressing your own imaginal body with love and healing, being aware of your feelings in response to it. . .

24. See how much of these feelings of love and self-acceptance you are willing to bring back with you when you later open your eyes. But for now spend as much time as you like simply being with yourself and the feelings that you have, whatever they are. . . And then open your eyes.

Worksheet

1. How are you feeling in and about your body right now?
2. Describe your experience in the present tense including any feelings, surprises, or obstacles that came up for you.
3. Were there differences for you in being massaged by another and being massaged by your own hands?
4. Comments.

Guiding Words

Imaginal Massage is usually the single most powerful and healing process in my workshops. It is the sequence that most former workshop members say they practice with on tape long after our association ends.

Here is Carla's experience:

> "I got in touch with the same part of me I discovered when I wrote my letter from my body to me. It feels so warm, loving, safe, tolerant of any mistakes or regrets — loving them and accepting them only for what they are. So warm, safe, loving, happy, pleasant — incredible! Wonderful!"

As for her feelings about her body:

> "A little part of me is still niggling at me — 'You're *not* how you *want* to look' — but that sounds old. I can use that warm, loving, unconditional part of me to answer it back and say — 'I'm O.K., no matter what — all of me.'. . . It's the first time I've ever consciously been able to apply this loving feeling to myself — tolerant of any & every mistake & 'unpleasant-ness' — I love me. What a base to have!"

The experience does not have to be so dramatic in order to be healing; transformation often happens quite quietly. Sometimes shifts in feelings and behavior can be recognized only in hindsight. Looking back you may say, "Ah, that experience was the turning point for me."

If you found yourself resistant to letting in positive energy, you need to practice this exercise over and over until it becomes second nature to surrender to such feelings. The process of being able to let in good feelings is much like the incoming tide of the ocean. Each new wave expands the ocean's reach onto the shore. Each time you practice a new experience, there is a further erosion of your self-imposed barriers. When you are willing to let down those barriers, you will be ready to heal yourself.

It is a good policy to treat your real body to the healing experiences of massage, lovemaking, or self-touch. Healing can also come by awakening your body to other possibilities: the feeling of a soft breeze on your skin, of your body as it moves to music, the feel of satin or fur against your skin. The possibilities are limitless. Indulging yourself in these ways can help to give you a more positive experience of living in your body. Try it and see.

XIII
PUTTING IT
ALL TOGETHER

In this next exercise you will be moving to a new level of exploration and healing, actively creating your own healing metaphor or myth of transformation. Fables, myths, and tales have long been used to instruct or to change attitudes. A metaphor is a way of expressing a complex idea in a small package (a word or a phrase) and in novel form. It is precisely this novelty that can often shed new light on an old issue. Metaphor frees us from some of the limitations that confront our ordinary waking minds.

Our dreams are one form of spontaneous, metaphorical thinking. Their interpretation can frequently reveal the state of our minds or offer solutions to problems hidden from our waking mind. Talking to the subconscious mind in metaphorical language can be very powerful since the message is frequently allowed to slip in under the radar of our defenses. It is a way of tricking ourselves into healing a wound or solving a problem—in this instance, tricking us into accepting a new body image.

In this next exercise you will be led through a process that will help you create a metaphor to represent coming to terms with your body. This will become clearer as you begin to work through the exercise. To help you further, I will illustrate each step with my own metaphor.

EXERCISE 22
Transformational Body Myth

Finding Your Metaphor

1. The first step is to connect with the *essential* kinesthetic experience of your body, not those feelings that are transitory. Stand up and close your eyes and tune in to your body and *experience* how your body *feels*. . .

2. Write a list of adjectives or phrases that capture your felt experience, and title this list, *"now."*

EXAMPLE:

I came up with an *essential* kinesthetic experience of my body as compressed, stumpy, short, wide, squat, close to the ground, and immobile. Transitory qualities not listed were fatigued and hungry.

3. Stand up again, close your eyes, and go into your body. This time get in touch with how you would *like* to feel in your body. Make a second list of adjectives and phrases that *capture* that experience. Call this list *"future."*

EXAMPLE:

I wanted to feel longer, more upward sweeping, more vertical, flowing, fluid, and mobile.

4. So you now have two lists of important attributes and qualities — one describing how you feel now, and one describing how you want to feel — that you want to make into a metaphor.

NOW	FUTURE
1.	1.
2.	2.
3.	3.
4.	4.

5. Keeping in mind the attributes and qualities of your *now* list ask yourself the following questions to help you find an apt metaphor for this set of qualities. Try to let your answers be as spontaneous as possible. Don't be concerned if you can't find something in every category.

- If these qualities were to be represented by an animal, what kind of animal would it be?
- If these qualities were to be represented by a plant, what kind of plant would it be?
- If these qualities were to be represented by a vehicle, what kind of vehicle would it be?
- If these qualities were to be represented by a kind of food, what would it be?
- If these qualities were to be represented by a raw material of any kind, what would it be?
- If these qualities were to be represented by a building, what would it be?
- If these qualities were to be represented by a landscape, what would it be?
- If these qualities were to be represented by an object, what would it be?
- If these qualities were to be represented by a work of art, what would it be?
- If these qualities were to be represented by a mythological creature, what would it be?

6. If one of these questions suggested an apt metaphor that best captures the essential attributes of your *now* list use that one. Otherwise, let your mind wander freely until you can find any object to represent your body experience. (I found that the image of a tree stump best captured my experience of my body as described in my *now* list.)

7. You hopefully have a starting image or metaphor, Point A. Now you want to find an ending image or metaphor, Point B, capturing the qualities in your *future* list — an object within the same family as your beginning metaphor, *e.g.,* if A is an animal, then B should also be an animal. (I found that a tall, willowy, graceful tree best expressed the attributes — elongation, verticality, fluidity, mobility — that I wished to build into my kinesthetic body experience.)

8. Between these beginning (Point A) and ending points (Point B), there exists a great *middle* that describes a process of transformation that reflects the change that you want in your body. This is where the real work of this exercise comes in.

A ---------------------- transformation process --------------------> B

Discovering The Transformation Process

You will be working with your metaphors using movement as a way of connecting with the kinesthetic level of the change process.
1. Find a space where you can stand and have plenty of room to move around.
2. Close your eyes, and really *become* your beginning metaphoric object. Completely identify with it. . .
 — How do you feel?
 — What do you look like?
 — Experience your mass, shape, and energy.
 — If you can move, notice how you move.
 — Do you make any sounds?
 — What do you feel like to the touch?
3. Take some time to move around as if you were your object until you get a real feel for it.
4. Now do the same thing with your ending metaphoric object, repeating Steps No. 2 and No. 3.
5. In movement, *experience* the feeling of transforming from your beginning object to your ending object. Move very slowly as in time lapse photography so that you can grasp the essential kinesthetic transformation process at work here. Really *feel* what it means to your body, your movement, and your inner experience to move back and forth between the two images. Try this for several minutes.

Creating Your Myth

Through movement you were able to grasp the kinesthetic level of the transformation process. Now it is time to create a story or myth about how A becomes B, your own unique myth of transformation. There may be many natural ways that your object can transform, as was true for my metaphor. The tree stump was able to send up new growth and to become a tall, graceful tree. You may have to make up a change process. But that is the beauty of myth—anything is possible.

Try not to worry about making it good literature. That is not the point. What you are after is transformation—internal transformation—not Pulitzer prizes. As you work your way through this process, trying one plan after another, you are doing important psychological work. In creating your myth, you are giving your subconscious mind new messages in a form it can accept.

Working With Your Myth

1. Illustrate your myth, drawing what the transformational process looks like including all the characters or objects involved in the process. Perhaps it would look like individual frames in an animated film. Once again, artistry is not the point—use stick figures if you like. The words of your myth will be communicating with the left half of your brain while your pictures will reach the right half. This way you will have a whole-brain experience which is always the best route to learning.

2. Create a *programmed visualization* out of your myth. In your imagination, enact your myth as an unfolding drama of transformation with you starring in the role of your metaphoric objects. *Experience* it with all your imaginal senses. Run this through in the theater of your mind at least once a day for 10-15 minutes for at least one week or longer if you can. As always, the more you work with it the more deeply this can penetrate into your subconscious mind and the more profound your transformation.

Guiding Words

Although many women in my workshops are hesitant as they approach the task of creating their myths, nearly all of them end up having a wonderful time. Even if it does not turn out to be fun for you, it is still a very important piece of the work of *Transforming Body Image*. It is an opportunity to take everything you have learned about your self and your body image, and everything that you know that still needs to change and out of that to write your own transformation story. The myth you create will be, in some profoundly true way, a metaphor for the real transformation you are going through in relation to your body. It is a way of putting it all together. To give you some idea of what is possible, I would like to share with you the myth that one woman wrote. I have so many clever, inspiring, and touching stories that it was not easy to choose only one. I leave you with Antoinette's Story because it says it all.

"Once there was a concrete block who was thick and heavy and clumsy and terribly dowdy. She couldn't wear anything that didn't make her look like a concrete block; very thick through the middle, at the same time tremendously broad through the base. She knew she was a concrete block and disliked the fact and so she wore the same few things all the time and never looked in mirrors. Occasionally she caught glimpses of herself in shop windows and was distressed and depressed.

"It must be understood that she felt she was a block, and always was a block, and would always be so. Yet there were times when she was a gleeful graceful wild strong song of a creature. These times came when she forgot her material being and laughed and enjoyed other people or her lover. But she wanted to feel free moving all the time and to not have her concrete block self rule her. She knew it had reasons for being there, but she battled with it anyway. She was quite tired of this battle for it stole energy needed elsewhere.

"This went on for many years until one day she sat down with herself and said, 'Block, you weigh me down. I'm tired of this struggle. State your purpose and be gone!'

"Of course, the block-self laughed and said, 'I admire your bravado. But you must understand that we are not to be separated as easily as that! In fact, I doubt that we can be separated at all. So we must learn tolerance and live together. I refuse to be painted as the villain. I pulled you through some terrible spots. I came in handy when you ran up against wolf-men. I prevented unwanted comments and whistles that make you so angry you can't think. And being less than perfect physically certainly kept your father from believing he fathered perfectly.'

"She answered, 'Now wait just a minute! I can be all those things without feeling like a ton of concrete! This better-feeling self is due for a coming out and staying out. So let's get used to it. From now on, whenever you feel the need for me to be more human just tap me on the shoulder and whisper in my ear. *I'll* take care of everything.'

"The block-self smiled. 'It's not that easy! I agree that a compromise is in order, but we have been functioning the other way so long that it will take a plan to turn things around.'

"So the woman stood in her concrete block and concentrated on the kernel of good-feeling inside. The tiny seed was so packed with potential and growth that with the slightest encouragement, it began to sprout, pushing bit by bit up through the cement, around and past each grain of concrete sand, between and over and around each grain, until the first little nubbin of growth gained access to the light and hoisted itself, bringing more sprouts with it. Soon the block was poking out all over with flexible, firm growth. And the sprouts began to grow together. Then, with a little sound, the block cracked and a crevice appeared. The good-feeling rejoiced and redoubled its business, until the block cracked wider. The crack stretched like an earthquake across the expanse of cement. The sprouts took shape in the form of a woman, a smiling woman. She took a deep, deep breath and split the block wide open into many pieces which fell around her. Then stepping lightly over the crumbled cement she twirled and pirouetted into the spaces where the ungraceful block could never take her.

"This scene was repeated many times, for old habits are not easily broken, and each time it was easier and the song-woman gradually gained control of the material self and lived intensely with the advice of her concrete self."

Now it is your turn to tell *your* story.

Section 3
The Road Home

XIV
FOUR WOMEN IN PROCESS

We like to think that transformation happens overnight. That occasionally happens, although not to the extent that our push-button, miracle-cure-oriented society would have us believe. The profound, inner transformation that leads to self-acceptance does not have a discrete beginning and ending—it is a gradual process of unfolding that can take many years.

I have asked four women who participated in the *Transforming Body Image* workshop at least a year and a half ago to tell their stories. My choice of these women was based on several factors. Most important was the time that had lapsed since completing the workshop so that the process could be seen in perspective. All four women are capable of communicating the richness of their experiences. All of them conscientiously attended the workshop and practiced at home.

Denise

Denise is a nursing supervisor in her mid-forties who completed the workshop nearly two years ago. Denise's body image was an issue for her from very early childhood. Her mother, who had lost her first baby, overfed her other children to keep them healthy. Denise was forced to eat as a child, and by age 10 her weight reached crisis proportions. That was when her father had a nervous breakdown. Before his hospitalization he tried to kill his wife and children. Denise's mother was left alone to support three children with no family to help her.

> "That was my protection, being fat. It created boundaries, it padded my nerves. It gave me a sense of some distance between all of that stuff that was going on and my inner world."

Denise was taken to the hospital and evaluated as obese. Then came the regime of strict diets and thyroid medication. Meals became a nightmare. She longingly watched her tall, thin brother wolf down bread and cookies while she drank her skim milk. Denise was enraged.

She was always plump and large boned, larger than her peers who tormented her for being fat and awkward. There was little comfort from her parents. Her father had always preferred thin women. Her mother struggled with her own weight.

By adolescence Denise became tall and for a time thin. The males in her world began to make sexual overtures. Denise was enraged. She didn't want to be seen as an extension of men's needs, sexual or otherwise.

These conflicting elements in her background were central to Denise's struggles. One part of her wanted to be thin and beautiful, the only way her father and society would accept and value her. The part of her trained to be a person reacted with rage and defiance when she was viewed as an object. Her conflict was played out on her body. Being fat allowed her to be herself.

"I came into the workshop with the dawning awareness that it wasn't just my problem, that I didn't know any women who felt good about their bodies. If they were thin and gorgeous, they hated their ears, or their breasts were too big—there was always something. I knew that I had to begin to get in touch with my body, that I couldn't go on like this, living in my head and living that terrible ambivalence with the diets and the terrible self-hatred. There were three things that happened for me in the workshop.

"I was the only fat one in my group! Everyone else was skinny. I still had this feeling that if only I could be thin that would take care of everything. Here were these thin women who were struggling with exactly the same problem, some of them much worse than me! That was an eye opener.

"I got a sense from you of your own beauty and your own acceptance of who you were as a woman even though you weren't thin. That made me feel that it might be possible for me to come to terms with my own large body.

"The guided imagery was very powerful stuff. I kept coming through to myself as very, very beautiful. And I don't mean in the sense that the world talks about, but more like a. . . wonderful soul. It has helped a lot. It's something that I'm going to have to work with for the rest of my life.

"It used to be that no day would go by when I wouldn't say to myself 'I have to lose weight,' 'I've got to go on a diet,' or 'If only I were as thin as she is.' I don't do that much any more. I'm never going to go on a diet again. Just this spring I gave myself permission to eat and I realized that I have never done that in my life. I had felt guilty about every piece of food I put in my mouth. What I eat now I enjoy. I used to eat in secret, quickly so no one would see me. Now I can appreciate the food and most of the time know when I'm full and need to stop. Sometimes I feel that I could eat the world just to become numb. Sometimes I eat to the point where I can't breathe. . . I don't feel good about it, but I don't whip myself over it. I just start fresh. I refuse to weigh myself. I want to find out who I am from the inside.

"Whatever I do has to come from inside. It cannot be imposed by somebody else's standards. That decision came from the workshop and from my life, too. There was a convergence. That trust and understanding also began to come in the workshop. I can work from that.

"I don't talk to myself a lot about being fat these days. . . part of me loves my big body. And part of me thinks it's wonderful. And I would be very content if I were not in this society, if I didn't pick up all the junk from men and women that I do pick up. There are times when I pick it up and run with it and get into despair and depression and rage. I yell and scream and carry on with my friends. And sometimes I keep quiet and try not to turn my rage in on myself as I used to do.

"I still sense in me this incredible ambivalence, this incredible desire to be thin. And yet now that I am thinner, I know that men are looking at me as an object. On the one hand I'm flattered. But on the other hand I'm enraged."

Toward the end of the workshop Denise ruptured a spinal disc and has spent the last several years learning to deal with chronic pain.

"It's been a time of tremendous growth, actually. It has forced me to try and look at my body, what I've done to it, how I've refused to live in it. It's made me begin to think of taking care of it in a loving and accepting way. . . And I'm trying to become more conscious. . . I'm trying to learn to live in my body.

"I got an idea that it was possible to be free *in my body*. It was in that workshop that I began to have a sense that I could do it. I began to see who I was inside and not focus on whether people were looking at me and what they were thinking. The inner became more important than the outer. My inner life is the most important thing to me in the world and the most astounding. The wonderful imagery work helped me get in touch with my inner life in a new way.

"I keep coming back again and again to those little voices—the *saboteurs*—and tell them to shut up and leave me alone, to get out. I laugh at them and challenge them. There's a new voice in me that doesn't take the *saboteurs* seriously, who's really more in command, 'Let's not be ridiculous!'

"Why does this culture hate women's bodies so much? Why is it necessary for us to be filled with self-hatred? That terrific self-hatred that I've struggled with is not just my own. It is part of every woman around me. That gives me perspective."

Ginny

Ginny, a social worker in her late thirties, came from a family with a history of body image trouble. Her mother, father, and brothers struggled with weight while her two sisters were bulimic. Ginny herself had been a fat child but had begun to normalize her weight as a young adult. Several knee operations kept her from being physically active and left her with a mistrust of her body.

The imagery she tapped early in the workshop shocked her with the level of self-hatred that it revealed.

> "I came to the workshop feeling disassociated from and angry with my body. I had expected to do a lot of work on weight and not being pretty and that sort of thing, but it was the real basic stuff—'I hate my body because it doesn't work for me'—that was incredibly painful.

> "When we lay on the floor and measured different parts of the body, I was accurate until I came to my hips. Every single time I thought I was eight inches wider in that area than I really am. I still do that. . . And I still do this exercise to remind myself that my images aren't always in tune with reality, because I still go through some of these trips, but now I know they're trips!

> "I got in touch with my parents' past messages to me and I was able to say 'That's them and those are *their* messages, and I'm here, I'm me.'

> "The ultimate moment for me was when I wrote my myth, which ended up with an image of me dancing with a woman, circling, and loving and being loved by this woman. This very beautiful woman that I was dancing with (whom I recognized as myself) and I merged. The dance that I danced with myself I mark as a turning point in my life, but I didn't know the ramifications of what had happened for some time. First I felt myself at home and O.K. And I liked who I was. I liked being in my body. That was so different.

> "I can literally date from that time a change in my energy, including my sexual energy. I was able to open myself up to loving myself at a very deep level. Something shifted and I loved myself. And most of the time I still do. There are times when I have my spinnings and my distortions, but there just isn't the same level of self separation and rejection that I had before. I don't feel separate any more from my body.

> "There have been many profound changes for me. I'm in a relationship, very close to getting married. I'm starting a doctoral program. I got involved with 'Color Me Beautiful' and I really enjoy the vitality and brightness of that way of thinking about color. I've come to enjoy walking just in the last few months, feeling myself move in my body and enjoying it. I feel like I'm O.K., I'm not going to get let down. I've taken some steps to deal with some of my physical stuff like going to a chiropractor. I am certainly aware now. I don't live in my head all the time or from the neck up. I'm feeling vibrant.

"It's an ongoing process. I have the tapes [of the exercises] and sometimes I play one. Sometimes all it takes is stopping and counting to ten and remembering to listen to myself. Let's say I'm walking down the street and I'm feeling fat and ugly and yukky and I've been eating too much. I'm looking in the windows and thinking, 'Ick.' And usually another side will come on and say 'Boy, are you being hard on yourself today.' 'Oh! that's what's going on.' So I stop and listen and do some countering. . . What I usually do is go back to that dance, to my myth when I was dancing with myself.

"I have a new voice that I listen to which has grown stronger. That's what it was about, identifying the old voices and getting the new one to grow in strength and be clearer. The ultimate challenge has been for me to listen to myself and to be open to the messages that I have. It doesn't always work. There are times when I am in periods of great stress when the old voices are most profound. But I find that I at least have a sense that there *is* a new voice. I may not be able to hear it all the time but I at least know it's in there.

"At times I still think I'm too fat. But I've been noticing recently as I look at fashion magazines that I think they're too thin! That's not what I want to be. No way.

"I see it all going back to self-acceptance and to the place where I danced and held myself. My changes weren't all overnight. It was like a little plant that grew. The seeds were strong and they were rooted when I left the workshop and they grew. And I kept on growing. And I expect to continue."

Margie

Margie, a teacher in her late twenties, had struggled on the diet/binge seesaw since puberty. She had spent puberty trying to lose ten to fifteen pounds. She was deeply affected by media images of thin women. Compared to them her body never looked right. She began to feel awkward, ungainly, and inhibited, and she wouldn't buy clothes. Her confusion about her body spread to her emerging sexuality. Feeling disapproval from her parents, her sisters, and her friends, she began to retreat socially. Her experience in the workshop, although healing and illuminating, helped her to acknowledge her need for additional therapy. She tells her story.

"The journal writing in *Transforming Body Image* really forced me to understand my background. I began to learn to accept my body more and to forgive the people who caused me pain. Mirror-Breathing and Chains and Woman in a Trap, especially that one, really helped me a lot because I literally felt that I was in a trap, letting life go by, confining myself to limited choices because I didn't feel O.K. enough to go out and be exposed. I was forced to look at my body and find the things I liked about it, to look into myself and realize that these negative feelings were ingrained but not really necessary. There were things I could like about my body and there were lots of positive feelings way deep inside that had been buried for so long. I loved the exercise where you look in the mirror and at every part of your body and find things that you love. It was so wonderful to me to discover that I could love my body and that was such a revelation, really meaning it. One Pill Makes You Larger gave me the opportunity to feel how it would be to be lighter and heavier. All the different exercises to explore how you feel in your body and the Feldenkrais movements. . . I learned so much about what I could do to myself in negative ways and how I could change that in positive ways. I felt that I had a renewed sense of myself and I felt very comfortable in my body.

"I think that compulsive eating and body image go together. When I eat compulsively it's because I'm unhappy about something. So I eat compulsively, and transfer the negative feelings about myself to my body. Whatever it is that's really bothering me gets numbed out, pushed away, and I focus on the food and on my body.

"I'm more socially oriented these days. . . I had been using my body and my weight as an excuse to isolate myself. It's very rare that I do that now. Because I feel happier and more confident in myself I can project a happier person to other people on my job and relate better and feel that other people accept me. Before I felt that no one would want to relate to me, feeling and looking the way I do.

"I started taking dance classes. I don't think I would have felt O.K. doing that before the workshop. I've also started taking bubble baths and really caring about myself. That's what I learned: that I was O.K. and that I was somebody I should take care of and give to.

"It's a slow process. You might not think that you're making progress at all but then you realize that you're thinking in a different way or you're doing something in a different way than you used to. The things that I learned are going to be helping me slowly and gradually throughout my life."

Francine

Francine is a photographer and art museum curator in her mid-thirties. Throughout school Francine was extremely quiet and so shy that she withdrew from other people. Her struggle with her body began very early. To protect herself she created a split between her body and the inner Francine. The war raged on with recurrent headaches beginning at age three and culminating in adolescence with migraines.

She suffered subtle and not so subtle bodily rejection from her family. Her looks even from infancy were a disappointment to her parents, and the contrast with her older, more beautiful brother made matters even worse. She was the butt of hostile teasing from him and his friends. Her parents never protected her from the abuse — they tacitly supported it. Francine was large boned and stocky. Her mother had weight problems of her own and projected them onto Francine. She took over control of her daughter's body: she chose her clothing, her diet, and sent her to a doctor for diet pills.

"I'm still very definitely in the process of trying to bring my inner realm and my outside together. I just got back from visiting my family whom I haven't seen in about two years. My mother really doesn't affect me anymore. I'm not trying to hide or pretend that I'm not overweight. Since I accept the fact that I am overweight, my mother's perception of me can't hurt.

"I feel much more confident about who I am. The workshop was a good piece of the work. I find that my body image is much more stable. When I'm not dealing with something that's bothering me — when I have some emotions that I'm not really owning up to — usually the first thing that happens to me is that I start feeling *real* ugly and start avoiding looking at myself in the mirror and start feeling like all of a sudden — maybe overnight — I've gotten much huger than the day before. Now I recognize that when I'm under stress I tend to immediately go to my body image and distort it. I've been able to say to myself 'Well what *really* is the problem? You know you didn't gain fifty pounds overnight. What *is* the problem?' That way I can keep things in perspective and not get involved in a distraction. . . and I'm able to relax and find out what's really bothering me. I have definitely developed a different voice — or maybe it was there all along — but I listen to it a lot more. I used to have pretty heated battles within myself. They [the voices] would be yelling at each other. Now my voice is much more compassionate.

"My therapist commented how much more open I was after the workshop. I really wasn't so available for the work of therapy before.

"After the workshop I was a lot more aware of my body and decided that I really wanted to wake my body up so I started seeing a bodywork person — once a month — and we did some emotional work together. It's something that two years ago I wouldn't have considered as being important. I'm still doing it and it's been very good for me. My headaches have decreased. . . I'm living a lot more physically than I did before. I had so much resistance to getting back in my body. I'm still in the process. Just the fact that I'm dealing with a lot of issues like sexuality that I never would have dealt with before is a very significant change. When I was denying my body so much I was not willing to even acknowledge myself as a sexual being. For the first time in my life I feel ready to explore in a non-threatening way what I actually feel. I've been able to acknowledge to myself that I am a bisexual. That has felt very freeing. I don't have to hide anything. I'm still working a lot of this out, but I know now that I'm not so frightened of the thought of becoming vulnerable to another person.

"I am a lot more comfortable with how I dress, experimenting with clothes and with my hair style. With my new job [at an art college] I feel that I can indulge that more flamboyant part of me that likes to dress crazy. I don't feel that I'm too fat to do that. Before I would dress in a funky manner because I couldn't pull off a straight way of dressing. I don't feel that way at all anymore. The way I dress now is a choice, a positive statement. It fits the way I feel inside. I have a confidence that is coming out and is actually showing to other people.

"I feel so much more supported in women's groups, much less vulnerable, less judged physically. I had always felt victimized and angered by the image that society has foisted upon women. I don't feel so controlled by my family or by society. I feel a lot more in control of my own life, and I don't have to be that angry anymore. I have more tolerance for other people and standpoints.

"The other thing that has been important to me is an ongoing support group—formal or informal. I had always pooh-poohed such things—I could make it on my own. I also meditate every day. No matter what is going on in the exterior world, I can go inside and contact my Self. That for me has been a real coping tool.

"Compassion really helps, especially in a stress period. I used to tell myself, 'You're too fat and you can't eat!' That's the worst thing I could do to myself at a time like that—it would send me off on a binge. Now I say to myself 'I'm going to eat something that will make me feel good because I need it.' I don't feel bad about it so I don't put pressure on myself and I don't binge. I'm much more sane about my eating now. Having a weight problem and a distorted body image has been a major portion of my life—my cross to bear. It has affected the way that I deal with the world. It has affected me—now I am able to realize—in positive as well as negative ways. My own struggles have helped me to be a more sensitive and compassionate person, personally and politically. I'm now working to be more compassionate with myself as well."

In their own words these women share the richness of their own transformations. Each one finds herself somewhere along the road homeward—still clearly in process. Their stories are unique, but some themes are shared.

Each woman has come to a place where compassion is the preferred way of dealing with herself, whether through self-talk or through self-caring. At any moment we have the choice to be kind or cruel, to affirm or negate ourselves. Each time we choose the path of compassion we nurture ourselves and grow in self-respect. This inner growth makes it easier to choose to continue being kind to ourselves.

And so on. This shift in attitude, although small in itself, can have a powerful and pervasive effect.

Each woman was able to gain access to her inner being and to experience that core of herself as both beautiful and lovable. This profound self-love is the key to being able to love our bodies, imperfections and all. It opens us to feelings of compassion and permissiveness with ourselves. In some fundamental way it allows us to transcend the identification with our bodies as the reflection of who we are. It allows us to stand back and be a witness to ourselves. Who we are is beautiful. And the body that self inhabits is beautiful by association. Not the other way around.

In going inside, each woman was able to tap the power of her own mind and imagination to heal herself. This realm of mind holds an important key to self-knowledge and self-transformation. Experiencing her inner wealth and the control that she could exert over it gave each woman a feeling of empowerment. It is our own power that can sustain our visions of ourselves as human beings who have bodies.

In transforming herself, each woman was able to sense her needs for further growth — dance lessons, individual therapy, keeping a journal, joining a woman's support group, bodywork, or medical attention. To know what we need we must first be able to know ourselves. To give ourselves what we need we must be willing to love ourselves. This is what coming home to our bodies is all about.

AFTERWORD

No man remains quite what he was when he recognizes himself.
Thomas Mann

I hope that the testimony of these four women will illuminate and inspire your own commitment to making peace with your body. This kind of change takes time. It is a process of chipping away at your assumptions until you reveal the truth that lies buried inside. It is being willing to be yourself rather than the person everyone else wants you to be. It involves learning a kind of unswerving gentleness toward yourself that reflects your desire to heal your wounds through love. It requires a deep commitment to yourself.

Throughout history Woman has been associated with Body and Nature while Man has represented Mind and Technology. Man has soared the spiritual heights while Woman has remained mistress of the dark, mysterious, and powerful realm of the flesh, her body associated with instinct, irrationality, unpredictability, sensuality, uncleanness, evil, the power to give and take life itself. Because Woman has been seen as essential but feared, she has been controlled, as has Body, by being objectified and placed under restraints. This continued objectification of woman's body by society and by ourselves has sustained our disembodiment and disempowerment.

We women today are pioneers breaking new ground and shedding confining roles that no longer suit us. The road is often lonely. In breaking free of the narrow and unnatural standards of our culture we are going against a very powerful historical current.

You have identified many of the voices that express these beliefs in you. You have made at least initial contact with that part of you that is a clear and direct expression of your true self. This part of you also has a voice, at this point perhaps small and faint. This voice will be your greatest ally.

Your challenge is this: To listen to that inner voice that speaks with clarity. To allow that voice to grow in force until it can overwhelm the other voices that compete for your attention. By acknowledging and listening to it, you will be nurturing that part of you that has the wisdom and true vision to know what is right for you. This is not necessarily easy as Ginny, Denise, Margie, and Francine learned, but it is possible.

Our task is to hold on to the vision of how we want our lives to be. The work of this book has been to bring you to a place of greater self-knowledge and self-acceptance. It has also hopefully heightened the clarity of your vision of how you want and deserve to live in your body. By holding this vision above all—and surrounding yourself with others who share your vision—you can surmount whatever obstacles a non-supportive environment throws your way.

You probably know by now that I feel passionately about this subject. I hope that some of that passion has come through in my writing. My zeal comes from a deep place of respect for women—who we are and what we have to offer to the world. It is also fueled by an abhorrence of waste, especially human waste. I have experienced it in my own life, and I have witnessed it in the lives of many other women who have made a career out of agonizing over their bodies.

I wrote this book to give constructive expression to my personal rage about the oppressive standards that I and other western women confront in living out our lives. From a larger perspective, I am both frightened and saddened as I watch today's women trying to conform to these standards at the expense of much of their human potential. This is a tragic waste, and it is my passionate belief that something must be done about this on a cultural and ideological level. It is my hope that this book will serve not only as a vehicle for self-improvement but as a way of sensitizing women to the need for change on a much larger scale.

When enough people change their consciousness to embrace a new set of values, the values of their culture change. We have all witnessed this in the major societal changes set in motion by the Women's Movement. When I lead my workshops or teach classes in body image I feel like a small voice in the wilderness. I can touch relatively few women at a time. Their changes cause a tiny ripple that is easily overwhelmed by the cultural currents they confront in their lives. A book can reach a larger audience. It is my hope that you will come away from reading this book with greater enlightenment than you had before, with a more profound and respectful sense of who you are as a person. Then those of you who have been touched by this process will in turn touch and support others until the ripple becomes a wave and finally a tide that cannot be ignored.

Many women — and therapists — fail to take the subject of woman's body image seriously, seeing it as a superficial concern. For many, this lack of concern comes from ignorance of the facts. While our outer appearances may indeed be superficial when compared to the depth of our inner beings, there is nothing shallow about the pain of separation between a woman and her body, nothing light about the waste of lives spent in trying to be something other than what we are.

Isn't it about time we all learned to love the bodies we have?

RESOURCES
BODY IMAGE, EATING, WEIGHT, and RELATED TOPICS

Atrens, Dale M. *Don't Diet*. NY: Morrow, 1988.

Bass, Ellen, and Davis, Laura. *The Courage to Heal: A Guide for Women Survivors of Child Sexual Abuse*. NY: Harper & Row, 1988.

Beller, Ann Scott. *Fat and Thin - A Natural History of Obesity*. Farrar, Straus: 1977.

Bennett, W.G., and Gurin, J. *The Dieter's Dilemma: Eating Less and Weighing More*. NY: Basic Books, 1982.

Boston Women's Health Collective. *The New Our Bodies Ourselves*. NY: Simon & Schuster, 1992.

Brownell, Kelly D., and Foreyt, John P., eds. *Handbook of Eating Disorders*. NY: Basic Books, 1986.

Brownmiller, Susan. *Femininity*. NY: Simon and Schuster, 1984.

Brown, Laura S., and Rothblum, Esther, eds. *Fat Oppression and Psychotherapy: A Feminist Perspective*. Binghamton: Haworth Press, 1990.

Cash, T., and Pruzinsky, T., eds. *Body Images: Development, Deviance, & Change*. NY: Guilford Press, 1990.

Chapkis, Wendy. *Beauty Secrets*. Boston: South End Press, 1986.

Chernin, Kim. *The Obsession: Reflections on the Tyranny of Slenderness*. NY: Harper & Row, 1981.
_____. *The Hungry Self: Women, Eating, and Identity*. NY: Harper & Row, 1985.
_____. *Reinventing Eve: Modern Woman in Search of Herself*. NY: Harper/Collins, 1988.

Ciliska, Donna. *Beyond Dieting - Psychoeducational Interventions for Chronically Obese Women: A Non-dieting Approach*. NY: Brunner/Mazel, 1990.

Dally, P., and Gomez, J. *Obesity and Anorexia Nervose: A Question of Shape*. Boston: Faber and Faber, 1980.

Doress, Paula, and Siegel, Diana, and the Midlife and Older Women Book Project. *Ourselves, Growing Older*. NY: Simon and Schuster, 1987.

Ernsberger, Paul, and Haskew, Paul. *Rethinking Obesity*. Journal of Obesity and Weight Regulation. 6, 58-137.

Faludi, Susan. *Backlash: The Undeclared War Against American Women*. NY: Doubleday, 1991.

Freedman, Rita. *Beauty Bound: Why We Pursue The Myth in the Mirror*. Lexington: Lexington Books, 1986.
_____. *Body Love*. NY: Harper & Row, 1988.

Garner, David, and Garfinkel, Paul E. *Handbook of Psychotherapy for Anorexia & Bulimia*. NY: Guilford, 1985.

Hatfied, Elaine, and Sprecher, Susan. *Mirror, Mirror...: The Importance of Looks in Everyday Life*. Albany: State University of New York Press, 1986.

Hirschmann, Jane R., and Munter, Carol H. *Overcoming Overeating*. NY: Fawcett Columbine, 1988.

Hirschmann, J., and Zaphiropoulos, L. *Solving Your Child's Eating Problems*. NY:.Fawcett Columbine,1985.

Hutchinson, Marcia Germaine. "Transforming Body Image: Your Body Friend or Foe?" *Women and Therapy*. Vol. 1, #3. Fall, 1982. (See also Sankowsky, M.H.)
_____. "Imagining Ourselves Whole." Chapter in *Feminist Perspectives on Eating Disorders*. S. Wooley, P. Fallon, and M. Katzman, eds. Guilford Publications, (scheduled for publication in 1993).
_____. "What it Means to be Recovered and Fat." Chapter in *Full Lives: A Woman's Guide to Freedom from Obsession with Food and Weight*. Lindsey Hall, ed. Gurze Books, (scheduled for publication in 1993).
_____. "Transforming Body Image." *Woman of Power*. #18, Women's Bodies. Fall, 1990.

Jasper, Karin. *Are You Too Fat, Ginny?*. (Children's Book) Toronto: Is Five Press.

Kano, Susan. *Making Peace With Food: A Step-by-Step Guide to Freedom From Diet/Weight Conflict*. NY: Harper & Row, 1989.

Latimer, Jane E. *Living Binge-Free*. Boulder: Living Quest, 1988.

Levine, Michael P. *How Schools Can Help Combat Student Eating Disorder: Anorexia Nervosa and Bulimia*. Washington, DC: NEA Professional Library, 1987.

Lyons, Patricia, and Burgard, Deborah L. *Great Shape: The First Exercise Guide for Large Women*. NY: Arbor House, 1988.

Meadow, Rosalyn, and Weiss, Lillie. *Women's Conflicts About Eating and Sexuality*. Binghamton: Haworth Press, 1992.

Millman, Marcia. *Such A Pretty Face: Being Fat in America*. NY: W.W. Norton, 1980.

Orbach, Susie. *Fat Is a Feminist Issue*. NY: Berkeley, 1978.
____. *Fat Is a Feminist Issue II*. NY: Berkeley, 1978.
____. *Hunger Strike*. NY: Norton, 1987.

Pinkola-Estes, Clarissa. *Women Who Run With The Wolves*. NY: Ballantine Books, 1992.

Polivy, J., and Herman, C.P. *Breaking the Diet Habit*. NY: Basic Books, 1983.

Roberts, Nancy. *Breaking All The Rules: Feeling Good and Looking Great No Matter What Your Size*. NY: Viking, 1986.

Rodin, Judith. *Body Traps*. NY: William Morrow and Co., 1992.

Sanford, Linda, and Donovan, Mary Ellen. *Women and Self-Esteem*. Garden City: Anchor Doubleday, 1984.

Sankowsky, Marcia H. (aka Marcia Germaine Hutchinson). *"The effect of a treatment based on the use of guided visuo-kinesthetic imager on the alteration of negative body-cathexis in women."* Doctoral dissertation. Boston University, 1981. (Available from University Microfilms International, P.O. Box 1764, Ann Arbor, MI.)

Schoenfielder, Lisa, and Wieser, Barbara, eds. *Shadow on a Tightrope: Writings by Women on Fat Oppression*. Iowa City: Aunt Lute Book Co., 1983.

Seid, Roberta Pollack. *Never Too Thin: Why Women Are at War with Their Bodies*. NY: Prentice Hall, 1989.

Steinhem, Gloria. *Revolution from Within*. Little, Brown, 1992.

Thompson, J.K. *Body Image Disturbance: Assessment & Treatment*. NY: Pergamon Press, 1990.

Wolf, Naomi. *The Beauty Myth*. NY: William Morrow and Co., 1991.

Woodman, Marion. *The Owl Was a Baker's Daughter: Obesity, Anorexia Nervosa, and the Repressed Feminine*. Toronto: Inner City Books, 1980.
____. *Addiction to Perfection: The Still Unravished Bride*. Toronto: Inner City Books, 1982.

Information about
***Transforming Body Image* Companion Audiocassettes**
and *Transforming Body Image* Workshops
by Marcia Germaine Hutchinson
Body-Mind Productions. 88 West Goulding St., Sherborn, MA 01770.

Films
Gilday, Katherine. *The Famine Within*. McNabb & Connelly. 65 Heward Avenue, Suite 209, Toronto, Ontario M4M 2T5, 1990.
Kilbourne, Jean. *Still Killing Us Softly*. Cambridge Documentary Films, Inc. P.O. Box 385, Cambridge, MA 02139, 1987.

Periodicals Relating to Size Acceptance
Radiance: The Magazine for Large Women. Oakland, CA.
Big Beautiful Woman (BBW). Beverly Hills, CA.
Magna (for men). P.O. Box 286, Cabin John, MD.
Ample Information. P.O. Box 40621, Portland, OR 97240-0621.

Organizations
NAAFA (National Association to Advance Fat Acceptance). P.O. Box 188620, Sacramento, CA.

Council on Size & Weight Discrimination, Inc. P.O. Box 238, Columbia, MD, (215) 426-9023.

Hersize: Weight Prejudice Action Group. 222 Concord Avenue, Toronto, Ontario M6H 2P4.

Miscellaneous
Gurze Eating Disorders Bookshelf Catalogue. Box 2238, Carlsbad, CA, (619) 434-7533.

Resources for Change: A directory of resources and activist groups dealing with Eating Disorders, Equality, Media Awareness, Sex - Role Stereotyping, Corporate Action, Recovery, etc. Contact: Jean Klibourne, 51 Church Street Boston, MA 02116.

Information about the Feldenkrais Method [R]
Body-Mind Productions. (Catalog of movement lessons on audiocassette for home study). 88 West Goulding Street, Sherborn, MA 01770.

Feldenkrais Resources. (Catalog of books and tapes on the Feldenkrais Method). P.O. Box 2067, Berkeley, CA 94702, (800) 765-1907.

Notes

Praise for

urning Sk

"Lori Benton gives us seasons in her debut novel *Burning Sky*. Seasons of planting corn, beans, and pumpkins as backdrops to the ripening and challenges of lives working through chaos after a war and a terrible personal tragedy. The author gives us seasons of the journey through loss, risk, family, and love. The author's voice is mesmerizing with evocative phrases like 'The air inside the cabin swirled with stale memories, echoes of once-familiar voices trapped within, awaiting her coming to free them.' Set on a frontier homestead in New York in 1784, we meet distinctive characters I came quickly to care about. And the promises of the opening poetic question of Burning Sky / Willa, 'Will the land remember?' is answered with passion and grace and the satisfaction of a good harvest. Enjoy this wonderful novel."

—JANE KIRKPATRICK, award-winning author
of *One Glorious Ambition*

"In *Burning Sky*, Lori Benton brings to turbulent life the bitter aftermath of the Revolution, when those who fought on opposing sides returned to ravaged homes, soul scarred by horrifying acts they both suffered and committed. With lyrical imagery and finely drawn characters who rise from the page, *Burning Sky* vividly portrays how God restores the bruised reed and the dimly burning wick and brings new life from the ashes of the past."

—J. M. HOCHSTETLER, author of the American Patriot
series

"*Burning Sky* is a beautifully written story of courage, love, and new beginnings. Author Lori Benton introduces us to a great cast of characters while keeping the action strong in every vividly drawn scene. *Burning Sky* had me reading deep into the night to see if Willa would find a way to leave her unhappy past behind and open her heart to love again. Highly recommended to fiction lovers everywhere."

—ANN H. GABHART, author of *Angel Sister, The Outsider,*
and other stories

"An authentic rendering of frontier life, full of heart and hope. *Burning Sky* takes the reader on a vivid journey into New York's wilderness at a time when cultures collided and lives were forever changed. A memorable debut!"
> —LAURA FRANTZ, author of *The Colonel's Lady*
> and *Love's Reckoning*

"Easily the best debut novel I've ever read. *Burning Sky* is a powerful account of a white woman born Wilhelmina Obenchain who lived as Burning Sky, a daughter of a Mohawk clan. Lori Benton writes with a colorful, spirited pen. Her distinct and compelling voice seizes the reader and holds them captive until the last line of this remarkable book."
> —BONNIE LEON, author of the Sydney Cove series
> and Alaskan Skies series

"By turns exciting and heart-wrenching, *Burning Sky* is a deeply engaging story with a tender, thoughtful heart."
> —DIANA GABALDON, author of the Outlander series

"In this classical frontier adventure, Lori Benton brings to readers a journey of the heart. *Burning Sky* is a vivid portrait of life in post-Revolutionary War New York. Ms. Benton's prose is beautifully written, with a romantic edge reminiscent of *The Last of the Mohicans* and *The Deerslayer*, but with a bold heroine whose struggles through the harsh realities of life in the wilderness bring her to the realization there is something greater than herself."
> —RITA GERLACH, author of the Daughters of the Potomac
> series and other inspirational fiction

"There are any number of novelists who can make history come to life, but Lori Benton does so with writing so beautiful that you wish the story would never end. From the first line to the last, her characters and story transported me. Take notice, friends; Lori isn't just a novelist. She's an artist. I can't wait for her next book."
> —KAREN BALL, award-winning editor and best-selling
> author of *Shattered Justice*

"Lori does an incredible job of using the characters, the setting, and the scene to wash the reader into the story's flow. *Burning Sky* is captivating from its very first phrase; I sighed and wept with her characters. I yearned for their well-being—and missed them like old friends when I turned the last page. Lori Benton's debut novel is one I'll keep on my shelf to read again. It's *that* good."

—MESU ANDREWS, author of *Love Amid the Ashes*,
2012 ECPA Book of the Year—New Author

"Lori Benton expertly and vividly captures the challenges of life on the American frontier in this remarkable debut novel. An unforgettable story of a young woman's brave journey to discover not only herself but the God who loves her."

—SUSAN MEISSNER, author of *The Girl in the Glass*

"Lori Benton's writing is magnetic, drawing you deeper and deeper into her debut novel *Burning Sky*. The woman who had been Burning Sky has loved two families and lived two lives, and hasn't the strength to care anymore. But when she is needed, her heart is stirred and again threatened by loss. Lori Benton is a word-artist, crafting every captivating line to keep you turning the pages of *Burning Sky*."

—MONA HODGSON, author of the Sinclair Sisters of
Cripple Creek series, the Quilted Heart novellas, and
Prairie Song

BURNING SKY

A NOVEL OF THE
AMERICAN
FRONTIER

LORI BENTON

WATERBROOK
PRESS

BURNING SKY
PUBLISHED BY WATERBROOK PRESS
12265 Oracle Boulevard, Suite 200
Colorado Springs, Colorado 80921

All Scripture quotations are taken from the King James Version.

The characters and events in this book are fictional, and any resemblance to actual persons or events is coincidental.

Trade Paperback ISBN 978-0-307-73147-0
eBook ISBN 978-0-307-73148-7

Cover design by Kristopher K. Orr; cover photography (Willa) by Mike Heath, Magnus Creative; cover photography (landscape) by Tai Power Seeff, Getty Images

Published in the United States by WaterBrook Multnomah, an imprint of the Crown Publishing Group, a division of Random House Inc., New York.

WATERBROOK and its deer colophon are registered trademarks of Random House Inc.

Library of Congress Cataloging-in-Publication Data
Benton, Lori.
    Burning sky : a novel of the American frontier / Lori Benton. — First edition
        pages cm
    ISBN 978-0-307-73147-0 (pbk.) — ISBN 978-0-307-73148-7 (electronic)
    1. Women—Fiction. 2. Frontier and pioneer life—New York (State)—Fiction. 3. New York (State)—History—1775–1865—Fiction. I. Title.
    PS3602.E6974B87 2013
    813'.6—dc23

                                        2013007114

Printed in the United States of America
2013—First Edition

10 9 8 7 6 5 4 3 2 1

◈

In memory of two special women...

*My grandmother, Margaret Johnson,
who kept my first story.*

*And Lauri Klobas,
without whom the journey would have taken longer
and included a lot less confetti.*

I remember the borders of our land, though I have been gone from them nearly half the moons of my life. They are these: the hilltop stone to the north; Black Kettle Creek to the south; to the east, the lake where the warriors found me; and west, the bottomland acres where the corn and wheat were sown, hard by the track that led to Shiloh.

But who there will remember me? Who will know these sun-browned arms, these callused hands, these legs that stride mountains without tiring and stand me taller than other women? What I have seen, what I have done, it has changed me.

I am the place where two rivers meet, silted with upheaval and loss.

Yet memory of our land is a clear stream. I shall know it as a mother knows the faces of her children. I will walk its borders. I will search its ground for what was taken, and what was left behind. It may be I will find me there.

If the land remembers.

ONERAHTÓKHA

The Budding Time—April

ONE

T he woman who had been Burning Sky had kept off the warrior
path that came down from the north through mountains, along the
courses of rivers and creeks. Doing so meant traveling slow, over steep
ground unfriendly to trudging feet, but she had not wanted to be seen by
men on the path. Red men or white men.

She'd slept on the cold ground thirteen times before she saw the stone
that marked the end of her journey—and the boundary of her papa's land,
the place she once called home. Time had not dimmed it in her memory.
The stone, tall as a man and pointed as a blade, thrust from the crest of a
ridge. But with her step quickened and her gaze fixed on it as she neared,
she failed to notice the dog slithering out of the laurel thicket below the
stone, until the muddy animal stood in her path and showed its teeth.

The woman who had been Burning Sky halted, shaken less by the dog
than by her own inattention. If Tames-His-Horse had been there, he
would have scolded her for it.

He was not there, but another was.

The sun had slipped from behind clouds and sent a shaft of light lanc-
ing down the ridge into the laurels, full across the man lying in the thicket,
showing her a booted foot, a length of knee breeches, a hand cradled on
the breast of a brown coat. A white hand.

She caught her breath, while the blood thundered in her ears. When
neither the man nor the dog moved, fear began to sift from her like chaff
through a winnowing basket. The dog was only standing guard. But over
the living or the dead?

It was tempting to assume the latter, but for this: the man lay on her papa's side of the boundary stone. The significance of that settled on her, a heavier burden than the long-trail basket she'd carried on her back these many days. Maybe the man was dead and it would not matter what she did, but she could not turn her back and walk on as though she had not seen him.

There was still the problem of the dog in her way. It was one of those bred for bullying sheep, black and white, rough coated. The English word for it surfaced in her mind: *collie*.

The woman who had been Burning Sky slipped the tumpline from her forehead and the cord loops from her arms, lowering the basket to the ground. She gripped the musket slung at her side, even as she spoke kindly in the language of the People. "You are a good dog, guarding your man. *Tohske' wahi*. It is so?"

The collie did not alter its rigid stance.

It occurred to her the dog might not know the speech of the *Kanien'kehá:ka*, called Mohawks by the whites. She tried English, which felt to her like speaking with pebbles in the mouth.

"You will let me near him, yes?" She took a step toward the laurels. The collie moved its matted tail side to side. "Good dog."

She set her musket within reach and turned her attention to the man. He was too tangled in the laurels to have crawled in. Likely he'd fallen from the ridge above. Not a long drop, but steep. Closer now, she could see his face. Even for a white man, it was pale, the hollows of his closed eyes bruised, sickly. Hair almost black stuck to his brow in stiffened curls.

While the dog nosed her heels, she wrenched away twigs, keeping one eye on the man's still face. With the small hatchet from her sash, she hacked away larger branches, sending down a shower of leaves and insects, until she knelt beside the man. He had not stirred, but the warmth of his breath against her palm told her he lived. From the way he cradled his right arm across his chest, she knew it to be injured. His legs lay straight and seemed undamaged, save for scrapes where his leg coverings had torn in the fall.

Not leg coverings, she thought. *Stockings.*

She did not know about his ribs, or what hurts might lurk beneath them. Moving him might cause further injury, but he could not remain as he was, unless she stayed and cared for him. She tipped back her head, lifting her eyes to the boundary stone, then to the sky at which it pointed.

Why the man? Why now, so near her journey's end?

Neither the stone nor its Maker gave answer. For whatever inscrutable reason, the Great Good God—the Almighty—had placed this man in her path, as He'd removed so many others from it.

It did not seem a fair exchange. But sitting there, wishing it was not so, would change nothing. This she well knew.

Returning to the basket, she found a length of sturdy basswood cord. With the hatchet, she cut cedar saplings to serve for poles and crosspieces, then retrieved the elk hide from her bedding. Through all this and the building of the travois, the dog milled about, whining. She met its fretful gaze but had no promises to make it. She would do what she could.

Though she was strong for a woman, and tall, the man's deadweight proved no easy burden. While she maneuvered him out of the laurels, she expected him to rouse. But not until she knelt to secure him to the travois, sweating from the exertion, did she look up to find his eyes open. He had blue eyes—the drenching blue of trade beads—and they were fixed on her in glittering bewilderment and pain.

Responding to his pain, she touched his face to reassure him. His beard was coming in. The rasp of it against her palm stirred memories. Papa's face had sometimes rasped with stubble, against the touch of her childish hand. Not black stubble—reddish brown like her own hair. Was it red still, or had the years made it white?

Then she thought she should stop touching the face of this man who was not Papa, whatever memories he stirred, but her fingers stayed pressed to the cold, bristly cheek.

While she hesitated, bewilderment fled the man's blue-bead eyes, replaced by something like awe, then a look she had not seen in another face since the day she watched the longhouse burn. He was gazing at her with the trust of a child, innocent and complete.

"Oh, aye, that's all right, then," he said. The warmth of his breath brushed her face as he exhaled, closing his startling eyes.

The woman who had been Burning Sky sat back on her heels, stabbed beneath her ribs by a blade so sharp she wanted to beat her breasts to drive it out. Never again had she wanted to see that look of trust on the face of the sick, the dying. She'd fled far, thinking she could outdistance that sorrowful pairing. Had she not seen suffering enough to fill a lifetime?

A bruised reed shall he not break, and the smoking flax shall he not quench. The words settled in her mind like a hand on the shoulder, large and steadying. She drew a breath through lungs that fought with grief for space inside her, and looked at the man on the travois. *A bruised reed.* There would be many such scattered over the land, broken and uprooted by the war just past. She was not the only one.

Though she was no longer adept at judging the ages of white men, this one seemed young. Not as young as she, though she doubted he was past thirty winters. No white threaded his hair, and the lines at the corners of his eyes were faintly drawn. The quality of his woolen coat marked him a man of consequence. *Not a farmer,* she thought.

She could not begin to guess why he was there, fallen on the edge of what the whites called the Great Northern Wilderness, a sea of forest rolling away in mounting crests to Canada, where the redcoat soldiers of the defeated English king had retreated since the war to lick their wounds. Was he someone Papa knew, here by his leave? If so, Papa would be glad she helped him.

She wanted Papa to be glad when he saw her again. *If* he saw her again.

Though the long winter had finally ended, the day was chill for the moon of budding leaves. She unrolled her rabbit-skin cloak and spread it over the man. She gathered the few belongings she found scattered around him and secured them on the travois. One of those was a small glass bottle, dark with the liquid it contained. She uncorked the glass, put it to her nose, and grimaced at the bittersweetness of opium dissolved in spirits. Was this the reason he'd fallen, or had he found it afterward and dosed himself to bear his injuries? It explained why he had remained unconscious, save for that brief moment.

Perhaps, even then, he had been in a dream's grip and had not really seen her. Perhaps that look of trust had been for someone else. She greatly hoped so.

She corked the bottle and dropped it into her carrying basket.

The snow thaw had passed on the lower slopes, leaving only the marshy places impassable with mud. There on the ridge, the ground was moist but not saturated. Gripping the travois poles, she hoisted her burden and picked herself a path through the wide-spaced trees, while the dog followed.

Though the going now was even slower, the land beneath her feet grew more familiar with each step. In her mind she rushed ahead, seeing it in memory—its fertile dips and rocky ridges, the broad noisy creek called Black Kettle, the lake with its tiny islet, the broad flats where Papa grew his corn and wheat. The clearing where the barn and cabin stood. So close now.

Relief and dread warred in her belly.

She found the little stream where she remembered it to be, and the footpath that followed its winding course south, then east, then south again. She saw no tracks of men, but the deer had kept it clear. Though the travois passed with little hindrance, the man's weight dragged at her shoulders, causing a burn across the muscles of her back and arms. The basket's tumpline, tight across her brow, strained the bones of her neck. She turned her mind from the pain, continuing as she had done through each day of her journey. One foot, then the other. A step, and another. As she went, she spoke aloud a name, one she had not heard for many years, and so she said it with care, her enunciation precise.

"Wil-helm-ina O-ben-chain."

The collie trotted up beside her, ears perked, already accustomed to her voice. The woman who had been Burning Sky nodded to the dog, whose name she did not know.

"Wilhelmina Obenchain," she said, more assuredly this time. "But you may call me Willa."

TWO

S he came down off the last ridge and halted at the northern edge of the long clearing. At the other end, on a slight rise near the far tree line, the cabin still stood. That much could be said.

A sweeping glance took in the rest of the homestead, or what remained of it. The charred bits of what had been the barn and crib and smokehouse. The pasture where the horse and cattle had grazed, choked with brush. The saplings advancing on the clearing her papa, Dieter Obenchain, had hacked from wilderness over twenty winters ago.

For more than half those winters, far to the north, she had pictured her parents, and Oma, going about their lives in this place, believing she would never see them again but comforted by such thoughts all the same.

Where was comfort to be found now? Where was Papa? Mama? With shaking arms she lowered the heavy travois to the weeds, then folded to her knees. Whatever army had done this burning, redcoat, bluecoat, or Long-house warriors, they'd left no one to welcome her home.

And no one to spurn your homecoming, a dark voice countered.

She cringed from the voice, though it was no stranger. Had it not with every step of her journey insisted she was foolish to go back? She was better off alone, for to clear a path to her heart for another to tread was only to invite more grief. Had she not done so twice—loved two families, lived two lives? Both had been torn from her, ripping out great pieces of her soul in the taking. Why should she gather in that spilling wound again?

She should have listened to that voice. It had been right in its dark warning. Now it was taunting her, saying, *Why not sit in the weeds and wait to follow your precious lost ones?*

Why not, indeed?

The dog, bossy creature, would not let her do so. It shoved its nose under her hand. It trotted toward the cabin, turned, and fixed her with expectant eyes. "Come, you," it said, clear as speech.

It had some sense, that dog. She might not care whether she lived or died, but the man she'd hauled out of the laurel thicket would no doubt wish her to choose living. For now at least.

Willa Obenchain thrust down her grief and refused to think of past or future. The past could not be altered. The future would bring what it would. There was a now to deal with, and it needed all her strength to stand and meet it.

"All right. Let's get your man inside and see what can be done for him, hen'en?"

The air inside the cabin swirled with stale memories, echoes of once-familiar voices trapped within, awaiting her coming to free them.

"Do ye gather in the eggs, Daughter, then help your mama with the bread."

"Willa, it is well done. Turn and show me the back seams."

"She'd make a passable sempstress, could she pull her nose from those frivolous books for more than an hour."

The onslaught dizzied her as she lowered the travois and the man it supported—dragged in over the porch steps—before the hearth. As her eyes adjusted to the dimness, the memories receded, flowing past her and away. She propped the carrying basket against the paneled wall and looked about, heart thudding like a water drum, with the strangeness of hardwood under her feet again.

And it was hard. The main room of the cabin appeared reasonably sound. The roof had not leaked, nor the floor rotted. This was not too surprising. Her papa possessed a German sense of craftsmanship. What he'd made, he had made well.

Even so, something felt at odds with the cabin's obvious abandonment. The open door admitted light enough to show the main room swept clean. Hardly a cobweb draped the corners, except high up among the roof beams.

The cabin's state of cleanliness was not all that felt strange. There was order here, in contrast to the neglect outside. Kindling for a fire was laid in the hearth, wood stacked at the ready nearby. From the old iron cooking crane hung a battered kettle. She lifted the lid to find it scoured clean, half-filled with water. Most puzzling of all were the wildflowers tied with string, dried to brown now but clearly placed there by some caring hand, as one might put flowers on a grave.

Unease tightened Willa's chest.

The cabin's front room was stripped of furnishings, save for a trestle bench once belonging to their table. She began for the first time to wonder if her parents had survived the burning—and whatever violence attended it—taken away their belongings and gone east to Albany, or south to German Flats.

Or had the place been raided and stripped clean?

She'd heard accounts of the devastation the war between the Americans and the British had wrought upon New York's frontier. Homes and crops burned. Settlers murdered, captured, driven off their land. For all she knew, Papa's cabin now stood in the midst of an unpeopled wilderness—if not for the flowers, wood, and water.

The man on the travois did not stir while she coaxed a fire to life and swung the kettle over the flames. She did not think *he* had left the cabin thus. His dog had come inside with her, but with a wariness that told her this was not a place it knew. It watched her, sniffed the man over, and went out again.

She set the items she'd found among the laurels beside the hearth: canteen; satchel; a small glass that made things seen through it loom large; an odd container made of tin, round-sided and long, with a leather strap for carrying and a sliding pin for a clasp.

The man moved his head, turning it toward the hearth. The firelight revealed a faintly reddened patch of skin, high above his left eyebrow. Most of his hair was tailed back, but shorter wisps curled on his brow. Thinking she might have overlooked a wound that needed tending, she brushed the stiffened hair aside.

It was a wound, but one long since healed. The pinkish scar sliced a messy line along the man's hairline, from his temple halfway across his brow.

A knife blade had left that scar. A scalping blade.

She drew back from the man, a little shaken, and went to fetch her herb pouch, from which she extracted a measure of willow bark. When steam rose off the water in the kettle, she dipped a gourd cup full, added the bark, and set it on the hearth to steep. Whatever hurts he might have besides the arm, the bark would ease their pain. When the laudanum wore off.

Turning, she nearly stumbled over the man's satchel.

Before she could think twice, she crouched and reached inside. The first thing she touched was flat, broad, and leather covered. She pulled it out. With a furtive glance at the man, she unwound the string from the horn toggle that secured its flap.

She'd expected a journal, something written down that might give understanding of who the man was. What she found instead were drawings. In pencil, in ink, even in colored paint. Page after page of them, mostly of plants and flowers, now and then a bird or insect with the plant— all recognizable by their remarkable detail. They were carefully labeled, with notes on the borders. Or most of them were. No writing accompanied the last dozen likenesses.

The stillness outside the cabin was broken by the dog's sudden barking. Willa returned the sketchbook to the satchel, took up her musket, crossed to the door, and stood there blinking in surprise.

Somewhere the dog had found a nanny goat, a half-starved, brindled creature, and was attempting to herd it across the cabin yard, creeping, crouching, circling around when the harried goat made a dash for the woods. Where it had come from was a mystery and made her wonder if it had belonged to her parents, or perhaps some other farm nearby, burned and abandoned like her own. She searched the sky above the wooded horizon, expecting to see smoke from another chimney.

There was no sign of neighbors.

After propping the musket by the door, she stepped off the porch and bent to wrench up a tuft of new spring grass. "Dog! Bring it this way. *Hahnio!*"

It was the goat that responded. Breaking off its escape with a protesting *bla-a-at*, it trotted straight to her outstretched hand.

Rolling its odd-pupiled eyes at the lurking collie, the goat followed Willa—or her handful of grass—around the porch to the addition her father had built when Opa died and Oma came up the creek from German Flats to live with them. This was the only part of the cabin that had fallen into disrepair. Half the roof was open to the sky, and the front timbers had rotted with rain and snow. The far corner timbers still stood solid, and the door to the main cabin was shut firm.

With some arranging of the fallen logs, Willa made a pen and with the help of the dog persuaded the goat inside it. She snatched up handfuls of grass for the creature, wondering after all that effort if it was not better to leave it loose and chance its staying. How would she feed it otherwise? She could not spare her seed corn. She needed every precious kernel. Perhaps she could build a proper pen…

If she decided to stay. Or to stay alive.

She was hearing voices again—women's voices. The singing and chatter that flew above brown hands busy planting; tending kettles, fires, babies; scraping hides; weaving mats; piecing moccasins and dying quills. So many hands to make the work fly. The memories pierced like arrows through her chest, her throat, her burning eyes.

Desperately, she reached back to dimmer memories—Mama and Oma making soap, dipping candles, sewing quilts, husking corn—but even their time-blunted points could wound.

The dog nudged her palm, and with a shake of her head, she came back to the present, where no hands offered help. Did she have it in her to go on? Was there any point in it now?

The dog whined. Willa sighed.

"I have not forgotten your man." She'd taken him into her care and under her roof—if she could call it that. She was obligated to see that decision through. What first, then? There was that arm she suspected was broken. If it needed to be set, best to do it before the laudanum wore off.

But when she came into the cabin, she found she was too late. The man had freed himself from the travois and was sitting up on it, looking about, blinking those eyes as blue as bits of sky fallen to earth. Dark brows soared at the sight of her, before he offered a tentative smile.

"'Tis not the first time I've waked to find myself cast upon the mercy of strangers," he said, the words rolling over her, thick as corn porridge. "Though come to that—"

Whatever more he meant to say was cut short when the dog, hearing his voice, pushed past her, bolted joyfully across the cabin, and hurled itself at the man.

THREE

Neil MacGregor got an arm half-raised before the filthy mass of fur vaguely resembling his dog barreled into him. Shielding his injured parts from the wriggling onslaught left his face open to a slobbery barrage. "Easy, sir—down, I say!"

He'd meant to say a deal more, but the collie swung its rump, tail whirling like a pinwheel, and swiped the wagging appendage against his swollen wrist. Pain forked like lightning up his arm, searing the words to his tongue.

"Dog. Come away."

The command came from the Indian who'd entered the cabin. From his glimpse of her stroud cloth and deerskin garments, Neil hadn't expected her to speak a word of English. More startling was his dog's response. The collie backed away and sat, pressed against the rock hearth, two paces from where Neil had awakened, lashed to what appeared to be a travois.

Removing his teeth from his lower lip, he peered at the woman in the doorway, squinting to bear the daylight streaming past her. Not an Indian, he realized. The thick braid of hair fallen over her shoulder was a light brown, glinting nearly auburn in the glare of sunlight. Her face, while tight-skinned and high-boned, had a golden cast, not the bronze of the Indians he'd encountered.

"D'ye mind terribly shutting the door?" he asked her, shooting a warning look at the dog lest it think itself released. The collie glanced at the woman and lay down. Neil was likewise tempted, but warring with a pounding, woozy head was the need to make sense of his circumstances— a far cry from the last he recalled—and to ascertain the extent of his injuries. Nothing too alarming, save for his right arm. Fractured, judging from the splintering pain when he moved it, and the bruised swelling of the wrist.

The woman did as he'd asked, bringing a blessed dimness to the cabin. She made no reply, however, nor any other indication she'd understood him. Perhaps she'd shut the door of her volition, not at his request. She *had* spoken English, hadn't she? The fading imprint of blinding pain told him he'd had another of the cursed headaches. They could scramble his brains for hours after waking.

Unnerved by the woman's silence, he looked at his dog. "Ye reek to high heaven, lad—and you're a sorry sight, forby."

The collie thumped the floor with its tail, pleased to be addressed.

"He is as I found him," the woman said. "Or as he found me."

That had been English, though the sound of it was odd, spoken with a faint accent Neil couldn't place, and a careful, almost halting manner, as though she was thinking hard about the words she chose to speak.

"Aye, well, he's inclined to attach himself to passersby. He found me near Schenectady—down on the Mohawk River. What his given name is I canna say, but I call him Capercaillie. That's a kind of bird," he explained at her blank stare. "In Scotland. Cap does for short."

He checked his blethering and dropped his gaze. The woman's feet were encased in stitched moccasins, beaded or quilled—he couldn't tell from that distance—in a flower design, their edges dark with moisture and mud. Above them, leggings of faded scarlet, similarly decorated, disappeared beneath a wrapped skirt of tanned hide, its edges fringed. Over this she wore a long tunic of stroud cloth like the leggings, only blue, and much worn. From her neck hung a necklace of shells and a bone-handled knife sheathed in beaded leather. It was the most rustic costume he'd yet seen on the frontier—on a white woman.

"He found you, did ye say?"

"Near the laurels. With you."

Images skittered at the edges of his memory. A laurel thicket…and a hawk in flight. A red-tailed hawk. It had circled up and over a curious stone on a ridge. A thin stone that rose to a point like a scalpel's blade. Wanting a closer look, he'd led the horse around to it by an easier ascent, made a sketch, then slipped the book into his satchel and unlaced a saddle-bag. A canteen had fallen. He'd grabbed for it...

Next he kent, he was lying in the laurels with Cap's frantic barking driving spikes into his skull, his vision occluded, and his wrist screaming in pain. At some point he'd roused and found the laudanum in his coat pocket, the glass thankfully unbroken. Black draft for the black spells. He hated the stuff. Hated worse his need of it.

So the woman had found him there, still in the laurels. "Ye dinna mean to say you brought me here, on your own?"

The woman's deep-set eyes narrowed, but she nodded.

"How? Oh, aye, the travois," he said, answering his own question. How had she gotten his horse to pull the contraption? Too distracted for the moment by a fresh stab of pain to ask, he ran light fingers over his swollen wrist, hissing in a breath.

The woman's moccasins drew near, and he saw that it was beads, not quills, that adorned them. Very pretty they were, though, where mud did not obscure the designs.

Her braid swung down in the firelight, the russet of autumn in its brown coils, as she reached for a gourd cup set by the hearth. She had capable-looking hands, long and shapely, but work roughened.

"Drink. It will help some. Your arm is broken?"

"Aye. I'm all but sure." He looked up as he accepted the gourd, and nearly spilled its contents into his lap. It was the first close look he'd had at her features. While his initial reaction was one of concern—the wide cheekbones, the deep hollows of her eyes, the line of her jaw, were sharply jutting in what was clearly a half-starved face—what caused the heat to rise to the roots of his hair was the thrill of recognition that shot through him.

He'd taken her for an angel when he opened his eyes to her the first time, thinking himself about to step through heaven's door.

Well, so. He wasn't dead. And she was no angel. Only striking in the remote and daunting way he'd imagined angels to be, with her straight back and long limbs and thick hair drawn back from those fiercely sculpted bones. And those eyes. He thought them green. Maybe hazel. With the firelight behind her, he couldn't tell for certain.

She pulled back from his scrutiny, the wide curve of her mouth pressed flat.

Disconcerted in his own right, Neil raised the gourd cup to his nose and sniffed. *Salix...*willow bark. The woman had some knowledge of herbs. He found that reassuring. He sipped the bitter tea, grimacing reflexively as his ministering angel backed away.

"Would ye be so kind," he ventured, "as to bring in my saddlebags? I'll be needing some things out of them if I'm to deal with this arm proper-like."

That got him another blank stare. "Saddlebags?"

"Aye. The ones on my horse."

"Horse?"

For an instant, he wondered if this—the woman, the cabin, the cup in his hand—was a laudanum-induced dream he was having. Why else would she commence to parroting his words as though she didn't comprehend them, when they'd been having reasonably fluent discourse a moment ago? Was it his accent? He'd taken pains to tamp it down some in recent years, but it did come creeping back thick as Highland mist if he didn't watch it.

"Did you not see a horse where you found me? A bay roan. Answers to the name of Seamus."

"There was no horse."

Her certainty was unfeigned, and he felt too wretched to be anything but full waking. Dash it all, his horse must have strayed after he fell.

Neil felt a plummeting in his gut as the magnitude of his situation drew clear. By necessity, he'd traveled light into the back country, but there were things in his saddlebags he could ill afford to lose. His medical case. The field desk and its contents. His cooking gear. The plant press!

He stifled a groan. Was this the end then? Was his hope of creating a collection of botanical drawings of the Adirondack Mountains—in the spirit of Catesby's work, and Colden, and the Bartrams—to terminate in such ignominious defeat? Must he return to Philadelphia with his tail between his legs…if he could find the courage to show his face to the Philosophical Society members and explain why their long-suffering faith in him—not to mention their monetary investment—had been woefully misplaced?

And he would be making that journey afoot, without Seamus. He'd never been much of a horseman, but he'd managed to acquire a fondness for the roan—not a mutual regard, apparently. Still, the horse ought to have been his first thought, not the last.

"Lord Almighty, he's Thy creature. I'll trust Thee to watch o'er him and lead him, if not back to me, then to someone who'll ken his worth and treat him kindly. In the name of our Lord Jesus Christ…" He looked up to find the woman staring.

"Amen," she finished for him, as if in startled reflex.

He gave her a half-embarrassed smile. "I've fallen into the habit of conversing aloud with the Almighty, alone on the trail." When that garnered no response, he added, "Well, then. Since I havena got my own supplies to hand, I'll need something for bandaging. Splinting as well."

"I will find sticks for the splinting."

Before he could reply, the woman ducked out of the cabin. Cap lifted his head, looking after her, then settled back with a sigh.

"You've reached an understanding with yon woman, I see." Neil supposed that was reassuring too, but was glad for her departure. What had to be done next was a thing best attempted in solitude, by chance the need to emit unmanly noises got the better of him.

"Physician, heal thyself," he muttered, and clenched his teeth.

A cracked distal radius was his best diagnosis, though for all his stoic teeth grinding as he probed the inner workings of his wrist, it might only be a bad sprain, absent an obviously misaligned bone. Since the treatments were identical—prolonged immobility—he saw no reason to prolong the agony too, when his arm already felt jammed through with a heated poker in place of bone. He was near to swooning from the pain when he felt the woman's hands easing him back to lie down again.

"You ought to have waited."

"'Tis no matter," he said, sounding weak as a half-drowned kitten. "I'm a physician—or trained as one."

The spinning cabin settled into place. He was between the woman and the fire now, its light falling full on her face. Neil found himself staring again, at her eyes.

They were the most peculiar he had ever seen. Both were large and thick lashed, well set—at the same slight tilt as her cheekbones—but otherwise they might have belonged to different faces. While the left was hazel, predominantly green, the right was a warm, vivid brown, nearly the same shade as her hair.

He tried but couldn't look away from them.

As if accustomed to such rude gaping—and not best pleased by it—the woman frowned and looked away. "I have the sticks for splinting. We should make a sling for the arm, yes?"

She started to rise, but Neil sat up, and despite his spinning head managed to grasp her wrist. "Aye, but wait. I've not asked your name."

She stiffened at his touch, and he released her.

"I am called—" She paused, then with a little huff of breath said, "I am Wilhelmina, daughter of Dieter Obenchain."

She had named her father but not a husband. "'Tis *Miss* Obenchain, is it?"

She leveled a look at him. "You may call me Willa. I expect you also have a name?"

Heat touched his cheeks again. "Neil MacGregor, your servant, ma'am. At least in time I mean to be, to repay your kindness." He reached to doff his hat, felt only hair, and realized only then he'd lost it—hat and head, too, it must appear.

The gesture brought faint amusement to the woman's mismatched eyes. "Then let us see to your mending, Neil MacGregor."

Wrist wrapped and splinted, Neil sat cross-legged on the elk hide spread near the hearth and watched the preparation of a meal—if a handful of parched corn and two cornmeal cakes cooked in the ashes counted as such. Provisions were scarce, it seemed.

He'd tried without success to ascertain the cabin's function. The structure was nearly bereft of plenishings. No tables, no chairs, no presses or shelves or even trunks. No kegs or barrels lined the walls. There was a bench. A kettle over the hearth. A musket leaned in the corner, beside the travois and that capacious basket from which the woman had removed the bits and things needed to make the cakes she now transferred to the hearthstones.

The smell of them baking stirred his empty wame, making him think with longing of the provisions lost with the horse: a slab of cured bacon; a sack of flour, another of beans; sugar, salt, dried apples, and cherries. Coffee. All of which could be replaced but…his field equipment. His horse.

He closed his eyes, caught in a thicket far more tangled than the one Willa Obenchain had extracted him from. Without the horse and his equipment, with weeks lost because of his injury, he saw no way forward. Only back. He promptly took the matter up with the Almighty. *I dinna understand why You let me come so far, only to end it so. If You didna want me out here, doing this, why did Ye not take away the passion for it, like I asked, over and again, all the months I waited out the war and hoped for healing? Have You some other path for me, after all? If so, I'd be much obliged did You spell it out for me.*

He waited, but the Almighty made no answer to his prayer born more of frustration than faith. Then he realized how he'd phrased that last bit in his mind and didn't ken whether to laugh or groan. *All right, then. I didna mean literally spell it for me. How about simply showing me, when You're ready?*

He'd been so sure his season of waiting had passed.

Seeking distraction before he worked himself into another headache, he opened his eyes and blurted, "I take it this cabin isna in general use?"

Squatting before the hearth, Willa Obenchain glanced at him. "It is. Now."

Unsure what to make of that, he noticed the bundled flowers on the hearthstones. Even dried, he knew them. *Trillium erectum. Erythronium americanum.* He ran Linnaeus's classifications through his mind by habit—and necessity—watching her turn the cakes. "Have you only just arrived yourself?"

"*Hen*—yes. I found you in my path." She sighed as she spoke that last. "You were alone when ye found me?"

"Yes."

And his horse had strayed. He cast another look at the basket, noticing for the first time its corded tumpline. If she'd borne that large a burden, it was likely she had no pack animal of her own.

Realization dawned at last. The woman, burdened on a journey from…somewhere…had found him unconscious, built the travois, put him on it, and hauled him and her burden through the wilderness to this cabin. How many miles?

One or a dozen, it was a stunning feat of endurance and strength.

"I left the Mohawk River near Johnstown," he said, hoping to gauge exactly where in the state of New York he was at present, "and traveled north for a bit, then west." And found as yet small indication of reoccupation of that frontier landscape, though plenty of burned homesteads, razed by one side or another in the late war between the former colonies and the Crown. "Are we near a settlement? A fort, maybe?" They could not be as far south as Fort Dayton. He could not credit her having brought him *that* far.

Willa set the corn cakes on the bench between them. "There was a settlement, Shiloh, about three miles from here. I do not know what is there now, if anything."

He'd never heard of Shiloh. "What river does it lie on?"

"No river. Black Kettle Creek. That flows into the West Canada." Willa handed him his canteen, which had been filled.

West Canada Creek. He'd never been that far west but recognized the name from maps he'd poured over years ago, when he first conceived of this venture.

He thanked Willa Obenchain for the food and bowed his head to thank the Almighty. When he raised it again, she was across the cabin, rummaging through her basket. He realized the cakes and parched corn were meant solely for him. Had she eaten before he woke?

He broke one of the cakes and, behind her back, tossed half of it to Cap. The collie gulped it down and stared at him, hopeful. Neil took a bite and closed his eyes, washed in comfort by its simple warmth and taste.

Across the cabin, Willa stood and faced him. "I am thinking of the horse. I did not know to look for it. Perhaps it did not stray far. There could be signs to follow." She took up the musket, slung a powder horn and shot bag over her shoulder, and was making for the cabin door before she finished speaking.

Neil choked down his mouthful. "You're going now? Back to where ye found me?"

She set her lips in resolve. "The longer the horse strays, the less chance I will have to track it."

"You can do that?"

Her level stare was answer enough. "I will be back by nightfall."

She opened the cabin door. Cap bounded up and rushed out past her. She started to call the collie back, then looked at Neil, who shrugged. "He'll be after his own supper."

She went out, shutting the door behind her.

"Aye, then." He let out his breath, chafing at his infirmities and at finding himself dependent on a stranger's mercy—again. He was torn between the hope that she might find his horse, and chagrin that after everything else she'd done, she felt compelled to go back and look for it.

For himself, he wanted a look at what lay beyond the cabin door. Perhaps it would tell him something about this woman who'd found him in her path, and where that path had led her. But he decided a rest wouldn't come amiss. Besides, he already had a fair notion of what he'd find. Wherever she'd come from, wherever she'd brought him to, Willa Obenchain, daughter of Dieter, was alone.

FOUR

B ehind the cabin near the woods' edge stood a privy, ventilated as a corn crib and listing slightly to port, yet Neil MacGregor stepped from the structure with a prayer of thanksgiving on his lips. Thanking the Almighty for a privy, and the strength to reach it, doubtless was a prayer uncommon to men his age, but he'd learned to count his blessings where he found them. They seemed thin on the ground just now.

The previous evening, while Willa Obenchain was out tracking his horse, he'd climbed a ladder propped to one side of the hearth and peered into a loft recess. Empty, like the room behind the central hearth. Opening a door at the side of the cabin, he'd found himself confronted by half a room open to the sky, containing a nanny goat, for which he'd obligingly gathered grass. He'd found a springhouse in the woods and filled his canteen and Willa's kettle. He was back at the makeshift goat pen, holding the gourd cup for the animal to drink from, when he'd felt the sensation of being watched.

Not a shadow moved out of place when he looked around, yet the feeling drove him back inside the cabin. Eventually, exhausted from the slight exertion, he'd slept, never hearing Willa's return or her rising that morning. That she'd done both was evident. Another cornmeal cake waited on the hearth for his breakfast.

He was embarrassed to have slept so long, but he was over the headache. Not even a twinge lingered at the back of his skull when he'd ventured out to the privy.

The sun, just topping the trees, gilded the line of low ridges to the north of the clearing. Birds were busy in the brush, twittering and rustling. The air was chill, but with a softened edge that spoke of green things awakening. He was still in his shirtsleeves—his only surviving shirt, creased and grubby after his misadventure.

He'd surmised by the absence of saddlebags that Willa's search had proved fruitless. Or nearly so. Beside his meager breakfast, he'd found his three-cornered hat of black felt and his tin cup, along with an item that hadn't been among his belongings. A book—or what had been a book. With its cover and pages pasted into a solid mass, by excessive water damage he guessed, its identity was as much a mystery as its origins. Though had the book been new with the smell of printer's ink ripe on its pages, its identity would still have eluded him.

Neil raised a hand to the scar on his brow. Blinding headaches weren't the only brain-scrambling affliction the events attending that particular wound had left him to suffer. He closed his eyes briefly, refusing the self-pity that sought to fill him at the reminder that the written word was barred to him. He had learned to manage. Harder to shake was this new blow—the loss of his horse and supplies, and the crushing weight of the choice now facing him. Not really a choice, just a matter of when he'd bring himself to admit the inevitable. He'd learned to function with a damaged brain, but what was he meant to accomplish without the tools of his trade? Paint with a twig and his own life's blood?

If there be any virtue, and if there be any praise, think on these things.

Neil took a deep breath, reminding himself to count the blessings and leave off the questioning. The Almighty hadn't forsaken him. His fall into the laurels, his horse going astray—those events hadn't gone unnoticed. Indeed, they'd been allowed to happen.

So, then. He was thankful for the kindness of strangers…and their rickety privies.

Visible from the present privy, the twin ruts of a track led off through a scrim of leafing trees to the west. The track passed through a swath of cleared ground before disappearing into deep woods. Leading, he presumed, to the settlement called Shiloh.

Was that where Willa Obenchain had gone? And Cap with her? He hadn't seen his dog since yesterday either.

"Turncoat," he muttered, but with amusement rather than annoyance. No surprise if the collie had latched onto the woman as the more engaging prospect at present.

Or had it been the other way around?

For the first time, it occurred to him to wonder if *she* had taken his horse, and now his dog, and gone off and left him here. He supposed he would suspect it, if it weren't for the fact that her belongings, such as they were, were still in the cabin. Including the goat. Still, he realized he had no real reason to trust her…save what his gut—or mayhap his spirit—was telling him. That she did not mean him ill.

He rubbed his bristled jaw, wishing for a shave. No chance of it, not with his razor bouncing about the wilderness in the saddlebag of a riderless horse. Resigning himself to being temporarily bearded, he started for the cabin.

The crack and crash of a large body moving through the nearby brush brought him up short.

Deer? But the tumult was loud even for a deer. Did moose range that far south? He'd yet to see *Alces americanus,* save in the pages of other naturalists' work.

His breath quickened as, nearer the cabin, a screen of witch-hobble set to thrashing. The foliage parted. Through it stumbled not moose or deer or ungulate of any sort, but a woman. And not Willa. This woman was shorter and better fed—though she appeared to be of an age with his enigmatic hostess. Freeing herself from the brush, she shook out her petticoats, tucked up a stray blond curl and straightened her cap, then sprinted to the porch, hidden from his view from behind the cabin.

He heard her calling, "Is it you? Are you here? Willa!"

Neil rounded the cabin's porch as the woman stepped outside again. She halted at the sight of him, wide eyed and pink cheeked.

"You aren't Willa," she said with disappointment so acute Neil laughed.

"Sorry, no. But I expect she's about the place."

"Is she?" The woman took a step toward him. Her eyes were a light, clear blue, fixed on him in hope. "Willa Obenchain? It's just we thought... It was understood she... But who are *you*?"

"Anni?"

Neither of them had noticed Willa's approach. She stood at the head of the track, gripping a long-handled spade, musket slung at her back.

"It can't be," the blond woman whispered. Despite the professed disbelief, she leaped from the porch and crossed the cabin yard to halt before Willa, who topped her by neck and head. "Let me see your eyes."

She cupped one of Willa's sharp-boned cheeks and turned her face to the morning sun, then with a glad cry threw her arms around Willa's long waist. "I barely recognize the rest of you, but I'd know those eyes anywhere!"

If she'd been the taller of the two instead of the stouter, Neil was certain the woman would have hoisted Willa off her feet and spun her around.

Over her shoulder, Willa was smiling. Not at him, Neil knew, but the effect was the same. In the dimness of the cabin, he had thought her striking, if a bit intimidating. Now, with her stern features softened by joy, she radiated a beauty that stole his breath.

"Anni," she said through that dazzling smile, "my heart is glad to see you, but you are breaking my ribs."

"Oh!" The woman released Willa, her face going pink. "Don't know my own strength, Charles says. But, you! Who'd have thought you'd shoot up like a cornstalk? Makes me feel positively *dumpy*. But never mind... I didn't know what to make of it when Francis showed up at our cabin this morning saying he'd seen you here—always lurking, our Francis—but he said nothing about..."

She turned abruptly, as if recalling Neil. "Willa, is this Scotsman with the bonny blue eyes your husband?"

Willa's radiance dimmed, taking the softness with it. "I have no husband. He... I..."

Neil took the matter in hand, coming forward to bow awkwardly with his pinioned arm. "Neil MacGregor, ma'am. I took a fall yesterday morn, and my horse, giving me up for dead, absconded with nigh all my earthly goods. Miss Obenchain brought me along here with her, like the stray that I am. Me and..." But the other member of his expedition had yet to reappear.

Willa pointed toward the ridgeline. "Chasing breakfast. Squirrel, I think."

"Ach, well. And you, ma'am?" Neil inquired of the blond woman. "A friend of Miss Obenchain's, are ye?"

"I am," the woman said, and dropped into a curtsy. "Anni—Annaliese Waring Keppler."

"Keppler?" Willa echoed.

Anni's smile brightened. "You remember Charles. His father ran the mill—Charles has it now. He asked the Colonel for my hand six years ago, and now we've Samuel and Samantha. Twins—heaven help me."

A shadow passed across Willa's eyes, though her mouth pulled into another smile. "I am happy for you, Anni." She raised a hand to brush back the hair escaped from her braid.

Her palm was blistered raw.

"What've you been about, Willa?" Neil reached for her hand.

She raised the spade as if to ward him off. "I found this—near the upper field. I am using it to break ground for planting."

It was a wide blade, solid and sharp. No cast-off tool left to rust. "You found it there? Abandoned? By whom, I wonder?"

"I do not know."

"I might." Anni Keppler had an unguarded face—soft and round cheeked. Now her expression shifted from wry amusement to discomfort. "And, Willa, I hate to have to say this so soon, but someone has to give you fair warning."

Bewilderment stared from Willa's eyes. "Warning?"

It was then Neil caught a drumming sound, faint in the distance, and glanced toward the track. It sounded like a horse's hooves, but he saw nothing.

"We never supposed you would come back," Anni was saying, distracting him from the noise. "Not that I'm not over the moon that you have...but after all these years, and since your parents—"

"Where are my parents, Anni?" Willa broke in. "Where is Oma?"

Anni's expression twisted with sympathy and deepening unease. "I'm sorry, Willa. Your parents were suspected Tories—Loyalists to the British. Richard was certain of it before the end, and you know he—"

The approach of hoofbeats, unmistakable now, silenced Anni.

At last Neil glimpsed a horse through the trees bordering the yard. A large bay, raw boned and white blazed, brought its rider into view, a man in a good blue coat, wide shouldered and very tall in the saddle. His clothing and bearing were that of a gentleman, but he was hatless. Fair hair unbound on his shoulders lent him a disconcertingly wild appearance. His face bore a coarser echo of Anni Keppler's features, only there was no softness there.

The man pulled the bay up short in front of them, yanking it in a series of tight turns, making it snort and prance. Ignoring Neil and Anni, the man's pale eyes blazed at Willa Obenchain, whose face drained of color as she mouthed a name. *Richard.*

Anni stepped between them, reaching for the horse's bridle. The man shifted his searing gaze to her. "I caught Francis skulking in the woods west of town. He left the twins on their own."

Anni held her ground. "Who minds them now?"

"Goodenough came into town with me. I sent her to mind them. As you ought to have done."

"And Francis?"

"Locked in the smokehouse with the rest of the game."

Anni grimaced. "Richard, Francis isn't an *animal*."

"Wasted fretting, Anni. He'll get himself loose within the hour and will be haring off to the hills. But I didn't come to talk of our brother." His gaze snapped back to Willa. "It's her?"

"She can speak, Richard. And can't you see her eyes?"

From atop the tall bay, the man's gaze raked Willa from beaded moccasins to braided hair. "So. What name did they give you?"

Neil comprehended neither the question nor the resentment behind it.

Anni apparently grasped both. "Richard—Alan—Waring! There's a time and a place." She started to move protectively toward Willa, who warded her off with a look.

Standing straight and unshrinking under Richard Waring's glare, Willa spoke a word in a language Neil didn't know, though the sound of it struck a chord of familiarity.

It struck more than that in Anni's brother. Loathing rippled over his face. "Burning Sky?"

The skin across Willa's cheekbones tightened until the bones stood stark beneath. "You speak *Kanien'keha*?"

"More than I ever wanted to." Waring swung from the saddle with smooth, athletic grace—an impressive feat, given he had to be a full four inches over six feet, and thickly muscled with it. "What was the name of the buck they mated you with?"

The blood left Neil's face in a rush of visceral outrage, followed swiftly by comprehension. How ridiculously slow he'd been to grasp the truth when he'd been staring it eye to eye since yesterday—the carrying basket, the clothing, even the faint accent with which she spoke, an accent he'd last heard moments before the scar on his forehead was put there.

Willa Obenchain had been an Indian captive.

He knew of the practice, of course, how the tribes took captives to replace those lost through battle or disease, but he'd thought Willa just another refugee, dressed more rustic than most, returning to her frontier home like so many others from some place of shelter back east. But those few women he'd seen on the roads had come with wagons, stock, goods, and families. Not alone.

Willa had lifted her chin, unflinching before Anni's brother. "What need have you to know his name?"

Neil saw the twitch of Waring's big hand, the threat of violence in his eyes. With no conscious memory of moving, he found himself beside Willa, startled despite the tense situation that she stood nearly equal to his own six foot height.

Waring didn't so much as blink to acknowledge him, but the violence Neil had glimpsed in his eyes receded, replaced by anger, and pain. "What need? I meant you to be *my* wife, not despoiled by some red savage."

"You may have meant her to be your wife," Neil said. "But she isna now, and ye willna offer her further insult while I'm here to prevent it."

Waring flicked him a glance, taking in his splinted arm. "What have you to do with her—or need I ask?"

"If that's your manner of inquiring, I'm Neil MacGregor, member of the American Philosophical Society, associate of"—his thoughts raced, coming up with the most notable of his society acquaintances—"Dr. Benjamin Franklin, commissioned to compile a field guide of the flora north of the Mohawk River. Insult *me* all ye like, Mr. Waring, but I canna stand by while ye cast aspersions against Miss Obenchain, who's been naught to me but kindness itself."

Waring smiled at him, a full smile with an unexpected charm. "Can you not?" he inquired mildly, before he rammed his fist into Neil's gut. "Then by all means—sit."

It doubled Neil like a hammer blow, driving out his breath. He dropped to his knees, pain spiking up his injured arm as instinctively he tried to catch himself. A gray curtain dropped around him. At its margin was movement. Moccasins took a stride forward, stopping in a spurt of dust beside large boots.

Willa's voice sliced through the curtain like a blade. "This man has taken shelter under my roof. You will not touch him again."

Silence stretched while Neil fought for breath and the blood rushed loud in his ears. At last a deeper reply came, laden with disgust. "Not today."

The boots stepped away. Saddle leather creaked. Neil's lungs remembered how to work. He pulled in a desperate breath as Waring's parting shot issued from on high, aimed not at him, but Willa.

"You've no place here, Burning Sky. Go back where you came from, or *burning* is what you'll bring down on yourself if you stay."

FIVE

She could not stop shaking. Not after Anni led her to the cabin porch, or pried her fingers from the spade's handle to lean it against a post. Neil MacGregor came up to the cabin and lowered himself gingerly to sit beside her.

Anni stood with tears on her cheeks. "I wish you'd brained Richard over the head with that spade, Willa. It might've knocked some sense into him."

The image of Richard Waring's face, aged and hardened, hung before Willa's eyes. She was as rattled by it as if another soul had stolen the face she remembered, a malevolent soul that had distorted its shape with its darkness and wore it now like a mask. She had not recognized the person staring out of Richard's eyes. She had seen a Long Knife soldier. An enemy.

"Mr. MacGregor, are you all right? I'm so sorry for what my brother did to you."

Anni's words jarred Willa from her thoughts in time to see Neil Mac-Gregor shift on the porch, and wince. The man was clearly in pain, but if he regretted coming to her defense, he did not show it.

"Aye, Mrs. Keppler. It wasna your fault. But what he said there at the last—what did he mean by it? Why should he threaten Miss Obenchain?"

Anni wiped her cheeks. "It's the land—your father's land, Willa. I started to tell you he was suspected of being a Loyalist. This farm was confiscated as Tory property, years ago. Lots of farms were, and now they're being sold off to the highest bidder. Richard has had his eye on this one since the war's ending. He means to bid on it whenever the auction is held."

A coldness formed in the pit of Willa's stomach, as the news both chilled and confused her. Anni's words swirled through her mind. Tory property. Confiscated. Sold off. But all she could force past her lips was, "My parents were not Tories."

Even as she spoke, a niggle of doubt wormed through her thoughts. The Kanien'kehá:ka had taken her in the autumn of 1772, nearly twelve years ago, long before the outbreak of war. But even then there had been talk of its brewing, on that very cabin porch. She remembered Papa reading aloud letters exchanged with some relation back east. In Albany, she thought. Taxes, government, the English King George...those had been the subjects of those letters. Had Dieter Obenchain been a king's man? She could not remember. She'd been barely fourteen years old, with her nose buried in romantic novels, not letters about politics.

"'Tis a thing happening all over," Neil said, nodding as though the situation was beginning to come clear to him. "The war was a staggering drain on the states, not just New York. Debts are owing. Selling off Tory land is a means of paying down those debts."

"Now that there's no fighting," Anni said, "all Richard talks about are the committees of confiscation and which farms along Black Kettle Creek will be up for auction soon. I don't know how soon, Willa, but there's a man coming to assess the properties north of German Flats. Richard has made it no secret he expects to own this tract."

Willa clenched the porch's edge—planks Papa had hewn and set in place, planks her feet had helped to smooth. Her parents were gone. She wanted desperately to ask when, how, but could not in the face of this new shock find the words.

Neil MacGregor found them for her. "You were fixing to tell us what happened to Willa's parents?"

Anni shook her head and looked with sympathy at Willa. "They disappeared six years ago. Your grandmother with them, we think."

Six years. The coldness in Willa's belly spread, encompassing her heart. "Killed?"

"Maybe not. Their—forgive me—their bodies were never found."

"I do not understand, Anni. If the British or Long Knives did not kill them, where are they?"

"Long Knives? Is that what you—" Anni did not finish the question. But her voice hardened a tiny measure as she said, "Let me try to explain, Willa. There were so many raids during those years—a homestead burned by one side, then weeks later another by way of reprisal, sometimes many at once—but after such raids, the families who sympathized with the Tories, the ones that got spared, would pack up and flee, follow the raiders back to the British in Canada."

Neil frowned, glancing between them. "You're saying that's what Willa's parents did? They fled to Canada?"

Anni raised helpless hands. "They didn't come to Fort Dayton, or Herkimer, with the rest of us. Some would say that's proof enough where their loyalty lay."

"But our barn... It is nothing but ashes." Willa dragged the words past an aching throat. "If my parents fled during a British raid—fled with the redcoats to Canada—then why was our barn burned?"

There were no answers here, only endless questions. And now, Richard's threat. And behind him, this threat of confiscation.

The shaking had stopped. Willa took up the spade and stood, planting its handle firm on the ground when she swayed. There was little cornmeal left. She'd made a cake for Neil in the dark while he slept but had not broken her own fast.

There were green things growing now. Fiddleheads, wild lettuce, milkweed, dock. She would gather them...soon.

The sense of too little time pressed hard on her. There would be an auction, Anni said. An assessor was coming. Well, let him come. He would find her hard at work. On *her* land.

"I cannot listen anymore. There is too much to do." A distant barking drew her gaze to the hills. "There, your dog at least is come back," Willa said to Neil, and set out for the field, armed with spade and musket.

The soil of the upper field, nearest the cabin, was hard and weed choked. She had not broken another square yard of it before Anni came marching out after her and stood in her path.

"Go ahead and dig, Willa, but whether you want to listen or not, I have more to say."

Willa moved around Anni's worn shoes. She stabbed the earth with the spade, while Anni's voice stabbed her heart.

"You are very changed, and I can only imagine you suffered your own hell. But that's exactly what the past years were for us here. Hell—or the nearest I ever expect to come to it. The British and that red fiend, Brant—"

Willa clenched her teeth at the name. Joseph Brant—Thayendanegea of the Mohawk, schooled by the Reverend Wheelock as a young man, a warrior who'd done his utmost to preserve the People's land and independence—a *fiend*? She supposed Anni would see him so…

"And the militia being called up," Anni was saying, a tremble in her voice. "The murders, massacres, loyalties questioned, families torn apart—"

"Like mine."

"Like everyone's." Tears glistened in Anni's eyes when Willa looked up, but there was a spark of something sharper too. "We lost Mama and Edward to raiding Indians, just before your parents disappeared. That very same spring—before everyone forted up. We'd lost Nicholas and Samuel at Oriskany the summer before. Richard and the Colonel never found their bodies—a blessing, maybe, considering what the Indians did to the fallen after that battle. But Mama was never right in her mind again after the news. And Francis… The day Mama and Edward were killed, Francis hid in the woods and saw them scalped in the dooryard."

Willa clenched the spade's smooth handle. "Anni," she said, but there were no words to touch such grief and horror. She knew there were no words.

Her mind latched onto the last member of the Waring clan Anni had mentioned, the youngest, who had hidden in the woods and survived. Francis Waring had been seven years old the last time Willa saw him, a child who spoke rarely, and then with a stutter that often rendered him unintelligible. A boy prone to wander, feral and unkempt, causing no end of worry. Other children had shunned him. He'd discomfited many an adult with his strange ways. Yet whenever she had visited the Warings' home and found Francis mewed indoors, he'd followed her with timid, curious eyes.

Willa thought of the kettle, the wood, the flowers. She touched the spade with the toe of her moccasin. "Was it Francis who left this spade?"

"I can't think who else it could have been. He comes here sometimes. It vexes Richard." Anni drew a breath and released it with a sigh. "I didn't mean what I said about braining Richard, for all he boils my blood. He's still my brother, and I love him, but…he isn't the boy you remember. All through the war he rode with the militia, as a scout for part of that time, and saw more death and butchery than anyone should in a dozen lifetimes, and maybe did too much of the same himself—I'll never ask. But all that violence—it shattered something in him."

A bruised reed, Willa thought. So Richard was one too. But the pity that should have followed the thought found no purchase in her heart. Fear choked it out.

"He's full of hate," Anni said, "but he's not past healing. I have to believe that." Her eyes begged for understanding.

Willa looked away. "Hate for my people."

"Indians, you mean?" Anni grasped her arm, forcing Willa to look at her. "How can you call them so? They took you from your people, your life. Of course Richard hates them. He's the one who…" Anni bit her lip, searching Willa's face.

Willa freed her arm. "The one who what?"

The indecision on Anni's face dissolved. "He mightn't want me telling you this, but you need to know. Richard tried to find you."

Shock skittered up Willa's spine. "Find me?"

"He set out after those savages who took you, found their trail and followed them over the mountains, all the way to Canada. He lost the trail, but still he spent months looking for you, offering to buy you back. No one would admit to knowing anything about you."

"They hide the ones they mean to keep." She knew she must sound indifferent to Anni. The truth was she was stunned. They *had* hidden her. She remembered the terror and confusion of those first weeks, how she'd been snatched from some task without warning or woken in the night—to be whisked away into the forest or downriver by canoe, before they settled her at last in a village near the Saint Lawrence River, where in time she accepted the life into which she'd been thrust. Became Burning Sky. All that time Richard had been trying to bring her home.

The Richard she remembered, not the man she'd met this day. That man had no intention of rescuing her, but of seeing her kicked aside like a stone in his path.

"It's true what he said," Anni went on. "He wanted to marry you. He was only waiting till you were both old enough. Did you know?"

Willa stared at the ridgeline to the north, trying in her mind to see Anni's brother as he had been at sixteen, already big and strapping, his handsome face quick to light with a smile. Even at fourteen, with her girl's body late to blossom, destined to grow much taller before it did, she had imagined herself as Wilhelmina Waring and more than once caught the same speculation in Richard's eyes.

"I knew," she said.

"Then do you understand, about Richard?" Anni's question held an edge so faint it might have gone unnoticed.

But Willa did notice.

What was there to understand? Many warriors of the Longhouse people—the Iroquois—and her own northern Mohawk people, their close kin, had suffered as much as Richard, had seen horrors and committed them, had returned from the long campaign with bodies and hearts scarred. Some never returned in their souls, but became like wounded animals, lashing out at those who tried to tend them. Many had found their solace, and their shame, in traders' rum.

"He is not the only one to have suffered."

Anni grasped Willa's hand. "I know that. Your parents—"

"Not only them."

"And you, of course. But Richard is a man. He cannot understand that sometimes a woman has to do…what she'd rather not do, to survive." Anni's gaze was pained. "They forced you to do it, to be with one of their men. It's something I tried not to think about, but of course I knew, if you'd survived…"

Willa pulled her hand from Anni's. "The clan mothers made the match. I agreed to be the wife of the man they chose for me."

"But you had to agree. Those women—they didn't give you a choice." When Willa did not reply, Anni stared in dawning comprehension, visibly appalled. "Willa…you didn't *want* him, did you?"

"I wanted our children." The ache, that deepest ache of all the many that never left Willa's chest, swelled up tight and full, choking her. Making her want to beat at it again.

Anni made an attempt to rally after this new shock. "Children? Are they here…or did you have to leave them?"

"I would never have left them. But where they and their father have gone, I cannot follow." Willa saw what was coming, the questions one would ask of any friend who admitted to the death of her entire family. She raised a hand to halt them. "That is all I have to say about them, Anni."

After a silence that stretched taut between them, Willa glanced at Anni's waistline and asked, "When is your new one to be born?"

She'd surprised Anni. "I didn't think it showed yet, me still plump as a hen from the twins. I'm nigh four months along, so…early September."

"I am glad for you."

Anni's eyes pooled, but she blinked back her tears. "What will you do, for now?"

Until your land is sold from under you, Willa finished silently.

"I will stay." Seeing doubt rise in Anni's face, Willa took up the spade again and set to work.

Anni stepped out of the way. "How will you live?"

"I can plant enough to feed myself. Maybe a little more." If there was time enough left to harvest it.

Anni bit back whatever she might have said to that and gazed toward the cabin. "Will he be staying? The Scotsman."

"I do not see why he would."

Especially after today.

"He mentioned Benjamin Franklin," Anni persisted, still staring through the line of leafing trees between the field and cabin yard. "Something about a philosophical society…and *flora,* wasn't it?"

Willa shrugged, not admitting to her curiosity about Neil MacGregor or the drawings in his satchel. He seemed a good man, though a different sort than any she had known. Which mattered not at all because she'd no means to feed him. Even if she had, it was unwise to let curiosity turn to liking. After his show of backbone on her behalf—despite its outcome—she was in danger of it.

She was not the only one intrigued. Anni asked, "What do you know of him?"

"Little beyond his name. I found him yesterday near the north boundary stone." With renewed vigor, Willa pushed the spade into the earth with the ball of her foot. "When he gets hungry, he will go."

Anni was quick to understand. "I'll talk to Charles and bring what supplies we can spare. Or I'll send Francis with them. He'd like that, I think. He really does seem drawn to this place."

They stared at each other across the hard, forsaken ground, still worlds apart, Willa at a loss to find a bridge. "My parents were not Tories."

"I want to believe that," Anni said, regret in her eyes. "But how can you prove it? And do you truly want to? I'm not saying I wouldn't want you to stay, or that Charles wouldn't, or even the Colonel. But Richard isn't the only one who'll see things as he does."

And by things, *she means me.* But Willa said nothing—what could she say? A woman did not return from nearly twelve years with "the savages" and expect to be seen by most whites as anything but tainted, ruined. What was the word Richard had used? *Despoiled.*

"Not that Richard mightn't change," Anni added quickly. "Give him time to accustom himself to your being here. I'll talk to him and maybe…" She faltered, as if sensing the precarious ground beneath her words. She found her footing again, squarely in the practical. "I'll find you a proper gown. Then you can come into Shiloh and we'll see how things stand. I know the Colonel will want to see you."

Six

C ap bounded onto the porch and lay down panting, spent from roaming and studded with cockleburs. Neil leaned forward and bowed his head into his hand.

After Willa had stalked off to the field, he'd asked Anni only one question. "How long has she been gone?"

"Twelve years, nearly," she'd said before following her childhood friend, distress on her open countenance.

"Gracious Father," he said now. "A captive of the Mohawk, for what… half her life?"

'Twas no news to the Almighty, of course, but Neil couldn't push beyond the notion, with all its unspeakable horrors. Had she escaped after all this time, or been permitted to leave? Would they come looking to take her back?

Concern for Willa Obenchain was taking root in him. Surely whatever hopes she'd had for this homecoming had been dashed, however well she concealed the fact. Who wouldn't be sent reeling? Having returned from captivity to be greeted by an empty cabin, parents vanished and branded traitors, and a hulking frontiersman bent on evicting her from her refuge—by force if necessary, if the man's conduct this morning was any indication of his scope.

Blood mounted in Neil's face at the thought of his pitiful attempt to defend Willa. Thus far it was she who'd done the defending, offering him shelter, care, and sustenance, warding off Waring by force of indignation alone. *"You will not touch him again."*

A cold nose nudged his hand. He passed it over the dog's head, then glanced down at the animal. Drying blood specked the white fur around Cap's lips.

Chasing squirrels. Hadn't he better chase up something to feed the rest of them? His bruised wame gave a growl, having made short work of the cornmeal cake left for his breakfast. At least he'd kept it down after that blow and hadn't added *that* humiliation to the rest.

Movement in the distance distracted him. Through the trees he glimpsed Anni Keppler striding away down the track, presumably to collect her offspring from someone with the unlikely name of Goodenough. He watched Willa toiling determinately in the field, ignoring her departing friend, musket slung at her back, and decided questions about her recent history could wait.

He stood, tensing at the ache in his belly, wincing at the sharper pain in his wrist. He did need shelter, for a little while at least. But the last thing Willa needed was another burden to bear.

He wouldn't be one. Not even for a day. Or no more than he could help.

Using a stick in lieu of a pothook, Neil lifted the kettle from the crane and set it on the stones. Willa leaned in to peer at its steaming contents. "Rabbit stew?"

She hadn't quite hidden her startled pleasure. Neil bit down on a grin. "'Twas Cap caught the wee bautie. I contributed the green bits." He'd been foraging along the runnel from the springhouse when Cap started the rabbit in the ferns. Replete with squirrel, the dog hadn't minded his appropriating the kill.

"What green bits?" Willa asked warily. "Not all plants are safe for eating."

"I ken that well enough. 'Tis fiddleheads, in the main. I found a patch of *asclepias syriaca* as well, along that creek the spring empties into." At her puzzled stare, he amended, "Milkweed. The shoots are tender, early in the season."

"I know that well enough," she said with a lifted brow. "What other name did you call it?"

"Oh, aye. *Asclepias syriaca* is the Latin for it, by Linnaeus's system." He caught her sidelong glance at his satchel where his sketchbook resided. Had she gone looking while he slept?

"The creek the spring runs into is called Black Kettle." She took up the horn spoon he'd found among her belongings to taste the stew. Her face softened in reluctant approval. "You did not mention the wild onion."

Having but the one gourd bowl and spoon between them, they ate by turns. Willa watched him finish his share. "I ought to have set snares for rabbits. I will do so tomorrow."

"Would you instruct me in their setting? I canna help ye overmuch in the fields yet, but I'd like to make myself useful." His question drew a frown from her, and he realized the presumption his words had implied. "If you dinna mind my staying on, that is—just till I've the use of my hand again."

She regarded him in silence. He was learning it wasn't her way to speak without thought, but her inscrutable stare and those mismated eyes left him disconcerted.

"You made a brush pen for the goat."

"I did." He couldn't tell if she approved. "Easier to move the goat to fresh grazing than to bring the grazing to the goat, aye?" It was the only thing he'd accomplished besides the stew. "Did you bring it with ye, the goat?"

"Your dog has a knack for finding strays, as well as food. But this"— she gestured toward the kettle and their empty bowl—"making of food is for a woman to do."

"And field work isna a man's work?"

"It is not."

Her answer was prompt and decisive. His response was more hesitant. "So...'tis like that among the Mohawks?"

"It is different, yes. It is women who tend the crops," she explained. "And the cook fire. But these things are hers to tend—fields, children, and lodge—because they belong to her, not to her husband." She held his gaze, adding, "She allows him to live in her lodge with her, but the lodge is hers."

He took her meaning well enough. She was telling him this cabin was hers; that no man—least of all him—had any right to it save what she gave. "But you've none by to help ye here, Willa. Leaving aside yon Waring and his threats, d'ye truly think you can work this land, a woman alone, and survive?"

"I am as strong as a man, and many men come alone to the frontier. You came alone."

And look how that's gone awry, he thought, and wondered suddenly if his bid for time to stay beneath her roof was less about healing and more about putting off acknowledging defeat.

She wasn't taking favorably to the notion of extending his welcome in either case. He could see her drawing into herself, retreating. Not out of timidity he was sure. He doubted she possessed a timid fiber in her being. But there was something she didn't wish him to see, some reason she found thought of his continued presence there troubling. What it was he couldn't tell. She'd curled herself around it like a creature protecting its vulnerable parts. A porcupine, maybe, with all its quills a'bristle.

Deciding to let the subject rest, he indicated the ruined book still lying near the hearth. "Did ye find that with my hat and cup? It isna mine."

"It is my book. Or it was."

"Yours? Can ye read, then?"

She frowned at his surprise. "I have not had the chance for many years, but yes. I read."

"Aye, well. I expect there were no books among the Mohawks."

"You are wrong," she countered. "There were some. But none in English, or in German, which I can also read. I had a…friend. He had a Bible written in Kanien'keha."

"Someone translated the Scriptures into their tongue?"

Her glance strayed to his brow, where the hair curled over his scar. "That surprises you?"

He steered the subject back to safer waters. "So where did ye find your wee book?"

"Where I left it. Upstream along Black Kettle Creek there is a lake, with a little islet. That was my place for hiding books."

He'd seen the lake of which she spoke, he realized, early on the day he took his fall, having paused there to sketch a pair of nesting loons, before journeying north. "Why did you need to hide them? Did your parents disapprove of your reading?"

"Oma did not like it. My grandmother," she explained, when he questioned her with a look. "Dagna Mehler. She would hide my books if she found them lying about, so I hid them from her. Oma thought *reading* another word for *idleness*. I was going to the lake to read when the warriors found me." She glanced at the book with a fleeting sadness. "I never got to finish this one."

Before he could say a word to prevent her, Willa took up the ruined book and thrust it into the hearth. With the stick he'd used to lift the kettle, she pushed it into the fire's center. It had been beyond salvaging, but still he felt a catch of regret in his chest at the cremation.

The smell in the cabin sharpened with its burning.

"What book was it?"

Willa watched it taking flame. "I am trying to remember the author's name. Richardson, I think."

"Samuel Richardson," he said, faintly amused by her tastes. "*Clarissa* or *Pamela*?"

"*Pamela*. You have read it?" She looked at him expectantly, her face transformed, open, younger seeming. "Do you know what happened after Pamela's friend, that man, Mr. Williams, was attacked and arrested? That is the last of the story I remember."

"If I did," he said with a corner of his mouth lifted, "you wouldna appreciate my spoiling the story."

The book was a blackened lump on the embers now.

"I am not likely to see another copy," she said, "but would like to know how the story ends. I thought of it often."

Neil tried to imagine her in years past, far away among the Mohawks, perhaps stitching beads onto a pair of moccasins like the ones she wore, pausing in her labors to stare into the fire and think about Richardson's titular servant maid kept prisoner at an English estate.

"Dinna be so sure of never seeing another copy," he said. If nothing else he'd find one in Philadelphia and post it to her. Small repayment for her kindness. He looked up from the dying flames at the faint squeak of the hearth crane. Willa had taken the empty kettle and put the bowl and spoon into it. She'd be headed for the spring next. "You've worked the day long, Willa. Let me see to that."

"As have you," she replied, and went out of the cabin with the kettle.

Neil followed. The sun was setting, its mellow rays striking sparks in Willa's braid as she crossed the yard and passed through the fringe of shadowed trees to the spring. While she knelt to scrub the kettle with pebbles from the runnel's bed, he stood by, wishing she'd allow him the task, awkward as it might prove one-handed.

"If you dinna mind my asking, how old were ye when the Mohawk took ye away?"

She didn't look up as she rinsed the kettle. "Fourteen."

Which made her now...six and twenty, most like. "Could you write as well as read?"

She scooped another handful of pebbles to scrub the bowl. "Papa taught me to do both."

Neil sank his teeth into his bottom lip, thoughts hovering on the edge of a possibility. If she hadn't lost the skill, might she consider helping him write a letter...once he acquired ink and quill and explained why he should need such help? Anni Keppler's husband was a miller; perhaps there was a trade store in Shiloh as well...

He followed Willa back to the cabin, feeling like a trailing pup. "You didna answer my question before," he said as she hung the kettle, filled now with water, over the fire. "I find myself in need of shelter and would stay here with ye, if that's agreeable. Till my arm is healed. Under different circumstances I'd never suggest it, and if you're concerned about your reputation, I could apply to Anni Keppler and her husband."

Willa turned to look at him, faint amusement in her mismatched eyes. "I have no reputation to protect."

"'Tis more than that needs protecting, I'm thinking."

The flash of amusement in her eyes was more than faint now, and mildly insulting. Reining in a twist of a smile, she nodded her chin toward Cap. "I do not need protecting, but if that dog can go on filling my kettle as he did today, you may stay as well."

She didn't need to add "for now" for him to hear it.

A worn quilt was folded around a slender kitchen knife and a long-handled spoon. Beside it lay a felling ax, a hefty sack of beans and another of corn-meal, and a pouch containing precious salt. The items were arranged with precision, with barely a wrinkle in quilt or sacking. It was the third such offering to appear on the cabin porch since Anni's visit. Evidencing no surprise at the first—a skillet, a bushel of potatoes, a serviceable shift, stays, and gown wrapped in a linen sheet—Willa had explained Anni's promise to share what provisions could be spared.

She'd studied the goods while the collie sniffed them with interest, and a faint smile touched her lips. It had seemed strange to Neil that Anni had come and gone without even Cap noticing. Quiet did not seem to be Anni Keppler's way. He'd said as much.

"It will have been Francis."

"The one they lock in the smokehouse?" He'd wished he held his tongue when Willa's face darkened. Though there'd been no further sign of Richard Waring in the two days since their meeting, the specter of the man lingered like a bitter taste on the tongue. Or the sense of watching eyes.

Willa took her spade and musket to the field, leaving Neil to store the newest provisions, curious about this youngest Waring as he dragged in the beans and cornmeal to the corner of the front room he'd designated as their pantry. The quilt he put in the loft where Willa slept. He left the ax on the porch.

Around midmorning, with the breakfast cleared, the goat put to graze in its brush pen, and Cap off roaming, Neil took his sketchbook to the edge of the woods, to the ax-marked stump of an immense hickory likely felled when the yard was first cleared. He sat with his back to the cabin, conscious once again of being watched. The sensation unnerved him, but he had himself a theory about it and meant to put it to the test.

Balancing the sketchbook on his knee, he turned to a fresh page, fixed the lead stick between thumb and forefinger of his splinted hand, and made a cursory doodle on the paper's margin. It hurt. A lot. But not quite enough to thwart him.

He sketched a trillium, bright against the dark forest soil, then a caterpillar inching up a beech sapling. Between sketches he rested his throbbing wrist till the pain eased off, taking the time to perform his daily exercise of rehearsing the lengthy field notes that went with the drawings in his satchel, the ones that bore no description as yet.

His patience—and endurance—paid off twofold. First was a fox that stepped through the leafing grapevine draping a stand of maples. It paused in a band of sunlight, its pelt a flash of brazen fire. Moving naught but hand and eye, he began a likeness of the creature, which sat on its haunches a biscuit's toss away and nonchalantly eyed him back. It was a clumsy effort, compared to what he was capable of days ago, but leastwise it resembled a fox.

His second audience, every bit as stealthy, drew quite near before the fox alerted him with a flick of black-tipped ears. Neil finished the sketch seconds before *Vulpes vulpes* melded back into the grapevine shadows. Then Neil turned his head.

The lad stood a few paces away, watching him.

Neil's first surprise was how unlike his brother he was in stature—middling tall, whip thin, shirt and breeches slack on his undernourished frame. He went shoeless, and the mop of pale hair brushing his shoulders sported bits of leaf. His age was hard to fix, though the bony hands that clutched an empty sack between them were a man's.

"You were canny," Neil said. "And verra quiet. I appreciate that."

The eyes in the thin face were the pale blue of his siblings' but flinchingly shy, where his sister's had been amiable and unreserved, his brother's cold, aggressive. Inquisitive, too, but in the way of the fox—as a creature apart, having its own realm of preoccupations, which Neil could never fully comprehend.

"You'll be Francis, then?"

The blue eyes flicked to Neil's arm, nestled in its sling, then to the sketchbook on his knee.

Neil shifted the drawing so the lad could better see. The scrawny neck craned, but the long bare feet came no closer. It was like coaxing a bird to the hand, a thing Neil had done time enough to recognize the blade-thin balance between fear and curiosity. He took a small penknife from his coat and carefully trimmed the page from the book. When he rose, the boy stepped back.

"'Tis yours, if ye like." Leaving the drawing on the stump, he strode back to the cabin, pausing at the porch to inspect the items the lad had brought this time. Once again, each was aligned with the porch edge, even with the seams between the floor planks. Had he a means of measuring, Neil was certain he'd find the space between them exact to a hair.

"I am F-Francis. You're Willa's f-friend."

He hadn't heard a grass blade rustle beneath those dirty feet. He turned. Anni's brother had tucked the sack into his waistband and now held Neil's drawing between his hands.

"Aye, for my part, I am. She's shown me great kindness. As have ye, bringing us these things."

Francis Waring broke into a smile of the same startling charm as his brother's, with one difference—it was also blindingly sincere. Neil caught his breath but wasn't quick enough to speak before the lad was making for the woods, the drawing of the fox clutched like a prize.

He told Willa about his encounter with Francis while they sat on the floor and ate boiled potatoes salted to perfection, no longer needing to eat by turns, thanks to Anni's generosity.

Willa gazed through the open door to the yard and the falling dusk, hair still damp from her wash at the spring. "I never knew Francis to take to a stranger so easily." Across the bench that served as a table, Roman style, her glance was almost shy. "He showed me your likeness of the fox. It was…"

He leaned forward, anticipating her opinion, though he kent the effort undeserving of favor, but drew back as if from a slap. Half her face had abruptly disappeared behind a bank of flashing lights and shadows. It struck with no more warning, as the black spells always did.

Willa exclaimed when he lurched to his feet, toppling the bench between them and sending their plates to the floor. He barely made it to the porch before the pain burst through his skull, and the vomiting began.

"Sorry," he gasped between violent bouts as his belly emptied onto the trodden yard. "It will pass…"

When the retching stopped, leaving him spent and humiliated, he felt cool hands on his brow. She urged him to his feet and led him, half-blinded by the flickering occlusions in his vision and the pain building to a scream behind his eyes, back into the cabin. Firelight stabbed his brain like spear points. Then he stumbled into darkness, felt the scratch of wool against his cheek, kent he was in the back room Willa had permitted him to use.

A spoon touched his mouth. The taste and smell of laudanum made his lip curl, but he swallowed. She'd found the powder among his things, and the small flask of sherry he kept for its mixing. A cup rim pressed against his teeth. Water slipped cool down his throat, washing back bitterness.

He choked, coughed, tried to sit up. "The supper... I made a mess."

"Do not think of it."

She pushed him back, and he went down like a fevered child, lost to half-waking dreams of being hunted through fire and smoke and misted woods, a path through a chaos of screaming. He began to think he might make it through without being seen or scalped or murdered, when an Indian stepped across his path, painted and pierced, tomahawk raised. Musket fire cracked...near, distant, near again. Lead balls thwacked the trees, spitting bark and leaves. The Indian fell. So did he.

He woke, flailing, banged his injured arm, then froze in a clench of agony till the tide of pain receded. A cloth, damp with water from the spring, had slipped from over his eyes. Somewhere, Cap was barking, the noise stabbing his skull.

Was it an attack? Or did he yet dream?

Willa's voice rose, hushing the dog. He pushed to his knees, still uncertain whether he dreamed, and crawled toward the front room. His head throbbed. His eyes throbbed. His wrist, raised like a wounded dog's, throbbed. He reached the opening between the rooms and poked his head around the doorway.

Cap had fallen to growling, nose pointed at the cabin door. Willa held her musket pointed in the same direction, at a man who filled the night-black opening. A big man. Waring?

No. The face was wrong. Brown, not white. Framed in black hair, not yellow. An Indian, one as tall as Waring. Biggest Indian he'd ever seen.

Then he understood. They'd found her, the Mohawks.

Willa lowered the musket, said a word he didn't understand, her voice low with shock. He watched her set the weapon aside. She was moving toward the big Indian, surrendering without a fight.

He pulled himself upright against the door frame. Willa heard his scrabbling and turned, face drawn with surprise. The Indian looked startled, too, as Neil staggered from the dark—startled but immovable, planted in the doorway like a great oak tree.

He would fell him, then. Crash him over. Topple him out of the cabin.

He lunged, but before he could make contact, the Indian tree uprooted itself, stepped nimbly aside, and Neil went through the door instead. Darkness and the porch floor rushed to meet him.

SEVEN

C oncern for Neil MacGregor, fallen across the threshold of her cabin, urged her to move, but she could not move. She could not look away from the other man in her doorway.

"Tames-His-Horse," she said, as though speaking his name would render him more substantial than a tall, deep-chested ghost that might vanish with her next exhalation. She breathed, and still he stood there, rifle slung at his shoulder, solid and real as her beating heart. His face, bronzed in the cabin's firelight, was leaner than she remembered—a warrior's face, chiseled and stern.

"*Sekoh,* my sister," he said. "But in this place, better to call me Joseph."

His voice washed over her, deep like the beating of drums at the fire, summoning a thousand memories to make war in her heart. He'd taken the name of Joseph in the lands south and west of the Mohawk River, where he'd gone as a youth to acquaint himself with his father's people, the *Onyota'a:ka*—Oneida—only to return to his mother's Mohawk kin in Canada with the white man's writing words in his head and the Christian God's Son, Jesus, in his heart.

Words crowded now behind Willa's teeth, but they could not speak like this, with Neil MacGregor lying prostrate between them. She knelt to touch his face. He moaned but did not rouse. She raised her face to Joseph. "Will you help me? He is ill. We will have to carry him."

Joseph set down his rifle and squatted in the doorway, hair spilling shiny black over his shoulders. He was dressed much as she last saw him— many seasons ago, when he rode away to fight for the British in their war—in blue linen shirt and deerskin breechcloth, leggings tied with beaded cloth strips, tomahawk and knife thrust through a sash. The difference was his hair. Last time she saw him, it had been plucked into a warrior's scalp-lock, tied with hawk feathers. Now his hair fell long and full, though there were still feathers tied in back. She reached across Neil MacGregor and gently grasped a lock.

"This is good to see."

His face lifted. Firelight reflected off the jutting planes of his cheekbones and jaw. His eyes locked with hers. Though she knew it was to neither of their good, she could not help searching them for that secret fire he'd carried for her, despite its impossibility, despite her efforts to quench it, certain it must have turned to ash like the rest of her Mohawk past.

But no. There on the cabin porch, Joseph Tames-His-Horse opened his soul to her. He still burned.

She let go of his hair.

"It is two years since I left the warpath," he said.

What, she wanted to ask, had he done in that time? Where had he been doing it? Why had he not returned to their village?

She said none of these things as he pulled Neil MacGregor upright, got a shoulder into his chest and, hoisting him like a grain sack, carried him into the cabin.

Kneeling in the dark beside Neil's pallet—Joseph smelling of balsam fir and the smoke of fires, and the clean musky scent that was his own—she wanted to lean into Joseph's chest, feel his arms enfold her, but resisted the need.

Her words were barely audible. "How did you find me?"

He spoke softly too. "I saw the trail sign you left. It was not hard to guess where you were bound. Not Niagara."

Niagara, the fort in the west by the Great Falling Water, where so many had fled to shelter under the clipped wings of the British who led them to ruin in the war that shattered the Longhouse people—Mohawks, Oneidas, Tuscaroras, Onondagas, Cayugas, Senecas—and scattered the Great Council Fire that had burned for centuries. Where the beleaguered remnant of her northern village had gone as well, being too few to sustain themselves. Where she might be, had the man beside her now been a few weeks quicker in returning.

Crouched in the dark beside a sick white man in a cabin far from the life they'd known together, Joseph Tames-His-Horse still read her soul. "Why did you come here? The Kanien'kehá:ka washed this life from your blood."

"Not from my memory." Not from her heart. Not Papa, Mama...

"It is not good. This is not the place for you."

Because it was dark, because she did not look at him, she found she could speak with truth. "I think there is no place for me."

"Burning Sky." Joseph hesitated, but she knew what he longed to say. That wherever he was, she would always have a place. The words hovered between them, unspoken.

"Here I am called Willa Obenchain." She took Joseph's hand, urging him up. "Let us leave him to rest."

Joseph had a white mare, cinnamon-spotted and tall. In the cabin yard he relieved it of its burdens, and his bow and quiver, and hobbled it to forage, while Willa put wood on the fire. They sat on the covered porch, in the light from the doorway, breathing in the night and the smell of waking earth.

She looked at him, to find him looking back at her. He had changed, yes, but there was still the scar above his left eyebrow where a child's stray arrow had nicked him, a year after her adoption. It had bled profusely, that small gash. She'd staunched it with a pad of rabbit skin, while his dark eyes teased her through a mask of scarlet, as if the fuss she made was worth the wound's sting.

She wanted to drink in his face, craved its familiarity, its strength, but in it as well lived memories that swelled the grief in her chest. She raised her chin and stared at the stars gathered thick above the ridges to the north.

"The man who was your husband made a good death. This was told to me. I did not see it."

Willa glanced aside to see Joseph staring not at the stars, but still at her. She'd known of Kingfisher's passing for a year and more. As best she could reckon it, having pieced together the accounts that made their way back to their remote village, he'd died the spring their second child was born, in a raid against the Long Knives, somewhere in Pennsylvania.

"He never saw his youngest daughter. In this world."

A sound caught in Joseph's throat—of sorrow, not surprise. He'd been to the village. He'd seen the ashes. "Then they are together?"

"Both of my daughters are with him." She-Goes-Singing, her first-born. Sweet Rain, her tiny one… Willa clenched her teeth to control the swift scald of tears. "It was the spotting sickness. Smallpox."

Joseph raised a hand to her cheek, knuckles brushing her unblemished skin. "But it did not touch you. Who was left to mourn with you? To make condolence?"

The words were like arms seeking to hold her. Grief clawed her throat tight. He waited while she made her voice strong. "The others all left for Niagara—Bear Clan, Turtle, the few left of Wolf. I bid them go. Enough had sickened. I stayed to care for my children and the others too sick to travel. When it was over, I mourned alone, then I burned the lodges to thaw the ground, and put them in the earth."

Joseph groaned, leaning into her until their shoulders pressed together, but it was too much to contain. She heaved herself off the porch and faced him.

By clan tradition, he was the one who should provide the condolence she had not received. He was Wolf Clan, her brother, though they did not share a drop of blood. Should she ask it, he was obligated to bring her captives to replace those she'd lost—as she had once replaced another for the Mohawk woman who became her mother. But all was changed now. It was no longer reasonable to expect such a thing, even if her heart cried out for it. She'd left the Kanien'kehá:ka. Yet she had not found her white parents. She was adrift between two lives, unable to grieve. Unable to hope.

"Why did you wait so long to come back?" They'd been speaking in the language of her adopted people, but now she spoke in English, and it made the question jarring. Joseph flinched but remained as he was, powerful body folded on the cabin step, watching her with pain in his eyes.

"For many moons, I did not know your husband was no longer with you."

She understood. When Thayendanegea came among them, recruiting warriors to help the British fight the colonists, Joseph had gone with him in no small part because she had accepted Kingfisher as her husband. Thinking Kingfisher still living, Joseph would not have returned.

"After the fighting ended," he went on, "I was given other work to do, and I did it."

"What work?"

"Hunting deserters for the British Army," he said, falling back into the language of the People.

She stared at him. "Deserters?"

"The forts around the lakes are undermanned. The redcoat officers send trackers to bring back those who desert. So now I hunt men I once fought beside."

He said it without pride.

It was chilly in the yard. Willa hugged her arms to her ribs. "Why would you do this work?"

This time Joseph did not flinch. "They pay me well to do it, and I have a family with bellies to fill. There are thousands of our people at Niagara, living poor and hungry all around the fort, waiting for the British to find places for them. Game is hard to find and so are men to hunt what game there is. If I have learned a thing, then it is this: war does not end when bows and guns and cannons are put away."

"True," she said, her heart wrenched for all the Longhouse people and the remnant of her own village, living in such misery and uncertainty. "It does not."

His expression softened, as if he regretted his words. "I meant to come back to you. I always meant to do that. But I did not mean to come empty-handed. Tracking these soldiers takes time. Longer if they reach a settlement, find a place among the Long Knives."

An Indian would be a fool to walk openly into such a settlement if he valued his life. Even one such as Joseph, who could pass as Oneida—the tribe that had broken from the rest of the Longhouse people and allied themselves with the colonists in the war. With a creeping chill, Willa thought of Richard's hatred, of Anni's haunted eyes, and glanced around at the darkness. Were they watched even now? Then something else Joseph said registered and gripped her heart tight.

"You have a family? Do you mean a wife and children?"

Joseph held her gaze. "My father and uncles are gone. I speak of my mother, my sister and her children."

She remembered his mother and sister well, though they had moved to another village shortly after Joseph rode to war. The news should not have eased that clenching of her heart when she thought he might have found a wife at last. There should not be such a clenching. It was unfair of her to begrudge him loving elsewhere.

"Thayendanegea has promised them fields to sow," Joseph continued. "But until it is settled between the sachems and the Canadians, I am the one left to hunt or trade for them."

"Or track deserters." She paced to the side of the porch and back, hoping he had not seen the confusion in her heart showing on her face. "How many such men have you tracked?"

His eyes caught the light from the cabin as they followed her. "Four. I have brought in three living."

"And the fourth?"

"I am on that trail now."

"Then why have you come here?" She returned to the porch and sat beside him. From the corner of her eye, she watched his hands, resting on his knees. They were large and lean, with fingers strong and brown. She had always thought them beautiful.

"Because I saw you in a dream," he said.

The urge to smile overcame Willa. "Of course you did."

It was a dream that had brought him to her in the first place, after all, so many years ago.

Arriving home to Canada after three years at the Oneida town of Kanowalohale, where he had embraced the teachings of the missionary there, Samuel Kirkland, Joseph had not found his family eager to embrace his newfound love for the white man's God—at least not his insistence that being a Christian meant more than obeying rules. "It is about the heart and knowing the voice of the Great Good God in your spirit," he'd told them in his newborn fervor. "It is by grace we are saved. By His goodness, not our own."

His mother's brother had been particularly displeased, angry with Joseph's father for having sent him to the Oneidas. After that disappointing homecoming, Joseph had gone to the women's fields to think and pray, and there he'd found her, hiding among the cornstalks, hunched among the squash vines that shaded their ground, three months adopted, miserably homesick, and crying her heart out. She had bolted to her feet at sight of him.

He was taller than any Indian she had seen, and so lean he had looked like a giant heron standing there with one foot raised to take a step, gazing at her with brows shot high. Mindful of her tear-streaked face, her greased and braided hair, the hateful deerskin clothing she wore, she had raised her chin to him and said, "What do you want? I suppose you've killed something and want me to skin it for you. Well, I won't! You killed it—skin it yourself!"

In her defiance she spoke English, not expecting to be understood. She suspected some of the women, including the one who called herself her mother, spoke some English, but all she earned was disapproving silence if she spoke anything but their heathen tongue—and once, from a warrior, a cuff on the head. She expected as much now and braced herself for it.

The tall young Indian put his foot down. His eyebrows lowered like the wings of a blackbird settling. Beneath them his dark eyes shone. "You are her," he said, in a voice unexpectedly resonant for his gangly build. "At least the hair is right. Had I a rag, I would wash your grubby face and be sure."

She stared, mouth flung wide. He'd spoken English—heavily accented, but clearly understandable *English*. The sound of it made her knees buckle. She sat down hard among the squashes.

The tall Indian stepped gracefully through the bean-entwined cornstalks, trampling not so much as a leaf. He knelt and put a hand on her long skinny arm.

"Please," she said, fearing she'd imagined it. "Say that again."

"That your face needs washing?" His eyes met hers, and widened. "One brown, one green. You are her."

What did he mean? Had he been spying on her?

"I haven't seen *you*." She wiped at her eyes, hating the weakness of her tears, hating the eyes themselves with their contrary colors the Mohawks said made her special. And she wiped them to get a better look at this Indian. Most of her time with the Mohawks had been spent among women. Their men's faces still looked much alike to her, grim and fierce and ugly. But she would have remembered this one. He wasn't so ugly, not too grim...and he was so tall. She was nearly fifteen now, getting taller by the day, but he'd towered over her when they both stood. Now he smiled, and the smile did something very agreeable to his not-so-ugly face.

"You have not seen me because I have been in the south, with my father's people. I had a dream while I was with them. In that dream I saw you."

Despite her misery, she began to be interested. "How could you have dreamed about me?"

Instead of answering, he asked, as if it was of greatest importance, "What clan has adopted you?"

"No cla—" She broke off with a sigh. He could ask anyone about that horrible day the women took her to the river, stripped her and scrubbed her roughly with sand and water, to cleanse away her white blood. Then they dressed her in Indian clothes and marched her into a longhouse where they fed her and petted her and called her *daughter...sister.*

"Okwhaho," she said bitterly.

The Indian's face lost some of its color, as if her answer dismayed him. She found herself perversely insulted by his reaction.

"Is there something wrong with being Wolf Clan?"

"No...no. Only I thought it would be Turtle, or Bear." Despite his words, he was still frowning. "Do not be offended. I am Wolf Clan, your... brother." He looked at her with the strangest mingling of warmth and confusion in his dark eyes. "What name were you given?"

Loathe to make the hateful sounds, she said, "Burning Sky."

He held out his hand, like her father—her *real* father, Papa—would have greeted another man at the mill. It seemed an outlandish gesture for an Indian to make here in the middle of a cornfield, wherever in the world this might be, so it must have been because he smiled again, or had carried on this entire conversation in English, that she slipped her hand into his. His grip was warm, encompassing. And to her great surprise, steadying.

"Sister," said the Indian. "I am called Joseph Tames-His-Horse, and I have come far to say a thing to you. In my dream of you, I was saying it. Will you let me say it now?"

For the first time, she didn't recoil at a Mohawk calling her *sister.* She would listen to anything this Indian had to say, as long as he said it in English. But what he said was one of the very last things she'd expected. A verse of Holy Scripture.

"'A bruised reed shall he not break, and the smoking flax shall he not quench.' Believe this, my sister, because He who said it is both great and good, and cannot lie."

Sitting now on her cabin porch, Joseph told her his new dream of her, the dream that had brought him back to her at last. "You were walking a path alone, but at every bend in this path, you would stop and look behind you. You were looking for me to be following you. In the dream I knew this. Yet you were also laying branches across that path, as if part of you wished to hinder me too."

"Joseph..." She said his name both to comfort and to plead. That path he saw led to her heart, and he would remove every branch in his way if he could. *You cannot, brother. Please...do not try.*

"God still speaks to you in dreams," she managed to say. "I'm glad some things do not change."

Inside the cabin the fire had died to embers. Still, Willa could see the gleam of Joseph's teeth when he smiled. "He did not mention that white man in there, who I think would have killed me, had he the strength."

"Him?" she said, startled by the reminder. "He is called Neil Mac-Gregor, and he is no warrior. His dog is the better hunter, I think. But he is injured and sick, so I may do him discredit."

Joseph stood. Behind them in the doorway, Neil's collie leaped to its feet from where it had been lying, watching them. Ignoring it, Joseph went to his saddlebags. He returned with a leather pouch. It clinked when he placed it in her lap.

"That is part of what the British paid for the last man I returned to them. There's every type of coin under the sun there. It is not much, but... it is something."

Willa felt the weight of the coins against her thighs. "I cannot take this. Your mother and sister—"

Joseph knelt, silencing her with his fingertips. With his thumb he traced her jaw, then ran it along the line of her collarbone, sharp beneath her skin. "You are starving, my sister. Take it, or I am dishonored. And since you cannot eat coins, I will hunt for you...while I can."

She shook her head. "We will manage."

"You and the crippled one in there, whose dog is a better hunter? I saw you are planting the fields, but who will tend them while you hunt? Or does this dog have other skills uncommon to its kind?" He reached to ruffle the collie's ear. The dog stiffened, but Joseph made a soothing noise, and it wagged its tail.

Willa said, "It would please this dog to be put in charge of the goat."

Joseph smiled at that, then looked at her, sobering. "I do not doubt your strength. But what sort of man would not provide meat for his widowed sister if he could?"

"And your deserter?"

"Will keep," Joseph said, enigmatically. "You are my more sacred duty."

Willa searched his determined face, then sighed and gave in to what felt a great weariness. She leaned against his chest. He spread a hand over her head and held her against his beating heart.

"You asked what sort of man would fail to provide for his sister. Not the man I know you to be." She drew a breath of resignation, which did not altogether conceal from her the relief flooding her limbs. "*Nia:wen,* Joseph," she added, thanking him.

Then she straightened, relief all too quickly replaced by fear. "But it is not safe for you to be here."

"I know."

"Did your dream tell you this too?"

Joseph held her gaze unblinking. "Your eyes are telling me now."

"Then hear these words of mine," she said. "Because my hungry belly will not be your death." Though Joseph listened—with the respect men of the Kanien'kehá:ka were raised to show their clan sisters—while she told him about her parents, the land auction, and Richard Waring, she could not sway his resolution to stay and provide meat for her.

"And something on which to eat it."

Those were his last words on the subject early the next morning, before he strode into the woods with the felling ax, bent on hewing boards to make a table.

EIGHT

N eil MacGregor awoke on his pallet, in his nose the scent of stewing meat, in his mouth the lingering taste of laudanum. Muzzy headed, he lay there trying to recall taking the laudanum, but couldn't. He did recall an Indian, tall and brown as an autumn oak, filling the cabin door-way. Or had that been a dream where Richard Waring turned into an Indian, come to take Willa away?

Willa. Hearing the muffled rise and fall of conversation, he raised himself to listen and felt relief at recognizing her voice. Until he heard the man's. He tensed, his first thought again of Waring, come to cause more trouble. But the voice was different, too deep for Waring. He strained to catch their words.

"...neighbors near enough to hear your rifle fire," Willa was saying.

"I have not forgotten how to use my bow," the man said. "You say it is dangerous for me to be here, but is it not for you? This Waring you spoke of... I can protect you from him but not in a way that will help you win friends among these people."

"I am not concerned with winning friends." A pot lid clanged, punctuating the statement.

"You will need them if you mean to stay."

Willa made no answer to that. Instead, she picked up what must have been an earlier thread of conversation. "If my parents were not Loyalists, I will find a way to prove it."

"And if they were?"

But to this, she said nothing at all.

"Thayendanegea told me how it was with the people here—here and down along the Mohawk River," the man said into the silence, "after

William Johnson's death. The whites, who took sides in secret, declared themselves openly, Whig and Tory. Did not your parents obtain this land from Johnson?"

Neil recognized the name of Sir William Johnson, Superintendent of Indian Affairs among the northern tribes until his death just prior to the outbreak of war. Trusted by the Mohawks like no other white man, Johnson had remained loyal to the British, a legacy that led in no small part to most of the Iroquois fighting against the colonials.

"They did," Willa said. "But that was long ago. And it does not make them Loyalists."

The man's voice lowered. "Does it really matter, when this life for you is past?"

Neil rose from the pallet and waded through waves of dizziness to the doorway. Peering around the frame, he could see only a portion of the room. That portion contained what he'd assumed he'd dreamed—an Indian, seated on a block chair, black hair tied with hawk feathers hanging long down his blue-shirted back. His legs were folded under a table, a tin cup engulfed in one large hand.

When had Willa Obenchain acquired a table?

"Where would you have me go, Joseph?"

Neil couldn't see Willa, but he saw the Indian's shoulders tense beneath the pull of his shirt. "Come back to Niagara with me. Thayendanegea means to speak with the governor there about a settlement on Grand River. The Canadians promise mills and a school, ministers, teachers. There will be land for us. I will build a house for you there."

"A man goes to the house of his wife, not the other way."

That drew from the Indian a surprising response. His head tilted and his voice warmed to teasing. "Is this you asking me to do so?"

"Do not even make a jest of it," Willa replied sharply. "We could never be together like that. Not among the People. You know this."

"As my sister, then." The teasing was gone from the Indian's voice. "Still, you would be with me."

Fear prickled the scar at Neil's hairline. Did this Indian, wherever he'd come from, intend to coerce Willa back into captivity, or *woo* her back? Alarmed by either prospect, he stepped into the front room.

Willa stood at the hearth, bent over a steaming pot with a spoon poised to stir its contents, her face raised to the Indian with a look of naked emotion—affection, exasperation, and, unbelievably, indecision.

"Could it be enough for you if…," she began, but clamped her lips tight when she saw Neil. The Indian turned on the block chair to look at him.

Neil cleared his throat. "Willa. Everything all right here?"

Neil had misgivings about leaving the Indian alone at the cabin the next morning while he and Willa made the trek into Shiloh—she hoped to find there the provisions and necessities Anni's charity hadn't provided and was determined to do so now, before the planting demanded her attention—but decided to keep those misgivings to himself. The Indian had spent the night on the porch, despite Willa's protests—apparently he'd spent the previous night beside the hearth—and now was out in the yard splitting cordwood.

Willa had explained their relationship succinctly the previous evening. "I was adopted by his clan—Wolf Clan, of the Seven Nations Mohawk in Canada—near kin to the Mohawks of the Longhouse people. Joseph is my brother."

'Twas maybe a shadow thrown by the fire, but Neil could have sworn at the word *brother* a wave of deeper color darkened the Indian's face, before he'd left them and gone out to the yard.

Now Neil sat at the table the Indian had built, a rough puncheon affair but sturdily made, waiting for Willa to descend from the loft. He heard the splash of water, a mutter of discontent. Not best pleased with the results of her toilette, he supposed.

As for himself...he ran his hand over his sprouting beard, resisting the urge to scratch. If in the settlement 'twas a razor to be had, it would be his by day's end. He'd found a neck cloth at the bottom of his satchel and done his best to brush clean his frock coat with its wide, turned-down collar. The brown broadcloth seemed permanently creased, but at least it covered his filthy shirt.

When at last Willa made her descent, Neil stood. And stared.

She wore her quilled moccasins—the only footwear she possessed—but had dressed herself in the gown Anni Keppler sent, a faded blue linen trimmed in yellowed lace. The cut would have been woefully out of fashion on the streets of Philadelphia, and the elbow-length sleeves and the hemline were more than a tad short for its present wearer, who was blushing brighter than the braid she'd coiled around her head like a crown. Yet even in a borrowed gown, outrageously tall and painfully thin, Willa Obenchain appeared not only respectable but regal as a queen.

A straight-backed warrior queen, braced for battle.

"Boudicca in the flesh."

She raised a brow, and he realized he'd spoken the name of the ancient Celtic queen aloud.

"Anni chose well," he said quickly. "That color suits you, if ye dinna mind my saying."

Her expression softened minutely. "It must do."

To the gown she added the bone-handled knife, attached to its corded sheath passed around her neck so it hung between her breasts, distracting from respectability, but adding to the overall martial effect. Neil watched as she hoisted her capacious basket and secured its tumpline across her brow.

He kent he was gaping at her—in admiration, though his staring was discomfiting her. Forcing himself to look away, he clapped his hat on his head and took up his satchel. "Ready?"

She took up her musket and headed for the porch. Neil followed her out to the yard, where the air held the tang of fresh-cut wood.

Cap sprang from the porch and circled his knees while Willa paused to speak with the Indian, who heaved the ax into the chopping block to listen. With his shirt sleeves turned up over corded forearms and an indecent amount of thigh bared by breechcloth and leggings, he took in Willa's words with a grave face. They spoke too low to overhear, though once the Indian cast him a narrowed glance, then cupped a hand on Willa's shoulder and bent to speak into her ear. It was so nigh an embrace Neil looked away.

"Hen'en," he heard Willa say—a tad sharpish—then she was striding past him toward the track, gripping the musket that rode her shoulder. Cap trotted after her.

The Indian's gaze followed as well, black eyes above the shelf of his cheekbones intense, inscrutable. The eyes turned on Neil, who'd hesitated in the yard. The Indian closed the space between them in a few strides.

"They will not look kindly on her in that place. But she will go. See no one touches her."

Neil took an involuntary step back. "Aye, I mean to do so."

The Indian drilled him with a look, then turned his back and went to take up the ax.

From down the track, Cap barked, impatient with Neil's dawdling.

He had to trot to catch Willa, striding on as though she cared not whether he followed. "How far did ye say was this settlement?"

She glanced aside. "An hour's walk when I was a girl."

"An hour's walk at this pace? I'd make it a dozen miles then."

She huffed through her nose and said, "More like three," but didn't slow her stride. At least he felt well enough to match it. That was something, after another headache the night before.

It was a promising day, the sky an unmarred blue, the sun still low over the eastern tree line, taking the edge off the chill. Passing the near field, Neil noted the amount of ground Willa had turned in a few short days. The woman worked like two men.

"It is not enough," she said, apparently reading his thoughts.

"Enough for what?"

"To survive the winter and not starve before I can plant again next spring."

For a plan, it was straightforward enough. She might even manage it, provided she was let alone to see it through. Yet the amount of fallow ground surrounding them held potential for more than bare survival. He was tempted to pause and stoop for a handful of soil. It was surprisingly dark where turned and looked neither stony nor heavy with clay. A rich, well-drained field, begging for plow and team. Neil could see stretching out to the south more bottomland acres waiting to be cleared.

Little wonder Waring coveted it.

"I mean to help in the fields, soon as my wrist can bear it." Though he'd rewrapped and splinted it, he'd left off the sling, hoping to draw less attention to the injury. "If I canna dig, I can maybe plant."

Willa said nothing to his offer. He tried another. "I can tote that musket for you."

Whatever the Indian had said to agitate her, she seemed to have finally walked it off. She slowed her pace. "You could not fire it should the need arise. Not with only one hand."

"True," he said, thinking that with the arrival of her imminently capable-looking clan brother, she must think she'd all the help she needed. And protection. The Indian was a match for Waring physically. Whether in brutality... He'd rather not have occasion to learn.

They left the cleared land and passed into dense woods. The track curved away from the line of ridges, edging toward the south. The noise of the creek reached them through the trees. And lofty trees they were: soaring pine, sugar maples—some bearing scars of past tapping—beech, oak, hornbeam, and elm, many of prodigious girth. Here and there, dogwood was in bloom, a delicate mist of white among the darker trunks. *Cornus florida.* And was that *Aster acuminatus* in the open spot beyond that rotting blowdown? He'd started toward it before he caught himself, gave a shrug, and sent his eyes roaming elsewhere.

"Have you any near neighbors," he asked, "or is it all forest betwixt you and Shiloh?"

"I have been gone twelve years," Willa said, "so we will have to see. But before, this track led only to Papa's farm, upstream on Black Kettle, east and a little north of Shiloh. West and south of Shiloh, there were more farms, but this part of the woods is Papa's land. Or was. See there?" She pointed to a stand of the scarred maples. "There is where we made sugar, at winter's end when the sap began to run. I am too late for it, this year."

He glanced at her, hearing the sadness in her voice, but her face was carefully composed.

A woodpecker, startled at their coming, exploded into bobbing flight through the upper branches. A squirrel darted across the track ahead; Cap was away after it. Neil didn't bother to call him back.

They walked in silence through wooded gloom speared only occasionally by a clever shaft of sunlight, until without preamble Willa said, "You have no need to fear him."

The forest shade snuffed the copper in her hair, but the spark in her eyes made up for it.

He knew who she meant. "I'm not afraid." When her mouth flattened, he confessed, "I was startled, aye. But I see you trust the man."

"But you do not?"

Willa halted so abruptly Neil strode beyond her several steps before turning. Her gaze went to his forehead.

"Is it only his brown skin you distrust? If so, put your mind at ease. Joseph is a Christian. It was he who opened my eyes to the gospel. Yes—mine, odd and ugly as they are. I knew of God from a child, but I never *knew* Him." She fisted one hand over her heart, where the straps of gun and knife and carrying basket crossed. "Joseph gave me hope when I despaired and friendship when I thought myself friendless. I have seen the scar you hide beneath your hair, and I know what made it. But Joseph did not put it there. He is no threat to you. He's a threat only to—"

She clamped her lips shut, but Neil had seen what lay at the heart of this passionate defense. Not offense at what she perceived he thought of Indians, but fear for Joseph.

He searched her eyes, their difference muted in the dimness, and in them found full understanding of what he'd heard the night before and what had made him look away by the woodpile while they spoke. Clan brother or no, the Indian was in love with Willa, and she was troubled by it. Because she loved him in that way as well? Or because she did not?

"I see," he said.

Willa frowned at his scrutiny. "Joseph Tames-His-Horse is a man you would do well to count a friend. As he is to me. That is all I have to say."

She'd been too blunt with her words. Every stride that took her farther along the track drove the knowledge deeper, but the silence had lengthened far past the time she should have spoken of it. Soon enough her fear for Joseph crowded out this small shame. If anyone from the settlement discovered his presence… She should tell Neil MacGregor not to speak of him, but thought of the settlement stole the words. The track ran closer to Black Kettle Creek now. Its clear waters chattered over the stones in its bed. At a bend in the track, Willa glimpsed a timbered roof rising beyond a brow of land—the gristmill, straddling the creek halfway down the slope beyond.

"Seems we've arrived," Neil said, breaking the silence.

She halted where the track began its descent. She could see the mill and the land widening below it, cleared back to the hillsides to accommodate the settlement strewn along Black Kettle's western bank. Among the Mohawks, hers had been a traditional village where people still lived mostly in longhouses. She had not seen so many square log structures all together for many years.

Neil paused beside her. His dog had not returned to them, and she was glad. It might have barked and revealed their presence, and she did not know whether she meant to go forward another step. The stays beneath the borrowed gown constricted her ribs. Besides the fact that they were not made for her and fitted ill, she'd forgotten the feel of English clothing and did not like it now. She did not like the fear tearing through her. For a paralyzing second, she was certain Joseph was right. She was no longer meant for this life.

She could hear the millstones grinding, their rotor wheel fed by the falls over which the structure was built. It was the mill of her childhood, miraculously intact. How often had she stood outside it as a girl, giggling with Anni, waiting for Papa's corn to be ground?

She trembled to see it now.

"I'm guessing the mill's friendly ground," Neil said. "Anni's husband runs it, aye? Shall we stop there first?"

She gulped air like a drowning person. "Yes." She took a step forward but halted when Neil's fingers curled around her arm, warm through her linen sleeve.

"Never call them ugly."

"What?"

"Your eyes," he said. "They're unusual, aye. Extraordinary even, but verra beautiful, and I'm sure I'll ne'er see their like again."

Neil MacGregor's startling remark retreated to the back of Willa's mind when, after they'd descended the final slope, two men emerged from the gristmill's doorway, so engaged in conversation they nearly collided with her in the yard.

"Sorry, there!" said the younger of the two, a mild-faced man with dark blond hair bound in a queue, stepping back and bumping his companion instead.

The second man was shorter, with grizzled red hair that hung down his back in a thin tail. A battered hat shaded a face as bearded as Neil MacGregor's had become. The man stared at Willa, taking her in from the basket's tumpline across her brow to the beaded moccasins showing beneath the too-short hem of her petticoat. He did not seem to like what he saw. She shifted her attention back to the blond man, who had looked nowhere but at her face.

"You'll be Willa Obenchain," that man said, speaking to be heard above the mill noise, "or my memory's shot. Don't know as you'll remember me, Charles Keppler."

"Obenchain?" The red-whiskered man uttered her name with an accent that, though faint, told her he was not born to the Dutch or Germans or anyone else settled long on the frontier. He was from the east. Maybe even British born. He stepped back a pace, as if to distance himself from her. "She's the one the savages carried off?"

Willa's heart bumped hard, but she ignored the man, and his question. "You are Anni's Charles," she said to the other.

"The very one," Charles Keppler said. "And here's Anni coming from the house now, unless my ears play me false."

Above the falls' rumble, Willa heard her name called. She looked upslope beyond the mill, to see Anni on the path from a cabin east of the creek, set on a promontory overlooking the settlement. Two small figures bobbed behind her.

The sight caught at her heart.

"And you, sir?" Charles was saying. "MacGregor, isn't it?" He noticed the splint and bindings showing below Neil's coat sleeve, preventing a handshake. "Anni related your misadventures. I hope we can be of help outfitting you again for your travels." Charles turned to introduce the second man. "Aram Crane, my father-in-law's groom. The Colonel's already building up another stable of horses."

This last was directed at Willa, who remembered the fine herd of horses Anni's father once owned. But Aram Crane bristled at it.

"No easy task after the red devils drove off the last lot. Good horse-flesh gone to fill thieving bellies."

More than his words, the man's narrowed, raking eyes made Willa's face burn, as if he blamed her for the loss. She thought it best to go on ignoring him, but Neil MacGregor was of a different mind.

"D'ye rob a man of all he has, then rebuke him for stealing so he doesna starve? They've children to feed too, I'd reckon."

After their exchange on the road, it was not a thing Willa had expected him to say.

Crane was not pleased to hear it. Beneath his hat, his nose was high bridged and narrow, his jaw hung low and thrusting. Or perhaps his stance, belligerent and disdainful, made it seem so. "You'll be one of those, then, taking up with squaws...when they offer?"

Neil took a step toward the man, looking as if he wanted to strike the mouth now sneering at him, but Charles was quick to raise a hand. "Aram, be civil. You've no grudge against these two."

"Not yet, I don't." Crane relaxed his stance, the hardness in his eyes easing off like a rifle hammer grudgingly let down. "But don't tell me we owe the Mohawks anything. I was at Cherry Valley—and other places, all through the war. I could tell you about the children Brant and his savages butchered. Whose fault is it if theirs are hungry now?"

The spit dried in Willa's mouth as she sought for something to say that would not make matters worse.

Neil MacGregor startled her by stepping boldly up to Aram Crane, then removing his hat. The noise of the falls was too great to hear, but she was certain he spoke to Crane, whose gaze darted to Neil's hairline. He was showing the man his scar.

The look in Crane's eyes shifted from wariness to surprise, then... something sharper.

Without a word, the man stepped back from Neil, nodded curtly, then spun on a heel and headed down the track, leaving Willa stunned by what she'd last seen, or thought she'd seen, in his eyes before he strode away. But what could have caused the man to look at Neil MacGregor with fear?

Charles Keppler's brows tightened, frowning at Neil, who watched Crane retreat before he set his hat on his head and turned back to them.

"Willa!" Anni had arrived, having descended the path and passed through the mill that served the family as a footbridge into town.

Willa tried to shake off the unnerving encounter as another round of introductions was made for the benefit of Anni's twins, Samuel and Samantha, five years old and both as towheaded as Anni had been as a child. The boy hung back, but the girl, barefoot in a calico frock, looked at Willa with a frank curiosity.

"Did you really live wild with them Injuns up north?" Samantha asked in a high, clear voice. "And why are you wearing that strap across your forehead?"

A maternal hand clamped over her mouth, too late. Anni's face went pink with mortification. "Little pitchers...heard what didn't concern them."

Everyone seemed poised as if on needle points, awaiting her reaction. After Aram Crane's undisguised loathing, this innocent inquisition felt benign, apart from the wringing of her heart. Images of another girl, black haired and browner skinned, swam in her vision. *Goes-Singing.* Not as she'd last seen her, spotted with sores, face drawn with suffering, but curious and full of life, like Anni's daughter.

She pushed down grief and wrestled her face into a smile. "I did so, little one, yes, but they are not wild. They live in towns, most of them, as you do. This basket I wear is the kind they use when they have more to carry than they can hold in their hands, or are traveling a long distance. You see?"

She shrugged out of the basket and set it on the ground. The girl stepped close. Her brother came near. Both peered within.

"It's empty," Samantha protested, sounding exactly like Anni at her age.

"I mean to fill it at the trading store," Willa said, somehow finding another smile for the child, even as tears pricked her eyes. "Maybe you would like to help me? Both of you?" When the children nodded with enthusiasm, she looked to Anni, suddenly wondering. "Is there still a store?"

It was clear in Anni's eyes; she knew Willa had been thinking of her own children—her half-Indian children. Anni's expression was torn between compassion and a repulsion that perhaps she could not help. Willa swallowed, but the grief going down met anger coming up and lodged in her throat like a stone.

"The British tried to burn it, but it's still standing," Anni said, a little too brightly. "Old Maeve Keegan's still there. Well, in and out," she added, with a tap to her forehead. "Her son keeps the store now. There's linen—mostly homespun but not all—and caps."

Willa glanced at Anni's covered head. Even Samantha wore a tiny ruffled cap over her pale braids. "I never did like them much," she said, then looked down the slope to the cluster of cabins and log structures. "How many have come back?"

"Between Loyalists decamping and then Oriskany…" Anni looked at her with uncertain eyes, but Willa held her gaze, not wanting her to shy away from the truth of things. "More than half the neighbors you'd remember are dead, many of the rest gone back east. But it's early days. More may return."

When they do, Willa thought, and have finished filling up this place again, then what? Will their children move west after the People who have gone that way, like Joseph's sister and mother and thousands more? Or would peace between her two peoples finally come now? Her two peoples…

Such thoughts found no place to settle in her heart, so she did not speak them aloud. Instead, she reached through a slit in her petticoat to the leather pouch Joseph gave her, hung on a cord at her waist. She extended a handful of coins to Anni. "For the gown and the rest."

Anni raised a hand but not to receive the coins. "No, Willa. I don't want— But where did you come by the coin?"

It was a question she ought to have foreseen. Likely Anni was the only soul in Shiloh who knew just how destitute she'd been before the gifts of house plenishings and food—and Joseph's arrival. She glanced aside at Neil, who'd drifted into conversation with Charles, out of earshot in the noise of the falls. He did not know about the coins. How was she to explain to Anni without revealing Joseph's presence at the cabin?

Seeing her glance, Anni precluded the need. "Of course. Mr. MacGregor's paying for his board. But, Willa, Charles and I weren't the only ones to help—our blacksmith and his wife did as well. Besides, I never expected payment and don't want any. Having you back with us is enough."

"Thank you, Anni." Willa smiled at her friend and slipped the coins back into her pocket, letting the misinterpretation stand. Bending for her basket, she leaned close and asked, "Where is Richard?"

"He rode home that morning from your farm, told the Colonel you'd come back, packed his saddlebags and left. He's gone down to German Flats, to find the assessor." Anni cast a look at the tumpline once again crossing Willa's forehead, then resolutely linked their arms. "Never mind Richard. There's me and the children, and Mr. MacGregor on our heels, and none of us mean to leave your side for a moment."

NINE

A rumble of male laughter stilled as Willa entered the store. After the brightness outdoors, it was too dim for her to see the faces of those clustered at the far hearth—particularly when a veritable maze of barrels, tables, and shelves piled with trade goods rose between. She could smell them, their sour stink faint above the crowding odors of wood smoke and tobacco leaf, tallow and tanned hides. Heads craned and mutters rose, but Willa did not catch their words. It was too much to take in at once. Her eyes could find no rest among the clutter of iron, sacking, leather, cloth bolts, wood, glass, copper, tin, and fur.

She'd halted inside the door. Anni edged around her and with hands on hips surveyed the gaping faces emerging from the shadows. "Jack Keegan! Are you back there with that lot? You've folk here mean to give you custom."

During Willa's childhood, the store's elderly Irish proprietor, John Keegan, had kept a tap for whiskey and other liquors in a side room. From its doorway now, a long-faced man emerged, ducking the lintel and wiping his hands on an apron.

"Brought me customers, have you, Mrs. Keppler?"

Though white sprinkled his sandy hair, Willa guessed this was Irish John's son, who she was surprised to remember had gone away trapping down into the Ohio country when she was a small child.

Anni made introductions. "This is Willa Obenchain. And Neil Mac-Gregor, from Philadelphia. Charles and I would be obliged if you'd tend to them."

"That's what I'm here for." From under bushy brows, Keegan's gaze settled on Willa. "Shall we be starting with you, then, Miss?"

"You mean all of us at once, Jack?"

The crude remark was buried under too much sniggering for Willa to tell which man in back made it, but it stood the hair on her neck erect, as into her mind rose tales of what the militia soldiers had done to the women of the People during raids through the Mohawk Valley and elsewhere.

Jack Keegan, seeing her white-knuckled grip on the musket slung at her shoulder, shot a glower toward the hearth. "I'll have none of that talk with ladies present."

"Aw, Jack. She ain't no—"

"Shut yer trap," Jack snapped, "or consider my tap shut for the day. That's all I aim to say on the matter."

"I'm here as well, let's not forget!" Red faced with fury, Anni hustled her children back outside, telling them to wait on the porch.

Neil MacGregor's anger was plain in the set of his jaw. He made as if to study the wares on display, in so doing putting himself between Willa and the men at the hearth. He caught Keegan's eye. "Have you ink and quills, sir, and a razor and strop I might have a look at whilst ye see to Miss Obenchain?"

"Up front there, back of the counter." Jack Keegan indicated the long table just opposite the door, then shot Willa a look of apology. He peered at her carrying basket, which rode too high for any but the tallest man to see that it was empty. "Now, Miss, have ye something to barter, or shall I start an account in my book?"

"I have coin to pay." Hearing the edge in her voice, Willa struggled for calm. Despite her resolve, she tensed as a man she had not noticed seated behind a stack of pelts stood and stepped away from the others. Black haired, heavily muscled through the shoulders and arms, he clutched a worn hat as he stopped in front of Neil and spoke a stream of unintelligible words.

"*Ciamar a tha thu, a MhicGriogair? Tha e math do choinneachadh. Is mise Gavan MacNab.*"

"*Chan eil mi ro dhona, tapa leat.*" Neil's response was equally incomprehensible, but the surprise and delight sweeping his features made Willa understand he'd found himself a fellow Scotsman. She'd never heard the Gaelic tongue before but assumed they had exchanged some manner of greeting.

"That's Gavan MacNab," Keegan interjected, grinning at her bewilderment. "Our blacksmith since...what, Gavan? Thirteen years back?"

"Aye," Gavan MacNab agreed and, nodding at Willa, switched nimbly to English—or something near it, for the man's accent was twice as thick as Neil MacGregor's. "Ye maybe dinna mind me, lass, as I was new come to Shiloh the spring ye was carrit away, but I'd seen ye with Miss Anni here, lassies the pair o' ye. Can I be telling my Leda ye've come to town? She wouldna be averse to speaking a word to ye, I'm thinking."

A beat of silence passed before Willa realized a question had been asked her. She nodded, uncertain what she'd just agreed to, and was still frowning after the blacksmith's departing back when Anni leaned close. "He meant his wife. It was Leda MacNab gave you the gown you're wearing."

Sturdy leather shoes, woolen stockings, candles, a pair of horn lanterns, scrap lead for bullets...cornmeal, maple sugar, soap...a kneading trough, two pewter plates... Willa filled the carrying basket and piled the overflow by the door. Yards of ticking, enough checked linsey-woolsey for a skirt and short gown, half-bleached linen for shifts...thread, needles, buttons, shears. No ribbon. No lace. One cap. Neil's purchases, though few, added to the bulk so that when it came to reckoning the accounts, Willa wondered how they would get it all back to the farm.

Though no further comments were aimed at her directly, the men now playing draughts at the hearth spoke and laughed in low murmurs, and there was an ugliness to the sound that was difficult to ignore. Despite the blacksmith's friendly overture, Neil MacGregor was subdued, as mindful as she of the thin barrier of civility maintained by the presence of Anni and the proprietor. Willa saw his surprise when she took from her pocket some of Joseph's coins, but a warning glance prevented his asking about them.

Keegan had created separate accounts in his book. Neil bent over the counter to frown at the column indicated as his. A tide of red rose from the collar of his coat.

"Do you need for me to pay?" Willa asked, thinking it more than he could afford after his losses. She glanced at the total for the ink, quills, razor, and strop, and read it aloud. "I have enough," she added, but Neil's expression had cleared. He took from his satchel a small leather fold, picked out the exact amount of his purchases, and handed the few coins to Keegan.

Willa was still puzzling over his hesitation—or had it been confusion?—when behind her a high, wobbly Irish voice slurred out a name.

"Dagna Mehler?"

In a doorway behind the counter, beaming at Willa, stood a shrunken wisp of a woman with white hair pulled back from an age-spotted brow. Though one corner of her mouth now sagged and she was greatly aged, Willa recognized Maeve Keegan, old Irish John's wife. She'd been a friend of her grandmother's, the only friend Oma ever made in Shiloh.

Willa took a step toward the woman, remembering Anni's mention of her at the mill and thinking perhaps Maeve Keegan had mistaken her for Oma.

"No, Ma." Jack Keegan stepped between them. "This is Mrs. Mehler's granddaughter, Willa Obenchain."

"I know who it is!" the old woman snapped, as a thin string of drool moistened her chin. She was out from behind the counter faster than Jack could prevent, grasping Willa's arm. "Dagna Mehler."

Willa remembered Maeve Keegan as a robust and domineering figure. The change in her was shocking. It was like being clung to by a child.

"Jack, you gonna stand there letting an Indian hug on your ma?"

"Yeah, Jack. If she's of that mind, send her back here. Wager she's had worse than us."

Resolve forgotten, Willa put the old woman away from her and faced the back of the store, where the crude comments had issued. "What do you know of me that you speak such things? You know nothing."

"Richard Waring heard it from your own mouth," one of the men at the game board shot back. "So don't go pretending you kept yourself to yourself all them years with the Mohawks. You ain't fit to walk that street out there, much less to come around doing trade in your begged-for gown. There's other ways of doing trade for your likes."

The words struck like stones, stealing the air from her lungs.

"That's done it." Neil MacGregor started for the back of the store, then stopped, his face going white. Jack Keegan had grasped his arm—the splinted one.

"Sorry." He let go quick, then raised his voice to the back of the store. "Now didn't I tell you boys—"

"You *boys*," a third voice said, hurling like a lance across the cluttered trading post, a voice accustomed to authority. And obedience. "Abe, Dexter, Orram—clear out of here. Your game's done, and it won't be played again."

Willa turned and felt a jolt drop down her spine. She thought for an instant it was Richard. It was not, though the man filling the doorway, blocking the daylight beyond, was very like his eldest son and would have been nearly as tall if he had not been bent to the support of a walking stick.

Colonel Elias Waring's hair was still the dark gold she remembered, hardly touched by gray, though the years had lined his face with less mercy. He moved aside for the men to file out past him. When they were gone, he fixed her in his gaze.

"Wilhelmina. It seems you found your way back to us at last… God be thanked." It was all he had time to say before he was nudged aside by someone intent on wedging past him, someone not the least intimidated by his presence—a handsome woman on the cusp of middle age, wearing a calico turban, its yellow a striking contrast to the brown of her face.

With a leap of heart, Willa recognized the Warings' longtime housemaid, the slave who went by the name of Goodenough.

TEN

N ever mind the endless work needs doing for these Waring men— weren't nothin' keeping me homebound, not after Mister Crane come blatting that you was in town—and the Colonel knew better than to tell me different."

Though an intermittent clang from the smithy punctuated Goodenough's words, Colonel Waring was within earshot of her voice, kneeling to talk to his twin grandchildren in the smithy yard. The look she slanted him was met with a glance that hinted at amusement rather than reproof.

Goodenough turned her gleaming smile back to Willa. "Never thought to see a woman standing taller than my spare bones, but look at you now, growed up to prove me wrong."

Though she recalled Goodenough—undisputed mistress of the Warings' kitchen—as a towering figure from her childhood, Willa now topped her by three fingers' width. Goodenough had measured it.

Of greater surprise was the long-legged, barefoot boy that had danced around Goodenough's skirts while they shifted their purchases from the trading store to the log-built smithy, where Gavan MacNab's soft-spoken wife added two wicker cages with a laying hen in each to the pile.

"This here's my boy, Lemuel." Goodenough pulled the child's head to her hip. His skin was the color of smoked deer hide, and his brown hair curled loose like a floppy cap. "Tell Miss Willa how old you be, Lem."

"Six year old, ma'am," the boy said.

"Lem! Speak true."

"Almost six," the boy amended, with a grin so appealing even his mama laughed.

"Old enough to do a favor for me." The Colonel rose to his feet, aided by his walking stick. "Think you can manage Cicero to the stable and back, Lem?"

The boy gazed up at his master, then at the big bay gelding hitched to a post outside the smithy, and nodded hard enough to bounce his curls.

"Then ride home and tell Mr. Crane we've need of the mule. You can lead it back, but be sure he puts the packsaddle on it first."

"Yes sir, Colonel!"

Understanding dawned on Willa. "Do you mean the mule for me? Please...do not go to the trouble."

"Actually," Neil said, emerging from the smithy in time to hear her protest, "we'd be obliged by the loan. I dinna see how else we'll be getting this lot back to the cabin," he added, turning to her with a rueful glance at his injured arm.

Willa closed her lips over further protest. The Colonel swung Lemuel into the saddle. Small hands took up the reins, and heels far short of the stirrups kicked the bay into a jouncing trot along the track leading west from the village. Tiny on his high perch, the boy clung to the saddle with knees and dirty toes.

"He was on the back of a pony nigh afore he could walk," Goodenough told her. "And it ain't but a mile, you recall."

The Colonel's mouth pulled sideways. "He's pestered me to ride that horse unaided since he was four. Tall as he is, I've suspected he could do it since he turned five."

With a last glance at the boy disappearing over the wooded hill to the west, Willa realized she'd yet to hear his father named and opened her mouth to ask. Before she could, on the heels of that realization came another. She looked at the Colonel, then at Goodenough, but it was Anni, standing by uncharacteristically silent, who caught her eye. Willa sensed Anni had been watching her, following her glances—and the progression of her thoughts. Now she was staring at Willa with her blue eyes wide, in them a look both acknowledging and beseeching silence.

Willa looked away, knowing her question need never be asked.

It was as well, for she'd lost heart for talk. Her soul felt pressed by all the faces she'd seen in a short space of time, most of them strangers, settlers come since the war's ending. A few of Shiloh's inhabitants who remembered her had approached her, though none made mention of her parents. More had kept their distance, peering out of cabin doors only to step inside when she returned their gazes. Some had greeted Neil MacGregor and pretended not to see her standing there. The thoughts of most were easy to read. The thoughts she could not guess at were those of the man now talking with Neil.

In daylight she could see how sharply Elias Waring had aged. The stick he leaned upon explained the lines of pain around his mouth. Anni's news of their family's losses explained those of grief.

If his physical presence had diminished, his authority had increased, for he was now a county magistrate as well as colonel of militia. The temptation was strong to blurt out her concerns to this man who'd called off her harassers in the store—but she could not forget he was also Richard's father.

She let the talk swirl around her.

A breeze brushed her face. Rain clouds had risen above the trees in the west. From a distance a grumble of thunder sounded, all but muffled by the clanking and steamy hissing from the smithy.

She closed her eyes. The voices around her speaking rapid English, the half-forgotten smells and noises, seemed things from out of a dream, lacking substance to make them real. She did not feel real, standing in the middle of it all. *"You found your way back to us,"* Anni's father had said. But had she? Was she trying to wrestle back to life a person dead and buried? Maybe Joseph was right. She thought of him with affection and gratitude and not for the first time wondered at the inscrutable ways of the Almighty. Why had she not been adopted by a Bear Clan woman, or Turtle Clan? Why a woman from the same clan as Joseph Tames-His-Horse, who loved her with a devotion few women probably ever knew?

She could not help thinking of what he asked of her, to come back to the People. Was she meant to remain Burning Sky of the Wolf Clan? Should she have gone to Niagara? Should she still go?

Hearing the thud of approaching hooves, she opened her eyes. Lemuel had returned, proud and triumphant, leading the mule with its packsaddle.

With their purchases loaded and the chickens secured, Willa lifted the heavy carrying basket, settled the tumpline across her brow, and took hold of the mule's lead rein.

The Colonel stopped her with a hand to her arm.

"Wilhelmina. There are matters you and I should discuss." He searched her face. The look in his eyes...she could only call it cautious. "Let it be when you return the mule. I've explained to Richard—and will to anyone necessary—that until the auction, you're to be allowed to remain where you are."

Willa thought relief might buckle her knees. Neil was swiftly at her side, looking into her face. "Are you all right? Shall I take the mule?"

Willa shook her head. "I will lead it."

The Colonel looked at Neil. "Mr. MacGregor, I'd be obliged if you'd accompany Wilhelmina when she returns the mule. If 'twould be no inconvenience to you."

Willa saw the look of warning that passed between Neil and Elias Waring. She would not be made to leave her land, for the time being. The Colonel had said that. He had not said he could prevent all harm from touching her, out there on her isolated farm.

◆

The daylight grayed as clouds rose above the ridges, covering the sun. They had not gone far past the mill when the drumming of thunder came again. That was what Willa thought it at first, but it did not stop when thunder should, but grew louder, coming on.

Halting, they turned to see two mud-spattered horsemen coming up the track. One of them was Richard on his blazed bay. He rode his horse past them and halted in the track, blocking the way.

"That's our mule," he said.

He was two days bearded, and Willa could smell his sweat from where she stood, yet he looked less worn than the middle-aged man who accompanied him.

"Your father loaned us the beast," Neil MacGregor said. "He also means Willa to remain on her land—unmolested by you or anyone else—until the auction."

"But the land will be assessed," Richard replied. "Not even the Colonel can prevent that."

"I assume that is your business here, sir?" Neil MacGregor asked, addressing the second rider, who'd kept his horse to the side of the track.

"Wendell Stoltz," the man said, when Richard failed to introduce him. He opened a satchel at his side and removed a sheaf of papers, flipping through until he found the one he sought. "And this," he added, nodding at Willa, "is the woman concerned with the property of the Loyalist Dieter Obenchain?"

"She's his daughter, Willa Obenchain," Neil said. "Have you proof he was a Loyalist?"

Stoltz held up the paper. "The burden of proof isn't laid upon me. I'm merely authorized to assess the previously confiscated properties along West Canada Creek and its adjacent waters, for resale at auction." Turning to Willa, he inquired, "Are you able to read, Miss Obenchain?"

Willa stepped forward and took the paper. A quick scan of it showed her sentence after sentence composed of more words than needed to be there, words that writhed and turned upon themselves, twisting the language she'd been born to into knots. In desperation she thrust the paper at Neil, who would understand it and tell her whether it gave this man the authority he claimed.

Neil MacGregor took the paper in his uninjured hand, but though he looked at it, he seemed to make no more sense of it than she had. That made no sense to *her*.

The breeze picked up while they stood there, surrounded by massive trees creaking, their upper boughs swaying. Thunder muttered, nearer now.

Richard broke their baffled silence. "Enough of this. There's nothing here to question."

"If you are determined to see this done now," Stoltz said to him, looking as if he'd rather do anything else, "I suggest we hasten to it." He bent from the saddle to take the paper from Neil and returned it to the satchel.

"Miss Obenchain has reason to think her parents were falsely accused," Neil said, but Willa barely heard for the new dread washing over her. Mounted as they were, Richard and the assessor would reach her cabin long before she could. There was no way to warn Joseph of their coming.

Thinking this, she turned to gaze down the track. When she looked back at Richard, he was looking at her, his blue eyes intense.

"Willa, you understand the confiscation isn't my doing. This was put in motion years ago. But since we're here, I'd as soon see this part of it done."

Before she could speak, Richard wheeled his horse down the track toward her cabin. The assessor, with an audible sigh, turned his horse to follow. She watched them ride away, then looked at Neil.

Alarm swept his features; he had thought of Joseph too.

"I must hurry." She thrust the mule's lead at him and slipped her musket from her shoulder. Richard and the assessor had disappeared where the track made a bend through the woods. She broke into a run, the basket heavy on her hips, the tumpline straining across her brow, pulling hard on her neck. Neil called her name as thunder rolled, but she pretended not to hear.

Let him be gone—gone to hunt for me as he said he would do.

Willa came into the yard with the first drops of rain, side and back and shoulders aching, gasping in breath. Richard's and the assessor's mounts stood in the yard, cropping grass. A small distance from the cabin stood a new shed-stall made of undressed saplings, with a proper pen for the goat. Beneath the porch eaves, cordwood was stacked. There was no spotted mare in the yard, or telltale saddlebags. Or Joseph.

Hearing voices, she hurried around the cabin. Richard and the assessor were in the side yard, looking at the ground where Joseph's mare had been hobbled.

Hearing her, Richard turned. "Who came to see you, Willa?"

Sweat ran freely down Willa's face, gone clammy as the rain struck in pelts. She glanced back toward the track. Neil MacGregor and the mule had come into view, still far across the upper field. She eased the carrying basket from her back and set the heavy burden on the porch, then crossed the yard to Richard. On the ground at his feet was a horse turd, smashed into the trampled grass.

"I had the goat penned here, before that shed-stall was built."

Richard's mouth tightened at her obvious evasion. Before he could question further, thunder cracked like musket shot and the rain became more than a pelting.

Wendell Stoltz had had enough. "Listen, Waring. Stay if you're bull-headed enough. I'm heading back before this weather breaks in earnest."

The man was in the saddle and turning onto the track before Richard came toward her through the rain. She tensed but stood her ground. Instead of passing her by, he stopped. They stood unnervingly close, nearly sharing the other's breath. Fear clawed Willa's flesh as his hand rose, and instinctively she flinched.

He did not strike her. With his thumb he rubbed her brow, following the chafing mark she knew the basket's tumpline had left. "What I did before—to that man, MacGregor—and the things I said to you… I would take it back, if I could." A spasm took his features, and he grimaced. "God help me… I never thought to see you again."

He took his hand away—snatched it, as though her flesh had burned him. The rain came steady now, molding her gown to her arms, her thighs. It darkened Richard's hat and shoulders, the sun-bleached tail of his hair. He seemed to struggle with something more he meant to say.

"Willa, *wa'kenhaten'*."

I am sorry. The words were less shocking than was the language in which they'd been uttered, or the strange wounded sound Richard made in his throat as he stepped past her. She heard him mount his horse and ride from the yard, but she did not turn around, not wanting him to see he had rattled her.

Once he was away, she scanned the nearest trees and called to the one she suspected was lurking. Not Joseph, who would be well away by now.

"Francis?"

She started as Neil MacGregor's dog burst from the brush at the woods' edge. The collie spotted Neil leading the mule into the yard and raced to meet him. Willa searched the trees where the dog had emerged, certain now that Joseph had been warned. Rain fell, whipped to a slant by the wind. The dim afternoon brightened as lightning flared, trailed by heavy thunder.

Willa stood in the yard with the rain beating her face but saw no sign of movement in the brush.

"We'd best shift this lot inside," Neil called from the cabin porch, where he was settling the hens in their wicker cages.

"Thank you," Willa mouthed, looking at the place where the dog had come bursting out. Turning toward the cabin as lightning flashed again, she thought she glimpsed a skinny, pale-haired figure flitting between the shadowed trees.

ELEVEN

A sharp crack of thunder woke him, but it was a softer sound, just audible above the torrent of rainfall, that kept Neil wakeful: a faint scraping noise coming from the cabin's front room.

He sat up and reached for his shirt, shed before crawling into the blankets, feeling for it in the dark. The shirt was gone. So was Cap, who'd been curled at his feet, wet and stinking, last he'd seen. He pulled on his breeches, wrapped a blanket around his shoulders, and went to investigate.

Cap was stretched out before the blazing hearth, paws batting the air in a dream. By the fire's light, Willa worked, bending over a shirt spread on the table—his shirt, half-covered by new linen she was cutting with her shears, using the old shirt as a pattern.

"Did ye not mean that cloth for yourself?"

Cap started out of sleep with a yelp when Neil spoke.

Willa swung to face him, nearly as startled. Recovering herself, she pinched a grimy shirt cuff between her forefinger and thumb and wrinkled her nose. "You must have a second shirt…if that is what it takes to make you wash this one."

Faintly embarrassed, he pulled the blanket higher around his neck. She seemed to hold cleanliness in high regard, bathing each morning at the spring-fed runnel in the woods, often washing her hair as well. He couldn't admit to such diligent ablutions, though he'd shaved the stubble off his jaw before seeking his bed. No easy task, one-handed.

"Aye, well. I *had* a spare—" Dash it all, he sounded prickly. He began again with more grace. "You didna have to, but I appreciate it."

Nodding, she went on with her work, leaving him to wonder why she'd chosen to do it in the dead of night. Had the storm disturbed her sleep too? Was she worried for the Indian? Waring? her parents? her land?

Any and all, she could take her pick.

His gaze fell on a pile of netting by the door. "Did you make this as well?" Crossing to squat beside it, he discovered it was woven of the same basswood cordage that had lashed him to the travois. "What need have you for netting?"

The scrape of the shears rose above the fire's snap and the battering rain outside.

"For fish."

Thunder boomed on the heels of her words, lending them absurdly ominous import.

"Fish?" he prompted, when she added nothing to that. Among the belongings he'd lost with the horse was a line and hook for fishing, an activity he enjoyed, but did far too little of.

"For the planting."

"Not for eating?"

"That too. But mostly for the planting."

Still she did not elaborate. He supposed he would have to wait and see what fish had to do with it. "You'll be planting soon, then?"

He'd expected a simple yes, but Willa cut a length of thread and passed it through the eye of her store-bought needle, and said, "I will plant the corn first, and the squash and pumpkins to shade the ground. When the stalks are tall enough to bear them, I will plant the climbing beans."

It was the Indian way of planting, three crops in one field. Dr. Franklin had explained its merits during a memorable conversation just after Neil's admittance into the Philosophical Society. And now he remembered why *fish*. One went into the ground beneath each cornstalk.

He felt a small thrill of eagerness, anticipating seeing the method implemented...only to recall where he'd be before the crop would have time to grow. Back in Philadelphia or well on his way there.

He'd been right about the availability, or lack thereof, of the sort of

equipment he needed in Shiloh. Even if he'd some means for barter-
ing, Keegan's store had been bereft of watercolor paints, and plant presses,
and more than the most rudimentary of medical supplies and writing
implements.

Thunder murmured, loud still but no longer cracking over their heads.
Dispirited, Neil took the bar from the door and pulled it wide enough to
peer out, letting in a rush of damp air, chill against his bare feet and shins.

The porch roof kept the rain from the doorway, but there was little to
see beyond the spill of light from the hearth. Gazing into the blackness, he
pushed thoughts of his impending disgrace aside and thought instead of
Richard Waring—with a whole other set of mixed emotions.

The man had paused his horse in the rain, practically on the spot of
their first memorable encounter, and made him an apology for his brutality at that meeting. He'd said much the same to Willa, she'd confessed
over their supper.

Fair enough. But remorse seemed not to have altered Waring's intentions to have the Obenchains' land, and Neil couldn't help wondering—
would the man have shown a conciliatory face had he found a Mohawk
warrior at the cabin?

Behind him Willa spoke, revealing where her thoughts lay.

"Joseph will have found shelter. He knows what to do in a storm."

No doubt he did. The Indian had built the table on which she worked,
had cut the wood that burned in the hearth, built a shelter for the goat—
all things Neil would have done, if he could.

He turned to look at her. "Why has he not come back?"

"He will come back. But not without a deer, or an elk...or both. He is
determined to see me set for meat for the winter."

Yet another task for which Neil was ill-suited. He'd never been a
hunter, aside from plants. Had never needed to be.

Noticing the woodpile by the hearth had dwindled, he went out to gather more, checking to see the hens in their cages were dry. He made three trips to the woodpile before it occurred to him to wonder why it mattered so much that he couldn't do the things Willa needed an extra set of hands to do. Had he not injured himself, practically in her path, he'd have been miles away, sitting out this storm in like manner to Joseph, never having known Willa Obenchain existed.

But he had, and if it hadn't been for the horse gone missing, he wasn't sure he'd mind it overmuch. He made one more trip to the porch, pondering a subtle shift in his thinking, a tentative tug on his soul, suspecting that his wrist, and his impending humiliation, weren't the only reasons he was finding it easy to put off thought of leaving.

He barred the door on the falling rain, stacked the wood by the hearth, then knelt to warm the blanket's folds. Cap beat the floor with his tail and stretched, content to be under Willa's roof. As was he, for the time being. Another week, maybe two—if she'd suffer him there that long—then he'd face what he must.

Willa settled on a block chair, close to the fire for the added light as she began to sew. Neil sat at the table on the other hewn block and watched her. Her hair was unbraided, spilling in long waves over her shoulders as she bent to her work.

It truly was a lovely color, her hair, the quiet russet of oak leaves that cling through winter's snow. Not often had he seen a woman's hair down loose like this. It was hard to look away.

She pushed the needle through the new linen, then looked up at him. "You seemed happy today to meet another Scotsman."

Embarrassed to be caught staring, he made a show of adjusting his splinted arm more comfortably on the table. "Aye, 'twas a surprise right enough, hearing the Gaelic in such a place." He glanced up, but she had her eyes on her work now.

"How did you come to leave it," she asked, "your home in Scotland? Did your parents come over the water and bring you with them?"

It was the first sign of interest she'd shown in him, other than his physical needs, and he felt a warmth quite apart from that of the fire.

"Ach, no," he said, hearing the Scotch burr thicken in his voice. "'Twas all my doing, that. I grew up on an estate where my da kept the grounds. I'd likely be keeping those grounds myself now, hadna the physician who owned the land, a Dr. Graham, caught me with a filched bit of foolscap and a quill, drawing flowers in one of his gardens—or trying to."

All of eight at the time, Neil had figured himself in for a tanned backside or worse, but the old man had been impressed rather than vexed.

"That is where you come by your interest in plants?"

"Aye, that was the start. Though I trained as a physician, in Edinburgh and Philadelphia, before I decided botany was the calling I wanted to follow."

Willa snapped off a thread and held up the shirt, now boasting one finished sleeve. "I have wanted to ask you about that...calling."

Neil rose to add more wood to the fire, then sat cross-legged in front of it. "Ask whatever ye wish."

Her face went dusky in the firelight. "First I have to confess. I looked at your drawings, the day I brought you here."

He'd half-guessed as much. "Then you'll have noticed that some are lacking in notes?"

She nodded. "I wondered why."

He looked into the fire, at the leaping, devouring flames. "Are ye up for another tale? This one's of more recent vintage—the autumn of '79."

"During the war."

"Smack in the middle of it, aye. And it happened not too terribly far from here." He paused, after all this time still reluctant to speak the name. "A settlement called Cherry Valley, south of the Mohawk River."

Willa's head lifted. Her needle stilled. "That is the place the Colonel's groom named today."

"The same."

"Bad things happened there?"

"They did so."

"Is that why he looked at you the way he did? He looked almost...
afraid. And then he went away."

Neil had been as baffled by the man's reaction as Willa seemed to be.
"I told him I was at Cherry Valley as well, that I'd seen what was done to
the people there. But why that should have rattled him so..." He shrugged.
So much unpleasantness had passed since that moment in the mill yard
he'd nearly forgotten Aram Crane.

"War does not end when the arrows and guns and cannons are put
away," she murmured, then caught his questioning look. "Something Joseph said to me. But you were going to tell me about your drawings, the
ones with no words written?"

"Right. Well. To shorten a rather longish tale, I was caught in a raid on
Cherry Valley that autumn of '78. I made it through that unscathed, only
to get myself knocked on the head by a guide I'd trusted to lead me to safer
quarters, who decided rather belatedly he was for the British, after all."

He mustered a half-smile, finding the subject discomfiting. But he
supposed if he meant to ask her aid, he had to tell her something by way
of explanation for the need.

"While his turncoating didna kill me—quite—it left me with the
headaches, as ye've witnessed, and one other...challenge. Since that day,
I've not been able to make sense of words on a page. However clear ye set
them down, the letters willna march straight for me now, but stagger about
like soldiers in their cups."

Willa's hands stilled again over the shirt in her lap. "In Keegan's store,
when you did not know at first how much to pay, then with the assessor,
that government paper..."

"I couldna read a word, either time."

Understanding lit her face. Then her brows puckered as she considered him. "That is a great loss for you, a great difficulty."

She acknowledged the fact with gravity, not pity, for which he was thankful.

"But you mean to go on with it—your work—or you would not be here. How have you managed?"

He would get no better opening than this. "I've kept the notes in my head for the drawings I've done, saying them over to myself before I sleep. But I'll lose the knowledge if I canna get it set in writing soon, which brings me to a thing I've wanted to ask ye." He drew a breath and plunged ahead. "Would you be agreeable to helping me with the writing, while my arm's on the mend?"

Instead of answering, she asked the one question he'd hoped *he* wouldn't have to answer. "When your arm is healed, what will you do then? You will need a horse, yes? And...other things?"

"Aye."

Resignation must have shown in his face. Her brow creased. "This troubles you?"

He sighed. "I havena wanted to say it, but I think losing my field kit is the feather that broke the horse's back, as they say. I dinna think I can go on without it."

Now her face was grave, her eyes full of concern. "Why can you not go on?"

"You've seen the inside of Keegan's store. I'd have to journey back to Schenectady, maybe even Albany, to replace what I lost—paints, brushes, the plant press, all the rest. Even if I did, I wasna given provision to outfit myself twice over." He set his teeth, then forced himself to say it aloud. "No. I'm done."

"After you have been through so much? That does not seem right."

Any less right than Willa's enduring twelve years of captivity, only to return to find her family's land about to be snatched out from under her? She looked away from him, at the fire, as if thinking hard about something—his request? His predicament? Her own?

"It matters to you," she said at last. "To set down the words for the drawings you have already finished, even if you do not mean to go on?"

"Aye. At least I'll have proof that I tried, when I explain my failure to the Society." His face flamed as he spoke, and he looked away, hoping she wouldn't notice the guilt thoughts of his mentors in Philadelphia stirred.

The American Philosophical Society had for the most part ceased to meet during the war years, the very years Neil had waited for the tumult—that inside his head as well as on the frontier—to cease. The one at least had done so, and at winter's end he'd received a letter from Benjamin Rush, in which the good doctor declared the Society's intention of resuming their interrupted gatherings. He'd encouraged Neil to strike out for the Great Northern Wilderness, if he still intended to do so, that they would expect word from him later in the season.

Had he been completely forthcoming about his condition, he was certain Rush's encouragement would have turned to dissuasion.

Neil forced himself to meet Willa's gaze, half believing she'd be so minded herself.

"I will help you," she said. "Some each day. But it must wait until the sun sleeps."

He smiled at her phrasing, as gratitude dispelled his embarrassment. Perhaps it would mean little in the end, whether or not the drawings he'd finished were annotated, but her willingness buoyed his spirits. "Thank you," he said.

There had been no thunder for some time. He rose and went to the door, opening it again to the night. The rain still pattered but no longer beat the ground. Feeling a nudge at his knee, he looked down. Cap had padded after him. "Ye dinna want to go out there."

The collie whined.

"I'll not be letting ye back in, do you get yourself all-over mud. You'll stay on the porch till you've dried."

Amber eyes fixed on him, unblinking.

"On your own head be it, lad." He let the dog out, calling after it, "Dinna pester the hens!"

When he glanced at the hearth, Willa was bent over her sewing, trying unsuccessfully to hide a smile. "Did I say something funny?"

"It is how you are with that dog that is funny. Talking to it as if it were a child."

Her smile dimmed suddenly, but he answered in the same light vein, "I suspect he sees it the other way 'round."

The cold was seeping in, raising gooseflesh up his shins, but he stayed at the door.

"Where was the village ye lived in? With the Mohawks, I mean. Was it one of those burned by—what was that general's name? Sullivan?"

Willa kept her gaze on her sewing. "My village was far to the north, not part of the Longhouse people. In that I was fortunate. No Town Destroyers like Sullivan or Clinton burned our crops or our houses. A sickness destroyed it. Smallpox."

Destroyed. He didn't think she used the word carelessly. Who had she lost to the pox? Her husband? Those who'd adopted her? He wanted to ask, but she'd turned closer to the fire, putting her shoulder to him. Protecting a wound she didn't want him probing, he sensed. He suspected he had only the vaguest idea as yet of what Willa Obenchain—or Burning Sky—had endured the past twelve years. But it was that day's events that came rushing in to fill his mind now.

By the Colonel's decree, Willa wouldn't be run off her land. Not by Richard or any other meddlesome neighbor. Not yet. But the eyes of one county magistrate couldn't be everywhere at once. Her Indian brother wasn't to be counted on for protection, save at the utmost extreme. In fact, his presence could make matters worse for Willa, if it was discovered.

Then there's me, he thought. While he couldn't for the moment chop wood or build a table or dig the ground, might he afford Willa the kind of protection that would discourage attack, rather than invite it? Or was he only looking for another excuse to delay his ignominious return to Philadelphia?

He had a week, he reminded himself, maybe two, to figure that out.

Gripping the spade in hands hardened to the work, Willa drew the earth into small scattered hillocks—earth too wet from last night's rain to work easily, earth smelling of the rawness of open graves.

She tried to drive back that last thought, but it was no good. The talking in the night had done it. Being with a man under her roof, hearing his voice, stitching a shirt for him, the fire warming their faces... It had felt too much like the life she'd known with Kingfisher and their children, and now she could not stop thinking of her daughters.

Goes-Singing, slender and quick, running between the mounds at last year's planting, bringing fish to replenish the earth. Sweet Rain, still fat and wobbly on her legs, tiny fist clenched around three kernels of seed corn, determined to help.

At the creek that morning, she'd caught a few small fish but had not wanted to take the time to throw the net again and again. A fish went into every hillock to nourish the plants as they grew. She could not catch enough and prepare the ground too. She would have to cut the fish into pieces, a stingy portion for each cornstalk. She worried the earth would feel neglected, that the crop would suffer. Thus she worked the ground in sorrow, and it wasn't good.

Planting was meant to be a time of joy, a singing time for the women and children of the clans. She had no children to catch the fish or bang the gourds to keep the birds from stealing the seeds and kernels after sowing. And in summer, when the bean pods came and the corn ripened and the squash vines blossomed, there would be no children to help guard the crop from the deer, raccoon, and rabbit that would steal it.

Letting the spade fall, she dropped to her knees and plunged her hands into the earth, grabbing up wet fistfuls of it to smear down the front of her tunic, the deerskin skirt covering her thighs. She did not care. She wanted to be covered. Buried.

Take my heart and hide it in this ground, for the pain of it in me is too great to bear.

Her throat was too tight for the scream building inside her to come out. Only a groan slipped past.

"Willa?"

She had not heard Neil MacGregor come across the field. He was simply there, kneeling to put his good hand on her shoulder. A sob escaped her throat at the touch, and his arm came around her.

Though she was as stiff and bent as a crone, filthy with dirt, she let him hold her as a brother might. As Joseph would have done. His hair was loose on his shoulders. It brushed her cheek, wet from bathing, cold.

"What d'ye need, Willa? Tell me."

My children. She swallowed back that answer and said, "Fish."

She felt a tremor go through him, as though her words made him laugh, but when he spoke, there was no mirth in his voice, only kindness.

"Then I'll get ye some." He gave her shoulder a gentle squeeze. Then he left her.

But somehow, he left her changed. She still had no children, no sisters to help her, but she'd remembered there was one thing more she could do. She could pray as she planted.

On her feet, covered in earth, she took up the spade and went back to making hillocks and beseeched the same God she'd always prayed to, even if sometimes it had been in silence, while others around her prayed in different ways—asking blessing for the ground, the seeds that would go into it, the crop that would spring from it. Asking for favor, asking for deliverance. Asking for a miracle.

TWELVE

The British had burned Richard's homestead, south of the Colonel's adjoining fields—so Anni told Willa when she and Neil stopped briefly at the mill on their way to return the Colonel's mule. In the months since Shiloh's surviving inhabitants left the forts on the Mohawk River and returned to pick up the pieces of their lives, Richard had not rebuilt his cabin. He'd slept and taken meals in the Colonel's six-room stone house—a structure impervious to flame—while he worked his land for all the profit he could wrest from it.

Willa prayed he was away tending that work the second morning after the storm.

They'd seen Richard and the assessor the previous day. Still covered in the mud of her grieving, Willa had seen them coming in time to slip from the field to the cabin yard, where she shot Neil MacGregor a pleading glance and, at his nod, hurried into the wood near the spring. To her shame, she'd been grateful he was stranded at her cabin, willing to spare her an encounter with Richard she was in no frame of mind, or heart, to endure. She was thankful to have him with her now, even if Richard was nowhere in sight and it was Goodenough's boy, Lem, who led them to the stable, where the Colonel's groom took the mule into custody.

Lem raced off to the cellar kitchen to tell his mama they'd arrived. Willa made to follow but halted at the stable door when she realized Neil was not behind her. She turned to see him standing by the mule, looking as if he meant to engage Aram Crane in conversation.

"Do you mean to come with me to the house?" she called.

He glanced at her, then back at Crane—who'd ducked into a tack room with the packsaddle, out of sight—then shrugged. "Aye."

"Is he still afraid of you?" Willa asked as they fell into step toward the stone house. It was hard to hide the smile tugging at her mouth. It did not escape Neil's notice.

"Think it funny, do ye?" he asked, pretending mild insult. "Aye," he muttered, with a glance behind him at the stable. "I suppose it is rather funny."

But the word she knew he was thinking, the word she was thinking, was *strange*.

Willa had let the tea in the cup go cold. Goodenough made a soft *tsk* as she warmed it with a fresh pouring, but her eyes lingered kindly as she served the Colonel, Neil, and Wendell Stoltz. On the table between the dishes lay the assessor's papers, including a map showing the boundaries of her land. Stoltz had explained his mapping, based on the original deed, and had inquired—from courtesy, Willa suspected—whether the borders he'd drawn and described in his notes coincided with her memory of them.

> *All that certain Farm or Tract of Land situate in upper Shiloh and*
> *County of Montgomery, formerly Tryon, being Bounded as follows*
> *Viz. Beginning at the South West corner of said Farm thence running*
> *Easterly by Woodland along the north bank of Black Kettle Creek to a*
> *Lake...*

She assured him that they were correct, and swallowed a sip of strong black tea. Another time she would have savored the half-forgotten taste, but today in the Colonel's paneled parlor, her throat felt lined with ashes, the tea bitter on her tongue. The assessor's notes had also contained these words: "Comprising about Ninety Acres more or less Forfeited to the People of this State by the Conviction of Dieter Obenchain."

"I'll leave you with a detailing of my assessment." Stoltz pushed a sheet of foolscap across the table. "An estimate. The final price will be fixed before the auction and will no doubt increase with the bidding."

Beside her, Neil MacGregor shifted in his chair. "When is it to be, the auction?"

"Also yet to be fixed, but Miss Obenchain may look to the autumn."

Stoltz rolled the map as Willa read the value set on her land, the ransom she must pay to redeem what she considered hers, a sum slightly nearer two hundred pounds than three hundred. It might as well have been ten thousand, for all she could imagine ever paying it.

"If present company holds me pardoned, there's a final property along Black Kettle to assess." Stoltz hesitated, gazing at her apologetically. "Miss Obenchain, there are times when my duties as assessor bring me no joy. And should you disprove what is commonly held against your father, that he never declared himself for the Patriot cause because he was, in fact, a Loyalist, then rest assured I shall do what I can to bring that proof before the commissioners of confiscation, to forestall these proceedings. But it must be unmitigated proof."

Though she wanted to, Willa could not dislike the man. "I will find that proof." Her assertion hung in the air, feeble words with nothing behind them but determination.

Goodenough followed the assessor out, leaving Willa and Neil alone with the Colonel.

The parlor had changed in the years since Willa last stepped foot inside it. Small reminder remained of Anni's mother, Sarah Waring. The room smelled of tobacco now. The furnishings were sparser, the tables unadorned. An oak-wood fire burned in the hearth, and a clock ticked on the wide-molded mantel. She remembered the clock. It and the fire were the only sounds in the room, until the Colonel spoke.

"You've begun planting, Richard tells me."

"I am still breaking ground, but I will plant soon."

The Colonel reached for a pipe, which he'd smoked earlier but had let go out. He tapped the bowl gently against the table, scattering dottle over the polished surface. "I'd ask you to consider leaving the land at rest for the present and coming here to live."

Willa opened her mouth, but the Colonel raised his pipe against a hasty response. "Dieter Obenchain, whatever his politics, was a good neighbor, an honest man. In his place—as a father, if you will—I offer you shelter, while you consider what you may wish to do…"

Willa stiffened in her chair. "You would see me admit defeat without trying to prove my parents' innocence?"

Elias Waring sighed, as if with a great weariness. "*Innocence* is a word I've learned to ascribe in strictest moderation, Wilhelmina. After the war we've come through, we are none of us innocent."

Neil MacGregor cleared his throat. "Respectfully, sir, are ye saying her parents deserved what happened to them?"

Willa caught the guarded look that crossed the Colonel's face.

"Anni has said she does not know what happened to them," she said. "Perhaps it is that you know?"

Abandoning the pipe, Anni's father rose from the table and crossed to the hearth, his limp more pronounced without the aid of his walking stick. He took up a poker and pushed at the logs in the grate, raising a spurt of flame.

"Has Anni told you about Oriskany, where we lost Sam and Nick?" he asked, instead of answering her question. "It was in that battle," he went on when Willa nodded, "that I took a ball through the thigh. The wound was slow healing. I was here abed from August until November of that year, 1777. Sarah and Edward died the spring after Oriskany. Afterward, and until the war ended, I spent little time in Shiloh."

The Colonel leaned against the mantel, watching the flames, firelight showing plain the deep-etched lines of his face. "Richard and I rode with the militia up and down West Canada Creek and between the forts on the

Mohawk, that last summer your parents were seen. There were countless
raids on settlements from here down into Pennsylvania. Impossible to
know who was responsible for them all."

"Was there reason to think Indians were involved?" Neil asked. "In
her parents' case."

The Colonel's gaze lifted. "If an arrow found embedded in the cabin
door counts as such. But as our worthy assessor would say, that cannot be
counted as *unmitigated* proof of who was behind that raid. Some of the
Iroquois fought on our side."

It was the Oneida who had sided with the Long Knives against the
British and the rest of the Longhouse nations, in large part due to their
beloved missionary, Samuel Kirkland—the man she had to thank for Joseph's faith. And her own.

Yet Willa felt herself deflate in disappointment. How could she ever
learn what had happened to her parents, what they might have thought or
said or did, when the world she'd left them in so long ago had been scattered to the winds, just like the Great Council Fire of the Longhouse
people? If anyone knew the truth of what happened to the Obenchains,
surely they would have come forward about it by now.

"I know about the Oneida." At her words, the air seemed to crackle
like the fire in the hearth. The Colonel studied her, curious, questioning.
"What is it you wish to ask me, Colonel?"

Elias Waring's eyes were sober. "I would be lying if I say the question
hasn't preyed on my mind—and been the subject of many a prayer. If I
may ask, were you treated kindly during your captivity?"

Captivity. How long since she had thought of her life with the
Kanien'kehá:ka in such a way?

"Except for the journey north after I was taken," she said, aware of
Neil MacGregor beside her, listening, "when I was pressed to travel swiftly,
I was treated well enough. It was longer before I learned to appreciate it,
but from the beginning, I was valued, though white."

Anni's father looked at her sharply, as though trying to discern a slight in her words. "Did you never attempt escape?"

The Colonel's question jarred. "How should I have? For weeks I was closely guarded, moved from place to place. By the time I was settled..." By then, she'd been adopted, named, and she had met Joseph Tames-His-Horse.

She couldn't say when it happened, but sometime during the months after that meeting in the cornfield, as she allowed herself to be drawn into the life of the Kanien'kehá:ka, into the family who patiently taught her their ways and words, a day had dawned when her first thought had not been suffused with longing for the family and the life from which she'd been torn.

The Colonel abandoned the mantel for the chair across the table, grimacing as he sat. "Far be it from me to judge a situation I have not, by God's grace, been forced to endure. You were young and alone and did what needs must to survive. You chose to return to us in the end. We will leave it there."

Willa did not wish to leave it there. "I returned because the mother who adopted me died. And the man who was my husband fell in battle. And then when the smallpox took—"

"Wilhelmina. I'm aware the Mohawks have suffered—those in Canada as well as here. The British tossed them aside like a spent weapon on the field as they fled." The Colonel must have seen her flinch at his words, for he made an effort to soften his voice. "I wonder if Anni told you one other thing. Did she tell you Richard spent weeks searching for you, as far afield as Montreal? He was barely more than a boy, but he made that journey. For you."

"She told me."

When she said no more, he asked, "Does that soften your opinion of him?"

Neil drew breath to speak, but Willa forestalled him with a look. She did not know what to make of Richard's painful attempt at apology, or the news that he had tried to find her so long ago, before giving up. But one thing had not been retracted or erased.

"Richard made it plain he will take my land from me. I have made it plain I will stop him—and anyone else who tries—if I can. The land is all I have, Colonel." Knowing she risked making an enemy of the one man in Shiloh who could be of help to her, she said, "That is why I cannot accept your invitation, as generous as it is. Not as long as Richard dwells under your roof."

A sharp light flared in the Colonel's eyes. "I have forbidden him to harass you, but it would help to keep the peace if you don't provoke him."

"Provoke him?" Neil replied, but again Willa's look forestalled his saying more. She'd glimpsed a truth in the Colonel's eyes when the sharpness came into them. Elias Waring did not see—or would not admit to seeing—what the war had done to his eldest son. Perhaps in all fairness he could not see it clearly, having witnessed a change that must have happened in stages. Perhaps, too, Richard had grown adept at hiding from his father the darkness in his heart. A darkness she'd seen staring from his eyes when he first rode into her cabin yard. She wanted to believe Richard was sincere in his repentance, but the knot of dread she'd carried in her chest since that meeting had not been dispelled by any words he or his father had said since.

They took their leave of the Colonel on the front steps, but had not gone a dozen paces toward the track that would take them back to Shiloh before Richard came striding around the house from the direction of the stables, face set with a determination to match his pace. Aram Crane trailed behind him but stopped at sight of Willa and Neil.

Richard hesitated, then squared his shoulders and came toward her. Willa halted.

Colonel Waring, standing in the doorway, blurted his son's name. "Richard!"

Perhaps it was only surprise at his appearance, but it sounded like a warning in Willa's ears. Richard's expression worked itself into something perceptibly softer. His breeches and long work frock were stained. He'd clearly come straight from his fields. He wore no hat, and his bound hair was streaked from sun and sweat.

"Willa," he said. "I heard you brought the mule back."

Aram Crane had obviously run to fetch him. Of his own accord, or had Richard requested he do so?

She was conscious of Neil MacGregor rooted at her side. They both looked to where they had seen Crane, but the man had retreated behind the big stone house.

"I hoped for a chance to talk to you. Alone." Richard made something less than rudeness of the word by bending his head to acknowledge Neil MacGregor.

"Ye dinna need speak to him," Neil said to her, low near her ear.

"He will do nothing untoward," Willa replied. "Not in front of his father." She nodded at Richard and crossed the yard, stopping to face him when they were out of earshot of the others. He stood too close for her comfort—she could smell the earth and sweat clinging to his clothes and skin—but she did not step back. "What do you wish to say to me?"

As they had in the rain outside her cabin, his words came with struggle. "Did the Colonel... Did he tell you... Did he offer the invitation?"

"To come and live here with you? He did."

Richard's brow furrowed. "And?"

"I mean to live on my land, to plant and tend it."

The muscles in Richard's jaw stiffened. "It gave me grief to see you grubbing in the dirt yesterday, to see the drudge those savages have made of you."

She had thought she'd slipped away before he saw her. Then his words penetrated. Grubbing? Drudge? For a woman to bring forth sustenance from the land was a sacred thing, not shameful. Willa contained the urge to rake her nails down the front of his work-stained chest.

"You have nothing to say to me that I wish to hear." She made to step past him, but he put a hand to her arm.

"Willa. That came out all wrong. Just…listen. Why won't you let us help you?"

For an instant she glimpsed a shadow of the younger Richard looking at her from this damaged mask—or imagined that she did—and she wanted to believe the person she'd known and admired still existed. Then she glanced past him to Neil MacGregor. He wasn't liking this. She could tell by the set of his jaw, the dark line of his brows. Even the Colonel had come down the steps of his stone house, watching them with worried eyes.

Tension thrummed in the air and through her very flesh. It was coming from the hand still gripping her arm, as though some immense tide of feeling inside Richard were building and building and it needed all his strength to contain it.

She pulled her arm free to hide the shudder she couldn't suppress. "I am going now. Do not hinder me."

Moving past him, she strode to where Neil waited, and he fell in beside her. But Richard was not finished. Across the distance widening between them, he called, "Has anyone told you that I came for you?"

She did not look back.

"I tried to find you—did you know?" Frustration, anger, maybe even loss, clogged the words. The sound of it touched a place in Willa's soul that she did not want anyone, least of all Richard Waring, to touch. She quickened her stride.

"Willa! No, Pa, let me—"

Neil glanced back, but Willa did not. She knew what she would see. Colonel Waring had stepped in front of Richard, perhaps taken hold of him, to prevent his coming after her.

Neil muttered something low that might have been a prayer. It did not drown the Colonel's voice, the last to reach them as they started down the track to Shiloh.

"There'll be another time, Richard. Let her go."

"There must be someone who kens what happened to your parents," Neil MacGregor was saying as they came in sight of the mill. He'd been talking since they left the stone house, as if enough words spoken might blot out the awful scene Richard had made in the dooryard. "Is it possible they went back east? Albany, perhaps?"

Willa had only half-listened, but now her rattled mind produced a memory. The cabin porch... Papa reading letters exchanged with a cousin—or someone—in Albany.

Who had it been? She could not remember a name.

"It is possible," she began, but Neil put out a hand to halt her. A tall, thin figure of a man was hurrying up the track toward the mill, coming from the town.

"Is that Jack Keegan?" Neil asked.

It was. But Keegan did not notice them. "Sorry, Mrs. Keppler! Turned my back and she slipped out again."

They continued on, until the point where the track crested the rise of land behind the mill, before it took its eastward turn toward Willa's land, was visible. And there was Anni, an arm around old Maeve Keegan, waiting for Jack to reach them.

In seconds he had his mother in tow, leading her back down to the cluster of log buildings that included their store, his body blocking the sight of Neil and Willa as they passed. Willa halted—not because of the quick, distracted nod Jack Keegan shot her, but for the words the old woman was muttering: "Dagna. Dagna... For the love of... 'Tis gone now. Gone..."

Neil halted too. "That's your grandmother's name she's saying, aye?"

"It is." Willa watched the old woman totter down the slope, dwarfed by her tall son.

Staring after Jack, Willa hadn't noticed Anni coming down to meet them until she stopped beside her, puffing out a breath. "That's the second time she's done that. She's got Mrs. Mehler fixed in her mind. She must be trying to head out to your farm, Willa, thinking your grandmother's still there. Poor thing gets as far as the mill, then wanders in circles."

Willa's heart was beating hard. "Did she do this before she saw me again?"

"No. But you do resemble your grandmother." Anni brushed the rounded slope of her apron, flecked with bits of cornmeal. "How was your talk with the Colonel?"

Willa tore her gaze from the Keegans, still making their slow way to the store, and saw in Anni's face that she knew what her father had asked of her. "We returned the mule, and now I must get back. There is still—"

"Much to be done," Anni finished for her, disappointment in her tone. "I take it you declined his invitation."

"Was that your notion?" Neil asked her.

"I'm not sure if it was Richard's or the Colonel's. But I thought it a good one. Still, you'll do as you think best, Willa."

Though her friend embraced her before hurrying back to the mill, her words left Willa smarting, convinced even Anni thought her foolish for laying up provisions for a winter no one believed she would—or should—spend in the cabin Dieter Obenchain had built.

THIRTEEN

Throughout the night of the storm, and during the days following, Joseph Tames-His-Horse's thoughts were less focused on the game he hunted than on the woman he hunted it for. Even so, he'd gotten his deer. The buck, quartered in its hide, rode his shoulders as he retraced his trail to the mare, concealed in a tamarack thicket he'd camped in the previous night, a day's ride north of the cabin Burning Sky's father had built.

Her white father.

The notion rested in Joseph's mind as easy as a switch of stinging nettle. As he picked his way through pines dotting a stony ridge, the musky tang of blood and deer hair was strong in his nose.

Stronger was the memory of Burning Sky's scent as he held her on the cabin porch. The memory made him ache with longing and cringe with self-reproach.

We could never be together like that. Not among the People. You know this. Her words still made his heart writhe.

That she was adopted did not matter. That she was born white did not matter. Even his dream of her—the one that came before they met, the one he'd assumed meant God had intended her for him—could not change the fact that every person in a clan was considered kin to every other person in that clan. And marriage within one's clan was forbidden.

Yet on this day, with the sun high and his kill made, a fresh thought crossed that troubled path his mind had worn like an ancient trace. Perhaps what Burning Sky had done in returning to the whites wasn't a mistake, but a step on a path to a future they could share. Perhaps what his father had done in sending him to Kanowalohale all those years ago had been a step on that path, one he would walk not with Burning Sky of the Wolf Clan, but with Willa Obenchain.

The name held no meaning for him—no more than did Roussard, the name he could claim from the Frenchman who was his father's father— not like the name bestowed at her adoption.

Joseph had not seen that ceremony, but he'd heard the story of her naming, how one night the woman who would be her mother stood in the doorway of their lodge, unable to sleep for pondering the name she would give her soon-to-be daughter. She had lost many family members. Which should be requickened in the soul of this new one the warriors had brought to her and she accepted?

While she stood gazing, the northern sky began to pulse with ribbons of light, undulating in greens and russets so like the vivid coloring of her soon-to-be-daughter's strange eyes. Watching them, she recalled the name her own mother had borne as a girl.

Now it was *Willa* she wished to be called, as he himself was known by his Christian name among the soldiers and traders at the forts, rather than the one given him in his thirteenth year, when he had caught a horse that had gone wild and gentled it again.

A name was one thing. A man might wear many in a lifetime. But what of his heart? Could he make that white? Could he forget his family, his clan, and make a place among a people he once fought, a people whose ways he barely comprehended, to have Burning Sky—Willa—as his wife?

And would she have him so? There was love between them. What manner of love, for her part, he could not be certain. She'd always been more careful with her heart than he had been with his.

He sent his thoughts rising like smoke, fragrant with longing, to the Great Good God, and followed a dry creek bed into the stand of tamarack where he'd left the horse.

All was quiet. Too quiet. His mare was not a creature to announce herself to all who came near, but it was a rare thing when she did not scent him coming and give a ruckle of welcome.

Joseph pushed through dripping boughs into the open space where the fire ring he had made lay black on the earth. Kneeling to lower his kill to the needled ground, he saw his blanket tied to the bough where he'd left it, saddle and bags concealed in the dry underbelly of a tree.

But there was no mare.

It is an easy thing to read the sign a thief leaves when the ground is soft from rain, and the thief is barefoot and in haste, and the thing stolen is a horse. The tracks leading from the tamaracks were fresh and deep, but the thief's barefoot prints were too small for a man. A woman had taken his horse.

Joseph shouldered his rifle, fit an arrow to his bowstring, and set out after the thief. For a mile and more, he went swiftly, the moist ground muffling his steps and revealing the passage of the mare and her shoeless abductor, until the tracks turned aside into a rocky defile edging a narrow stream. Arrow at the ready, he went forward, straining to hear above the stream's gentle purl. He reached the first jut of rock, a lichen-fuzzed outcrop that topped his head. Beyond it, the trace of his quarry led up a rise where the stones thinned and pines grew. He edged around the outcrop.

Movement glimpsed from the corner of his eye gave him warning enough to duck. The blow glanced off the back of his head instead of striking true. Even so, he staggered to a knee as the stick that clubbed him clattered to the ground.

Feet scrabbled on stone. Joseph looked up through a surge of pain as a slender figure slipped into the pines above. From deeper in the thicket, the mare whinnied.

Joseph gave a piercing whistle. From above came the thud of a body hitting the earth, then the mare broke from the trees, riderless.

After lurching to his feet, Joseph caught her bridle, quieted her with a word, then loosed her, knowing she would wait, and barreled his way through the pines still clutching his bow, though the arrow had fallen.

His barefoot thief lay face down on the needled ground, unmoving. Black hair tangled in Joseph's hands as he flipped her over, pinning her across the chest with the bow. His rifle slid around from his back. He grabbed it one-handed and tossed it aside, then got a look at what manner of person he had caught.

A face golden brown, grubby, boyish. Hair cropped at the shoulders. A body straight as bundled sticks.

Impressions collided in Joseph's mind, adding up to revelation. His horse stealer wasn't a woman but a boy—an Indian, though lighter skinned than Joseph and dressed like a white. And unmoving only because the fall had stolen his breath. He got it back, and with lips drawn in a snarl, he burst into a struggle, churning the matted needles that had broken his fall and landing a kick to Joseph's shin.

"*Yah. Se'nikònrarak.*" Joseph tossed aside the bow to wrestle the boy, keeping out of range of callused heels. "Do not fight me!"

The words, or the language in which he spoke them, checked the boy's struggle. Brown eyes darted to Joseph's face, to the tattoos marking his forearms. "You—you are Kanien'kehá:ka?"

"Hen'en." Joseph sat back on his heels, keeping one hand splayed on the boy's heaving chest. "I am Joseph Tames-His-Horse."

The boy's eyes narrowed. "Joseph is a white man's name."

Joseph admitted this was so. "Call me Tames-His-Horse, if it suits you. But I am thinking your mother or father is probably as white as was my grandfather."

The observation did not please the boy. "My mother was Wolf Clan."

Was. And he didn't name his father.

"I am also born to the Wolf Clan," Joseph told him calmly, "and do not mean you harm. But I cannot let you take my horse."

The boy glowered at him, face half-buried in pine straw. "I need the horse! Ours is lame, and my sister cannot walk."

To Joseph's surprise, tears gathered in the boy's angry eyes. He was young. No more than ten winters. Joseph took his hand away. "What are you called, young brother?"

"Owl."

"And you have a sister? Where is she?"

Owl sat up. "Our horse called to your horse when we passed by your camp, so I went into the trees to see, and found it. I led my sister away and came back for it."

The boy watched warily, as if waiting for Joseph to notice he hadn't answered his question. Whatever the child was doing in the woods, it wasn't going well for him. His clothes were turning to rags. His bare feet bled where the ground had torn them. Hunger was in his face.

Joseph took his time answering. "Will you take me to your sister and this horse that is lame?"

The boy's jaw tightened. Clearly he was reluctant to put himself into a stranger's hands, even one claiming kinship. Though he'd no intention of letting the boy go without first seeing this sister who couldn't walk, Joseph gave him the dignity of appearing to make the choice for himself. "We are both Wolf Clan, young brother. It is my place to help you if I can. Will you let me?"

Owl got to his feet, wincing as he did. Though his eyes widened when Joseph stood to his full height, he nodded his head and said, with a little more haughtiness than needful, "Hen'en. I will let you follow me to where my sister waits."

The boy spurned Joseph's offer to ride and spare his feet. He strode straight backed and limping over the rocky forest ground. Behind him Joseph led the mare, by turns amused, exasperated, and impressed by such stubborn endurance. It reminded him of Burning Sky.

It was the lame horse that announced the girl's whereabouts, a dark bay roan, its good saddle and baggage in contrast to the bedraggled appearance of the child who claimed it. Joseph raised a brow at the boy but was more interested in the girl, tucked into an oval of tree roots at the base of a slope.

Owl went to his sister, who had watched Joseph's approach with eyes too big for her thin face, dark eyes that spoke of pain and suffering. A look Joseph's heart twisted to see. The boy spoke too low for Joseph to hear, so he watched the girl's face as she listened. Younger than Owl by several years, she showed the same evidence of mixed blood in her coloring. But where the boy's features were molded in determined lines, already showing the man he would be, his sister's face was delicate, her likeness to her brother no more than a wistful echo.

"He is called Tames-His-Horse," he heard the boy say with a shrug. "That is probably why the mare chose to stay with him."

Joseph managed not to smile as he tethered his horse near the roan. He approached Owl's sister and knelt, making himself smaller and, he hoped, less intimidating. "*Sekoh,* young sister. I am here because your brother says you are not able to walk and that concerned me. He has not told me what you are called."

"Margaret Kershaw."

The child's voice was thin, like the call of a wren, and went straight to Joseph's heart. He hadn't expected her to give an English name. "Kershaw is the name of your father?"

"Her name is Pine Bird." Owl stepped near, frowning at his sister, who gazed down at the soiled quilt that wrapped her. "We have no father. He's dead."

Joseph asked the girl, "Which name do you wish to be called?"

She didn't look up. "Pine Bird?"

"A good name," he said. "Will you show me why it is you cannot walk?"

Pine Bird let the quilt fall open. A pair of too-big moccasins—her brother's, Joseph realized—were bound to her feet by strips torn from the hem of her homespun frock, over which she wore a man's linen shirt, the wide sleeves rolled above her slender wrists. The child hiked up her tattered skirt. Joseph didn't wince at the gash that tore the flesh below her knee in a long and ragged line, but it took effort. No bone showed in the raw wound, and the flesh around it wasn't badly inflamed, but it needed to be cleaned and drawn together with stitches.

"How did this happen?" He asked the question of her brother, who told the tale.

It had happened the night of the storm. Hoping to find shelter before it burst upon them, the children had approached a cabin miles to the east, only to be halted in the yard by a man with a musket. When Owl tried to bring the horse near enough to explain their need, the man shot at them.

"The ball grazed my sister's leg, but she clung hard to me and didn't fall from the saddle."

Joseph held the boy's gaze. "Is my brother certain he wasn't shot at for stealing that horse?"

"I didn't steal it! We found it."

There was, Joseph mused, no indignation so great as a thief accused when innocent. He couldn't help prodding such bruised pride. "As you found my mare?"

The boy glared, unabashed. "The roan wasn't tied in a camp. It was wandering, just as you see. It lost a shoe before we found it, and I made it carry us fast from that cabin where my sister was shot. Now the horse limps and can be no use to us." Words tumbled from the boy, borne of a desperation he'd struggled to hide. "If you give us your mare, I will give you the roan and all that it carries—if you get a new shoe soon, I'm sure it will be well. A barebacked horse for a horse with saddle and bags, that is a good trade."

Amused by this brazen attempt to trade for a horse he'd failed to steal, Joseph set aside the issue for the moment. "Have you people living near who can dress this wound? If so, you should take your sister to them."

Owl opened his mouth, then glanced at his sister. The girl was look-ing between them, not admitting to the hope Joseph read in her eyes. A hope as fragile as sparrows' eggs.

"There's no one," Owl said. "When soldiers killed our parents, white neighbors took us in so we didn't starve, but they did not want us. They let their children call us dirty Indians and treat us bad. We're going to our mother's people, and we will not be dirty among them."

Joseph pressed his mouth tight, saddened and angered by the chil-dren's plight, but he contained his feelings. "Do you know where these people are?"

Owl pointed west.

Joseph sighed. "Listen, brother. Our people are living in many places since the war and not living well. Do you know the names of your Wolf Clan uncles? A grandmother? An aunt?"

It took further coaxing, but at last he had from the boy the full truth. Owl didn't know where his mother's Mohawk clan had lived before the war, much less where they had gone since.

"Our father took our mother to live in a town on the Hudson River. He made her speak white and dress white." Their mother had tried to teach them her language and given them names of the People, but they couldn't remember hearing her speak the names of her kin. "But we are Wolf Clan. It comes from the mother. We know that much." Owl stood, feet planted in defiance, as if daring Joseph to disagree.

Joseph sat back on his heels, thinking. The boy was right, as far as it went. A child was born to his mother's clan. Perhaps someone at Niagara would take in these children if their kin could not be found. But the boy could have no idea the distance they had to travel or how hard it would prove to outwit the traders at the posts where they must go to look, men who would deceive and misuse them. Owl might have it in him to survive it, but the girl? He couldn't send her down such a treacherous path.

Joseph sent up a silent petition that the boy would prove as sensible as he was brave. "I cannot give you a sound horse for a lame one." He raised a hand before Owl could protest. "Listen. Here is a thing for you to think about. I, too, have a sister. It is for her I hunt. I have a deer, left at the place you found my mare." He hoped this was still true. He hadn't liked leaving the meat, but there had been nothing to do but hide it in the tamaracks and hope no predator found it before he retrieved his horse. "I will feed you both and in the morning take you to my sister. She will tend this wound. When your sister can travel again, you can decide what to do."

Owl crouched beside his sister, indecision in the set of his lips. Joseph had seen the longing in Pine Bird's eyes, but knew that to press too hard might harden her brother to his course and make what must happen next more difficult.

Joseph stood. "I will look at your horse now. You and your sister think on what I have said."

The roan shied a little as Joseph approached. It was a gelding, and by its trappings and the amount of gear it bore, it was a white man's horse. He stroked its head, then moved around the animal until he found the shoeless hoof. He removed a stone embedded in the soft tissue, but the hoof appeared sound, no cracks or bruising. He found no evidence of strain or swelling in the leg. But the boy was right. It must be reshod or it would go lame.

Movement made him turn to see the boy on his feet, his unhappy face resolved. "We'll go with you to your sister and be glad if she can make my sister's leg well. But if we don't like her, we must be allowed to go."

Joseph no longer suppressed the urge to smile. "This thing you have chosen makes my heart glad. And do not worry. You will like my sister."

Though Willa's fingers proved long of memory, an hour's writing had cramped her hand. On this second evening of taking up a goose quill— unlike the first practice turn—Neil MacGregor had spread his drawings across the table. One by one she'd added the notations he had long carried in his memory. It was start-and-stop work. Often he began speaking, only to halt her so he could rephrase his words.

"Aye," he said after such a pause. "Begin with this: 'The petal's shadings impart a liveliness to the whole, being of a luminous pink.'" He waited for her to write that much, then went on. "'When an insect alights upon the blossom cups, the stamens, which are fit into pockets in the petals, rise and powder it with pollen.'"

Beautiful as were his drawings, it was the glimpse into Neil Mac-Gregor's mind Willa found most absorbing. She dipped the quill and penned his words below the colorful likeness of bog laurel.

When last she'd turned to look, he'd been bending to place a pine knot onto the sinking flames in the hearth, using his uninjured left hand. Now she sensed him standing right behind her, blocking the fire's warmth.

"Ye're doing well."

She poised the quill above the small glass inkwell. "You can tell?"

His soft, self-deprecating laughter was another kind of warmth. "I dinna see any blotches or crossings out. Will ye read back to me what we've managed so far?"

She did so, and he pronounced it good.

"It is not so good."

Leaning his left arm on the table, he frowned at the page. "Why d'ye say that?"

She reached for a drawing that bore descriptions made before the injury that robbed him of the ability and placed it alongside the one on which she labored. "Your writing was much finer. Look. Mine is like the scratches chickens make in dirt."

He laughed again. "Dinna be hard on yourself. Ye havena held a quill in what, twelve years? You're doing bonnily."

Now she tried not to laugh. "Bonnily?"

"I mean, you're doing fine."

The candle on the table illumined his eyes—and his relief at finally getting these words out of his head and onto paper. Willa found she could not meet his gaze and looked instead at his injured arm. He'd wrapped it fresh but without the splints. The binding kept the wrist immobile, leaving his fingers free. She reached to touch them where they lay upon the table. "It is healing well, your arm?"

His fingers jerked beneath hers. His face had gained some color since she found him, but not enough to hide the red suffusing it now. She pulled her hand away.

"Faster than expected. Perhaps 'twas only sprained." His gaze on her seemed suddenly intense, before he blinked and looked away. "Aye, then. Where was I?"

Again she read the last words she'd set down, and with a creased brow, Neil MacGregor strode the cabin floor. He seemed better able to order his thoughts while on his feet. During an unusually long silence, Willa watched him pace. She'd never troubled to notice how he moved. He had a certain grace about him, as one at home in his skin. For all that he'd seemed strange before, the first white man she'd come near in years, he wasn't an ill-made man.

Just now he was dressed in shirtsleeves tucked into his breeches, and though the shirt was loose fitted, she could tell his belly was flat, his shoulders wide in proportion. She'd thought him rather slight of build. Next to men like Joseph or Richard, perhaps he was. Yet he was taller than her by a little, and while his lines were lean—her gaze dropped down his straight thighs to the curve of his stockinged calves—he did have some muscle to him. He was, she realized with a frisson of physical memory, the very height and build of the man she'd called husband. She knew exactly how their bodies would mold together, should they ever—

Across the cabin Neil MacGregor turned, retracing his steps toward her. The face emerging into the fire's light was as different from King-fisher's as one man could be from another. Yet it was a pleasing face. He had a good jaw on him, and no one could say his eyes were anything but beautiful—blue as a sky-reflecting lake, rimmed in black lashes below brows strongly marked. His hair always seemed in need of a comb, as if he'd run his hands through it, forgetting it was tied back, but the shorter wisps that curled over his scarred brow were pretty enough for a woman to envy. And he had a kind mouth, with lips shaped for smiling.

They were not smiling now, nor pressed together in thought. A prickle of heat washed across Willa's face. Neil MacGregor had stopped his pacing and spoken at last, and she hadn't heard a word of it. Now he was looking at her in the way she had looked at him. At her hair, her eyes, her mouth.

"Willa?"

She'd never heard him say her name in such a way, low and husky. It made her belly tighten with a flutter both pleasurable and panicking. She looked quickly at the drawing before her, cheeks blazing. "I am sorry. Say again…that last part you were saying."

After a moment he repeated the words she'd missed. This time she didn't let her mind, or her eyes, stray from the task at hand.

FOURTEEN

Cap's barking brought them rushing from the cabin, abandoning the remains of a midday meal. First to reach the porch, Neil halted so abruptly Willa ran into him, jabbing him with the butt of the musket she'd snatched up. He barely noticed for his astonishment at the sight that greeted him in the yard. The Indian had returned, leading his spotted mare, upon which two children rode. Tied to the mare's saddle was another horse—his horse.

"Seamus!" The gelding shot its ears forward and strode to the reach of its lead, yanking the mare sideways. Neil came down off the porch and took the horse by the bridle. "Where did ye find the wee gomeral? Is he sound?"

He ran his hands over warm, familiar horseflesh, finding scratches on chest and flanks and legs, some healed, some fresh. New scuffs to the saddle. A stain that looked like blood. But the bags were there, if battered, and to his relief, still wrapped in canvas was his plant press and the small field desk, though obviously it had been unwrapped by inquisitive hands; the knots in the bindings were clumsily retied.

Still, if it contained all it once had…there need be no returning to Philadelphia. No humiliation. No defeat.

"Yah, Joseph!" Willa suddenly exclaimed. "You were meant to be getting meat for me. That is all."

With his soul sending up silent *hallelujahs* to the Almighty for this restoration, this miraculous reprieve, Neil had paid scant heed to the rising voices nearby. Joseph had taken the children off his horse, and Willa had put aside her musket and come to stand before the Indian, her face gone a bloodless white.

"Their parents are lost to them. They have no white kin to take them in." Joseph's tone was reasoning. "They wish to find our people, but the girl is—"

Willa took a step back, shaking her head. "You must find some other way."

Frowning, Neil moved to peer around the wall of horseflesh to better see the children, black haired and grubby, clasping each other with skinny arms while Cap sniffed at their knees. Glaring at Joseph Tames-His-Horse, the older of the pair, a boy, spoke a hot stream of words Neil recognized as Mohawk.

Joseph turned to him. "I have not lied to you. She is one of the People. Our sister."

The girl, dressed in what suspiciously resembled his own spare shirt, turned her face to Neil—a small face marked with suffering. As her dark eyes met his, something tugged at his heart, making him want to gather her in comforting arms.

The boy dropped his scowl to the collie, sniffing at the girl's skirt. With a muttered oath, he kicked the dog.

"Hey, now," Neil began, just as the girl's small face crumpled and she slumped against the boy, who grabbed her to keep her from falling.

Neil moved swiftly, catching the girl as she slipped from the boy's grasp, bending low to support her. She'd fainted—he felt the sag of her full weight, slight as it was, and his knees met the ground as she sprawled across his lap. The impact jarred his injured wrist, but he hardly heeded it. There was only the dirty little face fallen limp against his chest, and the child's ragged skirt rucked up to bare a wound deeply scored from calve to ankle, broken open and bleeding.

The girl roused almost at once, looking up at him with eyes full of pain. His heart wrenched again. "'Twill be all right, lass. We'll see to it. Ye're safe with us."

Willa stood as if rooted, face set and white. He looked a wordless plea at her and saw in her eyes a battle being waged.

Whatever the conflict, she put it aside and with a jerk of her chin said, "Bring her inside." She strode past him toward the cabin but halted at the door. "Wait. The light is better on the porch. You will need light, yes? I will bring a quilt."

He held the injured girl propped across a knee until Willa returned and spread the quilt from her loft pallet between the door and the steps. Joseph lifted the child from Neil's arms, careful of her bloodied leg, and carried her to the quilt.

Neil knelt beside her, while the boy hunkered at her shoulder, distrustful eyes on him. "What will you do to my sister? She's only seven. You can see she's afraid."

Not the only one, Neil guessed, though the boy was putting up a brave, if belligerent, front. "I'm going to see to this wound. With a bit of help."

Willa had vanished into the cabin again, but she was filling a bowl with heated water, gathering linen for bandaging, moving now with reassuring efficiency. He turned to find Joseph on the porch step, watching. "My saddlebags—I've things in them will help." Or he did have, he amended silently, catching the boy's unrepentant glare. "Will you bring them?"

Joseph went to oblige.

Willa returned with the water and stepped across the girl to kneel beside her. "The wound is filthy. No wonder it is broken open."

The child shrank from her, scooting toward Neil until she was nearly in his lap again. Her brother stared darkly at Willa's face.

"What is wrong with her eyes?"

"There's not a thing wrong with her eyes." Neil shot Willa a quick smile, which she didn't return. "What's your name, lass?" he asked the girl, a hand to her tangled hair. She didn't seem to mind his touch, but she darted a look at her brother, as if expecting him to answer for her.

The saddlebags came down with a thump beside him.

"She is called Pine Bird," Joseph said. "The boy is Owl. That is what the woman who was their mother called them. Their father's name was Kershaw. By him, they were called Margaret and…?" Joseph's gaze drilled into the boy, who gave no name but Owl.

Willa held a soaked wad of linen at the ready. "The wound is deep at the one end. Can you close it?"

"I mean to," Neil said. "Now then, Margaret, Willa's going to clean your wound while I see what's left of my supplies."

"I did not steal that horse."

Already deep in the bags, Neil glanced up to find Owl looking at him, narrow eyed.

"I never accused you of it, lad. Ah… God be thanked." He extracted the small case of medical supplies he'd brought along to doctor himself and the horse as need arose. The weight of the polished wooden case bolstered him.

"Did ye by chance mislay anything 'twas *in* the bags?" he asked the boy, with the mildest hint of wryness.

"It's all there. Except the food. And my sister is wearing—"

"Yah!"

The girl's cry of protest startled them. Neil reached for her but not quick enough to prevent her kicking out with her sound leg and catching Willa's forearm, knocking the wad of bloodied linen from her hand. She grasped the girl by the ankle.

"Aki! Satahonhsatat, tha'tesato:tat."

Both children stilled, gaping at her. Willa stared them back, her face fierce in its sternness.

Neil put a hand to her shoulder. She was trembling. "Willa, if this is upsetting you, Joseph can help—"

"Yes. He can." Willa released the girl and went into the cabin.

Neil stared after her until the child's fingers touched the wrappings he still wore on his wrist and hand. Her eyes looked up at him, trusting.

"I'll need to stitch it shut, lass," he said, unwinding the linen from his wrist so he could better use the fingers of that hand. "'Twill hurt, and I'm sorry for it. Can ye be a braw lassie and verra still, and let me do what I must?"

His accent tended to thicken at such moments. He doubted she'd understood half of what he'd said, but when it came to it, she clenched her eyes and her brother's hand and endured the suturing without a sound, though tears streaked the grime on her cheeks and tremors shook the flesh beneath his hand. Then he was knotting the last of the stitches, and the worst was over. For the lass. He was aware now of a sharp throb in his right wrist, which had borne the brunt of the work.

"Right, then, wee Maggie. Go on and cry now—"

The girl reached skinny arms for him; by instinct he gathered her in, one-handed, looking over her tousled hair at her brother, who was staring at him with eyes far older than the rest of his face.

"She has not been called Maggie," the boy said, "since the redcoats killed our father."

They settled the children in the cabin's front room and fed them what remained of the midday meal. Neil sat at the table, resting his arm. He wanted to see to Seamus, but Willa had taken their dirtied bowls and the kettle to the spring to scrub, and he didn't wish to leave the children alone. From the corner of the room where the quilt had been spread, they stared at Neil, the boy with open distrust.

Hearing Willa's voice in the yard, he went to the door. She stood near the horses, kettle clenched to her chest, confronting the Indian, who was lifting the mare's saddle to the ground.

"Do not ask it of me, Joseph. I have no heart in me for this."

The Indian straightened. "It is not only I who ask."

"What do you mean?"

"They are Wolf Clan," the Indian said, sorrow in his look. "That should be reason enough."

Willa bowed her head over the kettle. Neil saw her throat work in a swallow. "'A bruised reed…'"

Joseph touched her cheek. "'Shall he not break.'"

Neil's heart jumped at the scripture, his own soul quickening to its promise. *And the smoking flax shall he not quench.* Aye, he thought, uncertain still as to the cause of Willa's pain, but wanting her to see past it—as apparently Joseph was hoping she would do.

Willa leaned her cheek into his large brown hand, but her face remained pale, pinched, and more vulnerable than Neil had ever seen.

"Until the leg is healed," she said.

"Awiyo." A tender exultation chased the sadness from Joseph's face. "It is good."

Willa's voice was flat. "We will see."

Neil stepped back inside the cabin before they caught him listening. In a moment Willa brushed past him and went to hang the kettle at the hearth. Her face was composed now.

"You will want to see to your horse," she said to him. "Go, then. I will plant no more today."

Neil hesitated, glancing at the children on their pallet. The boy glared, mistrusting them equally. The girl watched Willa with half-fearful eyes. "Ye'll be all right, then?" he asked.

Willa did not turn to him. "Yes. Go."

He went, his last glimpse that of the girl's clinging gaze.

Joseph had removed the roan's saddle and burdens and was busy going over the horse as Neil had done before, checking for injury. Ignoring a proprietary twinge, he crouched beside his field desk, unwrapped the oiled canvas, and opened the lid. His paints, the white clamshells he used for mixing them, the good paper stock, pencils, ink, quills—it was all as he'd left it. *Oh, the joy.*

"Those children in there found this horse wandering alone."

Neil tipped his head back to see the tall Indian was through going over his horse. "So I gathered. It strayed when I took my fall, before Willa found me."

As he stood, Joseph grunted. "It is missing a shoe. The hoof is sound. I do not think the horse is bad lame."

"There's a smith in Shiloh." Neil began to see the shape the rest of his day was to take. It meant leaving Willa and the children alone, unless Joseph planned to linger for a while.

He wondered at the depth of her distress over the children. Certainly their arrival was unexpected, and it was reasonable to assume two children to look after were the last thing she needed. That didn't seem sufficient to explain her upset. Or that poignant scene in the yard he'd witnessed. Was it because they were Mohawks?

"It is not even three moons since her children were taken."

Joseph's startling, low-spoken words worked themselves into Neil's brain but found no purchase there. "Her children? She'd bairns?"

Surprise flickered in the Indian's eyes, and wariness. "Two daughters. She has not told you of them?"

Neil knew of a husband. Willa had as much as admitted to one the day Richard Waring rode into the yard. But not that she'd borne him children…daughters. Dead but months past?

He started for the cabin.

Joseph's hand clamped around his arm, stopping him. "I should not have spoken. I thought she must have told you."

Neil pulled free. "How old were they, her daughters?"

At first Neil thought the Indian would say no more. But at length, he relented. "One was six winters, the other not yet two. That is all I will say.

Let her say more if she chooses. I must build a better shelter for the animals, now that you have your horse back."

Joseph moved away. Neil caught him up as he reached the chopping block and wrenched free the felling ax. "I'd like to help."

Black eyes above chiseled cheekbones regarded Neil, their assessing scrutiny settling on his wrist. "There is no need."

The eyes had said something less kind. Or so Neil thought. That enigmatic face could be as stern and closed as Willa's.

Swallowing his smarting pride, he watched the Indian head for the trees beyond the cabin, armed with his rifle, ax balanced easily across one broad shoulder, determination—and a not-so-subtle disdain—communicated with every fluid stride.

At least he meant to stick close by for the present. He would pray Joseph found the words to help Willa past her heartache, to show these children kindness. He'd have tried to speak such words himself, but the Indian was right. Unless Willa chose to share her grief, he hadn't the right.

Behind him Seamus nickered, reminding him of other needs, and his blessings. The weather was fine, the sun high and warm in the vaulted blue sky, and he'd just recovered all that he had lost.

"Aye, then," he said. "Let me fetch my satchel and we'll be off to see MacNab."

After cleaning Seamus's hoof, MacNab shaped a fitting shoe. While the smith did his work in the yard, filling the air with the acrid smell of burning hoof, Neil ducked inside the smithy. At the drinking bucket kept inside the wide-open doors, he dipped a gourd to quench the thirst worked up on the walk into the settlement. He still had the gourd to his lips when the smith's hammer stilled and Neil heard him say, "Och, aye. A moment, then, and I'll see t' the Colonel's mares."

Neil hadn't heard any new arrivals over the hammering and had no

time to react before a figure stepped within, headed for the bucket Neil
was drinking from. With his eyes already accustomed to the dim interior,
Neil caught the blaze of red hair as the new arrival doffed his hat and
scratched behind an ear, recognizing Aram Crane, Colonel Waring's
groom. The man caught sight of him next instant. He drew up short, as if
he meant to duck back out without so much as an acknowledgment, then
seemed to change his mind.

"MacGregor, isn't it?" Crane tossed a glance at the yard and asked in
some surprise, "That roan MacNab's shoeing, is it yours?"

"That he is."

"Where did you come by him?"

Neil explained how he'd lost the horse but kept the particulars of its
finding vague. He raised the gourd, still dripping in his grasp. "Water?"

Crane hesitated, then came forward and took the dipper. He downed
a swallow and hung the gourd on the bucket. "That's a turn of luck, it
showing up again."

"I'm inclined to think it the hand of Providence."

Crane's mouth twisted. "Anyway, looks to be in fair condition. Guess
you'll be moving on now?"

Moving on. The very thing Neil had pondered with every step into
town, though with less enthusiasm than he'd have thought would be the
case. The shame of returning to Philadelphia in defeat was no longer an
issue, thanks be to the Almighty and Joseph Tames-His-Horse. But that
first flush of joy had abated; with the return of his horse and supplies,
other decisions loomed.

Moving on. *Soon,* he thought. *But not quite yet.* Giving his wrist another week of rest wouldn't come amiss. 'Twas throbbing with a vengeance
after tending to the girl. Thought of saddling a horse each day, shifting
gear to and fro, was enough to make him wince.

And then there was Willa. Now she had the children to tend as well as
her fields, while the issue of her parents' loyalties still hung over her uncertain

future. The likelihood of her carrying out the brave promise spoken to Elias Waring seemed slim, while she was tied by strings of necessity to hearth and field. Was there some way he could help her, before moving on?

But what of his own duties, his own promises? He couldn't deny the call of pen and brush and plant press, of solitude and wilderness, but he felt a twinge of guilt to think of leaving now.

"Aye," he said. "I suppose I must do. Soon enough."

It struck him as odd that Waring's groom should look relieved at his words.

"What is it exactly you're doing out here, wandering about?"

"I'm sent by the American Philosophical Society to catalog—to create a field guide of sorts—the mountain flora north of the Mohawk River. I'd lost most of my equipment for the work along with the horse. But that's all restored now."

"The boy, Lem, he's told me the tale of you falling from that boundary stone half a dozen times. I suppose by now you're wishing it'd been just about anyone else come along to drag you home like a load of deer meat." Crane finished with a significant look at Neil's hairline, or where it would be if his hat wasn't covering it.

Neil had revealed his scar at their first meeting at the mill, in an effort to show Crane he wasn't the only one to have suffered during that raid, and that such blanketing hatred he seemed to hold for the entire race of red men was unwarranted. Perhaps it had been a misguided action on his part. Was the man now attempting to sympathize with him by insinuating he, too, must hold Willa in low regard?

"What happened to me at Cherry Valley had naught to do with Willa Obenchain. 'Twas years ago, and she wasna there."

"No," Crane said. "But maybe some of her red brothers were. Anyway, she's drawn you into her troubles, hasn't she?"

"No more than I've drawn her into mine." Neil raised his right hand, wrapped again after seeing to the girl. "And whatever this interruption has cost me, what the British did at Cherry Valley cost a hundred times dearer."

Crane's whole posture changed, like a dog bristling at a threat.

"The British? The Eighth would've kept to the fort and left the settlement alone. It was Brant's savages did the butchering. They wouldn't be controlled." The man's face seethed. Spittle flecked his lips as he added, "There was nothing the regular soldiers could do once the brutes got a taste of blood and burning."

Taken aback by such vehemence, Neil stared at Crane several moments before the meaning of the words sank in. "How is it ye ken so much about the British regulars and what they could or couldna do? 'Twas all a swirl of smoke and flame and chaos, as far as I could tell."

The hard line of Crane's lips parted, but only to gape in silence. The hammering in the smithy yard had fallen silent too. Neil looked toward Seamus, to find the sunlight of the yard blocked by the hulking figure that stepped into the smithy and took Aram Crane by the arm.

"MacNab's ready to tend our horses," Richard Waring said, low voiced. "I need you in the yard."

Crane jerked, as if Waring's grasp had broken a different sort of grip, and went out into the sunlight, leaving Waring facing Neil. Before stare or silence could resolve itself into anything concrete, the man nodded briefly and stepped into the yard, vanishing from sight beyond Seamus, where the Colonel's horses waited.

FIFTEEN

The spade had gone missing. It was not on the porch, where Willa had left it last evening. It was not by the new horse shed or corral, or anywhere in the yard or field. With the morning wearing on, she pushed her way back inside the cabin, decidedly vexed. It didn't help her mood to find Neil MacGregor seated at the table, the girl perched beside him peering round-eyed at his drawings spread across the boards—or that the boy still sulked in the corner as he'd done for the past two days. Even the collie was taking its ease, sprawled before the hearth where the fire had dwindled to embers.

Gripping the door's edge, she kept a precarious hold on her temper. "Which of you took away the spade, and where did you put it?"

Neil looked up. "Was it not right outside the door yesterev'n?"

"It is not there now." Furtive movement in the corner drew her narrowed gaze. "Two will find it faster. Owl, if you wish to stay here while your sister's leg heals, you will make yourself useful."

Without moving off the pallet, the boy muttered, "I don't know where it is."

"You'll speak to Willa with respect, Owl. Get up and do as she asked." Neil MacGregor stared the boy down until Owl heaved himself to his feet and started toward her.

Neil spoke again as she turned to go. "I'll be along to help as well. I meant to try my hand at drawing again today, but that can wait till dark."

"You should not be drawing or working in the field. Your wrist was made worse when..." Willa glanced at the girl, who quickly lowered her eyes.

"I think we're back on course with the healing." Neil turned to the child with an easy affection that made Willa's chest constrict. "What say ye, lass? With my legs and your hands, can we put in the work of one able-bodied farmer?"

At Pine Bird's shy nod, Willa's ribs squeezed tighter. She clenched the door. "No one will work if I cannot find—"

A *thunk* reverberated through the door with the force of a slamming fist. The impact shuddered up Willa's arm, choking off her words. The collie sprang up with a startled *woof.*

Yanking Owl out of the way, Willa shoved the door closed, shutting them within.

Neil shot to his feet. "What was that noise?"

Heart thundering, Willa snatched up her musket. "Stay back," she said to Owl. "Neil, move the girl to the hearth."

She waited until none of them could be seen from the doorway, then pulled the door open a crack. The metal hinges creaked, but there was no other sound. Soft air trickled in, smelling innocently of morning damp.

Neil was frowning, the girl pressed to his side. "Willa, what—?"

"This." Clutching the musket, she swung the door wide to reveal the feathered shaft of an arrow embedded in the wood, at exactly the height of her throat.

While the arrow's intent was clear to Willa, Neil had been less certain. Shaken as they stood on the spot at the woods' edge where they surmised the shooter had stood, he'd said, "Ye dinna think it was meant to…?"

"Kill me?" Had the arrow been so intended, the deed could have been accomplished a dozen times while she ran hither and yon in search of the missing spade. She clutched the arrow she'd wrenched from the door. "It is a warning. From Richard."

Neil had glanced around the underbrush, striped with sunlight, belying the dark intent it had so recently concealed. "Or someone delivering it for him."

He'd spoken the words under his breath, but Willa caught them, and the furrowing of his brow. "What is it you are thinking? Tell me."

His blue eyes focused on her. "'Tis a thing that happened at the smithy, when I took Seamus for shoeing. Richard was there."

Alarm flushed hot down her spine. "Did you tell him about the children or Joseph? Is that why this has happened?"

"No," he said. "I ken better than to do so. Anyway, I barely saw Richard. 'Twas Aram Crane I spoke to. I mentioned Cherry Valley again, and he said some things about it that made me think he wasna there. Not on the side of the settlement, I mean. 'Tis been a niggle at the back of my mind since, but I think, maybe, he was part of the British regiment attacking the fort."

Willa did her best to hide her startlement, to keep the suspicion that dawned from showing on her face. She might be wrong. There was no knowing. Not until Joseph came in from hunting and she could ask him whether he had another reason for being in Shiloh, besides her. Had he tracked his deserter there too? And was that deserter Aram Crane?

"It may mean nothing to the present situation," Neil was saying. "And 'tis no surprise if the man doesna want it spread about that he was once a British soldier—if he was so."

"Do you think," Willa ventured, unable to hold back such a burning curiosity, "he could be a deserter?"

That surprised Neil. "I hadna thought it, but I suppose 'tis possible. What makes you ask it?"

Willa shrugged the subject away. "No reason. It is the children that worry me. We must keep them close. Always within sight."

"Surely Richard wouldna harm the bairns?"

"I don't know." Richard wasn't the only man in Shiloh with cause to hate the Mohawks—nearly every man did, whether they would ever act on it or not—but she couldn't shake the suspicion that he was behind that arrow in some way. Despite his words of repentance, his professed desire to help her, her return to Shiloh had rattled him, stirring up memories she thought he would rather have kept buried.

"What I know is that this"—her grip on the arrow tightened—"cannot keep me from my work."

"How d'ye mean to work with no spade?"

She'd already started toward the cabin and did not look back. "If I do not have a metal blade, then I will dig the ground with sticks!"

In the end she found a tool more serviceable than a stick—a sharpened length of deer antler—but decided, once her temper cooled, that breaking more field ground could wait. She was on her hands and knees now, digging among a patch of burdock upstream along the bank of Black Kettle Creek. She'd lined her carrying basket with the coarse heart-shaped leaves, then added young roots to use for salves and wound washes. Two of the plants she'd harvested intact, roots packed in earth, meaning to start an herb garden.

Their musky scent, the feel of earth and growing things, the creek's burbling at her back, all combined to sooth her ruffled nerves. But her thoughts were still taken up with the arrow, the missing spade, and another theft discovered soon after. The magnifying glass had disappeared from Neil's satchel, left on the porch while they probed the woods for the place the arrow had been shot.

Fresh in her mind were thoughts of Aram Crane, and British deserters, and of Neil MacGregor unknowingly—if her guess was a right one—threatening the place that man had made for himself as Elias Waring's groom. And if so, then maybe Neil MacGregor was the target. Not the children. Not her.

That was one possibility. But there was another thing. She couldn't shake from her mind that the spade and the glass had gone missing after the children arrived. Was it coincidence, or might that unhappy boy be responsible? Not for the arrow, of course. But what of the rest? Owl *had* stolen Joseph's mare.

As she worked the sharpened antler tine around another plant, careful not to scar its roots, Willa remembered Joseph's tale of the would-be theft, told after Neil left with his horse and the children napped inside the cabin.

If it was the boy behind the thievery, how was she to deal with it? Among the Kanien'kehá:ka—those who lived still in longhouses— such items as a spade were held in common. Only what was stored above or beneath a sleeping platform was a person's property, not to be touched or taken without permission. Anyone could pick up a tool set aside and use it.

But if the boy had this understanding from his Mohawk mother, why not simply say where he left the glass or the spade when need of them arose?

Maybe the thief was someone else entirely. Whoever it was had come so silently even Cap was not aroused—a thought that brought to mind the gifts that had appeared on the cabin porch after Anni's first visit. Francis Waring had come and gone with such stealth.

But no. It couldn't have been Francis. He had his strangeness, his half-wild ways, but surely he would not have stolen from them.

She lifted the loosened plant from the earth and settled it in the basket. Burdock was a large plant. Already the basket was full. She needed to head back and transplant them into the plot near the cabin she'd marked for the garden. Brushing dirt from her hands, she sat back on her heels and looked up at a massive hickory that spread its shade right up to the burdock patch.

She stared straight at him without seeing him for several seconds, so still was he in the hickory's leaf shade, until a twitch of his hand made his shape distinct. "Francis!"

He flinched, and she knew at once he hadn't meant to startle her. It was his way to hang back—skulk, some said—when others would announce themselves. There was no dark intent in the watching. Not like the arrow shooter who'd lurked near the cabin.

Not at all like that.

Breaking the grip of irrational fear, Willa got to her feet.

"Francis, do you know about the arrow? The one shot at my door this morning?"

Francis blinked. And nodded.

Though she stood in sunlight, Willa felt a chill. "Do you know who put it there?"

She remembered the Colonel speaking of an arrow embedded in the cabin door at the time the homestead was razed. Not unmitigated proof of which side did the razing, since Indians fought for both.

No Indian shot that morning's arrow, she was all but certain.

"Francis, do you know?" Willa's gaze dropped to his hand. His fingers tapped against his thigh, a tense, repeated motion. She remembered it was a thing he did when he was agitated. Or afraid. "If the arrow was a warning, will you help me heed it, Francis?"

The hand twitching slowed.

"Joseph is hunting meat for me, but he needs to know not to come to the cabin again, unless it is by night and with caution."

She could warn Neil and guard the children, but she needed to get word to Joseph, who she could not so easily protect. Best to find a place where he could leave the meat for her to come and collect it. It would need to be someplace close enough to check frequently, yet not so close that anyone watching would notice the coming and going.

She took a step nearer Anni's brother. "You helped Joseph before, when the assessor came. You warned him, didn't you?" She smiled to show this was a thing that made her happy. "Will you find Joseph for me and give him this new warning and tell him the place he is to leave his kills?"

She'd thought of a place but decided to show Francis rather than try to explain. She hoisted her basket and settled its strap across her brow, then started walking upstream along the creek, glancing back once to see Francis sliding through the woods after her, silent as her shadow.

As a child, Willa had seen the lake as a vast watery world fringed by cattail reeds where geese nested and loons called their eerie cries through the drifting mist. In truth, it was not a large lake and took but half a day to walk its shore, which undulated in tiny coves where the hills rose wooded from its lapping waves.

In one of those coves was the islet where she'd often snatched an hour to read her books, away from Oma's disapproving stare, reachable through wading shallows at the lake's edge.

She had not returned since she retrieved the ruined copy of *Pamela*. Memories of her parents were sharp there. She didn't know why, save that it was where she was captured. Memories pierced her now, as did the fact that she'd done nothing to prove their loyalties hadn't lain with the British King George. One thing after another had distracted her, demanding her attention. Neil, Joseph, the children, the planting. But the need to feed herself for the winter was no more real than the need to prove her parents weren't traitors—if far more difficult a task.

Traitors. Not Papa, Mama. They'd wanted only to be left in quiet, to live their lives in peace and, as much as lay within their power, help others do the same. That was how she remembered them.

Willa rounded the last neck of land before the islet came in view, so deep in troubling thoughts she'd half-forgotten Francis moving through the brush behind her. She started when his fingers closed on her arm, firm enough to halt her.

"We are nearly there. See? That islet, where the birches grow, that is where I would have Joseph leave his kills. If you could tell him..."

Anni's brother was making agitated noises. His grip became a tug. He might seem childlike, but for all his slightness, he was a grown man now and as strong as one. Something just short of fear took hold of Willa. "Francis, let go of me."

He did so, backing away and beckoning her. Fear receded, replaced by puzzlement. "The lake is this way." She pointed at it, clearly visible through the trees.

Blue eyes pleading, Francis edged around a clump of holly until he was out of sight. Circling the holly on the opposite side, she ducked a low bough.

From the thicket a cardinal took flight, startling and red. She reared back, snagging her hair in the prickly leaves, wincing at the pull at her scalp. She untangled herself and hurried forward and was jolted to a halt by what lay across her path.

There were two of them, side by side in the holly's shade, distinguishable from the surrounding duff by the small white stones outlining their oblong borders. And the sticks tied into crosses, planted at the head of each. And the dried flowers tied with string, a bundle at each foot.

Francis materialized beside her, still agitated. She did not look at him. She couldn't tear her gaze from the crosses and the letters carved into their transverse pieces. *DO* on the left. *RO* on the right.

Dieter and Rebecca Obenchain.

A terrible ache was in her throat. She sank to her knees at the foot of the graves, as any remaining shred of hope that she might find her parents still living somewhere thinned like smoke on the wind and vanished. Her

parents were not gone away to Canada or Albany. They were dead. And no
one left in Shiloh must know or they would have told her.

Wouldn't they?

Someone carved those letters in the crosspieces. Someone placed flowers on their graves, like the flowers she'd found on the hearthstones in the
cabin. Surely that someone was Francis, who dropped into a crouch beside
her. She removed her carrying basket and, striving for calm, faced him.

"You tried to lead me away from this place. Did you not want me to
see them?"

Francis wrapped skinny arms around his shins and beat his brow
against his bony knees, rocking himself gently. Though it was a behavior
she had witnessed long ago, and came as no surprise, his distress was as
unsettling as the graves.

"Who did this, Francis? Who killed my parents? Or who found them
dead and put them here?"

Beside her, Francis rocked and whimpered. It would do no good to
grab his shoulders and shake him, as everything inside Willa screamed at
her to do. It would do no good even to press him with more words. Either
he did not know the answers to those questions, or he was so afraid of the
answers that the words were lost inside him, with no way out.

Willa put her hands over her face. After a moment she stood and
stared down at the stone-marked ovals in chilling realization. Two graves.
Only two. "Where is Oma's grave? Francis, where is my grandmother?"

But in the time it had taken her to realize there should have been three
graves, Francis Waring had slipped away into the woods.

The collie, sniffing behind the cabin, barked in welcome when she came
out of the trees.

Seeing her, Neil MacGregor left the children sitting on the end of the

porch and crossed the yard to meet her, doing all he could to tuck a grin
into the corners of his mouth.

Spying the cause of it, Willa halted. The plot of ground behind the
cabin, marked for a garden, had been partially broken and turned since she
left. Not a large area, but more than enough for the burdock. She stared,
blinking, at the rectangle of earth he must have labored over since the moment she walked into the woods. His hands were still soiled from it, the
knees of his breeches stained.

"You did this," she said. "With your wrist?"

She had not wept at her parents' graves, had found no tears on the
walk back. Now they burned hot behind her eyes. Tears of gratitude. Tears
of grief. Tears of emotions she feared to name and had no wish to feel.

"We all pitched in. Even Owl. We took your advice and used sticks…"
As Neil neared, the smile that had won out against his efforts faded.
"Willa, you're pale as if ye'd seen a ghost. Let me get that."

He meant the carrying basket. Before he could touch her, she stepped
from his reach, lips pressed tight. His hand fell to his side.

"Are you not pleased with what we've done? Did I mistake the spot ye
meant for the garden?"

"It is where I wanted it."

He studied her, concerned but baffled. From the porch, the children
peered warily. The need to say more pressed on her. She wanted to say
more. Where were the words?

"It will need a fence or the deer will get at it."

That wasn't right. That sounded as if she were displeased. She was
very pleased. She simply hadn't expected such a kindness. And she thought,
I do not deserve it.

Neil MacGregor searched her eyes. "Aye, a fence we can do. Now tell
me what's upset ye. Did something happen in the woods? Not another
arrow, sure?"

Willa wagged her head. "Not that."

Her throat closed, but Neil stood between her and the cabin, looking as though he could—and would—wait until the sun set for her to say what she didn't want to say. She knew she must just say it, but speaking it aloud would make it real beyond recanting.

"I found my parents. They are dead."

She pushed past him so she wouldn't have to see it become real to him as well, or the compassion that would come into his face. So she would not break.

NERAHTOHKO:WA

Time of Big Leaf—May

I don't know, Willa. Something doesn't feel right with this one. I've no energy at all. With the twins, I was mad with the urge to sweep and scrub for the whole nine months." Straightening from the wash kettle in her cabin yard, Anni pressed her fists to the small of her back, then caressed her rounding belly as she gazed down toward the mill's timbered roof.

Willa took the idle laundry stick and gave the boiling garments a prod. The day was overcast and cool, but the fire and the rising steam warmed her, dampening the tendrils escaped from her braid. "You do have the twins now and more work than when you carried them. That you're tired is no surprise."

Her words hid her true concern, for Anni did not look as well as when Willa had last seen her, back at the beginning of May, nearly three weeks past. Purple shadows hung beneath her eyes, and her face had thinned.

Willa lifted one of Charles's shirts with the stick, transferred it to the washtub, then bent for the chunk of hard soap on a bench.

Anni waved at the row of tubs and kettles. "I oughtn't to have attempted this today. Goodenough usually rides over to help, but Lem's taken fevered and she didn't like to leave him—Richard stopped by this morning to tell me."

Willa felt Anni's stare, though she was careful not to meet it.

"I do think he's trying, Willa."

She bent over the shirt, scrubbing the soap around the collar, the cuffs, all the places a man sweated. "What is he trying?"

"To make things right with you."

"If that is so, then it is for himself he does it. So his conscience is clean when he bids on my land." She put the shirt in the rinsing tub.

"I don't believe that." There was anger in Anni's voice, but she seemed too tired to sustain it. "Though I see you do. I hope he proves you wrong."

Willa didn't reply, and for a while they worked in silence until she asked, "Who is midwife in Shiloh now?"

Anni seemed glad for the shift in conversation. "The one we had went down to Fort Dayton when the raids were at their worst, but she never came back."

"There is no physician?"

Anni laughed bleakly at that. "We've not seen so much as a simples peddler since the war." The laughter faded as her hands cupped her belly.

Willa motioned her to a spot of grass in the sunlight. "Sit and rest. I will finish this batch, then help you ring them."

Garments were already spread on the bushes edging the yard: shirts, frocks, shifts, mended stockings. Anni had been at work since sunup. She groaned in relief. "Oh, Willa, bless you! But mustn't you be getting back to your fields?"

Always, no matter where she was, Willa felt the pull of her land, the work to be done, the pressing knowledge of a short growing season, of a harsh winter looming, and the uncertainty of where she would be by then. But she said, "There is time to help a friend."

It seemed answer enough for Anni, which was good, for Willa had no intention of admitting to her other reason for putting off her return to the farm.

She'd come into the village weeks ago to replace the missing spade. Now, with more hands willing to help, she'd finally broken away from the digging to acquire another. In the end she'd bought two blades from Keegan's store, spade and hoe. They lay in the grass nearby, tied in sacking. Even without them, some of the corn and squash had already gone into the ground, and she had planted her garden.

In the gray half light that morning, while Neil and the children slept, she'd gone out to water the herbs transplanted from the forest over the past few days. The plot, enlarged from the ground originally broke, was surrounded now by a six-foot wattle fence fitted with a gate Neil had fashioned. Spaced in rows and beds within were burdock, snakeroot, cohosh, sorrel, chamomile, sweet flag, pennyroyal, and more. Once the watering and a bit of weeding were done, she stood in the open gate, admiring the well-ordered sight. She didn't hear Neil cross the yard, soft footed in the moccasins she helped him to make the evening before, until he spoke.

"You've a canny hand with the green things," he said, so close behind her his breath stirred against her hair. "I dinna think ye lost a one."

She didn't let him see her surprise or her pleasure at his praise. He'd taken great interest in the herbs, quizzing her on their uses, impressing her with his knowledge of some of them.

As he peered into the green domain within, his shirt sleeve brushed the sleeve of her shift, all she wore. His voice rumbled near her ear, lightly teasing. "Maybe I should let ye bring them all to me and draw them in the comfort of our cabin yard."

Our cabin yard. She turned and faced him, struck by his words.

They stood nearly eye to eye, with the sky above them gone the color of a pearl, the sun sending its first rays darting through the tops of the trees. Below that arc of light, shadow turned his eyes a deeper blue, but they were clear enough to speak his soul. He'd come to think of her cabin as home, though she hadn't given him that right. It discomposed him to reveal it—she could see that—yet having done so, he stood by it, letting her receive it as she would.

What she'd done was fled. From the garden, and from what else she'd seen in his eyes, a well of tenderness and wanting that seemed to surprise him, but terrified her bone deep with the impulse it had stirred. She'd wanted to take his sleep-tousled head between her hands and press her mouth to his, to taste his lips and feel the roughness of his cheeks. Instead, she'd hurried away to put on more clothes and saddle his horse for the ride into Shiloh, thinking he had not read her so easily as she had him. Thinking she was safe.

"Samuel—give it back!"

"You had your turn. It's mine!"

The querulous voices of the twins inside the cabin jarred Willa from thought.

Anni started to heave herself up from the grass, an ominous hint of thunder on her brow. "They're meant to mind their lessons till dinner."

As if sensing the impending maternal storm by some thickening of the air, the twins ceased their argument. Peace descended, save for the mill noise and a distant clanging from the smithy.

"You haven't lost your knack with a needle, I see."

Willa smiled at Anni's words. With the small break in field work before she had replaced the spade, she'd found time to piece a petticoat and short gown from cloth purchased at Keegan's store. Her efforts pleased her, but it was still strange to be wearing English clothes again, with her hair pinned off her neck.

"Is your Scotsman still with you?"

She did not smile at those words. Already flushed from the kettle's steam, Willa felt a deeper warmth creep into her face. "He is not *my* Scotsman. But yes, he is still there."

She suspected Neil MacGregor could for some days now have managed to look after himself and his horse. Instead, he had stayed, making himself helpful, true, but also allowing himself to form an attachment with Joseph's foundlings. It was unwise of him to have let it happen. When their parting came, it would be painful. The sooner now it happened, the better. For everyone, she thought, shaking off a second time the memory of Neil's sleep-shadowed face.

"Is it true, what I hear?" Anni asked.

"That depends on what you have heard."

"That you have two children at your cabin as well. Indian children."

"It is true," Willa admitted, her mind spinning with ways Anni might have heard about them. "Did Francis see them?"

"What doesn't he see?" Anni hesitated. "They aren't yours, are they?"

"No, Anni. The parents of these two are dead. The girl was shot. Not badly. A gash on her leg. Neil has been tending her."

"Shot?" Anni's brows rose toward the ruffle of her cap. "And your Scotsman is tending her?"

"He is not my—" Willa drew a breath. "He's a physician."

"Is he?" Anni sounded delighted. "A man of many talents. Might he be convinced to stay in Shiloh, do you think?"

Such an arrangement might seem perfect to Anni, but the very thought of Neil MacGregor staying in Shiloh clenched her chest tight with a longing quickly smothered in fear.

"No. He has obligations elsewhere."

Anni widened her eyes at Willa's blunt reply. "All right. It was only— ouch!" She slapped her arm above her elbow, then rubbed the spot. "Oh, fiddle. It's started. Black flies."

Willa grimaced. Black flies were another reason she'd broken ground as quickly as she could. Their inevitable invasion would have made such work a misery had she waited, though she didn't seem as much to their tastes as some. The numerous bites Anni suffered as a girl had risen like marbles under her skin and tormented her with itching. "I will start praying for windy days."

That drew Anni's laughter. "I used to ask you to pray for wind in springtime, didn't I? Charles says I overreact, but I swear they come looking particularly for me." Anni glanced about with a hunted look and shifted closer to the smoky wash fire, where she peered up at Willa. "By the way...the Colonel was here for supper last night and mentioned talk of the government inviting the Iroquois to a peace council, down at Fort Stanwix. Maybe at the end of summer."

"A peace council? But there is already peace."

"I think it's more to do with the land," Anni said hesitantly, as if she didn't know how Willa would take her words. "Anyway, I thought it would be of interest to you."

"It is." A weight like stones settled in her heart. It seemed always to come down to land. She was no different than the rest of the People, trying to hold on to what remained of their ancient Longhouse territory against a tide of settlers pouring in. Maybe the Oneida, at least, would be allowed to stay where they had been for so many generations. But even if they were, it could never be the same for them, as it would never be the same for her.

Anni, watching her have these troubling thoughts, seemed to regret bringing up the subject. "So, did you find these children like you did Mr. MacGregor, astray in the woods?"

"They were brought to me." Willa paused with a petticoat lifted to wring. Anni rose and took it by one end and began twisting, while Willa turned from the opposite direction.

Across the dripping garment, their gazes met. Anni raised a brow. "Brought to you?"

Willa chewed her lip, realizing she should have better guarded her words. One moment talking to Anni felt like talking to a stranger, the next like being girls together again, with no secrets between them. "I will tell you, Anni, if you promise not to repeat my words to anyone. Please, for the sake of our friendship as girls."

"For the sake of our friendship now." Anni gave the petticoat a final twist and released it to Willa's grasp.

They walked the short distance to the hobblebush thicket growing along the edge of the yard where the land sloped off steep to the creek and the mill below. Willa shook out the petticoat and spread it to dry. She drew a breath and said, "I have a brother. A man born to my clan. He's called Joseph."

Willa didn't miss the confusion, then the shocked comprehension, that crossed Anni's face as she mouthed the word *clan,* though she recovered as they returned to the washing. "A brother?"

"He's helping me for a while. Hunting for me so I will have meat for the winter. I could not dissuade him from it."

She fished out another garment and held it up, dripping.

Anni didn't take it. "Orphans are one thing, Willa, but a warrior? Mohawks killed my mother and Edward. They mutilated our soldiers—probably my brothers—at Oriskany. And you're harboring one of them in your cabin?"

Willa looked into the eyes of her oldest friend. "You are washing your clothes with one of them."

Anni's face paled. "You wouldn't have chosen to be if they hadn't forced you."

"No. But—"

"But nothing, Willa. Do you know how dangerous it is, what you're doing? Even keeping those children is risky—"

"I am not keeping them. And Joseph isn't living at my cabin. As I said, he is hunting meat for me—that is how he found the children. Soon he will go. He will take the children when he does."

"It best be soon." Anni glanced down at the mill, where Neil's horse waited, tethered. She lowered her voice, though there was no one to hear. "There are men in Shiloh who'll shoot Indians on sight and ask questions later, if they ask at all."

Men like Richard? Willa almost asked.

"Aram Crane, for one," Anni said, as if she'd heard Willa's thought. "There's been more than one Indian found dead in the woods since the Colonel hired on that man. He swears he finds them stealing from his traps. There's never any witness to say otherwise."

She took hold of the garment Willa held waiting and began to twist, leaving Willa a moment to think. She hadn't had opportunity to tell Joseph what had passed between Neil and Aram Crane at the smithy, and aroused her suspicions that Crane was the deserter Joseph sought. Francis had gotten her warning to him; he'd been leaving kills at the islet and had not come to the cabin even once. Now, she wished very much he would risk it.

"Where did Aram Crane come from?" she asked. "And how long ago?"

Anni's hands stilled. "He wandered in with a few families returning from the fort, late last autumn. I don't know much about him, except that he's good with horses, and he has a powerful hate of Indians."

"Then it is not possible," Willa murmured.

"What isn't possible?"

"That he was the one who killed my parents."

Anni frowned. "But you don't know your parents were killed. They could be in Canada or—"

"I found their graves."

Anni took a step forward, the twisted garment clasped between them, sympathy contorting her features. "Willa, I'm so sorry. How did you find them? Where?"

"In the woods. Francis tried to lead me away before I saw them."

"Francis knew they were there? He *knew*?" Her eyes widened in such surprise there was no denying Anni had known nothing about the graves. Not that Willa had suspected she did.

"He seemed to, yes."

Anni's face paled from surprise to alarm. "You don't think he had anything to do with their deaths?"

Despite her passing suspicion weeks ago, Willa didn't believe it. "I doubt it, Anni. He was little more than a child at the time. But I did wonder… Francis can read and write, yes?"

Anni looked puzzled at the question. "We tried teaching him. Who can say what sticks in his mind? Why?"

"The graves are marked with my parents' initials. I thought maybe Francis did that much."

Someone besides whoever killed them must have buried her parents' bodies or at least marked the graves. Someone meaning to preserve the memory of Dieter and Rebecca Obenchain, hidden away in their sepulcher of holly. Not someone attempting to cover their deaths and leave their whereabouts clouded with suspicion.

Anni's thoughts had followed a different path. "You have to tell the Colonel, Willa. This could lead to proving your parents were murdered, that maybe they weren't Loyalists—"

"No, Anni." Whoever killed her parents might still be in Shiloh, near enough to cause more harm should he, or they, learn the graves had been discovered. "Say nothing of them. Not yet. I—"

From the corner of her eye, Willa caught sight of a figure below, beyond the creek. Old Maeve Keegan was hobbling up the road again.

"I'll be back, Anni," she said, and ran for the path to the mill.

The old woman had reached the dooryard by the time Willa exited the mill. "Mrs. Keegan!"

Maeve halted, swaying over her cane. Breathless from her trek, she greeted Willa with a grasping claw of a hand and bright blue eyes. Willa leaned in close to hear her creaky voice above the mill fall. "Wilhelmina. I was after comin' t' see...comin' t' tell..."

"Darn it, Ma!" a man's voice called over the faltering words. "Just hold her there, Miss Obenchain!"

Jack was already on his way up from the store, threatening to cut short the moment with her grandmother's friend.

"Mrs. Keegan, what is it you want to tell me? Something about Oma—your friend, Dagna?"

The old woman beamed. "Dagna Mehler."

"Do you know what happened to my grandmother?"

Maeve's brow puckered. Her voice thinned, quavering with uncertainty. "What...happened?"

Willa tightened her grasp on the frail hand. "Try to remember. Please."

She'd startled Maeve with her urgency. Now she watched, helpless, as whatever memory about her grandmother that had surfaced slipped away, receding into the depths of the old woman's failing mind. Maeve knew it too. She stamped her stick in frustration as Jack reached them.

"She's done it again," he said, puffing for breath. "Turned my back for an instant…"

Willa approved the man's attentiveness to his mother, if not his timing. "She's trying to tell me something about my grandmother."

Jack looked embarrassed. "You oughtn't to fret yourself over what she says. Gets the past jumbled with the here and now, she does. I'll just be taking her home." He nodded to Willa, then turned his mother back toward the store. "Now, Ma. Why must you bother Miss Obenchain so?"

Willa had the urge to stamp her foot too, watching the old woman being herded away. She started after them but stopped as Maeve uttered a bleat of protest loud enough to carry above the mill falls: "I *know* who I mean. Dagna Fruehauf Mehler!"

Willa halted, one of her own long-buried memories bursting to the surface at last. *Fruehauf.* That was her grandmother's name before she married *and* the name of the Albany relation with whom her father once exchanged letters—letters that might, if they still existed, give evidence of her parents' loyalties. And keep her lands from being auctioned.

Tilda Fruehauf. Her mother's spinster cousin.

SEVENTEEN

S omeone was yelling loud enough to raise the cabin roof. Willa slowed Neil's horse to a halt in the yard and was halfway out of the saddle when Owl rushed from the cabin, face twisted in defiance.

"I didn't do it—it wasn't me!" The boy saw Willa as he leaped from the porch and shot off toward the sheds that sheltered their animals.

"Owl? Come back! It isn't safe to—"

"I'm going to feed the chickens!"

But it was to the corral he ran, ducking behind the horse shed. Willa hitched the roan to a porch post and hurried into the cabin. Pine Bird huddled on the corner pallet, looking fearful. Neil MacGregor leaned over the table, hands planted flat. Between them were two of his drawings, completely defaced with ink splatters.

Raising his head, he looked at her with an expression she had never seen. There was anger in it, and bemusement, but more evident than either was a wrenching hurt.

And no wonder. *She* felt the wound of this violation like a hot twisting in her chest. "Did the boy do this?"

Not until she spoke did Neil appear to fully register her presence. His expression cleared. With surprising calm he said, "I expect so. Though ye'll have heard him deny it."

She came to his side and touched a fingertip to a ruined picture. The marring ink hadn't dried. "Your beautiful drawings."

"Aye, well…" A sudden smile crowded out the hurt in his eyes, warming their blue. "You thought them beautiful?"

"Of course." Had she never said so?

His anger seemed to have fled; hers had not. Owl had been persuaded to help her in the field by driving off the birds that would steal the kernels and seeds before they could sprout, shouting and whistling whenever one was bold enough to land among the hillocks. Though he maintained his prickly aloofness with her, Willa had thought he'd warmed to Neil. Not as the girl had done, but Owl had at least shown him civility. She'd misread the boy.

"You helped his sister, saved her leg and maybe her life, and this is how you are repaid? Now I wonder if it was not he who took the spade and your glass, after all."

Neil's mouth quirked. "D'ye think he shot that arrow at the door too, whilst he sat there moping in the corner?"

"Of course I do not think that, but if you didn't despoil the drawings, it must have been one of the children." Willa crossed to the corner and stood before Owl's huddled sister. "Did your brother put ink on those drawings? Did you see him do it?"

Pine Bird stared up at her, brown eyes huge in her thin face.

Feeling like a she-bear looming over a kitten, Willa repeated the questions. The girl flung herself beneath the quilt and set to crying. Willa bent to yank the quilt aside, but Neil stopped her, taking her by the arm.

She pulled free. "You cannot let this go without—"

"I ken that," Neil said with exasperating calm. "But ye'll get naught by frightening the lass. Let me talk to her, aye?"

Willa stared down at the shaking mound of quilt, and into her heart came a gladness that this bad thing had come between Neil and the children. *Gladness.* Why should she feel...?

Because she was jealous. Because even as the bond she had seen growing between Neil and the children had troubled her, her treacherous heart had been longing for the same thing to happen with her.

How could she? Neil MacGregor might not understand the pain he was letting himself and the children in for, but *she* knew.

"Talk, then." Barely aware of what she did, she took the kettle and went to fill it at the spring, not looking once toward the horse shed.

Neil and Pine Bird were still in the corner when she returned, but the girl had come out from under the quilt.

Willa hung the kettle on the crane. From an ember buried in ashes, she kindled a blaze. Putting her back to them, she knelt to rummage through their food stores, having no notion what she sought. She wasn't hungry. How could she be when her children were dead?

Goes-Singing. Sweet Rain. How could she have gone on eating, breathing, while they did neither? She put a hand to her mouth. Behind her, Neil MacGregor murmured, his voice drenched in kindness. It made her heart both swell and ache. Then came to her ears the sweetest sound she'd heard since the winter brought its bleak curtain over her world. A small girl's giggle.

Her whole being clenched against the sound, even as her heart yearned toward it with a need so visceral she'd have moaned if grief hadn't closed her throat.

When a hand touched her shoulder, she jumped, pressing her fingers hard against her mouth.

"'Twas Owl, right enough. Maggie saw him do it."

Willa stood. When she neither spoke nor turned, Neil touched her again. "Willa, you could be kinder to them."

The soft-spoken words burned like hornets' stings. She shrugged off his hand. "It is better this way."

"Better, how? Willa, look at me. How is it better?"

It was time to speak the truth, if he would not see it for himself. "It is good, this wrong that has come between you. It will wound them less when you go." She turned to see his beautiful, uncomprehending eyes. "Listen. Your wrist is well enough. Your horse and all your things are returned to you. Why have you stayed?"

Surprise sparked in his eyes and something else he hid too quickly for her to read. Something that reminded her unwillingly of that morning, in the garden.

"D'ye think I'd leave Maggie, 'twas the slightest chance she needed my care?"

She forgot the garden in a rush of frustration. "Why do you call her that? They wish her to be called Pine Bird."

"Owl wishes it. *She* asked me to call her Maggie."

"When?"

"The day after Joseph brought them. You were in the field." He shook his head. "Why does it trouble ye so?"

"It's what her father called her. Do you mean to take his place? Or only win her heart with the kindness of a father, then crush it when you go?"

She had hurt him with her accusation. That was plain. She braced herself when he started to speak, but he checked, studying her far too closely for comfort.

"That isna why you're angry. Is it?"

"No? Then tell me why I'm angry, if you know so much."

"I'd rather you tell me," he said, with something of the gentleness he'd used with the girl. It was a powerful thing. Little wonder the child had not withstood it. It took all her will to turn from it now. Even when she put her back to him, he waited, as if hoping she might yet speak. But would it bring her daughters back to speak of them now?

Silence stretched, as brittle and wounding as broken glass.

"I'm away to the yard," Neil finally said. "I mean to have a talk with the lad, who, incidentally, you've more in common with than ye may think."

Shirt sleeves rolled high, sweat streaming, Neil set the length of wood on the block and raised the ax. It split beneath his blow with a satisfying *chunk*. Less satisfying was the painful twinge that shot through his wrist.

The chore needed doing. In Joseph's absence the task had fallen to

Willa. Watching her chop the wood that cooked his meals and lighted his work of an evening had done his pride little good, never mind till recently it had been a task beyond his managing. It wasn't the wisest thing to be doing even now. Any second he expected Willa to appear and scold him for it.

It was Owl who came to him. From the corner of his eye, Neil spied the boy edging from behind the horse shed to creep along the corral fence. He went on cutting wood, flinging pieces into a haphazard pile, even when he knew Owl had circled the cabin and stood behind him. He sent up a prayer for the lad to muster whatever he meant to say, and quick. His wrist couldn't endure much more.

"I'm big enough to use an ax."

Neil heaved the ax into the block and turned, pushing back damp hair as he wiped his brow. Owl shot a startled look at his forehead, then stood scuffing one of the moccasins Willa had made for him in the chip-spattered grass.

"So you are. Help me sort this lot first. Then I mean to have a talk with ye."

That sounded more ominous than he'd intended, but he let the impression of impending reprimand stand.

The boy moved with the alacrity of a slug, dragging out the stacking of wood beneath the porch, reminding Neil of himself as a lad, sent to fetch a switch from the hedgerow—to be used on his backside in punishment for some mischief. He couldn't say the thought of tanning Owl in like manner hadn't crossed his mind, but Willa was right. The lad wasn't his son, and he sensed there was something besides mischief or ill will behind what the boy had done.

A breeze freshened the air as he took a seat on the end of the porch, looking out past the chopping block and the clearing that terminated in a wall of thickening green.

Inside the cabin, Willa spoke, too low for him to catch her words. She was talking to the girl, at least. That was good. He heard the kettle lid clang and hoped, vexed though she was, she meant to make something for their dinner.

Her need to speak of her own children was a kind of wound, open and bleeding, one he longed to wash and anoint and bind. Joseph had said she would speak of it when she was ready. What if she didn't recognize her need? So much had happened since her return—rescuing him, finding her parents dead, her home and livelihood threatened. Now she had these children, whom tragedy seemed to follow like a cloud of midges, to care for.

Aye, he kent it was a fine line he was walking. He had to leave them all, and soon, if he ever meant to complete his work. That didn't mean he must harden his heart and pretend he didn't see the need screaming from this lad's sullen, angry eyes.

And anyway, 'twas far too late for the leaving not to tear a hole through his heart.

He patted the edge of the porch. "Sit with me, Owl."

The boy obeyed, putting a careful distance between them.

They sat thus while Neil sought for words suitable to address what had been done and why such a thing was never to happen again.

"Why do you hate Indians?"

The lad's question caught him off guard, jumbling his thoughts like words on a page. "What makes ye think that of me?"

Owl stared at his hands, clenching the knees of his ragged breeches. "Most white people do, but I thought, at first, you would be different. Then Tames-His-Horse went away and hasn't come back. I didn't think he would do that unless—"

"Unless I made him leave?"

"And you have that scar on your forehead. I saw a scar like that once, on a man who'd been half-scalped." Owl thrust out his chin.

Neil resisted the urge to brush the hair down over his brow. At least he was beginning to understand the eruption of hostility against him. The boy felt himself abandoned—surely not for the first time in his young life—and had been holding him responsible. He wasn't. Or didn't think he was. But neither of them had thought to tell Owl or his sister why Joseph stayed away. Francis Waring had delivered Willa's message; they'd been collecting meat from the islet for over a fortnight.

"You ken that arrow on the mantel, aye? 'Twas meant as a warning, Willa thinks. Joseph's stayed away in case the warning was for him. That doesna mean he's abandoned you. He'll take you where ye wish to go, when he's able."

The boy thought about that and seemed to accept it. "Still... He didn't seem to like you. I didn't think it was because you were white. She is white." He jerked his head toward the cabin. "And he likes her well enough."

The notion—even so innocently stated—was disquieting. He liked her all too well, did Joseph.

"I canna speak for what Joseph Tames-His-Horse may think of my race as a whole. As for me, aye, there was a time when a brown face was enough to cause me fear. But not hate. Never that. As for the fear, I've been taught to think differently of late."

A faint scrape of a moccasin tread was the only indication Willa had come onto the porch to bring in wood. So soft was the sound it might have been the cabin settling, or a tree in the nearby forest creaking in the breeze blowing steady now from the west, piling up a cloud bank and, blessedly, keeping the flies at bay.

He touched his forehead, high up near the line of his hair. "Would ye care to hear the telling of how I came by this scar?"

Owl shot him a look through tangled hair—he hadn't permitted Willa to put a comb to it. His eyes still held wariness, but his grip on his knees was no longer a clench. "I will hear it."

He was a lad, after all. And a story was hard to resist.

EIGHTEEN

Neil had left Philadelphia in the summer of 1778, intending to compile his field guide and add his own contribution to the accumulated works of botanists like Catesby, Colden, and the Bartrams, while doing his best to stay clear of the escalating hostilities between the colonists and the Crown. He wanted no part in that quarrel, if he could avoid it.

He'd decided to traverse the Catskills first, though others before him had covered that ground, spend the winter in Schenectady, then head north of the Mohawk in the spring.

"I followed the Schoharie Creek north," he told Owl, gazing over the cabin yard as he spoke. "There'd been a raid by the Tories along that stretch earlier in the year, but it seemed the war had shifted to other parts of the frontier. I passed through the Catskills unhindered and made my way west along the Cobus Kill. By mid-autumn, I was just south of the Mohawk River, in a settlement called Cherry Valley."

There, he'd learned of trouble farther west along the Mohawk. The British and the Iroquois had struck from Fort Niagara and the west, burning homesteads and skirmishing with colonials, but he'd thought keeping to the east where the militia presence was stronger would render him secure while the colonists took their revenge.

"The Americans burned the crops and houses at a place called Onaquaga, where some of the Tories and Brant's warriors took refuge. You'll ken the name of Brant?"

Owl nodded. "He's a big chief of the Mohawk."

"Aye. Well, 'twas presumed that strike against Onaquaga would be the last of the trouble for the year. I took on a few provisions in Cherry Valley, planning to head north to Schenectady."

It was then November. It rained that night, snowing by fits as the temperature dropped. He'd hoped to lodge within the fort, but the commander there denied civilians entrance despite rumors of an enemy-raiding party being sighted, saying his scouts would give fair warning, need be.

Next morning at dawn found Neil breaking camp in the woods to the east, when the first war shrieks raked the hair of his scalp on end, and the sputtering pop of musket fire crackled on the cold, wet air.

He was told—weeks later, when he was able to pay heed to such things—that had the fort alone been attacked, Cherry Valley's settlers might have fled to the woods or remained barred inside their homes unmolested. But the Indians, impatient with the British regiment's assault that failed to immediately take the fort, spread through the settlement, eager to avenge Onaquaga. So the burning began, the plundering, the scalping.

"I was keeping to the woods, trying to skirt the attack and head north, when I came upon a warrior with a white woman and two lassies in tow." Neil had had a musket. Though no great shakes at firing the thing, he'd been prepared to use it. "But the warrior called to me in perfect English, asking would I be so obliging as to take the woman and her daughters into my custody, for he'd other friends in the village he aimed to protect."

Too stunned to refuse, Neil had dismounted and swung the children onto his horse. "We picked a way through the wood, stopping at the crack of brush or a shout nearby, moving on when it seemed safe, me all the while praying the Almighty Lord to blind the eyes of any who would show us less than that Indian's mercy."

While he spoke, Neil had grown aware of the smell of stewing venison. His stomach growled, answered by a gurgling from Owl's.

The boy started to return his grin, then firmed his mouth and looked away.

Cap, back from who knew whence and freshly tangled in cockleburs, had come onto the porch and crept between them to lie against Neil's thigh. He lifted a hand to the collie's head but drew back when he saw Owl's small hand doing the same. It was the first he'd seen the lad show his dog affection.

"The woman later told me that warrior was Brant," Neil said, catching up the thread of his tale. Having met with a band of Cherry Valley refugees a mile to the north, he left his charges in their care, to continue toward Schenectady. He'd been shaken, true, but he'd made it out of Cherry Valley alive and surely—surely—this squabble between the colonies and the Crown would be settled before the spring. "*Homo proponit, sed Deus disponit.* Man proposes, but God disposes."

"If you got away from Cherry Valley," Owl interrupted, "how did you get that scar?"

"I'm coming to that. I did get away. I just didna get far."

Among the band of refugees hiding from the attack was a young Oneida hunter who offered his service as a guide. He was vouched for as a friend to the Americans, as were most of the Oneida.

"So he proved, till we ran across a band of Tory Indians still bent on plunder." At which point his guide had experienced an alarming turnabout of allegiance. "All I mind is a screech in my ear and a blow to my head. I came to on the ground, in the midst of losing my scalp."

He'd come to screaming, sensible of what was being done to him, just as a rifle ball took his erstwhile guide in the chest. They'd both fallen back into the mud, whereupon he'd lost consciousness again, learning later he'd been rescued by a party of militia come too late to aid Cherry Valley, but soon enough to rescue one hapless naturalist.

"I was taken to Schenectady, laid out senseless in a wagon. I'm told I came nigh dying, but I canna call it to mind. There's a great lot of it—weeks—lost to me. Something was knocked awry," he said with a tap to his skull. "More than just my memory. Some things that came easy to me once, they're beyond me now."

Not until he attempted to pen a letter to Dr. Rush, and his benefactors in Philadelphia, apprising them of his situation, had he discovered the worst damage wrought upon him by that blow to his head. He closed his eyes briefly, recalling the horror of finding that he, a man of scientific study, fluent in the classic languages, could no longer read or write the simplest phrase—in any language.

"Things like reading?"

He looked at the boy, surprised. "How did ye ken that?"

"I've seen how she…Miss Willa…helps you with your work." The color deepened in Owl's dusky cheeks, but his gaze held steady. "I'm sorry for putting ink on your drawings. I don't know why I did it."

Neil now had a good idea why and felt more than a twinge of conscience about it after Willa's accusation. He hadn't sought the attachment Owl's sister had formed with him, but true, he'd done nothing to discourage it. Would his leaving be as hard on her as Willa predicted? Or on this troubled man-child beside him, awaiting an answer to his apology? He had a thing or two he wanted to say to the boy, before he addressed the issue of his ruined drawings.

"If ye'll suffer a word of advice, lad. Dinna put your trust in men—not foremost. Men will come and go from your life, even those who love you, some before you're ready to see them go. But I'll tell you this I've learnt: the Almighty loves you more than any man could, and He willna forsake ye. Not ever. D'ye ken that?"

He said the words with his whole heart behind them, having learned them again so recently himself.

Owl kept his eyes cast down, his hands busy pulling burs from Cap's belly hair. "That sounds like what our father would say."

"Well, he'd be speaking truth. And, lad, I'm sorry you lost him and your mother. I'm verra sorry for that."

Moisture welled in the boy's eyes. He brushed hastily at a tear, then jerked his chin in affirmation and picked another cocklebur from Cap's fur.

A lump grew in Neil's throat. His voice tightened around it as he went on. "As for my drawings, I willna say it didna do me hurt, what you did to them, but I accept your apology, and I forgive ye."

The boy looked up, relief on his face. "Can I fix them?"

"No, lad. Some things we do canna be undone. But maybe in a day or so, ye'll come out with me, see can we find those plants to draw again?"

As the boy accepted his offer, Neil grew conscious of Willa standing behind them in the cabin doorway. The porch boards creaked as she stepped nearer.

"Owl, there is meat on the table for you. Come inside and eat with your sister."

Whether on account of repentance or hunger, Owl got to his feet without being told twice and went into the cabin, leaving Neil with his legs dangling off the porch, the breeze in his face, glad for what had just passed between them. Cap leaped down and crossed the yard to investigate something his keen nose had discerned.

Willa's petticoat brushed Neil's shoulder. The sight of beaded moccasins beneath a homespun hem no longer seemed an incongruous sight.

"Today in Shiloh, I remembered something."

Compared to their last exchange, her tone was warm. Neil felt a knot inside him uncoil. He put a hand atop the moccasin nearest him. She didn't pull it away. "What was that, then?"

"The name of the one my parents wrote their letters to. Tilda Fruehauf, Mama's cousin in Albany."

Neil drew breath into his lungs, feeling a peace all the more comforting for the day's turmoil. "We'd best be writing a letter, then, aye?"

Birds were singing in the woods, but he didn't think of their names in Latin. He thought of Willa, barefoot in the garden, tall and slender in her shift. He thought of that instant she'd turned to him with eyes that seemed to drink him in, a little startled, and he'd wanted to take her into his arms before the children woke and—

"We will do that," she said, and he caught his breath before he realized she spoke of the letter, not—

"First," she said, "eat the food I made for you."

Before he could rise, he felt her hand on the crown of his head, touching him lightly.

"You didn't tell me before that the guide who betrayed you was an Indian."

Her touch, her words, felt like a benediction.

In that moment Neil MacGregor—physician, naturalist, possessed for years by a purpose unshaken by war or injury or loss of faculty— sensed something at the center of his being shift, like a compass needle turning to point in an unforeseen direction, toward a new purpose, a new path, at the end of which, he thought he could see her standing.

He was reaching up to catch her lifting hand, lips parting to spill to her what he had but half-glimpsed, when the report of a gun shattered the moment, silencing the unnamed birds.

NINETEEN

T he shot was too distant to deduce its origin. Neil thought it came from the west, toward Shiloh, a hunter maybe, and naught to do with them. Or with Joseph, the name that had obviously seared through Willa's mind. She wouldn't be dissuaded from making a trek to the islet. "To see if he is there, or a fresh kill, then I will know he is safe."

She took the travois.

Neil put food on a plate and sat at the table with the children, said a blessing over it and them, kept praying, and forgot to eat.

Willa returned after dark, dragging a butchered elk wrapped in its great hide. Neil met her in the yard and helped her bring the meat inside, to begin the task of cutting it for jerking.

The children helped but soon tired. Willa hauled water for them to wash. Afterward they lay down, Cap at their feet with his nose pointed toward the tantalizing meat. Willa and Neil talked softly into the night while they saw to the bloody task, using both table and hearth, rewarding Cap for his restraint with the occasional scrap.

"I searched the lakeshore," she told him, intent upon the knife in her hand as she sliced the dark red meat and piled it on the hide, spread fur down across the table. "There were only Joseph's tracks and his horse's leaving the islet. Those I lost with the light. The shot must have been a hunter's."

As I told ye, he thought, but held his tongue.

It was as well he did so.

Near midnight the task of preserving the meat was as complete as they could make it without daylight to build the fires for drying, when Cap sprang awake, trotted to the door and growled.

"I dinna hear—," Neil started to say, when the ruckle of a horse came, an instant before a *thump* reverberated through the boards under his feet. Cap erupted into ear-splitting alarm. The children started up with frightened cries. Neil grabbed the collie, muffling its noise.

Musket at the ready, Willa raised the bar and opened the door.

Joseph Tames-His-Horse, soaked in blood from the waist down, fell inward at their feet.

The musket ball had taken him in the side, missing bone and vitals, best as Neil could tell, but hadn't made an exit. He felt the bulge of it beneath the skin where Joseph's lean waist curved around to his back. "Right, then. I'll have to remove the ball before I can stop this bleeding. Willa, you'll need to hold the candle near. Owl, can ye help hold him still while—"

"No need." Joseph's words were strained, but Neil thought he caught amusement on the stern face of Willa's clan brother. "Do what you must. I will not move."

Neil raised a brow at the big Indian, lying on his side near the children's pallet, breechcloth and legging stiff with drying blood. "I'll have heard that before, aye?"

He directed Owl to sit on Joseph's opposite side, ready to take him by the shoulders if need be. He had his medical case open beside him, a pile of linen scraps, a bowl of water, a clean knife, a threaded needle ready.

"Willa?" He looked to the hearth where she'd been mixing a dressing of comfrey and burdock. She brought that now in a gourd bowl. The beeswax candle she'd lit shed better light than the tallow stubs they usually burned. She knelt beside him, impatiently whipping aside her petticoat. With one hand she held the candle close, with the other made ready to press a linen wad below the spot Neil indicated.

With Maggie behind him on the pallet, Owl watching him across Joseph's shoulder, Neil felt again for the embedded ball, wiped the area with a dampened cloth, and made his cut. It was done so quickly even

Willa gasped. The ball popped from the lips of Joseph's flesh and landed in Neil's palm in a bright red smear.

Blood welled from the small incision. Willa pressed the linen to it. "Good?" she asked.

"Aye. Just so." Neil took the candle and set it on the floor between them. He checked the ball carefully, determining it was whole.

As promised, Joseph hadn't so much as winced. Nor did he as Neil closed the incision with two neat stitches, leaving it partially open to drain. He took the grease Willa held out to rub onto the skin around it and the cleaned entry wound, before she applied the dressed poultices. Together they wrapped Joseph's midsection in linen to hold them in place.

Not until he helped the Indian sit up with his back against the wall did it occur to Neil how few words he and Willa had exchanged as they worked. "Ye did well," he told her now. "We'll watch for infection for a few days, while he lies about underfoot and you feed him full of elk."

"And make a new set of leggings," Willa added wryly.

Joseph grunted in amusement, then noticed the children staring, one to either side of him. "It will be well. You may sleep and not fear for me."

"Aye," Neil said mildly as he checked the bindings to be sure all the shifting about hadn't disturbed them. "You play the stoic brave like ye were born to it."

Joseph leveled him a look. "It is a thing that can be taught, if you wish to learn."

Willa rolled her eyes, in no mood for humor—or the tension it veiled. She wiped the musket ball clean, then stood and pinned her clan brother with a forbidding stare. "Who did this to you?"

Joseph glanced at the listening children. Willa made a huffing noise and retreated to the table, where she began cleaning up the mess left from the butchering. She set a kettle full of the meat to stew and wrapped the rest in the hide to deal with come morning. Which wasn't far off.

Silence stretched in the cabin's front room. Maggie curled onto her side and, despite the night's excitement, lost the battle with sleep. Neil gathered up his medical box and set it on a block chair, then put the blood-soaked linen scraps into what remained of the water in the bowl, to be scrubbed out later.

He was exhausted but too keyed up to sleep. Willa seemed in the same predicament. She scrubbed the table and fetched fresh water from the spring. Cap, put from the cabin during the surgery, came in with her. The collie gave Joseph a thorough sniffing over, then settled in a compact ball next to Owl, who sat wide awake, staring at them each in turn, his gaze settling lastly on Neil.

"How did you know to do that?"

At the table, Neil passed a hand over his face and blinked. "Do what, lad?"

Owl nodded at Joseph. "How did you know where to find the ball under his skin and get at it like you did?"

"I kent what to do because I went to university to learn such things, in a place called Edinburgh. I assisted a physician called Dr. Graham, there and in Philadelphia. After Cherry Valley, in Schenectady, I served as a doctor when needed."

So he had done—as well as a man could who had recovered in body, if not thoroughly in mind.

He'd hoped the answer was sufficient to satisfy the boy's curiosity, but Owl looked no more ready to sleep than moments ago. "Were you called Dr. MacGregor?"

"Aye, lad. I was so. Though lately I've spent more time with plants than patients."

The smell of blood—human and game—seemed of a sudden thick in the air. Neil rose and returned his medicine case to his room. While there, he fetched his Bible from its place in his bags. Willa had taken a seat at the table when he returned. Exhaustion shadowed her eyes, but when she saw the book in his hand, her gaze lighted. "Is that a Bible?"

"Aye. I havena read from it in some while, ken. Would ye care to? Read for us?"

Willa's glance went to Joseph. Hearing a small intake of breath, Neil turned to see him settling himself more comfortably against the paneled wall. Joseph caught him watching, and came near to smiling. "Even a warrior feels pain."

"There's laudanum, if ye wish it."

"No." Joseph canted his head, eying him. "Why do you not read your Bible?"

"He cannot," Owl answered for him. "An Indian—an Oneida—pretended to be his friend, then hit him over the head and tried to scalp him. It hurt him in his brain, and now he cannot read or write."

A twitch of brows was the only indication of Joseph's surprise, though Neil felt himself under a keener appraisal.

"I am half Oneida," the Indian said. "Small recompense it is for another's wrong, but I will read to you now, if you wish it."

Not to save himself could Neil tell if the man meant to mock him or not, but he handed the Bible over.

Owl watched the exchange, staring now at Joseph. "Are you a praying Indian?"

Joseph leaned his head back and narrowed his eyes to slits. The firelight barely reached him where he sat against the far wall, but the flickering light of the candle still burning beside him on the puncheon floor showed his face drawn with pain.

"When I was not many years older than you are now," he told the boy, "my father sent me to his Oneida people, to a town called Kanowalohale. A white man called Samuel Kirkland had come there to teach the People some of his English ways. My father wished me to know some of this learning and to know my Oneida kin in the south. That is why I was sent."

He shared a glance across the room with Willa, one that softened the angles of his face. "But Kirkland also taught about his God—the

Great Good God from this Book—and His Son who lived a short while as a man, called Jesus. Some of His words I had heard from the French black robes in the north, but some of it was new to me. The part about repentance—a changed heart—that was new. I listened for a long time before I began to know in *my* heart that Kirkland's words were true."

Joseph laid the Bible on his lap, drew the candle closer, and began to turn the pages, stopping near the middle—Psalms, Neil guessed. As the thin pages rustled and the fire sparked, his curiosity mounted. He made no suggestion, wanting to know what text an Indian would choose to read of his own free will.

Owl lay down beside his sleeping sister, eyes shining in the candlelight, half-lidded now.

Joseph found the passage he sought and began in a measured cadence, his voice barely touched by the pain that must be searing his torn flesh. "'He that dwelleth in the secret place of the most High shall abide under the shadow of the Almighty. I will say of the LORD, he is my refuge and my fortress: my God; in him will I trust. Surely he shall deliver thee from the snare of the fowler, and from the noisome pestilence. He shall cover thee with his feathers, and under his wings shalt thou trust: his truth shall be thy shield and buckler—'"

Joseph broke off, hissing in a breath. Neil waited, but when Joseph didn't continue, he picked up the passage from memory.

"'Thou shalt not be afraid for the terror by night; nor for the arrow that flieth by day; nor for the pestilence that walketh in darkness; nor for the destruction that wasteth at noonday.'"

He stopped when Joseph again opened his eyes.

"'A thousand shall fall at thy side,'" the Indian took up, "'and ten thousand at thy right hand; but it shall not come nigh thee. Only with thine eyes shalt thou behold and see the reward of the wicked.'"

In the silence following, Joseph stared long at Willa, his love for her unguarded on his face. Neil felt at once grateful…and more deeply stabbed with jealousy than he had any right to be.

He reminded himself of the obligations that should—that must—take him far from that cabin on Black Kettle Creek. At least for a time. Which seemed only to make the feeling worse. What he longed for was to be alone with Willa, to tell her of that possibility he'd glimpsed earlier, to confirm whether she had seen it too.

Joseph's dark eyes flicked to him, as if he could sense the tug of war going on inside Neil's soul. Neil looked away, at Willa, but her eyes were guarded, reflecting only firelight.

She rose from the table to spread a blanket over the sleeping children.

TWENTY

The fires in the yard were sending up good smoke. Willa had built them of green hickory laid over embers from the hearth, above which elk strips lay on trellises constructed of peeled poles. Soon the sun, just topping the trees, would lend its aid to the drying.

Willa lifted her face to its warmth, a burnished glow against her eyelids. Her hair and clothing smelled of smoke. Her mouth tasted of it. Longing for a wash in the spring runnel, even more for her loft pallet, she bent to check the nearest strip, pinching it between thumb and forefinger. Still too supple.

She looked toward the field where the corn now stood waist high in some spots, sheltering young squash plants and bean vines. The children's dark heads bobbed among the green stalks as they called to each other or whooped at the crows taking wing before them like drifts of blackened ash. The girl's leg was healing well.

The man responsible for that healing emerged from the smoke with reddened eyes and a mouth that smiled at her, showing his good teeth.

"Go and rest, Willa. You hardly slept at all last night."

He looked tempted to drop to the ground between the fires and take his own counsel. They were a sight, all but staggering with exhaustion, their faces, necks, and hands smeared with rendered grease—as were the children in the field—to ward off biting flies. Neil had balked at the smelly stuff, but when he saw how well it worked as a repellent, he'd given in and let the girl anoint his face and neck, making her giggle at the faces he had pulled.

"I ken how jerked meat looks when done," he said now. "I'll watch it—and the weans," he added, as a happy shriek came from the field beyond the scrim of trees.

Weans. Maybe it was exhaustion, but his word for the children struck her as funny. She was astonished to hear a giggle escape her own lips. It died when Neil stepped closer. Even with them red from sleeplessness and smoke, the pull of his eyes was strong.

She stepped back. "I will go in."

Her blood thrummed, warming her face as she shut herself within the cabin. She waited while her eyes adjusted to the dimness. Joseph was sitting against the wall, legs outstretched, Neil's Bible open on his lap.

Willa swayed, near to reeling with the need for sleep, but this was the first moment alone they'd had. Who could say in such a crowded cabin when one would come again? She crossed the room to stand before him. "It is time to tell me where you were and what you were doing to end up with a bullet in your side—though I think I know."

Joseph leaned his head back to look up at her, rounding his eyes in mock surprise. "Sit first. If you topple onto me, it will do my wound no good, big as you are."

He reached up a muscular arm and grasped her greasy hand. Though she wanted to give him a smarting remark, she sank down beside him and leaned her head against his bare shoulder, too lead weighted to pull her hand from his. He smelled of buckskin and blood, though it was hardly detectable beneath her own stink.

"Now you can tell me what I was doing."

She ignored his teasing tone. "You went near Shiloh and got yourself spotted."

"Why would I do that foolish thing?"

Joseph passed his thumb across the back of her hand. She closed her eyes, turning her palm over in his. He pressed the pad of his thumb deep into tired muscles, making her want to groan.

"Because you think your deserter is in Shiloh. Or nearby." The cabin floor made her backside hurt. She shifted, finding no comfort. "Is he?"

Joseph's thumb stilled. "I have seen him, coming and going from the place where he lives and works."

That could be many a man. "Is he the one who shot you?"

"That was another, but they live in the same place. A big man—bigger than me, maybe. Pale hair."

A spurt of alarm roused her. She sat up straight but was too surprised to speak Richard's name before Joseph added, "It is for that man the deserter is working. Tending horses."

"Aram Crane," Willa said, not bothering to clarify that it was for Richard's father he worked, for she saw recognition of the name in Joseph's face.

"How do you know this?"

"Neil told me—only he does not know that he did so. He does not know you are hunting a man."

"Then how is it he told you?"

"I am getting to that part," she said, cross and sounding it because she was so tired and worried. About so many things. "It was that place I keep hearing so much about: Cherry Valley. Neil was there when it was attacked, right before he was hurt by that Oneida. Crane said that he was there too, but he said things about the British attacking that made Neil think he might have been on their side of it, though he seems to be pretending otherwise."

"And so you guessed he was the man I sought." Joseph had begun kneading her hand again. She blinked and settled back against him, unable to resist relaxing despite the importance of what they were speaking about.

"It is true," he went on. "Crane was there as a soldier with the troops attacking the settlement. He is English born. Is that not apparent by his speech?"

"No," she murmured, then remembered the trace of an accent she'd thought was likely British. "Not so much. He must work to sound not English. How long has he been gone from his place at Niagara?"

"Since the autumn. I spent some time then looking and found some

Oneidas—good ones—who told me of a red-haired Englishman in German Flats, but they also said this man had left that place with settlers and gone north up the West Canada. It was coming on for winter, and I thought if he went to a settlement, he might well keep there. It was a chance I took, but there were other things I needed to do."

"Look for me?" She'd closed her eyes but could hear the smile in his voice.

"Yes. And bring in meat for my family."

With what remained to her of thought, she considered that it would be a good thing—for her—if Joseph removed Aram Crane from Shiloh. Though it might not prove an easy task. Crane was a killer of Indians, a dangerous man. And now that Richard had seen Joseph lurking…

"Will you tell the Scotsman?" Joseph asked, interrupting her bleary thoughts.

"Do you think he would try to stop you if he knew?"

"I do not know enough of him to say. But what he does not know, he cannot tell."

Willa's eyelids fluttered. The cabin swam in her vision. "I am learning to know him. He would do what is right. He has a good heart."

But she didn't want to think about Neil MacGregor's qualities or the warmth that filled her when she thought how he hadn't hesitated to help another Indian, perhaps saving his life. Had he taken her words about looking past a man's skin to heart, or had she misjudged him? Had she looked at his white skin and made her own presumptions?

She didn't know, but she felt ashamed of those words spoken on the road to Shiloh now.

"I will not tell him if you do not wish it," she hurried to say, but it was too late. She had said too much about Neil, and Joseph had noticed.

"It is different between you, from when I first found you here."

Willa lifted her head from his shoulder, feeling it sway on her neck. "What is different?"

"He grows to care for you." The weight of bullet lead was in Joseph's voice. In her chest too, of a sudden.

"He has helped me. As have you." Evading his gaze, she rested her head on his shoulder again. "I do not care about the British or what they want with the men who flee their forts. I would be happy to see Crane gone. But, Joseph, you have already been shot. Is there no other way to provide for your family?"

She felt his chest heave, then his wince as the sighing hurt his wound. She'd nearly drifted asleep against him before his voice roused her again. "There is one thing that would turn me from this path. If you leave this place and come west with me, I will let that man alone and never again be a dog to fetch for the British."

Protest rose in Willa's mind, but before she could decide how to again refuse him, she remembered something else she needed to tell him. "Anni said a thing to me that I think you will want to hear."

"What is that, my sister?"

She tried not to hear the sadness in his voice—sadness that she had not given him the answer he had long sought. "There is to be a council, some sort of peace talk, between the Longhouse nations and the Americans, at Fort Stanwix. It is about their lands here, I think."

"What else?" Joseph murmured. Her cheek rose and fell with the deep breath he drew. "When is it to be?"

"At the end of summer... I do not know exactly."

"Did she say whether Thayendanegea would be there?"

"Thayendanegea?" Willa said, or tried to say. She could not remember whether Anni had mentioned Brant by name or not, and she was too weary to make more words.

She felt herself sinking down and down, with Joseph's hand warm and heavy on her head.

◆

That was how Neil found them, coming in to retrieve the bark containers Willa meant to store the jerked meat in. He'd hoped she'd be asleep, just not in the lap of Joseph Tames-His-Horse, who looked at him with a faint smugness in the set of his mouth.

"I tried to lift her."

Neil crossed the cabin. "Dinna try it again. You'll undo all my work to patch ye up last night." He squatted to get his arms under Willa, grunting as he got his knees under him and pushed to his feet. Her long body sprawled across his sagging arms.

"Not exactly dainty, is she?"

Joseph grinned at that, rubbing his legs as though they'd lost feeling.

Neil eyed the ladder on the far side of the hearth. There was no hope of his climbing to the loft. "I'll put her in my bed."

Not till he'd wedged them both through the doorway to the back room did it strike him how Joseph might interpret that intention. He was the one grinning as Willa's head lolled and her eyelids fluttered open. Her voice slurred with fatigue. "Wha...?"

Neil grunted again with the strain as he lowered her to his blanket roll. "You're going to sleep if I have to tie ye hand and foot, that's what. Hush now, and do as I bid."

Amazingly she did, going limp even as he drew his blanket over her. He knelt, looking at her by the light from the papered window. After days in the fields, the sun had lightened her hair. It flowed like bright hanks of silken thread—brown, copper, and gold all spilled and tangled.

He lifted a strand and brushed it against his lips, before hurrying a little guiltily from the room.

To Tilda Fruehauf,

    I am Wilhelmina, daughter of Dieter and Rebecca, writing to you. You will know about me that I was Taken and I have lived with

the People north of here many Years and I was not Unhappy there but
for a while at First, and at the end. I am come back now to Shiloh but
here are no longer my Parents and I do not know about the Land.
There are men who say Papa did not side for the Americans but the
British. I do not believe this and I am writing to ask if you Know
if this is True or a Lie. If it is a Lie against Papa do you have a Letter
written in his Hand that will make it Plain to show these Men who
wish to take away Papa's Land from me? And where is Oma? I am
hoping for Word from you soon if you are still alive.
  Your Cousin,
  Willa Obenchain

A few days after the meat was jerked, Neil MacGregor braved the black
flies to ride into Shiloh and see the letter Willa had penned to her mother's
cousin added to the post bound for Albany. He returned with a smoked
ham, a gift from the MacNabs. As Willa squatted at the hearth to slice
enough to feed them supper, she dared to let herself feel hopeful about the
land for the first time since Richard rode into her yard and made his
threats, and she learned about the land auction.

Hope was tempered a few mornings later when she spotted Francis
skulking near the cabin. He came to her with a lip split open and an eye
swollen shut.

Later in the day, Richard came to call.

The children burst from between the cornstalks, panting from running, and found her crouched low, inspecting the squash plants. At their
breathless announcement of a rider on the track, she stood to look, and
there was Richard sitting on his blazed horse at the field's edge, looking
back across the distance at her.

"Go to the cabin," she told the children. When they didn't move, she
sharpened her voice. "Owl, take your sister inside."

The boy's eyes flicked to the motionless horseman. "Do I tell them?"

"Tell Neil you are hungry, that I sent you in. I am sure it's true."

"He's always hungry." Pine Bird gave her brother's arm a shove. Ignoring her, Owl looked doubtfully at Willa but took his sister's hand and did as she bid.

She watched until they were well away through the rustling stalks, then bent for her musket and began the long walk out to meet Richard, waiting where the field met the woods' edge and the track to Shiloh. He dismounted as she neared, his face impassive.

It wasn't his expression Willa sought to read, but his hand. The right one, holding his horse's reins. She expected the knuckles to be broken—by the bones of his brother's face.

"I wasn't m-meant to tell." It was all she'd coaxed from Francis to explain his injuries, while Neil raided her garden to make a salve to treat them.

It was enough. The graves. What else could it be that Francis wasn't meant to tell? This was her fault. Her fault for telling Anni about the graves, for mentioning Francis. Anni must not have considered the graves a secret she was meant to keep from Charles, who must have let it slip to Richard. Or had Anni been the one to let it slip?

Oh, Anni. Willa felt sick in the pit of her stomach as she reached Richard, who wore riding gloves against the black flies and hadn't removed them when he dismounted. A kerchief covered his neck, and high boots protected his legs. She was dressed in leggings and her deerskin skirt, her long stroud tunic. Bear grease smeared her face and hands. Richard's nostrils flared when she stopped.

Being so near him unnerved her. There was about him that barely contained animal energy, as if something feral lurked just beneath his skin. Something that longed to break free and—

"The crop looks well," he said.

He didn't say she looked well, yet he hadn't taken his eyes off her since she stood into his view. They bore into her now.

"It is a good crop. The land is rested."

Silence hummed with the chitter of cicadas, the scold of a jay, some other bird's more melodious call. She watched Richard's eyes, thinking them pale and cold, accustomed now to Neil MacGregor's warm, drenching blue.

Richard flicked a look along the track, though the cabin could barely be seen from that distance with the trees in full leaf. "Those children I saw with you... They're Mohawks?"

"Yes."

His gaze snapped back. "Yours?"

At least Anni had not related everything she'd shared.

"They are in my care for now."

Richard waited, but she had no more to say. It wasn't a warm day, but the air was thick and moist. Sweat made rivulets down the sides of his face. His throat moved as he swallowed. He had something to say to her. She wished he would say it. "The crop looks well, and the children look like they could be mine. Did you ride all this way to tell me things I know?"

That earned her a grimace, which he quickly wiped from his face. "I'm told you've found graves in the woods, that you think they're your parents'."

She tilted her head. "Who told you this?"

Richard raised a gloved hand as if to brush away the question. "I didn't come here to make trouble for you, Willa. I came to say I'm sorry about your parents."

She looked at him hard, wondering if she could trust this show of sympathy at all.

"I wish they'd fled to Canada."

"Rather than be murdered?"

Richard's jaw clenched, but he simply nodded.

"On that at least," Willa allowed, "we can agree."

He took a step toward her, but a cloud of black flies chose that moment to descend upon his horse. The animal tossed its head. Richard whipped off his hat and swatted at them, which did not please his horse any more than had the flies.

Willa watched him, trying to puzzle him out. She half-wished for the Richard who'd thundered into her cabin yard, the one who threatened and lashed out with his fist. This Richard was harder to read. Had he known her parents were dead? Had he anything to do with their deaths? Or concealing those deaths?

"You should go," she said. "Your horse is unhappy here."

Seeming to concur, Richard clapped his hat on his head and swung into the saddle, which creaked beneath his weight. "I also came here with a proposal for you—for how things might carry on between us after the auction, provided mine is the highest bid, of course."

Bristling at the idea of *things* carrying on between them, she bit down on the impulse to tell him about the cousin in Albany, or the letters that might have been saved. About unmitigated proof.

"What proposal?"

"I'm willing to let you go on living here. You can farm the land or plant an orchard—keep bees, if it suits you. I'll only ask a percentage of whatever you raise."

"As your tenant?"

"If that's as you want it." Richard stared at her with a look of speculation that made her queasy, as if he were envisioning her worth in the amount of milled corn and strings of beans he could expect to gain. But his next words banished that queasiness in a flush of fear.

"I saw an Indian in the woods, a few days back. On the Colonel's land, very near the house. I shot at him to drive him off. Don't know for sure whether I hit him, but I think so."

Willa watched his eyes, keeping her face still as stone. "Why do you tell me this? I have seen no Indians in the woods."

Richard held her in his scrutiny overlong, as if he took leave to doubt her, but finally he looked past her again toward the trees that hid the cabin. His mouth firmed in a harder line. "Is he there still?"

Fear washed over her again. Her thoughts were still dizzied with alarm over Joseph and whether Richard suspected her of sheltering him. "Who?"

Richard's mouth twisted. "The exalted member of the American Philosophical Society. Who did you think I meant?"

Before Willa could speak, from the trees behind Richard came the *snick* of a rifle being cocked.

"Aye. He's still here."

Willa stepped back, startled, and nearly raised her musket to the ready, though she knew the voice at once.

Richard swung his horse to face Neil MacGregor, standing beside an alder tree, Joseph's rifle held across his chest, pointing off into the woods. He must have circled around from the cabin, keeping all the while in cover, with such stealth even Willa hadn't sensed his approach. For a moment, she was irrationally furious that Owl had disobeyed her. Then she was as deeply relieved.

Neil didn't release the rifle's hammer. "Why are you here?"

"With a truer purpose than I reckon you can claim." The words were kept from belligerence by a wry edge. "I had a proposal to make. I've made it. I expect you'll hear all about it." Sparing her a last unreadable look, Richard touched his hat. "Think on it, Willa."

Richard kicked his horse into a canter, headed back to Shiloh. Leaving Willa staring at Neil.

He lowered the rifle's hammer, then propped it over his shoulder at rest, arching one thick brow at her. "A proposal?"

Willa shook her head. "Later. Where is Joseph?"

She looked around, expecting him to step from the trees as well—and ready to scold him for being on his feet when he did. When he didn't, she turned back in time to see the play of emotion cross Neil's face—hurt and embarrassment resolving into reluctant amusement—and she realized she'd wounded his pride in assuming him incapable of such woodcraft on his own.

"That is Joseph's rifle," she said. "That is why I asked."

He came out of the trees. "Aye. No doubt he'd have come here with it in my stead, if he could."

"Better that he didn't. He mustn't let himself be seen."

Neil stopped close beside her and touched her arm. "True, but that isna why he didna leave the cabin. He's taken a fever, Willa. You'd best come back with me now."

OHIARI:HA

Ripening Time—June

TWENTY-ONE

S ometimes he saw their faces or felt their hands on his burning flesh, turning him, bathing him, prodding his side where the ball had torn through him. More often their voices were all that reached him through the fiery veil.

"It is three days. Is there nothing more to do? Tell me what to do."

"You can go up to the loft and sleep."

"No."

"Ye canna help him by making yourself ill."

He took the sound of their words deep into his heat-ravaged flesh. Not only the words, but what lay beneath, emotion vivid enough to flay him. Her fear and helplessness. The Scotsman's frustration and tenderness. Both of their stubborn resolve.

"I willna close my eyes till you've opened yours again. The children are by to help, if I need it."

"You will call me if he wakes?"

"I promise."

He did not wake. His body was not through waging war with the flames, though every parched and aching fiber of him cried for water. His mouth must have made the word. A cup rim pressed against his lips. A strong hand supported his head. Cool relief on his tongue. He swallowed. Blue eyes swam in his vision.

The voices again. They troubled him, tethered him. The small frightened voice of the girl. The boy, masking worry with anger. The voice of the Scotsman. *Her* voice, scratched with weariness, speaking of a letter on which all her hope seemed to rest—someone in the east who might yet live, who could claim her as kin, who might hold her fast to this place where he knew now he could never be with her, even if he threw aside all that made him one of the People and his soul survived such a scouring. The Long Knives would not let him be with her. Never in peace.

"Do you think it has reached Albany? Do you think she has seen it?"

"Aye, maybe. Far too soon yet to expect a reply, though."

"There will be one. I have been thinking... It is like a miracle that Oma's name is still in Maeve Keegan's mind, when so much else is gone."

"Aye, it may be the Almighty kept it there. But we dinna ken what's to come of it yet."

"I wish we knew. The waiting—it is hard."

"'Tis dashed hard. But here's what I ken—the Almighty Lord has a path for ye to walk, and a place in mind for ye to be. But whether or not that place is here, d'ye trust Him to lead you into whatever is best?"

It was a good question. Joseph longed to know her answer, yearned for it as his tongue again craved water. He wanted her to say she would be at peace wherever the Great Good God chose to lead her. But the fire in his bones leaped high and crackling, writhing between them. If she answered, he did not hear it.

Time lost meaning again, day and night an inseparable blur.

Another time when the fire was not so high, he almost woke—or maybe did. He sensed them all around him. The children, asleep on their pallet. The dog lying by the hearth where another fire burned. The Scotsman seated at the table, head cradled on folded arms; Burning Sky coming up behind him in her English clothes, standing silent, taking in his weariness. Burning Sky putting a hand to his shoulder. The Scotsman's head rearing up, his hand groping for hers, pressing it to his cheek where the beard had come in like a shadow.

She pulled away, but not quick enough. "Now it is you who must sleep."

Her eyes followed the Scotsman as he half-staggered to his room, and there was so much behind the green and the brown of them, so much she was trying not to feel. Was afraid of feeling.

Joseph let his eyes close, but the images festered, deeper than the wound in his side.

Day. Night. Voices.

"She was not well when last I saw her. She is tired with this baby."

"Go to her. Help her. He's been like this nigh a week."

"I cannot leave him. I will go to Anni when I can."

Later...

"Wake up, Mister Joseph. Please, wake up."

He woke up. Pine Bird's small hand lay soft against his face, and the touch was no longer cool. The fire in him had burned itself out. The Master of Life meant him to live yet a while.

Though he was of two minds about that, he smiled at the girl, whose face lit like a candlewick dipped to flame. In her pipe-song voice, she called to the others to come and see.

Everyone slept the sleep of the exhausted, except for Joseph Tames-His-Horse. He lay wakeful until the darkest hour, then tied on the new leggings Burning Sky had made for him and let himself quietly out of the cabin. The Scotsman's dog, used to him now, barely raised its head as he passed it on the porch. He found his bags and saddled the mare and led her to the clearing's edge, where he paused to catch his breath—he was weak—and let his gaze rest on the cabin where she slept beneath its roof silvered in starlight. The night air was clammy against his skin.

It was hard to leave her, but he did so in hope. That was the fever in him now. Hope. It seemed impossible to quench. And though he knew it was a risk, what he hoped was that if he went away, there would be no reason for the Scotsman to stay. No one he need heal with the medicines in his box. Maybe Burning Sky would see this; maybe she would heed that fear he had seen in her and tell the Scotsman to go his way, take his paints and his plant press and be about the business that had brought him here.

Maybe that Albany letter would never come.

Maybe in the end she and the children would return with him to Niagara, to the People. There she would be his sister. Never more than that. But with him always. He could swallow back the love that must not be. He could spend the rest of his life swallowing it back, to be near her.

That is what he told himself.

Even such frayed hope had the power to tether him to this dangerous place. He would wait a little longer to do the other thing he had come here to do, to see if this was how it would be with Burning Sky.

Ohiari:ha, the time of ripening, had come while he lay fevered. Leaf cover lay thick on the ridges now, good for the hiding and watching he must do. The deserter was careful, well surrounded by those for whom he worked, rarely alone on the stretch of road between the big stone house and the village, and always mounted. He might be wary now, fearing the Indian the big Yellow Hair had shot at but not killed. He would know that the British Army sent warriors of the People to bring back their deserters.

But there would come a moment, if Joseph was patient, when the mind of the man was easy, his safety taken for granted. All he needed was to be watching when it came. But he must have his full strength when it did.

There was that peace council Burning Sky had told him about, the one to be held at Fort Stanwix at summer's end. An idea about that council was forming in his mind. An idea that had to do with Thayendanegea and the deserter.

For now he would head toward that fort, posing as one of his father's Oneida people—at least to any whites he could not avoid. He would see if he could gather news of who was coming to this meeting. The journey there and back would give him time to heal. And when his full strength returned, he would do his work for the British. One last time.

TWENTY-TWO

They would be, Neil MacGregor had informed her, "two laddies gone a' plant hunting."

Owl appeared as taken with the notion of spending the following day traipsing the hills in search of likely flora to put in Neil's book as was the naturalist himself. Willa didn't voice her misgivings about the time he was spending with the boy as the pair poured over each item to accompany them: plant press, specimen tin, the paints, brushes, quills, clamshells, pencils, and paper nested inside the field desk.

Next they gathered provisions—a sack of elk jerky and a batch of dubious-looking cornmeal cakes Neil was minding on the hearth.

Pine Bird, crestfallen that it was to be a males-only excursion, hung by Neil's side, gazing at the things laid out on the table. Her wistfulness cut straight to Willa's heart, but no one was more surprised than she to hear herself say, "Let these *laddies* get themselves scratched and bug bitten hunting plants in the hills. You and I will visit Anni tomorrow. She has children. Twins."

Pine Bird raised melting dark eyes to her. "Two born together?"

"Yes. A boy and a girl. Would you like to see them?"

"Are they babies?"

"They are five summers."

Owl shot his sister a smugly superior look. "Even you are older than that."

Pine Bird raised her chin. "I want to see them."

"I want to see a bear," Owl said. "Or a wolf. No—a panther!"

Neil looked up from the hearth, brows raised. "Whoa, young man. I dinna recall *Felis concolor* being on the list of things *I* aim to see."

"Yes," Willa said, catching his look across the children's heads. "We have enough to contend with without inviting panthers into it."

The two laddies and the dog were away into the hills before Willa finished tidying breakfast next morning. From the porch, she saw Pine Bird out by the shed, feeding the goat grass cut from the old horse pasture. The girl had taken over the animal's care and in the process made a pet of it.

"Time to go!" At her summons the child dumped her last armful over the slatted fence. Grass cascaded over the chewing goat, leaving it sprinkled in green. Willa had replaced the falling-to-rags garment the girl came to them wearing. As Pine Bird reached the porch, she saw the child's new petticoat was stained at the knees.

The sight brought a lump to her throat. It was all too easy, as the days passed and the children stayed, to fall into mothering them. Far too easy. She must guard her heart.

"Let me do something with your hair," she said briskly. "Would you like a braid?"

Pine Bird nodded and presented the back of her head to Willa, who quickly sectioned and plaited the long strands. The child's hair wasn't a true black, like her brother's. Sunlight revealed sparks of brown, like it did in Neil MacGregor's hair, though the girl's was as straight as if it had been ironed. Willa tied the braid with a leather whang threaded with two blue beads—beads the same rich shade as Neil's eyes, she thought, as the girl swung her braid around to admire them.

What was all this thinking of the man and his looks? She must stop it. She was letting him as well as the children too close, letting herself become used to them.

That path to her heart was becoming dangerously clear.

She was silently berating her foolishness, reminding herself that all of them were meant to follow their own paths away from her—including

Joseph—and that their going was for the best, when Pine Bird turned her sweet smile up to her and said, "*Istah* put beads in my hair too."

Istah. It was the Mohawk word for *Mother*.

The ache took Willa in the center of her chest. For the time it needed to draw a ragged breath around it, the face of the girl raised to her changed, became a little browner, wider, the eyes a startling hazel green. Goes-Singing's face.

Willa blinked, and it was a stranger's child looking up at her again, brown eyes sparkling because someone had thought to put beads in her hair. *Because I thought of it.*

It was exactly the sort of thing to put her heart in greater peril. The sort of thing she should not be doing.

"Come." Willa stepped off the porch. "It is a long walk."

She wasn't keen on leaving the cabin and fields unguarded, but there had been no cause for alarm in the days since Joseph left them. No unexpected visitations. No arrows shot from hiding. No sense even of being watched. Still she was more than half-regretting this decision; other threats existed, deer and rabbit foremost among them. She would probably spend the next few hours imagining voracious teeth chewing and chewing at her crops.

But there was another reason for going into Shiloh—a letter to mail, tucked inside her pocket. They'd received no reply to the first letter sent to Tilda Fruehauf in Albany. Neil had urged her to be patient with the vagaries of the post, but had agreed sending a second letter couldn't hurt.

Such were the thoughts the girl interrupted as they strode along the shortcut to Anni's.

"Where did Mister Joseph go, and when will he come back?"

It wasn't the first time the girl had asked such questions. "He is away hunting or else tending to business of his own. I do not know how long he will be about it. He will come for you when he can and take you and your brother to Niagara."

She doubted such answers satisfied the child, but it was all the answer Willa could give. She'd found it hard to conceal her own distress and frustration the morning they woke to Joseph's absence. For a week, they had seen nothing of him, then twice in the past few days, a fresh kill had appeared on the islet.

She'd begun to think Joseph didn't mean to come back to them, or not before he regained his strength and fetched his deserter back to the British, now that he knew where the man was hiding.

When Neil had asked why Joseph left so abruptly, before he was fully healed, she'd had nothing to say. She had only her suspicion, one it would be unwise to share.

It is different between you, from when I first found you here.

Still, he might have bothered to tell her what he planned to do, how long he thought it would take him to do it. She couldn't hope to feed herself and the children through the winter, even if she still had a roof over her head. Neil MacGregor would be gone by then at least. In fact, with Joseph no longer there to tend, and the girl's leg healed, there was no reason for Neil to stay another day. But was he gathering provisions and making plans to be on his way? No. He was off prowling the hills with the boy.

Willa set her face in a frown as her strides devoured the path, thoughts fixed on the vexing whims of men.

"I hope Mister Joseph doesn't come back."

Pine Bird's utterance was in such opposition to Willa's thoughts, and the thoughts she'd assumed were behind the girl's question, that she broke her stride to look at the child, who'd been trotting to keep up.

"Why wouldn't you want Joseph to come back?"

Pine Bird lowered her eyes, too shy to answer, but as Willa started off along the path again, she felt small fingers curl around her own.

"My Lem's taken with that girl," said Goodenough, the dark skin of her face glistening as she lifted a pair of breeches from the boiling kettle.

It was wash day again at Anni's. Goodenough and the smith's wife, Leda MacNab, were already deep into the backbreaking chore by the time Willa and Pine Bird arrived, but now many hands were making light of the work.

Manning the rinsing bucket, Willa looked to the children playing an energetic game of battledore and shuttlecock, using a whittled cork adorned with a feathered topknot. They'd divided into pairs to bat the shuttlecock back and forth using wooden paddles. Willa had assumed Anni's Samantha would have paired up with Pine Bird, but it was Lemuel who'd latched on to her, showing her how the game was played.

"One, two, three, four, Mary at the cottage door!"

Willa smiled at the rhyme. It was the same one she and Anni had used as girls, a line uttered each time the shuttlecock was batted, the goal to race through as many verses as possible before the shuttlecock fell to earth.

"Five, six, seven, eight, eating cherries off a plate!"

Pine Bird had proved agile, and quick to pick up the rhyming.

"She is used to boys," Willa said to Goodenough. "Her brother is with Neil MacGregor, looking for plants to put in the book he's making."

"I heard Mr. MacGregor telling Gavan about his field guide." Leda MacNab handed Willa a scrubbed frock, pausing to watch the scene of noisy play across the yard. "She's a pretty child. What did you call her?"

"Margaret Kershaw." Willa had thought better of introducing her as Pine Bird, but hadn't expected the girl's bright smile upon hearing her English name spoken.

"Had a white daddy," Goodenough said. "Thought so, to look at her. How old she be?"

"Seven." The age Goes-Singing would have been in a fortnight.

"On the puny side of seven. She need feeding up."

"She does." Anni returned from spreading pieces of wash on the hedges in time to catch Goodenough's comment. "Did you see the size of her eyes, Leda? She's half-starved, the little thing."

"She is not a *thing*. She's a child."

Willa's words hung in awkward silence.

"I didn't mean—" Anni broke off with a wince, rubbing her belly.

Goodenough eyed her sternly, wet hands on hips. "Didn't I tell you to rest whilst we're here to give you the chance? I brought you out that chair. Sit, afore you bring on the pains again."

"I think I will." Anni lowered herself into the straight-backed chair set near the wash kettle. At six months along, the baby seemed healthy and vigorous, but already Anni had twice feared she was losing the child. Leda and Goodenough came to help with chores as they could. Willa thought she should do likewise, but it would mean leaving the fields untended far too often for *their* health. Unless Neil stayed a little longer...

No. She must not find excuses for that. It was time—past time—for him to go.

What if he had left before Joseph came to the cabin with a bullet in his side? she wondered. Even if she'd removed the ball herself, would he have taken a worse fever and died of it?

What if Anni's baby was born too soon and needed a physician's skill to help it live?

"Willa, I meant no offense." Anni's voice held hurt.

Willa fished a small petticoat from the rinse bucket and began to squeeze out the excess water. "I did not mean to snap at you."

"The heat has all our tempers on edge," Leda ventured.

Though early in the day, it was already warm, the air muggy enough to mold shifts and gowns to sticky flesh. A heavy rain in the night hadn't lifted the humidity. Thick clouds still overhung the sky.

"The Colonel stopped by the smithy yesterday," Leda said, filling up the silence. "He'd news about that treaty with the Iroquois, over to Fort Stanwix. It's going to happen around the first of September."

"I pray God they don't let the Mohawks come back," Goodenough said. "I can't see it coming to nothin' but bad, after everything."

Willa felt the women's gazes, as if they'd each suddenly remembered where she'd spent the past twelve years. Her own heart constricted, not because of the awkward silence, but for thinking of the refugees gathered around the crowded British forts, among them Joseph's family. Her own clan. Ought she to have abandoned them?

But what good would the presence of one more widow have done? Another mouth to feed, that was all she'd have been. At least here she could make shift to sustain herself, if she found a way to keep the land. But her heart ached for those who didn't have even an acre of land to call their own now, whose choice of sides in the war had cost them everything— and pushed aside the thought that her parents' choice might yet cost *her* everything.

In the absence of conversation, the children's voices intruded, high spirited, carefree. Willa wrung the petticoat and took it to the hedge. She was smoothing out its wrinkles when she looked past the mill below to the tracks that converged just above the cluster of cabins around the trade store and smithy.

Coming down from the west, the direction of the Warings' land, was a solitary rider, tall in the saddle. Richard. He saw her there on the ridge above the mill and reined his horse to a halt. Thrice the space of a stone's throw lay between them, and a rushing creek tumbling over the mill falls, yet she felt the scorch of his stare as if they stood at arm's length.

Richard touched his hat before turning his horse down the track. He didn't look back at her.

"There he goes, my sweet boy."

Willa started. Beside her Goodenough stood, holding a pair of little

Sam's breeches. Her dark eyes, usually so snapping in her handsome face, had softened and saddened as she watched the Colonel's eldest son riding into the village.

"Did you know Richard was there in Albany, that day the Colonel bought me for his missus?"

This was unexpected. Goodenough had never spoken of how she came to be the Warings' slave. As a girl, Willa had never thought to ask.

"He weren't much bigger than my Lem is now. Me, though, I was a strapping girl, long since taken off my mama. But when that wagon started rolling, taking me off to this wild place, I couldn't help looking back to Albany and crying my eyes out."

Goodenough pressed her lips tight, then made a noise through them that might have been laughter. "There we was, back of that wagon heaped with plenishings bound for the Colonel's house, with that blue-eyed boy-child staring at me blubbing into a wad of my skirt. And what you think that little towhead up and do? He grab my hand and don't let go till that wagon stop for the night."

Willa blinked, reminded of a small hand clasping her own. The irre-pressible sweetness. The pain.

Goodenough's voice sank like a fire settling as she looked downslope. "'It'll be all right,' he say to me. 'You'll see. You'll be good enough to please my mama.'" Goodenough laughed, soft and low. "I didn't give a jot then what might please his mama, but I never forgot 'twas out of kindness he said it."

Richard had reached the smithy, was dismounting from his horse. Willa looked away from him, eying the woman beside her. "He said you would be *good enough*?"

Goodenough smiled. "Miz Sarah Waring see me climb down from the wagon in her yard and ask my name. I tell her, 'Ma'am, yo' boy say I'm good enough. Reckon, then, I am.'" She waved a hand, as if her name were of no matter. "All the Waring babies was good babies, even that Francis with his odd ways. But Richard was the kindest to me. Nothing but sweet temper did I ever get from him."

Goodenough turned her face to Willa, who still found it surprising to look another woman eye to eye. "Now Francis, Anni, and Richard be all that's left us."

"And Lem," Willa said softly.

Goodenough met her look and smiled. "Mm-hmm." She looked again toward the distant smithy, the smile fading.

"I know the war done things to him," she said, and she wasn't speaking of Lem. "I know he's changed. But what he is now ain't what I see when I look at him. I see that boy in the wagon taking hold of my hand."

Willa couldn't see that boy, or even the youth she'd known, in the hulking form of the man lingering in Jack Keegan's store. Though she'd ignored him from the moment he stepped in behind her, she knew exactly where he was—over by the cloth bolts, fingering a length of calico. He was like a wolf, she thought, a hungry wolf skulking beyond the circle of her fire, menacing those who would help her, waiting for her vigilance to falter that he might rush in for a strike.

She tried to turn so he couldn't see what she was doing, but her scalp prickled as Jack took the second letter to Tilda Fruehauf and put it with the small collection of sealed missives waiting for the post rider's next visit.

She'd known Richard was in town. She'd seen him ride in. She should have waited for another day to do this. But she was already as far as Anni's and couldn't spare the time to come back again.

"I'll make sure it goes out with the next batch," Jack told her, casting a look behind her. Willa thanked him before turning on her heel for the door.

Richard stood behind her, blocking the way.

"Willa, are you sending that letter for your houseguest?"

She stiffened at the question. "It is my business. I do not have to tell you."

His eyes flared at her sharpness, then narrowed. "True enough, only I didn't think you had anyone to be writing to, after all this time."

She'd done the last thing she meant to do—aroused his suspicion. Now he thought she was doing exactly what she was doing, hiding something from him.

"I'm sure you've been thinking about my offer," he said, moving on to an even more grievous subject. "I was hoping you'd come to the house, that we might discuss it further—with the Colonel, of course."

Her fraying patience snapped. "You think you know all that concerns me—my thoughts as well, apparently—but you do not know me, Richard." She looked him in the eye, wishing she could drill her words straight through his skull. "I am not who I was when we were younger, and neither are you, and now I ask you to step aside so that I might leave this place."

Richard held her stare long enough for heat to blaze in her face, long enough that she wondered if Jack would intervene, or if she would have to shove Richard out of her path. But he shifted, giving her room to pass.

"By all means," he said with chilling courtesy.

She slipped past, trying not to touch him, and wasn't sure over the banging of the door and that of her own heart whether she imagined the words he muttered after her. An echo of her own.

Leave this place.

They'd stayed longer at Anni's than Willa had intended. Watching Pine Bird with the other children, drawn out of her shyness into spirited play, she hadn't had the heart to cut short their time together. But after returning from Keegan's, she'd been almost terse in collecting the child and heading for home, so rattled she'd taken the road instead of the path.

She slowed her step now. Pine Bird had fallen behind while she trudged ahead, vexation over Richard driving her pace.

A more welcome image sprang to Willa's mind as she paused to wait—one of Lemuel tagging after the girl, even when Samantha brought out her cornhusk dolls, turning to more feminine play, leaving Sam sitting on the porch glumly rolling his eyes. The memory made her smile.

Pine Bird raced to catch up. As she had that morning, the child reached for her hand. The fingers curled around Willa's were grubby now. So was the child's face.

"We must get you cleaned up and supper started. If you gather some eggs, I will..." Her words died as she caught a scent on the air, pungent, sharp in her nose.

Pine Bird looked up at her. "Smoke."

"Hen'en," Willa answered without thinking. She did smell smoke. Were Neil and Owl returned early from their roaming and getting their own supper?

The smell was too strong. They weren't far from the place where the woods ended and the cornfield began, but still too far to scent smoke from the cabin's chimney.

Up through the trees, a gray haze drifted, faint against the bits of sky visible. Something was burning that shouldn't be.

Willa dropped Pine Bird's hand to run.

TWENTY-THREE

The corn was burning, the northwest corner of the field, farthest from the cabin. Long green leaves whipped Willa's face as she raced through the hillocks toward the crackle of flames.

Behind her Pine Bird cried out, and she whirled to see the child sprawled among the squash plants.

"Stay back from this! You cannot help!"

The words were barely out of her mouth when she heard her own name shouted. Neil MacGregor came plunging from the smoke, soot covered, clutching the hoe. He grasped her arm, coughing out breath in ragged spasms. "We're cutting a break. I dinna think you'll lose it all."

As he spoke, he tugged her toward the thickest smoke. She saw what he was doing, digging up a swathe of the crop several yards out from where it burned. She yanked free.

"Where is the spade?"

Neil cupped a hand to his mouth and bellowed into the smoke, "Owl!"

Seconds later the boy came leaping over vines dragging the spade, face streaked with dirt, eyes round with excitement and fear.

Willa yanked the spade from his grasp. "Find your sister. Get her to the cabin. Wait—first get the buckets off the porch. Fill them at the spring."

"I did that!"

"Good. Do it again!"

Two buckets, a hoe, a spade—against a burning crop. But a green crop still moist with rain. Did they have a chance?

"Show me where you left off digging!"

Neil showed her, then ran to where Owl had been working.

Through thickening smoke Willa saw the flames devouring her sustenance, her tenuous hope. She hacked at more of it, tearing down the beautiful stalks, ripping out the beans, shouting with the effort, raging against the need. There had been rain in the night but no lightning. It was no accident, this fire. Who had started it? Richard had been in town. And why would Richard wreak such havoc after making his offer to let her live there as his tenant?

The fire's heat was scorching. Grasshoppers and beetles fleeing the flames struck her face and hands. Sweat stung her eyes. Her palms rubbed sore as with the spade she attacked the earth, severing cornstalks, hurling them away, bending and lunging between hillocks like a warrior in a maddened dance.

Owl's slight figure rushed past. The boy hurled water against the creeping flames and made off again with the buckets.

It would not be enough.

Yet she kept tearing at the earth and its bounty, until her arms and shoulders screamed with the effort, until every breath was a searing in her lungs, a booming in her head. Until a warm, fat splash struck her face.

Willa staggered, caught herself...and listened.

The booming wasn't in her head but above her in the darkened clouds. Relief so profound it buckled her knees washed over her.

She turned her face to the sky as the rain came sweeping in.

He had prayed. Since the moment they paused on the ridge, spotted smoke rising from the field, and the first clench of dread had gripped him, he had prayed. While they raced Seamus back to the cabin, grabbed spade and hoe and buckets and ran to save the crop, he had prayed. But he hadn't prayed with such faith to warrant this glorious summer shower now doing the work he and Willa and the boy couldn't have accomplished. The crop was saved, minus a blackened half acre.

They stood at the field's edge, gulping moist air as the rain's drumming eased to a patter, as drenched now as they had been scorched with the fire's heat. From the cabin, they could hear Cap's muffled barking—Owl had shut the collie inside before racing to the spring—but over the three of them had settled a stunned silence.

Willa broke it, turning to Owl. She brushed rain-plastered hair from his face, then took up his hands to inspect them. "Let me see you. Are you hurt anywhere?"

Looking embarrassed, and pleased, by her attention, he said, "No. I'm not hurt."

He wasn't. Not physically. But his eyes told of another kind of hurt, and Neil recalled with an inner lurch what other devastation had been wrought in their absence. The rainfall swept away as abruptly as it had come, leaving behind a silence unbroken by birdsong or insect hum. It was then they heard it, a sound Neil sensed had been issuing for some while, masked by the drumming of the rain. A child's grief-stricken wail.

"Ach, no. I didna mean her to see. There wasna time to do aught about it, not with the fire."

Willa looked at him, dread reemerging on her rain-slick face.

Owl took off running down the track toward his sister's cries. Willa stared after the boy, her body straight as a sapling, but one storm-battered and swaying. It was all Neil could do to keep from wrapping his arms about her, to shelter her from the next blow.

Instead, it was left to him to deliver it.

"The goat, Willa. 'Tis been slaughtered."

Maggie was inconsolable. They'd told the children it might have been a wolf, come prowling while they were away. Owl had shot them a narrowed stare. A wolf would have dragged off the carcass or left considerably less of it to find. A wolf wouldn't have made a straight slash across the animal's tender throat.

"Aye," Neil said as they stood alone by the pen. "'Twas done by a wolf, right enough, but one that goes on two legs." He studied Willa as she gazed at the sodden carcass. Her own hair straggled wet about her shoulders, and the bones of her face looked high and stark.

"It will make a meal or two. If you could hang it to bleed, I will see to the rest."

"I'll do that," he said.

She started to move away, but hesitated. "I saw your plant press and desk on the porch. Did you find what you sought?"

His brief outing with the boy might have happened days ago. "I made a few new sketches. Let the lad try his hand at it too."

Instead of softening, her features hardened further. "It was foolish of me to leave the fields and yard unguarded. It will not happen again."

"Willa." He moved toward her, but she stepped away, leaving him only words to offer. "'Tis going to be all right, ken. Most of the crop was saved. 'Tis a pity about the goat, but I've coin enough to—"

"Thank you, but no, I do not need your coin," she said, rebuffing the offer before he could make it. Her eyes flicked up to his, almost pleading—for what, he wished he kent—then she tore them away and strode to the cabin, took up a cloth and soap she'd left on the porch, and headed toward the spring.

He let her go. There was the goat to see to and the children. He did both, then changed his shirt and breeches. But even after a cursory ablution in his room, Willa hadn't returned from the spring.

Maggie had cried herself to sleep. Owl lay unconscious beside her, spent from their early rising and the fire. He left them sleeping, Cap curled nearby, and went outside.

The sun was setting, streaking the sky above the hills to the west with banners of fiery gold. The startling beauty of it after such a harrowing few hours struck in him a chord of longing—not the old longing to be roaming those hills, eyes to the ground in hope of spying some as-yet-unnamed floral specimen. It was a longing to remain precisely where he was, with this view before his eyes, this land under his feet. And Willa Obenchain beside him.

He'd glimpsed the mother Willa had been when she looked to Owl's welfare in the fire's aftermath, and later, still rain soaked, sitting cross-legged beside the pallet where Maggie lay crying, stroking the girl, comforting her in murmurs. He wished he'd been close enough to hear what she'd said. There was a strength in her like no woman he'd known, yet there was also as great a capacity to embrace and console, though she let herself show it so rarely.

"Burning Sky," he whispered as the sunset blazed before his eyes, and for the first time wondered, was it this for which the Mohawks had named her? She could be as incandescent. Perhaps they'd been quick to see it and simply called her what she was.

Aye, she was still that daughter of the Wolf Clan, as much as she was Willa Obenchain, daughter of Dieter and Rebecca. If he could, if she'd let him, he would help her see she didn't have to choose. With him, and perhaps with these children, she could be both.

It felt like scales falling from his eyes, for what was only half-glimpsed before was now as clear as the sun's blazing glory. He could see now how the Almighty had led them each to this solitary cabin, had set them like the fragments of a shattered bone, knitting them into what Willa and the children had lost. Family. A gift he hadn't asked for, but one more precious than all the accolades he could receive from his peers. What matter that he'd never presumed himself anything but a temporary interloper on the frontier. Never seen himself as strong enough, hardened enough, that the notion of permanency in such a place should have ever crossed his mind.

Perhaps he didn't need to be.

"'And God hath chosen the weak things of the world to confound the things which are mighty,'" he said, and laughed softly at the irony of it.

He might be weak, even foolish. He was also sure.

With a prayer on his lips, he stepped off the porch and crossed the cabin yard, headed for the spring.

Stripped to her shift, kneeling by the spring, Willa rocked herself and let the tears flow like the rivulets streaming from her hair. She had tried so long to contain this grief, but it was clawing down the walls she'd built around it like a wild, caged thing, shredding its way out of her, raw in her throat, flooding from her eyes. *She-Goes-Singing. Sweet Rain.*

Mixed in with the faces of her daughters as she grieved were the faces of Pine Bird and Owl, her parents, Oma, Joseph…and Neil MacGregor.

She wanted to go back to the cabin, but whether to take Neil into her arms or simply to hold Pine Bird and weep and weep and maybe never stop, she didn't know. If she did the last, it would only frighten the child. If she did the first—that she was even having the thought terrified *her*.

She had to get hold of herself, to pull this grief back in, to cast down branches across the path to her heart before Neil came looking for her, before he found her like this. He would offer comfort, and she would be so tempted to let him give it…

No, *no*. She'd made her decision before ever she came back to this place. She would live alone. A solitary life. To consider weakening, allowing anything else—the love of a man, children—made her want to huddle there by the spring and pray never to get up again. It was too much pain to risk. Too much.

Oh, but to feel Neil MacGregor's arms around her, just for a moment… A sob escaped her as she snatched up the cloth to dry her hair.

Her hair hung down her back in a dripping mass, dark against her shift. She'd washed it, which explained her tardiness in returning from the spring.

Neil paused on the footpath while she knelt among the ferns edging the runnel, his heart both full and wrung at the sight of her. While he hesitated, she made a sound that carried above the spring's trickle. A sob?

Almost angrily she snatched up a cloth from the ground and yanked her wet locks forward to rub them dry—only to drop the towel with an indrawn hiss of breath.

He was at her side, kneeling in the rain-wet ferns, taking gentle hold of her hands to turn them palm up. Like his, they were rubbed almost to blisters. Unlike his, a reddened streak crossed her right palm at the base of all four fingers. A burn. A slight one, but obviously painful.

"What...? Did ye grab a burning stalk?"

She looked at her hands as though they belonged to someone else. "I don't remember."

She averted her face, letting the long wet curtain of her hair fall between them. He took up the cloth. "Let me."

The amber glow of sunset had cooled to shadow beneath the trees. The air around them hung warm, still, save for the tiny bright pulses of fireflies at the edge of the cabin yard. He took up her hair and squeezed the strands with the cloth. She didn't protest, but closed her still averted eyes and made another noise, this one of pleasure.

He felt a jolt through his belly as her hair slipped wet through his fingers. "'Tis the color of winter oak leaves, your hair." His hand brushed her throat. "So beautiful."

He felt her shiver at the touch. She turned her face to him. There wasn't light enough to distinguish the disparate colors of her eyes, but he could read the softening of her mouth.

"Willa." It was all he had time to say before she raised a hand to his face and drew his mouth down to hers.

For a second, he didn't breathe. Couldn't move. Then he dropped the towel and took her in his arms, his fingers tangled in the cool of her wet hair.

A groan rose from within her, a sound of surprise, and need. She slid her hand inside the open neck of his shirt, down the slope of his shoulder, her fingers cool on his skin, her mouth slanting more fully to his, at once hungry and yielding.

His thoughts were in chaos, fragments of reason beating against the tide of joy and desire sweeping over him, beating it back until he could grasp one shining thread. He wanted her, but not like this—not yet. Soon—*God Almighty, let it be soon*—but not now.

He thrust out a hand, landing it palm flat against the earth. "Willa—," he spoke against her lips. "Let me stay with ye."

"Yes." She strained to pull him closer. "Stay."

"No." He took her wrist. "I dinna mean now—this—though I want it." He let go of her wrist to touch her face, thrilled that her eagerness seemed to match his own. Groaning with the effort of restraint, he cradled her cheek.

"Willa, you're so like your eyes, the brown and the green. 'Tis like you've two souls in ye. Sometimes you're as wild and remote to me as if you were born Mohawk. Other times it seems I've kent ye my life long, and you're as near to me as my own heart. But whatever you've been, whatever else ye will be, I want you to be my wife."

Beneath his hands she went completely still. For an instant, even her breathing ceased. Then she choked out, "What?"

Twilight had engulfed them. He could no longer see her face as clearly as he longed to do. He ran his hands down her slackened arms, cupping her upturned hands in his. He raised her fingers to his lips, kissed the tips of them gently. "'Twas no coincidence, your finding me as ye did, no co-incidence these children came to us. 'Tis the Almighty's doing. Can ye not feel it?"

She pulled her hands away and stared, her eyes lost in shadowed hollows. "You do not wish to go away? You want to keep those children and… what? Raise them here with me?"

"Aye." She wasn't reacting to his offer of marriage as he'd hoped, nor as her embrace had convinced him she would. His head was still half-full of thoughts of things forbidden him—her taste, her scent, the feel of her bare skin—at least until they were wed proper. "Aye and amen to both. With all my heart. And with all my heart, I love you."

He barely had the words out before she bolted off the ground, leaving him kneeling at her feet, staring up at the long white flow of her shift, her damp hair swinging, the pale oval of her face. He stood more slowly, feeling a heaviness weighing him to the earth. Silence stretched with no break but the distant hoot of an owl.

A tightness built beneath his breastbone. He'd long since realized she was struggling with their nearness, that she feared to let him, the children—anyone—into her heart after all she'd lost. She clenched that grief to herself like a shield, keeping any risk of loving again at arm's length.

But she didn't know how much he knew.

"Willa," he said, as the tightness coiled in his chest. "I ken about the children."

"The children?" she asked, clearly confused.

"Your children. The daughters you had with your Mohawk husband."

Her arms came up, linking across her ribs. "How do you know?" She wielded the question like a weapon, meant to ward him off.

"Joseph told me, the day he brought us Owl and Maggie."

She stared at him, her face white in the near dark. "He wouldn't."

"He thought I kent or he'd not have spoken of them, or your need to let yourself grieve them. But he was right, Willa. You need to grieve, only let me be here while ye do. Let me help bear your burdens, give ye time to heal. And when you're ready, to love—"

She lunged for her clothing on the ground so abruptly he broke off. When she started to move past him, he tried to step in front of her. "Wait, Willa."

"No. Please. Get out of my path!" Dodging his grasp, she hurried down the footpath their feet had worn, returning to the cabin.

He lingered at the spring after she vanished, hardly mindful of the mosquitoes descending about his ears, whining, seeking his blood. They might've bitten him raw; it wouldn't have compared to the rawness within. Darkness gathered beneath the trees. Through their lacing branches, stars pricked the inky blue where the clouds had broken.

She'd have gone to skin the goat, to hang it in the smoking shed. Probably she'd put some of the meat to stew on the hearth, while the children were asleep and couldn't ask what sort of meat it was. Keeping herself too busy to think. Too busy to feel.

Hiding away her heart again, so he couldn't reach it.

He walked at last to the cabin yard still sparking here and there with fireflies. He raised his eyes to the glittering stars blazing a cloud-crossed trail toward the wilderness he had come to set down in paint and ink. And maybe that was what he was meant to be doing. Maybe he had heard wrong, there on the porch as the sun set. But the sight could not hold his heart. It was the solitary cabin under the stars and what it contained that drew his gaze, his soul, his prayers.

"I tried. You saw how it went, aye? What more would Ye have me do?"

He waited in the insect-humming dark until an answer came, and it wasn't the one he'd expected.

Stay.

"All right. But we've some convincing to be doing, then, aye?"

TWENTY-FOUR

Because she couldn't bear to stay inside the cabin feigning sleep, Willa was crouched in the garden pulling weeds with barely light enough to distinguish them from healing plants. Hearing a rustling beyond the fence, she assumed it the collie, which had come out with her, and went on with her work, sore hands digging into moist earth as the darkness lifted, head and eyes and heart aching.

"Willa?"

How long Neil MacGregor had stood in the gate behind her she didn't know—perhaps it had been him, not his collie, she heard.

She raised her head but didn't turn. "Yes?"

"I'd speak to ye before the children wake. May I come in?"

His voice washed over her as it had done that first day she found him awake on the travois, catching at her heart with that way he had of turning the simplest speech into lilting music, while underneath beat a rumble like distant drums.

"If you wish."

On the path between the aromatic beds, she stood to face him. The light was gray now, the garden a world of scent and shadow. She brushed her hands gingerly together, avoiding the burn, searching for words to undo what she'd done the previous night.

The fire, the goat, the children's distress, his kindness and strength, it had been too much all at once. It had weakened her, peeling back the layers she had built around that raw, wounded part in her soul. She had let down her guard against him when he found her at the spring, against the feelings he stirred in her despite all her efforts to keep them, and him, at bay. But she was past it now. She was strong again. She would tell him…

He came toward her along the garden path, but he didn't stop a pace away, as someone who wished to talk. Or listen. A glimpse of his eyes, blue shadowed in the dawn, was all she had before her face was between his hands and his mouth was on hers, tender and honest, and it was as if she hadn't lain awake the night long fighting the pull to go to him. The roughness of his whiskers against her chin. The smell of him. The warmth of his hands, his mouth. She was back at the spring.

When he pulled away, she stifled a groan. He had done it again, so easily. Broken through her defenses as if they weren't even there.

"You didna answer me last night," he said. He still held her face between his hands. She didn't have the strength to pull away.

"You will make me say it?"

"That's generally what's expected of a woman when a man proposes marriage."

The gentle humor in his voice almost undid her. She risked a look at his eyes, with their strong brows that gave them such expression, and saw what he'd said in the dark was true in the gray of dawn. He was offering her everything she'd lost, and more. He was offering her his heart in a way Kingfisher had never done, as good a husband as Kingfisher had been to her, and she knew that if she took it, she would be giving hers in exchange, in a way that she had never known. And because of that, she stood before him, more terrified than she had ever been, knowing only one thing she could do to save herself.

Despite the lightness of his speech, his eyes held a hope as deep and wide as the pearly sky above them. It was far too late to spare him hurt, even if she could spare herself.

"You have not had one of your headaches in weeks," she said. "Your wrist is healed. Pine Bird's leg is healed. There is no more reason for you to be here."

She found the will to step back from the warmth of his hands, but saw she hadn't rebuffed him.

"Setting aside for the moment my feelings—and yours—d'ye expect me just to go, to leave ye and the children unprotected? After yesterday?"

"Joseph—"

"Isna here," he said. "I ken he means to come back for the children, but, Willa, you do ken he'll ask ye again to go with him. Dinna tell me that's not what he still wants."

She couldn't meet his searching look. "It is what he wants."

"And will ye tell him no? Will ye force him to go and take the children away with him?"

"I will. And then I will be alone."

He flinched at that. "What will you do, God forbid something like that fire should happen again?"

"Whatever I must do." She met his gaze, hardening her resolve so that she could get the words out. "I do not want the children to stay, and I do not want you here."

She couldn't have made it plainer, but oh, his eyes. They were the only color in her landscape now. So blue, so filled with disappointment, bewilderment, hurt.

"What was that about, then, last night?" he demanded of her. "*You* kissed me, Willa. There's no pretending ye didna. Was it that you just needed a man's arms to hold you, and mine did for you, being most convenient?"

She couldn't stem the tide of heat rising in her face or pretend she did not feel the ache in her chest, the urgent need to tell him no, it had been his arms she wanted. Only his. But she said the word, knowing it would wound. "Yes."

"'Twas naught to do with me, then?"

"No."

The skin went taut across his cheekbones. Pain cut across his eyes. Still he said, "I dinna believe ye. Willa, dinna drive away the people who care for you."

She couldn't bear this. Not his words. Not his eyes. Not his heart, of-fered to her with such terrifying abandon. She turned her back, bent her knees, and resumed pulling weeds.

She went on pulling them as the silence stretched, bleeding out be-tween them.

When he spoke again, the hope was gone from his voice.

"You've tried verra hard not to let me, but I've seen deeper into your soul than ye ken. You're frozen as ice. But ice canna last, Willa. 'Tis either going to thaw or shatter. And a life of solitude doesna guarantee you'll never feel grief or pain again. But if you want me to leave, then I canna force ye to let me stay."

Another pause, another wounding silence, then his footsteps on the path. Leaving her.

The rising sun speared light through the treetops. It struck her face, but she didn't feel its warmth. The sun that might have melted her was setting fast behind her, leaving a chill hardened around her heart, and the image of his eyes, ravishing as the snowbound memory of a summer sky.

She left the garden after he'd cleared his things from the cabin and saddled his horse in the yard, and came down barefoot into the sound of his voice.

"No—listen to me. Dinna hold my leaving against her. She has every right to bid me go. 'Tis not fitting, my staying longer. Besides, I made promises to people back east. I must keep my word, aye?"

"Take us with you!" It was Owl imploring, sounding not the almost-man he wanted them to think him, but the child he was.

Neil's voice caught. "I would do—lad, I would was I bound west-ward. I'm headed east, back into the mountains, then down the Hudson where ye came from. I'm not likely to come this way again."

Willa halted at the end of the porch. In the yard Seamus stood bearing bags and canvas-wrapped burdens tied behind the saddle. The sight left her hollowed.

Then she saw Neil, on the porch, on his knees before the children, their hair and clothes still mussed from sleep. He had an arm encircling each, and they clung to him as if they wouldn't let him go. But gently he put them from him, never taking his eyes from their anguished faces.

"I'll pray for ye every day. Dinna be afraid, but trust the Almighty. For if I love you, being only human, then He does all the more. And because He loves you, He will keep you in the shelter of His hand. Will you remember that?"

Owl said he would. Pine Bird bobbed her chin, though it dripped with tears. Neil placed a hand upon each of their heads.

"Then may the Almighty Lord bless and keep thee, Owl and Maggie. May He make His face to shine upon thee and be gracious unto thee. May the Lord lift up His countenance upon thee, and give thee peace."

The ache in Willa's chest was unbearable.

"Do you have all you need?" The words came out like crow squawks, shattering the moment, startling the children.

Neil stood and stepped off the porch. "Willa, I wish you'd take—"

"I will not."

He'd been reaching into his coat as if he meant again to offer her coin. He withdrew his hand. "What provisions I need I'll get in Shiloh."

"Good," she said.

"Do you mean to send us away too?"

Though she'd anticipated resentment toward her, anger even, over Neil's leaving, Willa was taken aback by Owl's question.

"That is what you want," she said, turning to the children who stood with brown toes curled over the porch's edge, stricken faces lifted to her. "For Joseph to take you west to Niagara. To the People. Is it not?"

"No—yes. We want…" Owl's tight-knit brows unraveled in confusion, but Pine Bird thrust out her small quivering chin.

"We want to stay with you," she said.

Willa saw the revelation in Owl's eyes, unknown to him until his sister spoke for them. "Will you keep us, Miss Willa?"

She rocked back on her heels, mouth open, but no words to speak. Even for Neil, it seemed too much. As though he couldn't bear to hear her refuse them as well, he took up his hat and mounted his horse.

"Cap!" he called to the collie, lolling on the porch through this distressing farewell as if nothing of consequence were unfolding.

The dog sat up but didn't obey.

"Capercaillie! Let's go."

The collie sidled close to Owl, pressing against the boy's knee, ears flattened. Neil's mouth slanted in a grimace he might have meant for a smile. He raised his eyes to the boy. "Ye'll keep him for me, then?"

"I will." Tears coursed down Owl's face now too. Pine Bird was looking back and forth between them, as if expecting someone to say this wasn't happening. Willa pressed her lips tight together.

Neil MacGregor looked at her from the saddle. "God keep ye, Willa. And thank you, for everything." He chirruped softly, and the horse took its first steps away from her.

The morning air was sticky, smelling of coming heat. The birds seemed to sense it; their trills held a sense of urgency, but they couldn't drown the steady *clop* of the roan's departing hooves. Over Willa and the children, silence had fallen, as hobbling as fetters. Neil had reached the fringe of trees between the yard and the cornfield before Owl's shout broke its bonds.

"Mr. MacGregor, wait!"

Neil reined in the horse, twisting in the saddle to look back as the boy leaped off the porch and ran into the yard to stand, bare legged beneath his shirt, black hair straggling on his shoulders.

"Don't you want to know my name when you pray for me?"

"Lad," Neil said, "I've always wanted that. Tell me your name."

Willa was near enough to see the gladness and grief breaking on Neil MacGregor's face, but she couldn't see the boy's, to know if he smiled or wept as he shouted, "It's Matthew. My name is Matthew Kershaw!"

OHIARIHKO:WA

Time of Much Ripening—July

Outside the cabin, crickets were singing. Inside, supper was cleared away, plates and kettle scrubbed—as were the children, settled on their pallet in the corner but not sleeping. Or even sleepy, Willa observed as she gathered the trappings for bullet making: scrap lead, mold, and ladle.

Her shot pouch was nearly empty. She'd let Owl, or rather Matthew—the children insisted on their Christian names now—use her musket to practice his marksmanship. Though he recovered some of the spent balls, digging them from the stump into which he'd shot them, most were misshapen and useless. She added them to the pile of scrap lead on the hearth.

Maggie sang softly to a cornhusk doll, a gift from Anni's Samantha. Even with Maggie's small voice filling the room, Willa felt the absence of Neil MacGregor. Twelve evenings they had spent without him, not that she was keeping a count. She didn't want to admit how much she missed his easy conversation with the children or his sketches spread out on the table, missed him standing at her shoulder giving dictation while she labored to write legibly with his quill. She kept busy, clinging to the part of herself that was relieved Neil was gone, dismayed when that part shrank a little each day. More dismayed at how frequently her thoughts flitted back to those moments by the spring, the night before he left. It overcame her in unguarded moments, the memory of his mouth on hers, his lovely words…the horrible things she had said to drive him away.

It was harder than she'd expected, his absence. But the struggle would pass. If she would just cease thinking of the man, it would pass.

Annoyed with herself, she set the mold and ladle on the hearth, then glanced at the children's pallet, beside which a tallow stub burned in a wooden dish. The boy made a sudden movement when she looked his way, shoving something under a quilt.

He hadn't been quick enough to hide what it was. Willa straightened from the hearth, petticoat swishing around her ankles.

"Owl, where did you get a book?"

Maggie's singing ceased. "He's Matthew now," she reminded her. When Neil MacGregor rode from the cabin yard, he'd taken the girl's shyness with him. She'd since been bold to speak her mind, reminding Willa more of Goes-Singing every day.

"Matthew, then. You have a book. Let me see it."

To his credit, the boy didn't deny the book. He drew it from hiding and brought it to her. It was Neil's Bible.

"He didn't steal it," his sister said firmly. The boy's mouth twisted, then firmed.

"Mr. MacGregor gave it to me."

She took it into hands that trembled. "When?"

"The day he left. You were in your garden."

"Why?"

"Because you were angry with him."

Willa shook her head. "*Why* did he give you his Bible?"

"He cannot read it. He wanted me to read it."

Willa's grip on the Bible tightened. She wanted to climb to the loft, light a candle, pour through its pages, which looked to be marked with dozens of stray bits of paper. "Do you wish to read it?"

"Yes," Matthew said.

She searched his face, seeing only earnestness. "Do you know how to read?"

The boy lowered his gaze. "Yes."

Behind his back, his sister wagged her head. Matthew turned and caught her at it, scowled, then flushed. "I can read...some."

"You needn't hide it from me to do so," Willa said. Then on impulse added, "If you wish it, I will help you to read it."

The boy nodded, and she set the Bible on the table. The sight made her feel as if some bit of Neil MacGregor had come whispering back into her home.

She did not look too closely at the comfort she drew from that.

A scratching sounded at the door. Matthew let in the collie. In the seconds of the door's opening, Willa caught the flash of lightning away beyond the ridge to the north. She sent up a prayer for the wandering naturalist, that he was somewhere safe and dry.

The boy shut the door. The dog went to the pallet where Maggie sat, curling near her to sleep.

His Bible and his dog. Willa didn't know whether to smile or put a fist to the spot of pain that had bloomed beneath her ribs. She caught herself doing both as the girl set the doll aside and began grooming the dog with careful fingers, picking foxtails from its coat.

Willa settled cross-legged at the hearth and set about replenishing her shot pouch. She chose a piece from the pile of deformed bullets, broken buttons, and bits of lead, and placed it in the ladle. As she held the ladle to the fire, the boy crouched near to watch.

She was conscious of the tension that had existed between her and the children since Neil's leaving. It was never anything overt. She had no complaint to make of them. They did everything she bid them—including spending hours each day patrolling the cornfield to keep away deer and raccoon. Yet she had a sense of them withholding something from her. Had it been the Bible? The tension hadn't broken with its discovery.

Not a secret, then. More like a sense of waiting hanging over them. There could be only one thing they were waiting for—an answer to the question put to her the day of Neil MacGregor's leaving.

How could she give an answer? She couldn't bear the terror of *yes*. She just couldn't. But she could not bring herself to disappoint them with *no*. She would wait. Joseph would return. When he was there, ready to put them on the back of his horse, then she would say no.

Across the room the collie rolled onto its back, four paws in the air, showing its teeth in a foolish grin that drew giggles from Maggie. Closer to hand, Matthew stared at the lead in the ladle she held to the fire's heart, until it melted all at once into a shimmering puddle. He watched as she poured the liquid into the mold, holding her face away from the sharp metallic fumes.

"Who taught you to do that? Was it your white father?"

She remembered Dieter Obenchain kneeling before that very hearth, turning out musket balls while she sat on a bench at the table—a different table than the one there now—her legs too short to reach the floor. Papa had poured the bright stream of lead into the mold, then turned to her…

His smile flashed upon her mind with such searing clarity she was forced to blink back tears. She waved a hand before her face, pretending the fumes stung her eyes.

The memory vanished and another took its place. A fire in the center of a longhouse, sending up its smoke to the high bark roof. A pair of tattooed old warriors come to visit the even older man who was the father of her adoptive mother. The three sitting wrinkled and brown and smelling of bear grease, turning out round musket balls that clacked in the ashes like marbles, while she watched from a platform a few feet away. It was this memory she spoke of.

Maggie abandoned the dog and came to sit beside her brother, eyes trained on her. Their faces were sheened like copper in the firelight.

"They did not know how closely I watched them." Willa turned out the first musket ball into the ashes, to be filed smooth when cool. She took up a broken button and an unrecognizable twist of lead and dropped them into the ladle. "Or else they didn't mind. Not even when I moved to the fire and sat with them. That is one time I saw this done."

She didn't sense the tension so much when she spoke, so she kept talking. She told them of the day Joseph Tames-His-Horse got the small scar above his eyebrow, trying to teach three small boys to shoot their bows.

"All went well till I decided I wished to learn, though I was a girl. The boys were unhappy when I shot better than they on my first try. One leaped up with his bow and loosed an arrow to prove himself my match." Willa poured more molten lead into the bullet mold. "It was a good shot, except Joseph had not moved away from checking the arrow I had shot. He turned his face as the arrow nipped past him, nearly taking out his eye."

Maggie gasped. Matthew watched her face, holding back his own reaction until Willa showed him a smile. Then he smiled too.

"Joseph is still leaving meat for you, but when will we see him again?" The boy looked half-hopeful, but half-wary too. He had admired Joseph, but now there was this question between them. Did the child sense she had made up her mind to give them their answer when Joseph returned?

"Before the autumn he will come back." She didn't have the heart to add "for you."

The children shared a look, turned quiet for a time, until Matthew asked, "What was your name to them?"

At first the question itself surprised her. Then it struck Willa how the boy had phrased it. The Mohawks were *them*.

"Burning Sky."

"For your hair?" Maggie reached for Willa's braid. She'd been told its color changed with the light. In the fire's glow it was more auburn than brown.

'Tis the color of winter oak leaves, your hair.

Willa paused in reaching for the mold to turn out another ball. *Do not think of him.* She took a deep breath and could smell the girl's hair beside her, sweet and damp from washing, and another yearning nearly as sharp filled her. The yearning for the warm weight of a child in her arms.

"I suppose so," she said, her throat too tight for telling that story.

Matthew held a toy soldier broken at the knees, the last piece of lead she had to melt. He handed it to her, reluctant. "Were you happy being Mohawk?"

Willa set the soldier in the ladle and held it to the flames, watching for the moment when it would dissolve and be a soldier no more. "I learned to be."

"Why did you leave them?"

She jerked the soldier back from the fire, uncertain why she hesitated to turn him into a musket ball. She stared at him, afraid she was too late, but the soldier held his broken shape. "I left because my husband was dead. My mother was dead. My children were dead. Joseph was gone away, and I did not know whether he—"

Hearing such dreadful words on her lips, afraid she would lose control of the tears that burned her eyes, her nose, Willa set the ladle on the hearth. "If you want that soldier," she told the boy, "you may have him. But let him cool first."

She looked at the children, expecting more questions, wondering how she could answer without dissolving into a puddle of grief in front of them. But they looked back at her with eyes too old for their faces and said no more.

When the children slept, she sat at the table, a candle lighting the boards, and reached for the Bible. She held it in her hands, feeling the weight and wear of it, the tiny cracks in the leather of the spine and edges. She opened the cover to the first page. Inscribed in faded ink were names. James, Angus, Dougal…all MacGregors and the wives they'd married, down to Liam MacGregor and Morag Murray MacGregor…and the last name, Neil William Murray MacGregor. He'd given the boy his family Bible, as a man would pass it to a son.

She set it on its worn spine and let it open where it would. It chose a place near the middle. The book of Isaiah. Halfway down the page, a passage was underscored: "A bruised reed shall he not break, and the smoking flax shall he not quench: he shall bring forth judgment unto truth."

Even had they been unmarked, the words would have leaped off the page like an arrow aimed at her soul. *A bruised reed.* She had thought of this tender promise, clung to it in fact, when she found Neil MacGregor lying in the laurels below the boundary stone. It had compelled her to look past her own pain and see him. Broken. Wounded. Like herself.

Swallowing past a thick pain in her throat, she let her fingertip wander across the words. Turning the thin pages at random for a while, careful they didn't crinkle and disturb the children, she paused when she came to one of the papers tucked between. It wasn't folded or sealed, but was filled edge to edge with the neat slanted script she recognized from Neil's older drawings. His own writing. She turned the paper so she could read it.

Before she took in more than the first few words, she spread her hand across it, struck by the notion that she was intruding upon something not meant for her eyes. He'd given the Bible and all it contained to the boy. Not to her.

But might he have supposed she'd learn of the gift, be curious enough to open it for herself? Might he have hoped she would do so? This would have been her Bible, with her name beside his on that front page, if she'd given him what he asked of her.

Whatever you've been, whatever else ye will be, I want you to be my wife.

The words had struck terror in her soul when he spoke them, yet they insisted on replaying through her mind, rife with bittersweet regret. Why could she not have been strong until his leaving? Kept him at arm's length as she had meant to do. What did he think of her now? That she'd wanted to bed him there in the ferns, but not marry him? That she'd have let it get that far? She would not have. She hoped she would not have.

Did he despise her now?

She lifted her hand from the paper. The lines swam, then cleared before her eyes. Unaddressed, unsigned, the words began as a simple declaration.

I embark upon my Journey into the Hinterland of this troubled Colony to pursue the Vision for which I am entrusted. Though I go into the Unknown with no little Trepidation, I pray I shall not fail those who send me forth, my Fellows of the Philosophical Society. I do not consider myself a Man cut from Cloth suited for great Hardship or Endurance, yet I set out in Faith, believing that what I lack in my flesh the Almighty Lord shall by His Good Grace supply daily, whatever may come. Be Thou my Vision. Be Thou to me always my True North. May Providence once again use the foolish things of this World to confound the Wise, the Weak to confound the Mighty, all the better that He receive the Glory when I am safe delivered, my Journey finished, my Labor complete. In the Name of the Lord Jesus Christ.

Willa set the paper back into the pages of the Bible and shut the book, tasting the salt of tears on her lips. She stroked her fingertips across the cover, certain she'd never known a man with greater faith. Neil Mac-Gregor saw things as they could be, not as they were. It was how he'd insisted on seeing her. And the children. Everyone except himself. He saw *himself* all wrong. He was neither foolish nor weak. She might have thought so once. She knew better now.

'Twas no coincidence, your finding me as ye did, no coincidence these children came to us. 'Tis the Almighty's doing.

She put her hands over her face, as if to hide from his impassioned words at the spring. Through her fingers, she looked at the children, dark forms sprawled in the abandon of sleep. Trusting her. Like they would a mother.

"No," she whispered. "No."

Neil MacGregor was gone. Soon the children would go. Joseph would return and take them west to find their mother's kin or someone of the Wolf Clan willing to take them in. And with them would go the last terrible temptation to offer up her heart for breaking again.

Leaving the Bible for the boy to find come morning, she climbed the loft ladder, trying not to think of the empty room below where Neil Mac-Gregor no longer slept.

TWENTY-SIX

A fortnight and a day after riding from Willa's cabin yard, Neil Mac-Gregor had begun drawing uneasy parallels between himself and the prophet Jonah, who'd gone down to Joppa in search of a ship to take him in the opposite direction of Nineveh, where the Almighty had instructed him to go.

It began with a tempest of a mountain storm breaking over his head and nearly drowning him. In short order he'd found himself swallowed whole—by a cave little drier than a fish's belly. The air reeked of damp but was at least breathable. He had that over Jonah.

"In everything give thanks," Neil muttered, hunkered back from the cave's entrance at the close of this, his third day in the bowels of the earth. "For this is the will of God in Christ Jesus concerning you," he added, finishing the verse from Thessalonians—and wished immediately he hadn't. The will of God was a topic of thought he'd lately avoided pondering. Since leaving Willa and the children, in fact.

He never hoped to experience again such a heart-scouring as he'd endured that day. After that raw leave-taking in her cabin yard, he'd gone into Shiloh where, while purchasing provisions and checking a final time for a letter for Willa—there was none—he'd been forced to run a gauntlet of acquaintances, none happy to see him go. Jack Keegan, the MacNabs, the Kepplers.

It was near midday before he put the settlement behind him, taking a trail headed northward. Even then, he'd gone but a short way before Francis Waring stepped from the woods.

Neil had reined in Seamus to bid the lad farewell and request that he look in on Willa and the children from time to time—a thing Francis would likely have done regardless, but the asking assuaged Neil's guilt over leaving.

Like a scrap of linen over a disembowelment.

He gazed now at the cave's stony confines, half of which his horse occupied. The floor was sandy toward the back. There he'd spread his saddle, bags, and their contents, in the hope of their keeping dry, most particularly the drawings bearing Willa's rough but earnest penmanship. Wrapped in oilskin, they'd suffered no lasting damage from the rain. He thought of her bent over the table, ink-stained fingers clenched around a quill, mouth set in concentration as she took his dictation. And hastily pushed away the memory.

"Chamaedaphne calyculata." It was daily ritual again, reciting his mental field notes. "The shrub grows in open bog waters, forming dense colonies…doesna tolerate shade…leaves leathery, oblong, arranged alternately on stem…small remnant of bell-shaped blossoms, no fruit present in July."

How much knowledge could his brain hold before vital bits began slipping away and he ended with a set of pretty drawings bereft of annotation? In his university days, he'd met a fellow in a public house in Edinburgh who claimed to have the entire canon of Scripture put to memory. For hours, Neil had tested the assertion, flipping through his Bible for the most obscure verses he could find. The fellow never once misquoted a passage.

He'd given that Bible to the lad, a scene he couldn't recall without a hollowness opening under his ribs. He missed the children. He missed his Bible too—its presence had long been a comfort even if he couldn't read it—but he was glad to know Owl had it in his possession and, Neil hoped, would cherish it as he grew to manhood.

Not Owl, he reminded himself.

"Matthew Kershaw," he murmured, still blessed by the parting gift. Leaning his head against damp stone, he prayed. *Guard and keep them. Be a father to the fatherless. A husband to the widow…*

His thoughts had circled back to Willa. Neither in mind nor in heart had he truly left her. But he must. He would. Tomorrow.

Tomorrow he would stop thinking of her incessantly.

Beyond the cave the rain had slackened at long last. Because the clouds lay low and the land sloping from the cave was thickly wooded, it was hard to judge the time of day. He reckoned it getting on to dusk. Too late for traveling. Besides, there was likely no drier place to camp for a hundred miles around than where he was, stuck in the belly of the earth.

He plucked at the sleeve of his shirt, which clung like a second skin, and wrinkled his nose. He stank. His horse stank. The cave stank. The whole world stank.

Finished with his litany of field notes, he fed and watered Seamus, then glanced toward the cave entrance and automatically called, "Cap," then laid himself down in the cave's chill, missing his stinking dog.

Sometime later, sleep elusive and thoughts of Willa grown unbearable, he rose and sat on a damp lip of rock outside the cave. It was full dark now. The croaking of contented frogs had replaced the patter of rain.

He'd had little sense of the topography beyond the slope he'd been crossing when the storm broke. Now he could see a fair distance to the north and west, where a ragged line of peaks rose in silhouette against ever-broadening patches of stars. The air had cooled on the heels of the storm and held an autumnal freshness now, though it was yet high summer. He drew it in and breathed out prayer. For Willa. For the children. For Anni and her unborn baby. He even prayed for Joseph, knowing the Indian shared his pain, his longing, and had carried it longer.

The one he didn't pray for was himself, wary of what the Almighty might have to say about his recent actions. It was all well and good to be told "Stay." Neil wished it had been explained how he was meant to do so given Willa's resolve to the contrary.

"Ye might've consulted with her before telling me such a thing." He watched a shooting star arc a path across the heavens, two others hot on its tail. "Or maybe You did, and she simply wasna having it. Or me."

What, after all, did he have about his person to recommend him to a woman like Willa? He'd no great worldly goods to ease the burden of her poverty. He wasn't a farmer, though he supposed he could learn to be. He was certainly no warrior. In short, he wasn't the kind of man a woman like Willa Obenchain needed. Better suited was a man like Richard Waring, had he been less a brute. Or Joseph, had he not been her clan brother, which seemed to be how Willa still viewed him.

Neil hoped it was how she still viewed him.

But why should he hope such a thing? Capable as she was, he wanted to see her covered, shielded from those who would burn her crops and kill her livestock and shoot arrows into her cabin door. If Joseph could be that for her...

In everything give thanks.

He put his head in his hands and asked for the strength to expunge Willa from his heart. He asked for a revival of the passion that had called him to the frontier in the first place. The challenge and thrill of scientific discovery; the creative drive to render those discoveries on paper. It had once been all-consuming, sharp and clear in his mind, leaving no room for vague notions of wife, or family.

Such notions wore faces now. Beloved faces...

A sense of light and movement at the edge of his vision jerked his head up. He thought it must have been another shooting star, till a moment later, a curtain of greenish light materialized across the northern horizon.

Aurora borealis. He'd seen it before, but never heard of it happening so many weeks out from the equinox. The glowing, rippling curtain vanished, then reappeared. At its lowest edge, above the black undulation of the mountains, flowed a ribbon of scarlet. It gave him a queer sense of displacement, like seeing the sun rise from the wrong direction. He caught his breath at the savage beauty of the sight. And understanding struck.

"Burning Sky."

It wasn't the sunset for which the Mohawks had given Willa her name. Surely it had been for these fleeting, arresting, enchanting northern lights. A burning sky.

Four days deeper into the mountains, he saw a moose at last and, running along a distant ridge, a pair of hunting wolves. But no sign of another human being save the scattered black remains of small hunters' fires, many seasons old. This was the land of the eagle and hawk, of stealthy panthers and shy, lumbering bear, of falling cataracts and towering forest.

It was the place of his dreams, wider and wilder than his feeble imaginings had rendered it. He was meandering northeastward through it, planning eventually to strike Lake Champlain, then head southward toward Albany, and ultimately Philadelphia. Yet every morning he was forced to overcome a shackling resistance to pushing on.

Around midday, the day he saw the moose, he came across a game trail leading up to a saddle in the mountains. Neil let Seamus follow it, musing on what he'd name the peaks around him were he a mapmaker instead of a plant hunter.

That craggy summit to the north, with a rocky knob at the top, looking for all the world like his da's weathered profile. Old Man Peak? MacGregor's Pate?

No. He had it. Head-in-the-Clouds…or however one would say that in Mohawk. Willa could have told him. He wondered what she might be doing at that moment. Thinking of him?

Were he a man given to cursing, he'd have let loose with a few well-deserved invectives at himself. He focused all his effort on *not* thinking of

Willa, dismayed it should still require such vigilance. Surely it should get easier with practice, not harder.

The way had steepened. Ahead, the trees closed in, narrowing the trail, cutting off his view of the peaks. He'd do well to watch for snakes, as well as loose scree that might threaten Seamus's footing.

Even as he thought it, the horse lurched beneath him, hooves sending stones rattling down the incline to their right. The drop was only a few feet, but even a minor injury could prove life threatening with nothing but his meager medical kit to tend himself. He couldn't count again on a passing angel inclined to offer aid.

The trees pressed close, pine and balsam fir forming a corridor of green that swiped his knees as they passed. He urged the roan over a rise where the trail switched back on itself. Boughs brushed his face, fragrantly needled. They maneuvered another sharp turn, and Neil reined the roan to a halt. Thirty feet ahead the trail ended in a wall of rubble.

"Ye canna be serious." He hadn't been speaking to Seamus, but the gelding tossed its head, as though in the affirmative.

Stubbornness congealed in his chest. He wasn't going to retrace their steps, losing a day's travel to find another trail. He wanted to be over this pass and off the mountain. He'd envisioned a quiet stretch of water, a bit of fishing for his supper. Lake trout rolled in cornmeal, fried to perfection…

Leaning back, he gazed upslope, trying to recall his last glimpse of the saddle he was attempting to cross. From that vantage he couldn't see the forest—or the mountain—for the trees. But it couldn't be far. He could pick his way up the remainder of the slope, tangled and wooded as it was. Spotting a break in the trees, near where the trail ended in jumbled rock, he urged Seamus toward it.

The horse laid back its ears and didn't budge.

"None of that, now. I dinna mean to fight this mountain *and* you." He gave Seamus's sides a kick. The horse lurched forward.

At the break in the trees, the ground was fresh cut by cloven hooves.

Perhaps the slide had come down recently, forcing the game that used this trail to find a way around. This had to be it.

One hand on the slackened reins, the other raised as a shield, he urged Seamus up and through the break. With a scrabbling of hooves, the horse went, carrying him blind, scratched and poked by protruding branches.

Without warning Seamus balked again.

Caught in the thicket, unable even to see the horse's head, Neil felt more than saw what Seamus was attempting to do—turn on the steep ground back toward the trail. The horse swung sideways, thrusting him against a pine snag studded with broken branches, one of which gouged a furrow in his leg just above his boot top.

With a growl of pain and frustration, he got the leg up and over the roan's neck. He hit the ground, keeping hold of the reins, and shouldered his way to the horse's head.

Seamus was white eyed and snorting.

"Come on, wee gomeral. No way now but through it." Sweating and cross, he led the unhappy horse upward through the trees, coaxing it when he felt again like cursing.

Not two dozen paces on, he came across the trail again, winding up the pass as docile as you please. He'd been right. A short section of it had been buried in a slide, was all.

"See? Ye didna need to fash so."

But they'd barely reached the trail before the fool horse balked again, this time with conviction enough to nearly yank Neil's arm from its socket. He fumbled the reins as the horse shied across the broken ground, on the verge of bolting.

Above the clatter they were generating, he heard a noise, a deep animal grunt. He whirled to face upslope where the trail, still walled in by trees, topped another stony rise. On that rise in the center of the trail stood a bear, enormous and black, filling the gap in the trees like a sentry at a gate.

He ought to have been afraid; startled at the least. Likely on some level he was both, but what struck him most vividly in that moment was enlightenment—and a gripping amusement at the Almighty's sense of humor in its dispensing.

Though he hadn't in all his prayers dared broach the subject of his disobedience, God had been speaking pointedly to the matter all the while—in metaphorical language he ought sooner to have heeded. Biblical allusion. Signs in the heavens. Now they were back to Old Testament reference, with his horse engaged in the dialogue.

Standing not a dozen yards from the biggest bear he'd ever seen, Neil MacGregor began to laugh. He laughed till the force of it doubled him. "All right," he sputtered through the spasms. "I'll go back. Though heaven kens how I'm to explain it to her."

Or anyone else, for that matter.

When he got his breath back and looked again, the bear was gone. Seamus no longer showed the whites of his eyes, but had fixed him with a look of disgruntled accusation as eloquent as speech.

Hysteria threatened to bubble again, but the release of belated understanding—and his choice to obey—capped the urge. He managed a semblance of decorum as he apologized.

"I'm sorry, aye?" Taking bridle in hand, he turned the horse back the way they'd come. "But next time, save us both the bother, and just tell me 'tis an angel in the path."

# SESKEHA

Time of Freshness—August

Francis was sitting on the porch when Willa stepped from the cabin with a bucket, headed for the spring. The collie pushed past to sniff with interest at what was laid out across the steps at Francis's feet, the gutted carcass of a doe. Willa set down the bucket.

"Francis, did you—?" She broke off the question, spying the answer for herself—the arrow wound in the doe's neck. Instead, she asked, "Did you see him?"

Francis unbent his bony frame. "I f-found it. At the lake. I d-didn't see your Indian."

With the morning breeze on her face, Willa scanned the clearing's edge, struggling to control a surge of exasperation. Why did Joseph stay away? Did he not know Neil MacGregor was gone? What did he mean to do about Aram Crane? And the children?

Having heard her talking, the pair of them came sleep-tousled from the cabin, exchanging grins with Francis. Anni's brother had become a frequent visitor since Neil's leaving. Usually he spent his time with the children, helping them shoo crows and deer and rabbits from the field, or tagging along while they did their chores.

Today, he had a request to make of her.

"Anni says for m-me to say"—he pitched his voice in mimicry of his sister—"'Tell-Willa-Goodenough-is-bringing-Lem-to-visit-this-morning-while-we-quilt-and-he-has-asked-will-she-bring-Matthew-and-Maggie-to-play.'"

The children pealed with laughter, then promptly fell to begging, and though Willa chuckled too, her first instinct was to refuse the request. She didn't wish to leave the farm untended; she'd done so only twice since Neil went away—to check for an answer to her letters. Both times Jack Keegan had met her with a look of regret, finally telling her that if a letter came, he would send someone with it, so she needn't keep walking into town.

As anxious as she was for that letter to arrive, there was no pressing need for her to leave the farm now. Certainly not to take the children to Anni's to play. But she made the mistake of looking at their pleading faces.

"All right," she heard herself say. "For a short while—after chores."

They darted inside to wash and dress and soon were racing out again to gather the day's eggs, and kindling for the hearth.

"I will not go with you," Willa said on her way to the spring, Francis trailing her. "Will you promise to take them straight to Anni's and look after them?"

"Like he t-told me."

Willa halted. "Like who told you?"

"He t-told me," Francis repeated.

Willa frowned. "Joseph?"

Francis wouldn't look at her. If it wasn't Joseph…

"Francis, did you see Neil MacGregor before he left?"

She didn't need to catch the quick jerk of a nod to deduce the truth. Neil had set Francis to be their guardian angel. *Neil.*

"He didn't need to do that," she muttered, trying to be annoyed, or even amused, when in truth she was pathetically grateful, and touched.

With their chores done, Willa bade the children be back for their dinner. "Anni is meant to be resting. I do not want you wearing on her. And, Francis, don't take them by the road." That would be too dangerous. They must go by the path, straight to Anni's cabin.

"I never go b-by road," Francis said, which was true enough.

Willa smiled, remembering how he had, at three years of age, discovered the path she and Anni used to go between Shiloh and the Obenchain cabin. It crossed Black Kettle Creek upstream from the cabin that had been built above the mill by Charles Keppler's father.

They had had to skirt that cabin as girls, to keep from being seen. Now, it was Anni's home.

Francis had followed her and Anni that day, even at three years so stealthy they'd nearly reached the Obenchain's cabin before they found him out.

No one could conceal himself in the woods as well as Francis. He would be wary and watchful as a deer. She could trust the children to him, just to Anni's. She told herself this and believed it, but couldn't quite banish her worry as she watched them walk away into the green-shadowed woods.

The collie trotted to the clearing's edge and looked back at her. "Go, if you wish." She made a casting motion with her hand.

The dog went. As the brush closed behind it, a sense of solitude fell over her. Instead of relishing it, she grew jumpy as the clouds cleared and the sun rose and the air warmed to a swelter. She kept pausing to look toward the woods for Joseph. Or her mind would stray to Neil, out there somewhere too, with his nose in a thicket. Did he think of them? of her?

Annoyed with herself for wondering, she went into the field to check the corn and scare off any marauding deer. Though she planned to let most of the corn dry on the stalk, the green corn that was best for eating fresh had ripened. She picked six ears to boil for their dinner and stood at the edge of the field surveying the tasseled stalks, the beans and squash plants clustered around each, thought about her mother's cousin, and for the first time faced the possibility that no letter was coming.

She stopped seeing corn and squash. Instead, she saw the paths it seemed were left for her to choose.

She could take Richard up on his offer. She could stay on the land and be his tenant. Maybe one day she would have enough to buy the land back from him. But that path was fraught with perils, ones she could see coming, probably many she could not. Most of Richard's devising. Thought of being so closely linked to him made her recoil from that path.

There were others to look at. She could abandon this crop in a risky gamble and walk to Albany, there to go from house to house until she found her mother's cousin or determined she was never to be found. The problem with that path was the children. Unless Joseph came and got them very soon, how could she depart in time enough for it to make a difference? August was passing. Autumn, and the land auction, were rushing up fast.

There was a third path. It led back to the People, huddled up to that British fort at Niagara, waiting to be told what to do, where to go. There were many risks to her heart on that path. Joseph. The children. The People ready to embrace her, draw her back into their circle of mutual need and caring...

She turned from the field with her corn to boil and busied herself so she wouldn't think of paths anymore, telling herself to wait another day. Or two. The letter would come. It had to come.

She swept and tidied the cabin. Then the yard.

She found a shirt of the boy's needing mending and sat in the porch shade to stitch a rent in the sleeve.

She fetched water for the corn, lingering at the spring to cool her sweating face and neck, hoping to see the children coming along the path home. Save for the hum of insects, the wood was quiet. The air lay heavy as soaked muslin, sticking her shift to her flesh as she toted the bucket back to the cabin.

Not until the high sun began to slip westward in the milk-blue sky did she acknowledge her fear. With the musket primed and loaded, she pinned up her braid and, despite the heat, started down the path at a run.

The old foot log still spanned Black Kettle Creek at the narrow point where the path crossed it. It was another short stretch to the miller's cabin. Willa's breathless appearance, bursting from the woods, made Anni squeak in surprise and half-rise from her porch chair, thrusting aside the baby quilt she was stitching.

A glance told Willa no one else was present. She halted at the steps, streaming sweat, to say in breathless snatches, "Anni...don't get up. You are meant...to be resting."

Anni grimaced as she ran a hand across her belly. Tired half moons still hung beneath her eyes. "Willa, is everything all right?"

"Where is Goodenough? Where are the children?"

Anni's expression brightened. "They went down to the mill, though by now they've likely gone into town."

"Town?" Cold alarm gripped Willa. It wasn't safe for the children to be in town, even with Goodenough looking after them. What if Richard saw them? Or Aram Crane?

"Why did you let them go?" Leaving Anni on the porch, Willa hurried across the yard, long strides eating up the ground.

"Willa! There's no cause for worry. I was about to tell you—"

Anni's words were lost beneath the swell of the mill falls as Willa reached the descending path. A glance across the creek showed no sign of the children or Francis or Goodenough. The mill itself was silent, the great stones still. As she stepped inside, Willa heard voices in the yard beyond the far door, which had been blocked from her view at the top of the path by the mill itself. Even with the rush of water beneath the floor echoing off the high walls, one of the voices sounded very much like...

It couldn't be. But it was.

She halted just inside the mill as Neil MacGregor strode through the opposite door. He moved at the center of a knot of chattering children. His shirt sleeves were turned up, showing sun-browned forearms. Those arms encircled Maggie Kershaw, who rode his hip, skinny legs wrapped around his waist. Matthew walked beside him, clutching his sleeve as though Neil might vanish if he let go. Anni's twins and Lem bobbed around him like little moons, and the collie frisked like a shooting star at their edges.

There was an instant when his focus was on the children, when he was unaware of her, an instant when her heart jumped as if it meant to leap out of her chest and rush across the mill to him. Then he tilted back his head to laugh at something one of the children said and caught sight of her. He came to a halt. Lem bumped into his back.

Goodenough and Francis came into the mill. Goodenough said something Willa didn't hear above the muffled rush of the falls—or was it the rushing in her own head?

Neil MacGregor didn't seem to hear either. Bodies flowed around him like floodwaters past a rooted tree. His face had lit at the sight of her, as if he felt the same startled joy racing through her now.

"Willa," he said, and this she heard, for everyone else had fallen silent and was looking at her, smiling in expectation, and her mouth wanted to smile too because of the blazing joy, then a spark shot out of the blaze, a spark of bewildered anger. Its small heat jolted her to her senses. Neil MacGregor was *here*.

"Why are you here?" Her voice was a sharp-edged thing, though she hadn't meant it to be. His smile faltered at it. He slid Maggie to her feet. Goodenough and Francis came toward her, then passed on with Anni's children and Lem to climb the path to the cabin. Matthew and Maggie lingered.

"Mr. MacGregor came back," Maggie said, her smile undimmed by the tension searing the air above her head. Matthew, more wary of it, looked uneasily between them.

"Run on up to Miss Anni's cabin," Neil told the children, never taking his gaze from her. "I need to speak with Willa. Go on and dinna fash," he added when they made to protest. "Ye'll see me again, I promise."

Reluctantly they crept past her, two dark, sleek heads. The collie slipped out on their heels.

Neil came toward her across the dusty mill, creaking the aging boards beneath their feet. She watched him come, sweating now from more than running, each lungful of air filling her senses with the smells of creek water and corn chaff and old wet wood, until he stood in the sunlight that spilled through the door over her shoulders, hot on the back of her head. He didn't seem the least perturbed as silence stretched between them, a silence too heavy for her to bear.

"You have come back because you are unwell? More headaches?" Even as she asked, she knew it wasn't so. He looked in better health than she had ever seen. The sun had browned his face and arms, making his eyes more vivid, his complexion more robust. But there was something else changed about him. She couldn't put a name to it, but she'd never seen him look so whole, so strong, so assured in himself.

His teeth shone white against his skin when he smiled, and her heart made the little eager jump again.

"No headaches. I think this cracked head of mine has finally made its peace with the frontier. 'Tis awfully good to see you, Willa."

This time when he said her name, her belly turned over as well as her heart, as his eyes threatened to pull her straight into his arms, all good sense abandoned. It was like wrenching a knife from a wound, but she took a step back from him, nearly exiting the mill.

"Why are you here?"

He closed the space between them. "I should never have left."

She frowned at that. "You have your work to do."

"Willa—" His smile fell lopsided. He rubbed the back of his neck. "At least it didna take a talking donkey to turn me from my folly, just a canny horse and a bear. I have that over Balaam."

Willa shook her head. Absent or present, silent or talking, men were a complete exasperation. "I do not understand."

"You dinna need to just now," Neil said with maddening calm. "Listen, I dinna mean to intrude upon you. I willna come to the cabin if ye dinna wish me to. I'm staying with the blacksmith."

"With Gavan and Leda?"

"Aye. And I did get a bit of work done while I was away. Gavan's helping me with the annotation now."

"He is?" She sounded like a simpleton, questioning his every utterance, but none of it was making sense.

Voices interrupted as Charles and a customer entered the mill.

Neil put a hand to her arm. She jerked away. Disappointment flickered in his eyes but didn't dim his smile.

"I ken you'll be anxious, being away from the farm. Shall we go on up so you can collect the children and head back?"

It was an offer of escape, and she took it, turning her back on him to hurry up the path.

He followed in silence, yet she sensed it wasn't the silence of defeat. She suspected she'd find him smiling at her still, did she dare look back.

TWENTY-EIGHT

From the moment they left Anni's cabin, all the children could talk about was Neil. Across the creek on the foot log, through the long stretch of muggy woods, they strung their questions like beads on a thread with barely a breath between: "Why did he come back?" "Why isn't he living in your cabin?" "Why didn't he come to see us first?" "What does he mean to do?"

Glancing over field and yard to assure herself all was as she'd left it, Willa opened the cabin door. She tried to push aside the crowding collie with her knee, lost that battle, and turned on the children as the dog rushed in ahead of her.

"As I said the first time you asked, I do not know. How can I know? I have seen him for less time than you have."

She set about boiling the corn for their late dinner. The children hung back, stomachs growling. She could feel them casting glances at each other behind her back.

Matthew ventured, "He spoke to you in the mill. Did he say—"

"He told me nothing." That wasn't true, but what he had told her made her wonder if he'd lied about not having the headaches, the ones that could scramble his brains. Talking donkeys?

"He is staying with the smith," she added, hoping it would satisfy.

"We know," the children said in unison.

"Then you know as much as I know." Reaching for a chunk of wood, she turned her mind from the memory of Neil's gaze spilling over her, naked with the answer to all the children's questions. And her own.

She built up the fire, swung the kettle over it, and set about husking the corn. The children had gone out to the porch, where they went on asking each other questions in lowered voices. She dropped the corn into the water and sat down to watch for the first curls of steam to rise.

Her hands were shaking.

Despairing of sleep, Willa descended the loft ladder and stood over the boy and his sister to be sure they slept undisturbed. Even the collie lay curled and slumbering, barely cracking an eye at her when she lifted the bar from the door and slipped outside.

The heat had broken at sunset with a rain that rumbled through, intense and brief, then passed across the hills as twilight fell. A freshening breeze blew in its wake. The air felt scrubbed clean.

Having no real aim in mind, she crossed the yard barefoot under a moon so bright she could see her shadow. When she spotted a stray branch strewn by the storm, she picked it up. A few paces on, she bent for another. Making a circuit of the clearing, she gathered windblown limbs for kindling.

She stopped to feel the breeze on her skin, sensing in it a distant hint of autumn. And on the other side of autumn…where would she be? She had no more than caught that haunting worry from the corner of her mind before a well-worn memory slipped in to distract her: *'Tis the color of winter oak leaves, your hair…*

Kingfisher had never said such a thing to her. How could a man saying such a thing delight and terrify her in equal measure? She wasn't like Neil MacGregor, lacking a sense of self-preservation. From the day he stood up to Richard and was brought to his knees for it, she had seen this. Everything she'd learned of him since confirmed it. He didn't fear bodily pain. Nor the more terrible pain the heart could feel. He was unafraid to risk its breaking.

She'd left the cabin to stop thinking of Neil. Better to fix her mind on the land auction and the letter from her mother's cousin that had yet to come. Her hope in it had frayed to a desperate thread. The only thing that had changed since she stood at the edge of the cornfield, facing her three stark choices, was that Neil had come back.

Did that mean there was a fourth choice?

No. She dared not let there be. But since he *was* back, maybe he would agree to look after the children while she went to Albany to find Tilda Fruehauf. If he would not, and Joseph did not return in time, she saw little left for her here. It came hard to admit it, but probably it was already too late to make such a journey.

All her work. All her struggle. It had been for nothing. What else was left but to give up and go back to the People? At least that would make Joseph happy, for a time. But what about a year from now? five years from now? How would he feel then? Did he mean to live his life as no woman's husband, no child's father, because he couldn't have her in that way?

He deserved more.

Hugging the bundle of storm-cast limbs to her chest, she moved along the corral, weeds wetting her feet and the hem of her shift. Wind rattled the trees at the clearing's edge and ran cool fingers through her unbraided hair. Somewhere a night bird called, and she thought: *Neil could name it.*

With a sigh she turned back toward the cabin. As she reached the empty horse shed, the breeze kicked up again. It covered the small sounds that might have warned her before a horse nickered from the other side of the shed wall. Which wasn't empty.

Flinging aside all but the stoutest limb, she rounded the shed. A figure stepped out, towering and broad. With a half-choked cry, she swung.

Joseph caught the limb in an upraised hand, but the tip of it raked him below the eye. He recoiled a step but didn't let go.

"Burning Sky."

She snatched the limb from his grasp and flung it aside, fear ebbing, anger flaring. Moonlight revealed the scratch she'd left, dark across his cheek. "What do you mean, giving me such a fright?"

"I saw you leave the cabin. When you came close, I called to you."

"The bird call? That was you?"

His teeth in the moonlight were white when he smiled. She peered into the shed. He hadn't come empty-handed. A few feet from his mare, a gutted deer hung from a roof pole.

"I'd have suspected you crawled off to die in a thicket somewhere if you hadn't left us meat a few times—and I thank you for that—but now tell me where you have been. You couldn't have taken Aram Crane away or I would have heard of it. Did you decide you had the wrong man and go off to find the right one?"

Before her flood of questions abated, he was laughing softly, deep in his throat. She was mightily tempted to hit him again.

"Aram Crane is the right man," he told her, amusement fading. "But after what you told me about the peace talk, I wished more news of it and of Thayendanegea, so I went to that place to see what I could learn."

"So you did go to Fort Stanwix? All that way with your wound barely healed?"

"I had good reason, and not just for learning what might happen to our people." He was a tall shadow in the darkness, with the moon at his back. He moved closer. "Thayendanegea will come to this talk."

"I should think so," Willa cut in. "But how does that matter to you or me now?"

"Listen, this is how it matters. Because he comes to Fort Stanwix, I will not have to take Crane to Niagara but only as far as that fort. I can let Thayendanegea and the others take him the rest of the way. Then I can come back here to—for the children."

She wondered briefly what he'd started to say, before her mind moved on to the children. At last he would take them away. She closed her eyes, waiting for the relief to come.

It did not come. There was only emptiness and a stirring of something like panic.

"You've left me to wonder about all this for weeks," she said, hearing the scold in her voice, unable to temper it. "You might have said something before you went so that I wouldn't have worried and wondered."

"I am sorry," he said, one hand coming warm around her shoulder. "You worried for me?"

The way he said it, surprised and hopeful, made her cautious.

"Of course I did. When is it to be?" she asked, though she knew the answer.

As she'd hoped, the question diverted him. His hand fell away from her. "Not until *Seskeha* is past."

The time of freshness: August.

"That is barely more than a fortnight. What do you think will happen?"

"The Mohawks will not come back to live along the river. The Oneidas will want to stay on their lands—they have the favor of the Americans as allies, so this may be a thing that happens. But even much of their land is overrun with settlers, land takers. They would be as islands among them, even if they lived as the whites do, each man on his farm. You remember I told you Thayendanegea talks of land in Canada to resettle the Kanien'kehá:ka?"

His words fell like stones into the pool of Willa's thoughts, stirring questions that surfaced until she skimmed off the one that truly mattered. "Do you still mean to follow Thayendanegea?"

"That depends."

Joseph moved closer. He wore no shirt, only leggings and breechcloth. Willa felt the warmth coming off his skin. Her face was inches from the hollow of his bare throat.

"The Scotsman no longer sleeps beneath your roof?"

She was cautious again. "He went to the mountains for a time. But he has come back—to Shiloh."

"You spoke to him. I saw you at the mill." His dark eyes were fathomless in the moonlight. "I was on the ridge above you. I saw you leave. You did not look pleased with him, though him you did not hit with a branch."

"I didn't have one to hand, or I might have."

She saw the flash of his teeth, the slight wince as the skin across his cheekbone pulled at the scratches she'd made. She raised a hand to his face.

"I should take you in by the fire and clean that."

Joseph put a hand over hers, pressing it to the wound. His hand covered hers completely, making her feel small and delicate, both of which she was not. "Soon," he said.

She knew what he meant to do even before his face bent toward hers.

"Yah, Joseph." She spoke gently but with finality, and raised a hand so that it came between their lips before they touched.

He jerked back from her. Even in the moonlight, she could see the flooding sadness in his face, like the blood that pours from a wound when the knife is pulled free.

Sorrow came down on her. But not regret. "Joseph, I will always care for you. But you are my brother."

The ache of wanting her was thick in his voice. "What keeps us apart now? Is it our clan? Or is it *him*?"

She knew who he meant. Her mind rose up to deny it, but the words stuck in her throat.

"Answer me, Burning Sky. Or is it that you fear to love anyone again?"

She tried not to wince at that.

"You want me to go away and take those children with me." He took her in his arms then, too swiftly for her to prevent it.

Though she stiffened at first, she sensed this time he held her as the brother who'd comforted her in a cornfield far to the north, a lifetime ago that suddenly felt like yesterday.

"Do not let fear rule your heart," he whispered into her hair. "We are Wolf Clan, you and I. But even a wolf is not meant to walk alone."

She stayed in the shelter of his arms for a moment, then forced herself to leave it and move beneath the shed to the hanging deer, where the smell of blood was strong.

"Come. Help me build the fires, and we will smoke this good meat you've brought me."

Easing his weight off the balls of his feet, Joseph Tames-His-Horse settled his haunches on the earth and watched from a stand of pines west of the village. The clank and bang of the smithy had ceased for the day. On a bench behind the log structure, the Scotsman sat, using the last of the daylight to work. He had been at it long, but the light was fading.

There. He was gathering up the tools of his trade—field sketches, brushes, paints, the shell bowl; Joseph was too far away to recognize each object, but he'd seen them often enough to know what the man required to work. The Scotsman didn't walk to another cabin, nor to find his horse and ride away on it. He went inside the small lean-to at the back of the smithy. Soon, smoke was coming from the chimney.

Dusk was fading to twilight when another man rounded the building.

The blood in Joseph's veins quickened. He'd watched the deserter often enough to know his build, his stride, the small habitual movements that marked him, even without light enough to show his bright hair. So absorbed had he been in watching the Scotsman, Joseph had missed the man riding into the village. Now there he was, behind the smithy emptying his bladder against a sapling tree.

Thought of sending an arrow into some vital part of the man while his breeches were undone amused him, but he did not intend to kill Crane, if he could help it. Deserting soldiers brought back living were more useful to the British than dead ones. Most of the time. And he had better be about the business, now that Burning Sky had made her choice.

Did she even know it herself? She had not answered him about the Scotsman, so perhaps she didn't realize yet that she loved him, despite all her protesting that it was not so, that she wished only to be left alone.

If only the man had not come back.

He pushed up from his crouch and made his way to where he'd hidden the mare, emptiness in his heart where for years hope had clung. He wanted with all his being to hate the Scotsman, but the man had taken the lead ball out of his side and seen him through a fever. He'd showed Owl and Pine Bird affection and care. He was a man who took his God seriously, yet didn't take himself with the unassailable gravity of most white men, possessing instead a self-deprecating humor Joseph could appreciate.

He might actually have liked Neil MacGregor, had Burning Sky not stood between them.

Retrieving his mare, he moved off through the forest to find a place where he might bide the night in safety. He needed to pray and make ready his spirit for what he meant soon to do.

And put into practice for himself the trust in God he had always preached to Burning Sky.

TWENTY-NINE

Y ou sure it isn't twins, Dr. MacGregor?" Anni Keppler asked as she
straightened her garments and pushed herself upright on the bed.

"As sure as I can be," Neil said, having already admitted that he'd had
little practice tending expectant mothers, even before deciding he'd rather
be drawing plants than prescribing them. "I didna feel but the one head
and two wee feet."

Charles hovered at the foot of the bed. "That's a relief. Don't know
why you came back, Doc, but I'll be glad to have you by when Anni's time
comes."

Almost before Neil had unrolled his blankets on the spare bunk behind the smithy, folk began trickling in for doctoring. Despite the scarcity
of medicines to hand, their need filled up his days of waiting—on the
Lord, on the mail, and on Willa.

When Charles stepped into the front room, leaving them momentarily alone, Anni fixed him with a knowing look. "Have you seen Willa
since that day at the mill?"

Her expressive face reminded him of that first morning at Willa's
cabin, when she'd burst from the woods, eager to reunite with a friend
she'd thought forever lost. "No, I havena," he said as he helped Anni to her
feet.

For more than a week now, Willa had stayed rooted to her cabin and
fields. If only a letter would arrive, he'd have an excuse for riding out to her.

"I've wanted to ask"—Anni lowered her voice, glancing at the door
and the unshuttered window—"whether that brother of hers is still about.
The Mohawk, I mean."

"She told you about him?" he asked in surprise, though the answer
was obvious.

Anni's gaze was searching. "He was meant to go away and take those children with him."

"He was."

"Yesterday Francis came here from Willa's. He mentioned the children. They're still there. I guess that means *he* is still somewhere nearby." Anni sighed. "I told her it was dangerous. For everyone." She crossed the room with the waddling gait of advanced pregnancy.

"They both ken the danger," he said, remembering Joseph Tames-His-Horse lying in Willa's cabin with a bullet in his side.

At the bedroom door, Anni paused. "Has Willa ever told you how her grandmother used to hide her books? Mrs. Mehler thought reading a waste of time, that it bred laziness. So Willa took to keeping her books on that little islet in the lake near their cabin. . .where she was taken."

Neil minded the ruined copy of *Pamela*. "She told me."

"She was stubborn even then, was Willa, and yet"—Anni frowned, as if searching for words—"she's the nearest to a sister I ever had, and now that I have my sister back, I want to keep her. I know she's making it hard, but if you love her, don't give up on her."

She'd taken him so off guard with this plea Neil couldn't for the life of him make his jaw work to reply.

Into his silence she pressed, "Because if you do—love her, I mean—and she can be made to see what she has in you, maybe she won't fight so hard to hold on to what doesn't matter as much."

Anni placed a hand on his arm. "Not that her land isn't important, or that I want to see her lose it. It's only that something's broken in Willa, and instead of facing it, she's hiding behind her anger and resolve like the walls of a fort, shutting everyone out."

"Not broken," he said. "Bruised, and verra badly so, but. . ." *A bruised reed shall he not break.*

Please, he prayed, as he met Anni's earnest, troubled blue eyes. "Think of all she's lost. We went through the same war, but we at least can claim a remnant of who we were before. Willa lost two families, two lives, utterly. All but the land."

And Joseph. But he didn't say that.

"I fear what else she might lose, trying to save it." Anni let her hand fall from his sleeve. "And I fear losing her again."

"I willna give up on Willa," he said. "Before God, I promise ye that. Not unless a day comes I'm sure that's what He's asking of me." Even if that meant he lost everything, in the end.

Anni's eyes shone. "Then neither will I."

Neil followed her into the front room. The cabin door swung wide enough for a small blond head to poke in. Samuel.

"Mama? Can we come back in?"

While Charles tended the stew bubbling over the fire, Anni eased herself down at the table, rubbing at her back. "I hear your stomach gnawing your backbone from here. Come on."

Both the twins rushed in.

Neil, taking this as his cue to leave, was startled to find the Colonel had arrived and was tapping dottle from a pipe over the porch railing. He didn't follow his grandchildren in. Instead, he turned to walk with Neil beyond the light from the cabin door toward the mill path, his limp more noticeable without his stick, left on the porch.

Though twilight had fallen, the day's warmth lingered. The last of the season's fireflies lit random sparks in the grass. What Neil hoped was the last of the season's mosquitoes whined about his ears.

"I wanted to thank you for your care of my daughter," Waring said, holding his unlit pipe by the bowl, white stem resting along his forearm. "I'm relieved to see you return to Shiloh. We certainly stand in need of a doctor."

"I've been kept busy, true enough."

The Colonel made a sound of affirmation. "I cannot help but notice where you're bunking at present. Other arrangements could be made, if you intend to make this situation permanent. Or have you arrangements of your own in mind?"

Neil was glad for the twilight that hid his warming face. "I willna say my purpose in coming back had naught to do with Willa Obenchain. She's determined to have naught to do with me just now, though."

The Colonel gave a wry snort. "Determined, is she?"

Neil chuckled at that, but as always in the man's presence, he could not feel wholly at ease. Perhaps it was only the specter of his son, who as far as Neil could tell had kept himself on his own land since making his offer of tenancy and had left off plaguing Willa about hers. Unless that crop fire had been at his instigation.

When Elias Waring spoke again, it was clear his thoughts had gone to his eldest son as well, though in a very different light.

"You realize, had Willa never returned, there isn't a man in Shiloh who'd blink twice at Richard purchasing that land at auction." The Colonel put his pipe stem to his mouth, then lowered it. "While I've every sympathy for her plight, my son isn't the villain here."

Had Willa never returned... How many others in Shiloh had had the same thought? No doubt Richard Waring had chewed on it for months, like a dog worrying marrow from a bone. "Nor is Willa in the wrong for wanting to prove the government has no claim of confiscation."

"I've never thought her so," the Colonel said. "I do, however, have cause to think her unwise."

Neil felt a crawling up his spine. As supportive of Willa as the man had been, if forced to choose between her interests and his son's, Neil was in little doubt at this moment which way the man would lean. "What cause?"

The Colonel crossed his arms. "My daughter should learn to shutter her window before she speaks of things she'd rather not have overheard."

Neil tried to swallow, but his mouth had dried. "What d'ye mean by that, sir?"

The Colonel's pipe stem pointed at him like an accusing finger. "If what Anni said is true and there's a Mohawk involved in these matters—not a couple of half-breed children but a warrior, here by Willa's leave—then I'd be keen to hear what you know of him and his business in Shiloh."

Two days later, in the room behind the smithy, ostensibly at work, Neil couldn't put from his mind the final moments of his conversation with the Colonel in the Kepplers' yard.

"If what Anni said is true and there's a Mohawk involved in these matters…"

Neil had slapped at a mosquito biting his neck and rubbed at the spot, giving himself space to think through his reply. "His business in Shiloh, so far as I ken, has naught to do with anything but Willa. He's something of a brother to her, as the Mohawks reckon these things. He's hunting for her, is all."

That wasn't all, but he hadn't voiced his lingering worry that Joseph might, in the end, convince Willa to go back to their people. Perhaps the Colonel had sensed that hidden worry, for he'd rephrased his question several times to no avail. There was nothing more Neil could add.

He shook his head now and put pen to paper, but found the ink had dried on his quill. Spread on the table were his newest field sketches, a few plant specimens, and the sheet of foolscap he was meant to be filling with a drawing fit for the pages of a field guide. He was in no frame of mind for the work. He wanted companionship, conversation, but there was no one with whom he could discuss the matters troubling his soul. No one but Willa. The impulse to go to her was constant, despite the inner voice that cautioned doing so now would end badly.

He spread a cloth over his work, then went around to the smithy. Judging by the noise and heat from the forge, MacNab was busy, but the man didn't mind if he took a notion to sit by, provided he kept out of the way.

The tall blazed mare hitched in the yard brought him to a halt before the clang of metal ceased and Richard Waring's voice rose.

"It's the blasted right hind shoe again…"

Neil did an about-face and headed instead for Keegan's store. He glanced back when he reached the oak-shaded porch to find Richard standing in the smithy yard staring after him, looking on the verge of following.

Neil ducked inside the store. The only occupant of the densely stocked front room was Keegan's old mother, seated in a rocking chair near the counter, keeping herself in motion with one crooked bare foot.

"Good day to ye, ma'am," Neil said, though the vague blue eyes she flicked at him bore no recognition.

The sound of his voice brought Keegan from the taproom, wiping his hands on a rag. "Doc. Wondered when I'd be seeing your face today."

Neil's mouth lifted at the corner. He'd come in nearly every day since his return, checking for mail. "Aye. Though I'm also wondering after your mother here." Glancing at the woman's wispy head, bobbing as she rocked, he lowered his voice. "You dinna have her tied to that chair, do ye?"

Keegan grinned. "No need. Whatever bee she had in her cap to do with Willa Obenchain, it's flown. She ain't wandered off in weeks. Speaking of Willa, sorry. No mail for her. But there's a letter come for you."

"For me?" Neil replied.

"Before the sun was up. We've a rider on the route now will sometimes push on through the night, up from German Flats—which is jolly fine for those expecting mail, but not so convenient for those receiving it for 'em." Complaining happily, Keegan fished behind the counter, coming up with a battered letter he handed to Neil.

Though the seal wasn't broken, the original direction had been scratched through and another—presumably Shiloh—written in its place.

Neil paid for the letter, trying to decipher the return address. There was a *B.* He was almost certain of that. But did the surname begin with an *R* or a *K*?

"Looks to have taken some pains to sniff you out." Keegan craned his neck. "From a Benjamin Rush, in Philadelphia. Friend of yours?"

"Aye." Neil's stomach took a plunge. There was only one reason Dr. Rush would be attempting to reach him by post. Though he wanted badly to ask Keegan to read the letter to him, doing so would equate to telling all of Shiloh his business. "What I canna account for is its finding me here."

Someone in Schenectady, one of those few who knew where he'd gone, must have chosen the farthest settlement to the westward they could name and sent it on in hopes of it reaching him.

"Ironic that it did so," he added, "while the letter that should come for Willa never has."

"Not since the last one, anyway."

Neil looked up from the letter in his hand, to stare at Jack Keegan. "What d'ye mean—the last one?"

"The last letter."

"A letter came for Willa? You're sure?"

Keegan's brows rose. "Sure as I can read my own name."

Neil felt the blood drain from his face. He forced himself to enunciate each word. "Who sent it?"

"Dagna Mehler."

The thready voice came from behind Neil, but Jack only rolled his eyes. "Now, Ma. Don't start that again." He looked at Neil, apologetic. "Though I seem to recall it was from a woman…"

"Dagna Fruehauf Mehler." Maeve Keegan glared at her son, whose expression suddenly cleared.

"Well, now, it was *Fruehauf.* But a different front name. Not *Dagna,* Ma, for crying out loud."

Not Dagna. *Tilda.*

Neil heard himself ask how long ago this letter had passed through Keegan's store. It seemed an age before Keegan admitted he couldn't recall exactly when. "A while back. About the time you left. Or a bit after. Willa came in a time or two, and I finally told her should a letter come, I'd see it reached—"

"Aye, man," Neil cut in. "Whenever it came, where is it now?"

Keegan stared. "I expect Willa has it. Where else would it be?"

"You're the one took it to her. You tell me."

"No, I didn't," Keegan said deliberately, as if Neil was slow to grasp the obvious.

Neil felt his composure slipping.

"Listen," he began, then stopped. He could never say what made him turn to look at Keegan's mother again. She sat in the chair rocking it as before, yet something about the woman was different.

Then he knew. It was her eyes. They were clear now, penetrating as she gave him back his stare.

Enlightenment was dawning, almost as clear. He turned to Jack, his heart beating with an ominous thud. "If you didna take it to her, who did?"

"I'd meant to trot it over to the Kepplers, but didn't after all, on account of Waring stopping in that day. He said he was riding out to her cabin to check on things so he'd save everyone the trouble. He took the letter himself."

Something like a fist squeezed Neil's gut, reminding him of a certain morning in Willa's cabin yard. "D'ye mean the Colonel? Did he take it to Willa?"

"No," Keegan said. "It was Richard Waring took the letter."

'Twas clear now why they'd had no answer from Tilda Fruehauf— and why Waring had seemed content to leave Willa alone and bide his time; that letter had never reached her. Of this Neil was certain. Whether it had contained news in Willa's favor or not, Anni would have heard about it by now and would have told him. That the letter *had* contained news in Willa's favor he was also certain, else Waring would have passed it along to her, if only to dash her hopes. Easy enough to explain its seal being disturbed, after so long a journey from Albany.

Less apparent was what Neil was meant to do about it.

Waring wasn't likely to suffer a sudden pang of conscience and confess to stealing, and possibly destroying, the letter from Albany, along with whatever evidence—or promise of the same—in Willa's favor it might have contained. Confronting Waring about the theft would prove useless—dangerous even, should it spur the man out of his complacency to some reckless act.

Should he appeal to Elias Waring?

No. Richard was bound to learn of it, and the result could be the same.

Racing Seamus out to Willa's cabin to tell her what he'd learned was an impulse harder to ignore. Later, he paced his small room, praying, thinking he'd talk it over with MacNab. While he waited for the smith to finish work, Neil came the nearest he had yet to ignoring the internal warning against pushing his presence upon Willa.

It was while he waited that a curious—and worrying—thing occurred. Waring couldn't have kent, standing in the smithy yard watching him enter the store, that Neil was about to discover the existence of the missing letter, but it seemed he suspected as much, for soon after Waring rode his freshly shod horse back in the direction of his farm, Aram Crane had ridden into Shiloh.

Now the man was loitering at the mill, watching the track to Willa's farm—as well as the only way to reach the Keppler's cabin and the path that led from thence.

Going to Willa now would be as good as admitting his knowledge of the theft. At first he thought he'd wait until nightfall. Surely they couldn't mean to watch that track—and him—every hour of the day and night. But while he waited and paced, there came into Neil's mind another action he could take. As the initial tide of outrage over the letter theft ebbed, he grew increasingly certain it was the right course.

He could leave Shiloh—by a path no one would expect.

Benjamin Rush's letter, in reply to the letter he'd sent before leaving Schenectady that spring, didn't contain the news Neil had feared—that he'd been recalled from his wilderness sojourn—though what the man had to relate was bad enough. The crux of it was that the Society was losing interest in his long-delayed expedition, or at least their interest in reimbursing him for any further expenses he had or would incur, or printing the body of his work should it be completed. The doctor had stated tactfully that should his letter find Neil before he was beyond its reach, some evidence of his progress sent in earnest of the completed manuscript might serve to fan the members' flagging enthusiasm for the project. It was true that unavoidable delays had occurred, and that Neil was not to blame for them, but now that the war was over the Society was ready to regroup, and it was only natural that fresh visions, new directions, would supersede those that seemed of primary interest years ago…

MacNab set the letter aside. "Did ye ne'er tell this Rush all of what befell ye?" The smith tapped his own forehead below the line of his hair, indicating Neil's scar.

"No, I havena." Rush knew he'd been injured in the aftermath of Cherry Valley, months after he'd set out from Philadelphia, but Neil had made light of his condition. He'd admitted to the headaches, needing some reason to explain his letters being penned by other hands than his. But he hadn't told them the worst of it. His failure to be forthcoming had been a mistake.

Call it what it is. A lie of omission. For all his talk to Willa of trust, he was the one fallen short in that regard. He'd feared his fellow Society members would see him as damaged goods, unfit for the task they'd sent him to accomplish. In striving to protect his dream, he'd come to the brink of having it snatched from him.

"*Mea culpa*," he murmured, turning to the lean-to's tiny clay-and-wattle hearth to dish up the stewed rabbit he'd heated for his supper.

As he ladled the stew onto a tin plate, memory of the bear in his path returned with clarity. In that moment he'd known beyond doubt what he was meant to do. What the Almighty spoke to him on that mountainside hadn't changed. That Willa might never return his love, never want him as he did her, didn't alter the act of service that love asked of him now. Not *stay* this time. But *go*.

He turned from the hearth as MacNab rose to make for his own table. "I've decided a thing, Gavan. Come morning—"

A shadow in the open doorway checked him.

"Mister Neil," Goodenough said in greeting. "I see I've interrupted supper."

THIRTY

I'm on my way to Miss Anni's," Goodenough said, "but wanted to stop in and tell you, in case you see Miss Willa afore she or I do. They fixed a date for that land auction. The Colonel got it in a letter from that fella poked around here back in spring with his maps and deeds."

Wendell Stoltz. The assessor for the commissioners of confiscation.

"He's heading back this way soon," Goodenough added.

Neil swallowed past a knotted throat. "When is it to be?"

"Middle of September, the sixteenth, I think it is."

Less than three weeks away. If he'd needed confirmation, he had it. "Right, then." He leaned over the table, palms flat. "There's a thing I must do, and I must leave Shiloh to do it."

If Willa had a hope of gaining the proof she needed to save her land, then he must go to Albany and find Tilda Fruehauf—apparently alive and willing to communicate—and let the consequences shake themselves out as they may.

Goodenough looked less than pleased. "Seem like you just come back, saying leaving was a mistake. Where you aiming to go now, Mister Neil?"

"'Tis best I dinna say." The fewer who kent his business, the longer he'd have before Richard Waring deduced where he'd gone and why. "But there's a concern I have in going. 'Tis Anni. I've every reason to think she'll carry to term, or verra near it, but if she doesna, and I'm not by—"

Goodenough held up a hand. "I'm here. And there's Miss Leda. It'll be all right, and if it ain't, not much can be done even if you were here, is there?"

Her dark eyes defied him to offer argument or platitude. He'd none to give and less experience birthing bairns than she, in any case. "There's a thing more I must ask of ye. Both of ye," he said, turning to include MacNab. "Speak of my leaving to no one."

"Ye've my word," MacNab said without question.

Goodenough eyed him, less certain. "Folk gonna notice soon enough."

"Aye. Still, I'm asking you. Please."

Goodenough heaved a sigh. "All right, Mister Neil. If that's how you want it."

"That's how it has to be." He saw in her eyes she caught the difference and didn't know whether to be glad or worried. The last thing he wanted was for Waring—father *or* son—to get wind of his absence any sooner than was necessary. He was tempted to explain his journey to Goodenough, but word was far more likely to reach Willa in so doing, and he didn't want to make a promise to Willa he mightn't be able to keep.

There was one thing he needed to say to her, however. Once Goodenough took her leave, he asked Gavan MacNab to help him say it.

Neil folded the letter and sealed it with a candle's drippings. Not only had MacNab penned it for him, he'd agreed to ride to the cabin and see the letter into Willa's hands. Unavoidably privy to its contents, the man had been unable to hide his sympathy, which Neil pretended not to see.

"Just one thing, Gavan," Neil said. "I'm certain Aram Crane's watching that road, expecting *me* to go to Willa."

The smith's gaze sharpened. "Need I expect trouble out o' him?"

"I'll not put it past the man," Neil said, already turning his attention to provisioning the journey east. In brief he explained about the letter gone missing and why he was leaving for Albany—and why it needed to be in secret. "I mean to leave as soon after nightfall as I can slip away unseen."

Gavan's black brows drew low. "I ken Willa's been waitin' for word from back east, something that might be o' help to her—and the contrary to Waring. Even supposing he stole the letter, ye dinna think he'd do any-thin' worse to thwart her, do ye?"

Anything and everything, Neil thought.

"I'm asking you to trust me, Gavan—and take care. If the road past the mill is watched tomorrow, dinna go. Wait. But the soonest you can take it safely, I'd be obliged."

He picked his slow way along Black Kettle Creek, beneath a moonless sky, then south on a broader track from the point where the creek emptied into the West Canada, flowing down to the Mohawk River, but it wasn't until a few miles north of German Flats, with the sky beginning to gray, that he kent he was being tracked. While no more than the occasional snapped twig had struck him as anything other than normal nocturnal forest sounds, Seamus had sensed a presence, swiveling long black ears to catch at sounds beyond Neil's hearing.

Little he could do about it save press on. A chill settled in his bones as he rode. A mist rose off the broad creek, hanging low in the bordering woods as dawn's gray flushed rose gold. He welcomed the rising sun, not only in hope of catching a glimpse of the rider he was all but certain was keeping pace with him; he'd ridden the past hour with his bladder full and needed badly to find cover in which to stop.

The sun was spilling its liquid light through the trees when he could stand the discomfort no longer. He drew Seamus to a halt and scanned the track behind, which rose to a slight crest, blackly wooded either side, and deserted. Quickly he dismounted.

In the seconds it took him to do so, a rider had materialized in the road behind him, his horse turned sideways as if frozen in the act of cross-ing, a pale horse gleaming like marble, the mist coiling around its hooves.

Neil took a step toward Seamus, heart knocking like a fist. Then he stopped.

The man on the pale horse would have been immensely tall on his feet, but it wasn't Richard Waring, whom Neil had feared had followed him. It was Joseph Tames-His-Horse.

As shock and fear subsided, Neil's impulse was to close the distance between himself and Willa's clan brother, tell him where he was bound, what he hoped to accomplish, until it struck him that such a mission might be the last thing the man would want to see succeed. Was that why he'd followed him? To prevent his reaching Albany?

But no, he couldn't ken what Neil was doing. No one did, save MacNab, and he couldn't have taken his letter to Willa so soon.

Again he nearly started forward, but something in the way Joseph sat his horse, straight and aloof, held him back. Though it was a coin's toss whether it was reproach or approval he read in that bearing, he couldn't look away from the power of the Indian's stare.

Look away, or move.

Was this what the hypnotizing stare of a snake felt like to a field mouse? The thought almost made him smile.

The spell was broken as Joseph raised a hand, laying it flat against the place where Neil had cut out the musket ball and stitched the smooth brown flesh together again. Beyond the forest, the sun sent its light spearing down through tree and mist, to glint on Joseph's glossy hair as he dipped his head at Neil. Without visible gesture, he turned the spotted mare back into the trees. In an instant he was gone, leaving no more sign than a wind's rustle where the leaves shivered in his wake.

Had it been Godspeed, then? Or good riddance?

Neil couldn't say, though he thought there had been gratitude in the gesture.

With his heart thudding in his chest, he saw to his business, swung back into the saddle, and turned Seamus's nose into the rising sun.

SESKEHKO:WA

Time of Much Freshness—September

Experience warned him to clip its wings, but despite his efforts, hope once again soared in the chest of Joseph Tames-His-Horse, higher with every mile he'd trailed the Scotsman away from Shiloh. He had not expected the man to leave, not after he returned so soon from his wilderness wanderings. This time he'd gone south toward the white settlements, not north into the mountains. Could it be he wasn't coming back? Had Burning Sky rebuffed him one too many times?

More consuming to his heart, more pressing to his mind, was another question. Did his going mean that he, Joseph, might yet have a chance to woo her back to the People?

That was the hope he tried to push down, to cover with the heavy stone of duty. No matter how things may have changed between Burning Sky and the Scotsman, there was still the deserter to deal with. And that deserter was behaving strangely.

For the past days, Crane had taken to hanging about the village, which was how Joseph came to observe Neil MacGregor's going. But as he did not know what prompted the Scotsman's departure, he did not know why Crane had changed his habits, why he seemed intent on lingering by the mill each day, as though he waited for something, or someone, to pass. Not until the sun had set did he mount his horse and return along the track that led west of the village to the stable and pastures of the big stone house, where before he'd spent the majority of his time, tending to the horses there.

Joseph sat in concealment on a ridge north of the mill, watching the track just above the structure where it curved away eastward toward Burning Sky's distant fields. The sun had dipped behind the hills to the west. Daylight was dimming. He bent his head to peer through the laurel thicket that concealed him, and there went the deserter, swinging into the saddle and leaving the mill yard, headed back along the short but lonely stretch of track to the people called Waring, who had taken him in as groom.

Do it now, half of Joseph's mind urged. *Do not let him reach his place of refuge this night. Take the man and be gone with him to Fort Stanwix.*

The other half of his mind had the whole of his heart on its side, and was shouting louder—as it had since the Scotsman left. *Go to her,* it was saying. *See if she has changed her mind about being Burning Sky.*

That half of his mind won the battle. If Crane was at the mill again on the morrow, Joseph would take him at this hour, on his homeward journey. If all went as he hoped—oh, those sprouting wings hope had— Burning Sky and the children would be waiting for him, secured away from the village, when he brought the deserter along, and they would all leave this place together.

He did not go by the woodland track but kept it in sight as he made a slower way threading his horse through timber and brush. He wasn't far past the turn the track took above the mill when the thudding of hooves alerted him to a rider's approach. He slid from the mare's back to stroke her muzzle and keep her quiet. His own heart thumped a beat of alarm, and the place in his side the ball had torn pulled with a prickling ache, as if in warning. Had he been seen again?

He waited, eyes fixed on the brush that screened the track, which showed as a lighter patch beyond the darkening woods, a stone's throw away. He didn't see the horse, but the disembodied head and shoulders of its rider passed through a break in the brush with the up-and-down motion of an easy trot.

A face in profile. Bushy black hair tailed below a hat. Broad shoulders. Heavy arms and chest.

The deserter wasn't the only Shiloh man Joseph had come to recognize on site. It was the smith, the one the Scotsman had lodged with. The man rode with purpose, though not with haste.

Joseph knew of no one else living out that way. Only Burning Sky. Why would the smith be going to see her? An errand for the Scotsman?

He grasped a fistful of mane, ready to mount up again, annoyed as much as curious. He would have to wait until the man left her cabin before he could speak to Burning Sky. He'd tensed to swing onto the horse's back when he heard another rider coming along behind the smith. This one was moving fast.

Joseph shifted to where he could see the track, in time to glimpse the passing rider. Despite the swiftness of it, despite the failing light, he knew this horseman with more surety than he had the first. Aram Crane hadn't ridden home but doubled back to the track above the mill.

Was it the smith he'd been waiting for all this time?

Hearing a shout, then a scuffling of hooves as if both horses had paused, Joseph swung onto the mare, excitement singing through his blood. He was almost to the edge of the darkening woods when one of the riders came racing back toward the village.

Crane was past him when Joseph crashed the mare through the wooded strip, kicked her into a gallop on the open track, and tugged the tomahawk from his sash. Crane slowed and wheeled his horse. Joseph glimpsed wild eyes in a white face too startled to cry out, before he struck with the flat of the blade, a blow to the head measured to daze, not kill.

Crane landed on the dusty track and did not move.

Grasping the reins of the man's horse, Joseph slid down to settle the quivering creature, then slung his prisoner across its saddle, bound him, and led both horses off the track to the woods' edge.

He paused to look down the road for sign of the smith but couldn't see far in the gathering twilight. Nothing stirred on the track. He'd taken his quarry in near silence. No doubt the smith was already halfway to Burning Sky's cabin.

He'd also taken his quarry on impulse and was now revising his plans. He wouldn't take Crane to Burning Sky or risk lingering near Shiloh where the man could be aided or rescued, and so was more than ever certain his earlier journey to Fort Stanwix had been wise. The Scotsman was gone. The deserter was in custody. And now Thayendanegea was near. Joseph would ride straight to Fort Stanwix and give the deserter over to his war chief, if Thayendanegea was amenable—and there was little doubt in Joseph's mind that he would be.

Then he would return and do all in his power to persuade Willa Obenchain to leave this place, come back to the People, be Burning Sky again. Forever.

For the first time since he found her with the Scotsman in her cabin, Joseph dared to believe it could happen that way.

Before the next dawn, a snag in the hasty capture of Crane made itself apparent. Having decided to take the deserter to Fort Stanwix in hope of catching the Mohawk delegation before they returned to Niagara, Joseph found himself forced to hunt to feed him. Many miles west of Shiloh, he left the deserter tied to a tree, taking both horses and Crane's shoes as precautions against escape.

In the gray before sunrise, as the last ribbon of pink faded from the brightening eastern sky, he set out, pausing beneath a beech tree to swallow a few shriveled huckleberries—all that remained of his provisions. He was still leaning against the smooth trunk when a line of turkeys ambled into view.

Forgoing the rifle for silence's sake, he spent three arrows and gained two hens before the birds scattered. As he retrieved the third arrow, through his mind flashed the image of himself thrusting it through the neck of his prisoner. He was meant to return Crane alive or dead. Dead was more tempting than it had been one sleep ago.

Once Crane regained his senses after his capture and was made to understand his situation, Joseph had halted the horses long enough to set him upright in the saddle, securing him with hands bound, ankles tied beneath the horse's belly, another rope at his neck, which Joseph held like a leash.

"Good dog." He'd been unable to resist giving Crane's knee a pat, grinning as the man cursed him roundly and jerked in a futile attempt at a kick.

"Folk in Shiloh know about you." Crane glared in the moonlight as Joseph swung onto his mare and gave lead reins and neck rope a tug. Crane grunted at the pull, coughed, and spat. "They know you've been skulking about. Important folk. Colonel Waring, for one."

The deserter had taken pains to alter his speech. He sounded less an Englishman now than he did the people he'd attempted to hide among, though Joseph knew he'd been born in a place called Birmingham, over the great water in England.

He kept his tone light. "And the big yellow-haired one?"

"Was it you he shot?" Crane was silent for a time, obviously thinking, then said, "And I can guess who it was patched you up again—that Scotsman who's been hanging around Shiloh all summer."

Joseph made no answer to that.

"It's known who gave you shelter too. That's going to count against her with most, along with those half breeds she's still got under her roof."

Burning Sky. A coldness congealed in Joseph's belly. He kept his gaze ahead as he picked his way through the wooded dark, brushing aside clinging webs and trailing boughs.

"She is no concern to you."

"I suspect she is to you, though." Crane's voice, rising above the crackle and thud of hooves, held suggestion, and veiled threat. "Listen now... You and I could come to an agreement, one of benefit to us both."

Joseph's belly clenched around the cold knot. "You come along peaceful, and I do not cave in your skull. That is the agreement between you and me."

"There's something I need to do east of here and—"

"East of here?" Joseph cut in placidly. "You have no food for a journey. You carry a musket, one small satchel. You are lying."

"That's your doing. I was headed back to Waring's place. That cook of theirs was meant to be putting up provisions for me."

Joseph thought about this as he picked their slow way, a vague uneasiness stirring at the back of his mind. *East of here*...where the Scotsman had been headed?

Over his shoulder he asked, "What were you doing on that track above the mill?"

"Nothing that concerns you," Crane said, with more than a little sarcasm.

"Then we have no more to say to each other."

"Just hear me out." Crane's voice tightened with rage and what sounded like fear. "Don't take me back to Niagara and I give you my word to leave the Obenchain woman alone. I'll even do what I can to keep Waring from pestering her more."

What did the deserter think his word was worth? Joseph ducked as pine branches brushed his head, glancing back as they hit Crane in the face. Then the mare dipped and swayed and carried them down into a clearing bright with moonlight.

Crane had kept his seat.

More, he had said.

"What pestering has he done?" Joseph hoped he wouldn't have to return and kill the yellow-haired giant, if Burning Sky was still so stubborn as to want to stay among such people.

Crane did not answer his question. Nearly across the clearing, Joseph turned his horse back until they were knee to knee. He grasped the neck rope tight. Crane had lost his hat somewhere in the night's passage. The forehead beneath the line of his hair showed pale in the moonlight. Tempting.

"Tell me what Yellow Hair Waring has done to her, or I take your red scalp now. They will pay me for you, either way."

"A-all right," Crane choked, and Joseph eased his grip. "The fool wants her, but he wants her land more. He set me to scaring her off it—but I never touched her," he added. "Or those little half breeds."

Joseph pictured the revulsion he felt for this man like arrows scattered on the ground. In his mind he picked them up one by one and bundled them, until he had them back in their quiver and himself under control. He turned his horse to continue on, having knowledge of the acts the deserter hinted at—the arrow in the door, the crop fire, the goat. Burning Sky and the children had weathered them all.

"Just a matter of time before someone does," Crane added under his breath. In seconds Joseph had the man by the neck again.

"Who? Who is going to touch her?"

"Waring," the man bit out, the stink of his breath in Joseph's face. "Thinks he can stomach knowing what you savages did to her, make a wife of her, once he's rid of those half breeds. But I've seen the disgust in his face when he talks about what she—"

Joseph heard no more, for that was when he knocked the man senseless again.

Crane had been coming around to wakefulness as he was leaving to hunt— too late to fight the gag or the ropes Joseph knotted behind the tree, knots that would make struggling only draw them tighter. In the dark he'd rifled through the man's belongings, taking his shot bag and musket as well as his shoes, but leaving what other possessions the man had had on him. Precautions only. The man could not get himself free.

The sun had barely crested the tops of the trees before he was tying the turkey hens to the saddle of the deserter's mount and starting back. Avoiding paths, even those of game, had served him well so far. But on his return he followed a stream and strayed too near a trail he hadn't known the stream would cross and got himself spotted.

There were three of them, afoot. Oneidas, by the feather placement in the headpieces two of them wore. Those two were elders with gray braids on their chests. They weren't dressed for hunting, rather some occasion demanding of every scrap of silver and quilled and beaded ornamentation they owned, draped or sewn to their garments. The peace treaty at Fort Stanwix, no doubt.

The third was more boy than man, though he carried a musket.

The trio stopped to stare at him, so Joseph urged the mare forward, pulling the deserter's mount along, hooves splashing in the stream. One of the Oneidas gave greeting with wary civility. That was before he drew near enough for them to see his tattoos.

"Kanien'kehá:ka," the youngest said as Joseph halted in their path. He had the supple, arrogant bearing of a warrior, though his hair wasn't plucked. He'd probably been too young to fight in the war, but suspicion darkened his voice and narrowed his eyes.

Joseph felt the brokenness of the Great Council Fire like his own heart in pieces, even though he'd been born to the People who long ago removed to Canada. Still he was Mohawk, had fought for them with Thayendanegea's warriors. How long would he feel this breaking when he met with Oneidas or Tuscaroras, the nations of the Longhouse people who had fought with the Long Knives?

He saw the same bleak thoughts in the expressions of these three, especially the sad, seamed faces of the elders.

"I give you greeting, Grandfathers, Brother," he said in the language of his father, and slid from the saddle. The threesome gaped, for he towered over them still, shoulders as well as head. "Do you make for the council at Fort Stanwix?"

He hadn't wished to ask after their business so directly, but was in a hurry to see that his prisoner was still in his custody—though he was confident of his knot work.

The more wrinkled of the elders wore a British soldier's coat, too big for his frame. He said, "We have been to that council. Now we are going home."

"Has the talking ended so soon?" Joseph noticed the other elder was staring hard at him. His broad features were faintly pitted with old scars of the spotting sickness.

The old man's wrinkles gathered into a sudden smile, a true smile that reached his eyes. "You came to Kanowalohale, many summers past, before the whites started fighting one another and made us choose sides. You came as Tames-His-Horse, but after you listened to Brother Kirkland, you left that place as Joseph. You were born Mohawk, but your father was Oneida. Bear Clan, I think."

Joseph peered at the seamed face, studying the bones beneath the pitted skin, until the face of a slightly younger man formed in his mind. "You are the one called Clear Day—Daniel Clear Day?"

The old man nodded, pleased to be remembered in turn.

Joseph would have liked to speak at length to this man, about Kirkland and the people they had both known years ago, but his need to deliver his captive beat strong against the desire.

"Grandfather, was the war chief Thayendanegea, called Brant, at the fort with the sachems and the white chiefs?"

Wisps of hair lifted on the breeze as the old man looked up at him. "Brant was there, but he has gone back west to Niagara. He went yesterday, and all the Mohawks with him. But do not be cast down about it," he added when Joseph could not hide his dismay. "There is to be another council with the chiefs from all the Thirteen Fires."

"Another council? Was nothing decided at this one?"

Clear Day shrugged, the furrows around his mouth bowing downward.

"Only the chiefs from New York came to treat. We wanted to treat with those who are over all the Fires—the Great Chief Washington or one who speaks for him. The People wish to know about their hunting lands. The whites want to know about those same lands and say some of this land must be given up to them."

"The Long Knives will honor their promises to the Oneidas, who stood with them, and leave your land unsettled," Joseph said to encourage the man, but in his heart he didn't half-believe it.

Neither did Daniel Clear Day. "That is what I went to that fort thinking, but I have not told you all. When Brant stood to speak in his turn, he said he was not given leave to offer land in trade for peace, but that he would go back to the sachems at Niagara to speak of this request, for he deems it reasonable."

Clear Day's words stunned Joseph speechless.

The old man talked on. "But this is the question I am asking now: After all the lands are divided and all the peoples put in their places, what will be divided next? Will the white chiefs say to us, 'You Oneidas cannot have the sun for warmth because we have bought it from some other red men in another place, and now you must go live in darkness'?"

The bitter words settled low on the ground between them.

"I am very sorry for it, Grandfather. It is not right for you. For any of us." Half of Joseph's mind was flitting ahead to what he was going to do with his prisoner, since going to Fort Stanwix was pointless now, when his gaze snagged on a thing one of the Oneidas carried. The young one had turned away to look down the path, revealing not only his impatience to be moving on but a leather satchel slung across his back, one that Joseph had seen before. He'd left it in camp that morning, with Crane.

Clear Day caught his look and his surprised recognition.

"A short while ago," the old man said, "we found the man who claimed to own that bag. A white man tied to a tree. Someone had put him there beside a nest of ants, and he was in torment from their biting."

It had been dark still when Joseph left his prisoner. If there had been ants, he hadn't seen the nest. "Grandfather, did this man speak to you? Did he say anything of himself?"

"Once we freed his mouth, he asked us to help him. We took pity and cut him loose."

There was no point in showing the frustration that twisted his gut into knots tighter than any he'd tied for his prisoner. "Did he repay you for this kindness with that satchel?" he asked, pointing with his chin to the bag the young one wore.

That one barked a laugh. "Once he had the feeling back in his hands, he stole this grandfather's musket and shot bag. He tried to take our food too. That is how he repaid our kindness." The young man showed his teeth in a grin. "But I fought him and stole this bag from him instead. He got away with the rest, though. It was a good musket."

Clear Day was watching Joseph's face. "Part of me did not want to show that man kindness. I am thinking now I should have listened."

Joseph closed his eyes, already devising what his next move should be. "I do not fault you for it, Grandfather, but that man belongs to the British. He deserted his post with the army. I was sent to bring him back."

His options amounted to exactly one: return to the camp and track Crane from that point.

When he opened his eyes, Joseph caught the other elder eying the turkeys. "If you will give me the satchel that belonged to that man," he said on impulse, "I will give you these birds—and the musket I took from him when I left him in the camp, to repay you for the one he stole."

It was daylight now, and he wanted a look at the contents of the bag Crane had carried on his person; in the back of his mind was the memory of the smith and that strange encounter with Crane on the track to Burning Sky's cabin.

The warrior put a hand over the satchel, as if he meant to protest, but at a look from his elders, he relented and slipped it from his shoulder. "I should have killed him for you," he said, moving to the horse to take the turkeys and the gun. "Shall I go with you now? Help you bring him in?"

Joseph smiled. "It is well offered, young brother, but no. Go with these grandfathers and see them safe to their fires."

The young Oneida reached for his arm, and Joseph felt a warming in his soul as the warrior gripped it. "Good hunting, then."

He found the letter Neil MacGregor had meant to send to Burning Sky, its seal broken, in the satchel the Oneidas had taken from Aram Crane. Instantly, he understood why it was there. The Scotsman had not abandoned her, as Joseph had hoped, but Crane—or Yellow Hair Waring— wanted her to think he had.

Joseph hunkered at the edge of camp, where churning footprints in the pine straw led off from where Crane and the young Oneida had scuffled over guns and provisions. Headed east, where the man had said he needed to go.

Thought of the Scotsman stirred uneasily in his mind, but it was buried behind his more pressing worry for Burning Sky and the children and this onerous burden of recapturing Crane.

Though the stolen musket was worrying, with no horse, no food, no covering for his feet, Crane was as near to helpless as such a man could be. Briefly Joseph regretted knocking him unconscious so soon as he had done. He wished he'd learned more about what Waring had meant for Crane to do, sending him east.

He would follow the man for now. If his trail veered toward Shiloh after all, Joseph would have him again. But if Crane was intent on vanishing elsewhere, then so be it. Joseph knew where his own trail must now lead.

He stood, feeling release in his soul about the deserter.

Regretting more than anything that he hadn't captured Burning Sky instead, regardless of her protests, and ridden hard and fast with her to Canada, he took up the lead of Crane's horse and swung onto the mare to go to her now, his belly empty as if for war, his mind fixed like an arrow launched.

THIRTY-TWO

The corn had faded from its summer lushness. The drying leaves rattled in the wind now rather than rustled, and Willa prayed daily no heavy rain or damaging wind would sweep through before it was ready to harvest. There was work aplenty to occupy her and the children until then, with beans to pick and string, squash to slice and dry, and pumpkins soon to ripen.

The long grass edging the field had crackled as their feet passed through that morning, scattering grasshoppers with each step, some leaping up to smack their hands or land in the picking baskets they toted.

At the edges of the field, the trees were beginning to show red and gold. The morning air had been chill.

Even at midday, it was cool against Willa's face, but the sun was warm where it touched her skin. She'd worn a shawl to the field, but with the sun now high, she had it slung across her chest, filling it with more beans while she waited for the children to fill their baskets and walk back with her to the cabin.

It was the shawl she'd carried her babies in when she fed them or wanted them closer than a cradleboard. The weight of the beans sagging the cloth, the bulge it created against her breast, made an ache swell beneath it. An ache she hadn't felt in many days.

Fingers falling still, she stared at the bean vines twining green among the browning corn. *Goes-Singing. Sweet Rain.* She tried to call up their faces and found she couldn't do it.

Panic jolted through her limbs. She couldn't see the faces of her children.

Her heart slammed the way it had when Goes-Singing, at two years, wandered from their place in the longhouse while her back was turned.

Just as she had searched every corner of the long, bark-covered lodge that day, finally finding her daughter hiding under a neighbor's sleeping platform, Willa scoured her mind for the memory of her children's faces. *Goes-Singing had green eyes like my one. Sweet Rain's eyes were brown. But were they dark like her father's or light like my one?*

The pattering thump of moccasined feet intruded into her anxious search.

"Miss Willa, Miss Willa! Where are you?"

Willa opened her mouth, but like a fish out of water, her lips moved without sound, as Maggie's shining-eyed face came between her and her fraying memories.

"Miss Willa—a pumpkin!"

The girl took her by the hand and tugged. Willa made her lips move again. This time words came.

"Yes. I see them all around." Pumpkins sprawled around the base of every hillock, many of them still green, some with a faint blush of ripening orange. What had the child so excited about pumpkins?

"Not like these. Come and see!"

"You are meant to be picking beans. Have you filled your basket? Where is your brother?"

"Yes. I don't know." The child was nearly jumping up and down with impatience. "Come!"

Willa left her basket and followed the girl, winding in and out of the hillocks until they'd covered nearly half the field. Maggie raced ahead to where her basket lay on the ground, its contents listing.

Halting, the child pointed like a dog scenting quail. "Look!"

Willa looked, and in surprise said, "A pumpkin!"

She picked her way over vines to the one pumpkin in all the field a week ahead of the rest, fully ripened, smooth and deeply orange. As she looked from the bright squash to the child standing by with a smile as eager as her own daughter's might have been, something hard and shell-like inside Willa cracked and began to crumble. She felt an answering smile spread over her face, heard a sound leave her lips. Laughter.

"A pumpkin," she said again, and took the knife from its sheath at her breast. "We have picked beans enough for today. It's time to make a pie."

Willa was fairly certain they would make a pie, though thus far what they'd mostly made was a mess—of the hearth, the table, and the floor between. She didn't care. Not with the bright eyes and laughter of a little girl beside her. Matthew had gone to the hens for extra eggs and stood now watching Willa crack them. She looked up while Maggie, splattered with boiled pumpkin, mashed the soft flesh in a wooden bowl with the eggs. The boy had one foot outside the cabin, one inside.

"You needn't stay inside," Willa told him. "Take that dog out and find something to do. Or," she added, hiding a smile, "would you like to measure out flour for the crust?"

Betrayed by the longing in his eyes, the boy nevertheless lifted his chin. "Men don't make pies." He cast about for some task befitting his masculine attention. "I'll chop wood."

"That is a thing for a man to do." Willa kept her face sober long enough for Matthew to leave the cabin. Then she looked at his sister. The child burst into giggles.

"He's not big enough to chop wood," Maggie said.

Willa dabbed her small nose with a streak of flour. "Perhaps he will make kindling. He's helping without arguing. Awiyo. It's good."

"Helping like me."

"No." Willa nudged her with a hip. "In this I am helping *you*. Do you wish to make the crust while I see what spices I have?"

The girl nodded, pleased. "That is easy. I'll show you."

Though she recalled well enough how to make a piecrust, Willa stepped back and let the child be the teacher.

Outside the cabin came the *chunk* of the ax hitting the cutting stump, now and then a sharper *crack* when the blade made contact with a piece of firewood. Inside the cabin the pie had just gone into the oven beside the main hearth. Willa had been saying how long she expected it would take to bake, when the collie began barking.

The barking escalated, sharp with warning.

They were staring at the cabin door when the thump of feet sounded on the porch and Matthew entered, dragging the collie by the scruff. The dog was woofing low in its throat.

Willa heard a horse in the yard. Seconds later a heavy tread creaked the porch boards and Richard Waring filled the doorway, blocking out the light. He took in the mess she and the children had made—spilled flour, slimy pumpkin pulp and seeds spotting the table and floor, as well as themselves. He grimaced at Willa's clothes—the deerskin skirt and stroud tunic she still found most convenient to wear around the farm, those she'd worn the day she found Neil MacGregor in the laurels.

She shook away Neil's image and the regret that pierced her.

The collie was still growling low in its throat.

"Matthew, take that animal outside." The boy did as she said, edging past Richard with unconcealed dislike.

Maggie, unwilling to abandon her baking pie, was all but hugging the edge of the hearth.

"Don't scorch yourself," Willa told her with all the normalcy she could muster. "Stand at a safe distance from that oven."

Richard glanced at the girl, then back at Willa, looking as if he'd swallowed something bitter. "How long do you mean to keep them?"

Willa, concealing how deeply this unexpected visitation had her rattled, rounded the table and stepped onto the porch without answering the question.

A mother quail leading the wolf from her chick.

Richard followed her out.

Without looking she knew Matthew had taken the collie to the horse shed and was crouched there with it, watching her, uncertain what to do. She knew the small movements Maggie made inside the cabin—cleaning up their pie making without having to be asked. She was conscious of the ax embedded in the chopping stump and how many strides off the side of the porch it would take her to reach it.

The last thing she took in was Richard's mare. Something large was rolled and tied behind its saddle. Richard stepped off the porch. He took the rolled thing off the horse, and she realized what it was. A feather tick.

"Goodenough thought to send this to you." He looked at her with his pale eyes giving the lie to his words, ran a finger down a row of tiny stitches in the tick's muslin covering, then set it on the porch.

Willa made her hands into fists, then remembered he'd asked her a question before they stepped out of the cabin.

"I will keep these children as long as they need me to keep them." She'd been tempted to say "for always." Was it only to spite Richard, who clearly wished them gone? She couldn't look too closely at that thought. Doing so would lead to other thoughts. Thoughts about a blue-eyed botanist who had wanted her to keep them, who had wanted her to keep *him*...

Instead, she thought of Joseph, who meant to take the children away. But she mustn't think of Joseph either, not with Richard looking at her as if his eyes could burn through her skull to read her thoughts. He hadn't liked her answer, she could see that, but he swallowed it without argument.

He strode to the end of the porch and looked out at the fields past which he'd ridden. "Your corn is nearly ready for harvesting. I'll send Aram Crane to help you, once he returns."

Crane, the deserter, the Indian killer. Willa's skin crawled.

Then her senses pricked to that last word. "Returns? From where?"

"I sent him back east, on an errand I couldn't attend to myself." Richard still spoke with his back turned, sounding at ease and yet...evasive.

"What errand?" Willa said, unable now *not* to think of Joseph. If Richard had sent Crane back east, what did this mean for Joseph's plans to return the man to the British?

Richard chuckled low in his throat. "He was eager enough to do it—didn't even take the food Goodenough put together for him or wait till morning like he said he'd do. He'll have the deed done and be back in plenty of time for the harvest."

His tone, dark and smug, sent spikes of dread through Willa. Had this errand—whatever it could be—something to do with her? She was sorely tempted to tell him what sort of man he and his father had been harboring in their stable, but then Richard would want to know how she had come by such knowledge.

"I was wondering, though," Richard said. "Have you seen that Scotsman, MacGregor, of late? Has he sent you word?"

A sick feeling coiled in her belly, hearing Neil's name on Richard's lips. "Sent me word? Of what?"

"Nothing. I only wondered had you heard from him."

She wished Richard would turn around so she might see his eyes, though talking to the back of him gave her better courage.

"I have not been into Shiloh to see anyone for days." And it had been all she could do for each hour of those days not to abandon her fields, which seemed a cage and not a haven of late, and race down the path to Anni's, through the mill and down to the smithy to do a thing the very thought of which struck terror in her heart—throw herself, and her future, into Neil MacGregor's arms. "And I will not need Aram Crane's help in my fields. I—"

"You're right." Richard faced her and crossed the porch to halt so close she took an involuntary step back. "One man isn't enough. I'll come as well."

His inability to accept her refusal left her furious, and momentarily speechless.

Through the cabin door came the smell of baking pie, spicy and sweet. Relieved for the distraction, she opened her mouth to tell Maggie to check the oven to be sure it wasn't too hot.

The instant she looked away, Richard's arm snaked out like a grasping vine and pulled her tight against him.

The kiss was hard to the point of bruising, his hands on her like the jaws of a trap. She tried to pull away—not with undue force, fearing what might follow if she fought too hard and angered him. The children were within his reach.

He seemed not to notice her resistance. She abandoned it and with wooden patience bore the violation of his lips and hands until he drew back of his own accord and looked down at her.

"I know you don't love me, Willa, but you need me. I can give you what you want—this land—and I will, if you agree to one thing."

There was triumph in his eyes, hot and burning. She wanted only to wipe her mouth. "What is that?"

"Marry me."

Anger buzzed in her ears like the whirring of insects. She felt the crawl of insects too, down her spine, her flanks, her thighs, in the seconds of silence before Richard put his big hand to her face, his fingers at her temple, his thumb beneath her jaw.

There was more threat than tenderness in the touch.

"Think before you answer, Willa. I wanted no other when we were young and still don't—though God knows I've tried. Over and again I've filled my mind with every imagining of you that tormented me those first few years, hoping to crush what seeing you again made me feel, and still I want you. Even knowing..."

Even knowing that a savage had had her first. That was what he was thinking. And it was not enough to make him leave her be. Maybe she could make it easier for him.

"Did Anni tell you I bore him children?" she asked. "I rejoiced when each of them filled my belly, and had they lived, you would never have seen my face again. These children here you are so eager to see me send away? They could have been mine and Kingfisher's."

An ugliness rippled over Richard's face, and Willa feared she'd said too much, pushed him too far. Then something stirred in his eyes she hadn't expected and didn't know how to fight.

A tainted curiosity.

"I tried to spare you that," he said. "I tried to find you."

"That boy who looked for me is no more," Willa said, desperate now to make him leave, "and I will not be the wife of the man who stands before me now. Nor will I be your tenant. I have nothing to give you, Richard. I want nothing from you—save that you leave me in peace to live in quiet on my land."

It was there—in his eyes gone chill as winter, in the bulge of his jaw, in the whiteness of his cheekbones, sharp under the strain—the explosion Willa dreaded.

It was at that moment she glanced past him and saw Matthew.

While she'd had her focus solely on Richard, the boy had circled the cabin and was standing now behind Richard, at the end of the porch, the ax gripped in his hands.

For the flick of an instant, their eyes locked. Willa gave the tiniest shake of her head.

It was enough. The boy melted back around the side of the cabin as Richard turned to see what she was looking at. There was nothing to see but the empty chopping stump.

He took a step back from her and said with a curving lip, "Keep the tick. Winter's coming. It'll be a cold one for you."

Richard banged down the steps and heaved his big frame onto his horse. She did not expect him to say another word, but once settled in the saddle, he looked at her.

"You're friendly with the smith's wife, aren't you?"

The question left her blinking. He was asking about Leda MacNab, after all the terrible things they had just said to each other?

"What of her?"

"Not her. MacNab. He took a fall from his horse a few days back, out by the mill. Broke his leg. Pretty bad, I hear."

Willa frowned, trying to take this in. She'd seen no one in days, not Anni, not Francis, no one to tell her this bad thing had happened. Was Neil taking care of his friend? Surely he must be. Still, Willa's impulse was to go to Leda.

With her next breath, she knew she didn't dare. She'd made herself a prisoner to her land. If she left it, who would guard it? Only for the greatest necessity would she leave now.

Would this ever end? Even if she somehow saved her land from that auction and no one took it from her, would there ever come a day she could live there in peace, without some threat from Richard hanging over her?

Looking inexplicably amused at her concern and indecision, Richard nodded a farewell and rode away, leaving her more shaken than she had been since coming there to find her parents gone.

Once he was well out of the yard, off down the track past the fields, Matthew climbed the porch steps, still holding the ax, and stood beside her.

Maggie came out of the cabin, round eyed and grave.

Willa drew them to her, one in each arm. The girl pressed her face into her ribs.

Matthew's voice was tightly controlled. "I wish Mr. MacGregor was here."

"So do I," came his sister's tremulous reply, half-muffled against Willa's side. "Is he praying for us?"

"He said he would," her brother replied.

There was a thickening in Willa's throat as she hugged the children to her. "He is a man of his word," she said, sounding choked. "We are not defenseless. God is with us."

That was what Neil would have said, she was sure. It was what the children needed to hear—what she needed to hear. The words didn't sound as convincing when they came out of her mouth, but there was no other mouth to say them now.

Please. It was the first time she'd prayed, even in the quiet of her thoughts, for days. Too many days. But it came now from a raw place, a true place, far down inside her soul. *Please.*

They stood there together for a few seconds more. Then Willa gave the children's shoulders a squeeze and said, "Let's check on that pie. It would be a shame to let it burn, hen'en?"

Not until she lay in her bed, full of pie and worry, did it strike Willa: of the two men most concerned with their lives, the man the children had wanted to defend them wasn't the warrior, Joseph, but the healer, Neil.

As did I.

The knowledge swelled beneath her ribs, sharp as broken glass, and it was far into the night before she had smashed the shards small enough to draw a calming breath around them.

THIRTY-THREE

Francis was pacing the cabin yard when they came in from the field, laden with baskets full of gourds and squash. The collie, last seen sleeping on the porch, slunk behind him like a fretful shadow. Willa quickened her pace, belly twisting with dread.

"Francis...what is wrong?" Francis halted and stammered something unintelligible. Willa set her basket on the porch and told the children, "Take this into the cabin."

They cast wide looks at Anni's agitated brother as they climbed the porch steps. When they were inside, Willa did a thing she had never done—grabbed Francis by the arm and gave him a shake.

"Francis! Did Anni send you?"

Stringy blond hair whipped across his shoulders as Francis shook his head, a violent denial that startled Willa into releasing him.

"What is it, then? What is wrong?"

"I meant to s-s-say—" Francis stuttered to a halt, then blurted, "Anni needs you."

"So she did send you? Is it the baby coming?"

This was odd, even for Francis. First no. Then yes. And now he wouldn't look at her.

"Francis," she began impatiently, but stopped herself. Either Anni's baby was coming and she was needed, or it wasn't. But what ought to be straightforward for a person to say or do, Francis would come at it round-about, or not at all.

Willa reached for calm. She was going to have to go to Anni, and see. "It will be all right. You did well to come to me."

"I did well," Francis repeated under his breath, but he didn't look well.

His face was pinched, and he'd gone back to pacing, long skinny fingers all but snapping off like twigs against his leg. "I did well…"

With no time to spare for puzzling him out, she hurried up the cabin steps, only to be met at the door by Maggie, thrusting the carrying basket at her. "We put in everything. All your plant medicines, linen pads, salves. There's a skin of water. And the leftover corn cakes, in case you get hungry."

Amazed by the child's quick thinking, Willa turned and settled the arm straps and tumpline into place while Maggie supported the basket. Then she took the child's face between her hands, bent, and kissed her cheek. "You are a good girl."

She drew back, struck to her fast-beating heart by the child's blazing smile.

"Matthew helped," she said as her brother appeared behind her.

Willa didn't stop to consider the dignity the boy strived so hard to protect. She lifted a hand to his head and kissed him too, smelling his sweat-dampened hair and his young boy's scent. "Look after your sister. Do not leave the cabin, no matter how long I'm gone."

Francis stood at the foot of the porch steps, darting hunted glances all around as if he expected hungry wolves to come bursting into the clearing. A bruise was coming up on his cheekbone. Willa hadn't noticed until now. There was no time to ask about it.

"Francis, stay with them. And you both, stay inside—" She turned, admonishing the children once more, and nearly fell across the collie, still milling about. "And keep this dog back!"

Matthew grabbed the dog as she raced for the path to Anni's cabin.

She was halfway there before it occurred to her to wonder why she'd been sent for when Neil MacGregor was right there in town. Not to mention

Goodenough and Leda MacNab. Maybe Anni simply wanted her there at such a time. *For the sake of our friendship now...*

Memory of Anni's words to her weeks ago warmed her, and she smiled as she trotted along the path, thankful for how Anni had stood by her, even though it had been hard for her to accept all the ways in which her years with the Mohawks had remade her. And now there was to be a new addition to Anni's family, not born too soon, despite the trial this pregnancy had been for Anni. She ran on smiling through the woods, praying all would be well.

The smile faded as the sound of a moan, low with suffering, met her at the edge of Anni's yard.

Willa ran full out the final distance to the cabin. Anni was in the back room where the family slept, but a quick glance revealed that aside from her little daughter, she was alone. Samantha, hovering over a kettle at the hearth, pale hair plastered to her scalp with steam, burst into wails when Willa came through the cabin door.

"Miss Willa! Mama's dying!"

Anni, seeing her from the bed in the adjoining room, struggled to sit up. "I'm not dying, sweet—" A groan stifled the reassurance.

Willa hurried through the cabin, banging her carrying basket on the door frame, nearly staggering into the back room. An old quilt and straw tick had been spread over the bed ropes, the good feather tick and bed coverings stripped off and tossed in a corner. Anni wore a shift, half-drenched with sweat and birth waters.

"Why are you alone, Anni? Where is Charles?"

"There wasn't time. It's come on so fast—" Her face went a strained and livid red for a count of heartbeats. Then she went limp into the nest of sweaty pillows at her back. "Maybe I *am* dying..."

Willa slipped off the basket and set it on the floor. She found a rag and a basin half-filled with water and wiped Anni's gleaming brow. "Do not say such a thing," she began, but Anni grasped her hand, squeezing hard.

"This one's different." She kept her voice low, but Willa caught the current of panic surging just under the surface. "It hurts more. A lot more."

So had Willa's labors been nothing alike. Goes-Singing had taken an agonizing day and night to birth, while Sweet Rain had taken barely half a morning. That was the usual way of it. First births were long. Second births went faster. But not always.

She hid her concern behind a mask of calm and for the second time asked, "Anni, where is Charles?"

Anni moved her head across the pillows. "I was fine this morning. Feeling stronger. Charles had been talking for days about riding down to the ford at West Canada to talk to a cutter about a new stone for the mill. I told him to go on."

"What about Leda? Goodenough? Has no one sent for them?"

"Sam went for Leda just before you got here. She's closest."

Anni's fingers clamped down on Willa's again. Willa waited out the seconds before the contraction loosened its hold. "But why has Neil not come to tend you? He's the physician, after all. Where is he?"

Anni's eyes blanked. "You don't know?" She sat up, curling into the next swift pain, hands pressing the sides of her rounded belly. The pains were coming very close together.

"Mama? The water's boiling." Samantha hovered in the doorway, wringing her little hands. "What should I do about it?"

"I...have no...idea," Anni got out between breaths. Willa thought Anni was answering her daughter, until she added, "Dr. MacGregor left Shiloh—days ago."

Willa pushed herself off the bed and stood. "He's gone?"

The news, once she'd made of it what sense she could, left her hollowed, adrift, as if her last mooring had been yanked free and she was being swept away from what little in her life had been sure and safe.

Neil had left them again, without even a farewell.

What right had she to expect one? None at all, after all she'd done to push him away. And yet...her efforts to do so had been in vain. She knew it now, knew it clear past denying—as clear as the path he had made to her heart.

Her mouth shaped words, but she barely recognized her voice as she spoke. "Is that why you sent Francis for me?"

Anni blew out a gust of breath. "Sent him? I haven't seen Francis in days."

Anni's eyes cleared briefly of pain, but Willa knew her own had clouded as unease rose to fill her. Something was wrong here—beyond the hollow loss of Neil's departing. Her thoughts were too scattered, too distracted, to put a name to it, but something did not add up. If Anni had not sent Francis, then why—?

"Why did you have to be such a pigheaded fool, Willa?"

The sharpness of Anni's voice, as much as her words, struck Willa like a splash of cold water. "What?"

"Dr. MacGregor was a good man, and he loved you." Anni's face was screwing up again, not with her words, but another pain coming. "We could all see it. Why couldn't...you?"

Before Willa could untangle all the words inside her clamoring to get out—*I could see it, of course I could see it, and hear it and feel it too, but I was too afraid to trust it, to put my heart unshielded into his hands and the hands of the Almighty, one more time; and now it is too late*—the drumming of feet sounded on the cabin porch.

"Mama! Miss Leda can't come. Mr. Gavan's leg took bad, and she's taken him in a wagon down to German Flats. Mr. Keegan told me."

Anni moaned. "Oh, I forgot about poor Gavan."

So had Willa. Richard had told her. He hadn't told her about Neil leaving.

But he knew. She remembered now, his asking her about Neil. What had it been? Whether she had seen him lately? Had word from him? Had he been fishing to see if she knew he'd left?

She ought to have followed her first instinct and gone to Leda right away. Now she felt ashamed that she'd stayed on her farm in fear. Was any decision she'd made since the spring *not* founded on fear?

"It's all right, Sam." Anni reached from the bed, trying to comfort her children, trying to catch her breath.

Willa shoved aside the condemnation bearing down on her, knowing it would be there waiting when she had time for indulging in regret, and took Anni's small son by the shoulder.

"Sam, you must run again. This time go to Colonel Waring's for Goodenough. Tell her to bring you on a horse, because the baby is coming fast. Go now."

The boy groaned, but went, and Willa was left with her thoughts in a spin. Neil MacGregor had left Shiloh. She would have to tell the children when Anni's childbed was past. She would have to look into their faces and explain it to them.

The children.

She had chased concern for Anni all the way from her cabin, but now that she was here, concern flew straight back along that path and hovered now with Francis, who had lied to her, and the children she'd left him to watch over.

"I will stay with you, Anni, until Goodenough comes. Then I must go."

THIRTY-FOUR

I t was late in the season for deer flies. Were it not for one determined specimen convinced that his blood would make a fitting supper, Neil MacGregor would have called it a perfect day: warm enough with the sun in his face to ride in shirtsleeves, the air clear beneath a sky patched with clouds like billowing sails. Trees along the river's north bank wore autumn's first scarlet, and the near-to-setting sun bathed the whole of the Mohawk Valley in gold.

Still it was the news he carried across the pommel of his saddle, tucked in the breast of his shed coat, that buoyed him so he hardly noticed the accumulated aches of his swift journey to Albany.

Though he'd still some miles to go before he'd reach German Flats, near the mouth of West Canada Creek, he decided to press on; a full moon was rising, promising light. By next nightfall, God willing, he'd be riding into Willa's cabin yard. Guiding the roan past another of the rock outcrops that dotted the river's bank, he thought the Almighty would be willing, having thus far blessed his hasty venture beyond all Neil could have asked.

A dozen times he'd imagined handing Willa the packet of letters Dieter Obenchain had written during the war. Would she thank him? Or would she be riled at his taking liberty with her affairs after she'd so firmly set him at arm's length?

By now, Gavan MacNab would have delivered his letter. Had it made any difference to her?

Over and again he'd prayed it had, knowing he'd done what he could. He'd have to trust the Almighty Lord for whatever came of it. And not only concerning Willa.

While in Albany he had, with the help of Tilda Fruehauf, composed a long-overdue confession to Benjamin Rush, detailing the extent of his injuries after Cherry Valley. Along with the letter, he'd sent the work thus far completed, with the promise of more to come in spring. He'd made it clear he desired to finish what he'd begun, but that the Almighty had given him another task to see finished first, and he must be about it.

He touched the pocket of the coat draped across his lap, remembering the startled face of Tilda Fruehauf when she opened her door and he explained who he was, why he'd come; how she in turn had astonished him with her news of—

A pain like a needle's jab at the base of his neck jerked him from the recollection. Instinctively he ducked, slapping at his neck. "Blasted fly!"

His hand came away bloody, as his ears half-registered a report that seemed to strike the hills across the river and come rolling back in echo.

Musket fire. A hunter up in the hills behind him?

His mind filled with thoughts of venison steak as his stomach growled for supper. Wishing the hunter luck, he grasped the brim of his hat to ward off his biting nemesis, just as somewhere, closer than he'd thought at first, the hunter took another shot at his prey.

The deer fly made a buzzing pass at his head, this time striking his hat, which he'd have lost had he not been grasping it.

He halted Seamus and yanked off the hat to swat it wildly around his head—and stared at it instead. There was a hole through the felted brim where its sides met at a point. There'd been no hole when last he donned it, and surely a deer fly couldn't have…

With a fierce twisting in his wame, he kent it was no deer fly seeking his blood; whoever held that musket wasn't shooting at supper.

He wheeled Seamus, the horse beginning to quiver in reaction to his alarm, and looked wildly at tree and rock for cover, though he'd no idea from which direction he was being shot at. A stream came down just there from the higher hills, cutting through a small wooded draw. He turned the roan's head in that direction.

It took no more time than that for the shooter—wherever he hid—to reload the musket and fire again. And this time hit his mark.

He was soaking wet, staring up through sun-dazzled water at a fleet of passing sails. He blinked, blinked again, realized he wasn't breathing. Couldn't breathe. He'd fallen. Fresh in his mind was the impact of striking—what had it been? Ship's deck? Water? Of course, water. He was bone-cold wet. He was in the sea. That's why he couldn't breathe. God Almighty, he was drowning!

Man overboard screamed inside his head as panic sank hooks into his flesh. The will to live shot a current through his chest, which heaved and filled his lungs with...air. Not water. But there was water everywhere, cold water flowing around him.

Neil MacGregor sat up, and two facts became apparent.

First, he'd been lying on his back in the creek that tumbled from the hills; it wasn't sails on a sun-dazzled sea he'd seen, but clouds through an overhang of yellow leaves.

Second, he'd been shot. The creek's flow had made a broad pink stain of it, but already his shirt was blooming fresh crimson. The water's chill had numbed the pain, but it was building now, a white-hot scream in his flesh. He couldn't move his arm—the right arm *again,* dash it all—and could not bring himself to turn his face to see torn flesh, bone, whatever damage might show.

Why had he been shot? And where was Seamus?

He heard a snort, the thud of hooves, curses. Neil clamped his lips tight and turned to look behind him. Some half-dozen yards off, a man with a musket slung across his back clung to Seamus's reins, digging through the bags behind the saddle.

He'd fallen victim to a highway robber.

Thought came in desperate snatches. Let the man take what he wanted. Anything. Even Seamus. But not the letters. *Willa's letters.*

He thrashed about in the creek, trying to get to his knees. The man rifling his saddlebags turned.

It was Aram Crane.

Through pain and shock, Neil struggled to grasp what was happening. This had to be Richard Waring's doing. That stolen letter must have mentioned the proof Willa needed to keep her land from confiscation—her father's letters. Waring had been watching the post ever since for their arrival. And watching Neil more closely than he'd ever suspected. So closely he'd guessed the reason for Neil's journey and sent Crane to stop him. Or steal the letters that were Willa's only hope.

The letters. They were still in his coat. But where—?

Both men saw it in the same instant. The coat lay where it had fallen from the saddle, tails trailing in the creek, just beyond Neil's reach.

Crane abandoned Seamus and lunged for it as Neil fell across the shallow stream, making a grab. His left hand closed on a sleeve as Crane reached him. With his face half in water, he saw only the man's feet. They were shoeless, torn and bleeding.

"There's where you put them? Give them over to me, and I'll tell Waring you got away."

"You'll have to kill me!" With only the one hand free to swing or hold fast the coat, Neil couldn't do both. Crane's ginger-bristled face showed no fear, only irritation, as they struggled over the garment.

"Have it your way." The man swung his musket to hand and slammed the butt of it into Neil's head. The shock of the blow made him lose his grip on the coat. Crane tore the garment from his grasp and lurched away, running on bleeding feet for Seamus, who'd edged as far from their struggle as the terrain allowed.

Neil fell back into the creek, lay there until the pain in his arm and head receded enough that he could move, then rolled onto his side, scrambled to his knees, pushed to his feet. He staggered after Crane, streaming blood and water. The man had reached his horse. He wasn't going to catch him in time.

His shout was an inarticulate groan.

Seamus, unnerved the more by the stranger rushing at him, wheeled from Crane's reach and lashed out with his hooves, catching the man a glancing blow to the chest. Crane fell back hard.

The blood was coming down Neil's arm, running in rivulets, and he still couldn't move it. He staggered when he reached Crane, who'd had the breath knocked from him but had got it back and was sitting up. A wave of dizziness slammed Neil as he bent for the coat, but he was moving now without thinking, his body obeying the instinct to save the letters at whatever cost. With his left hand, he snatched up the coat and felt the brush of grasping fingers as he spun away, making for the horse he prayed would stand still for him.

Seamus did stand still, though the roan whinnied loud in agitation as Neil slung his coat across the horse's withers and somehow swung himself into the saddle, where stars burst across his vision and his arm blazed like fire. Crane was on his feet, yelling, cursing, but to no avail. Neil kicked the roan into a canter, and in moments they'd left the man behind, shoeless and afoot.

Neil rode a mile at a jarring gallop, clutching his coat to his chest, before he dared slow Seamus enough to check on the letters, his heart hammering in fear that in the scuffle and flight they'd slipped from that inner pocket and were strewn now along the road.

They were there, still bundled and intact, though he smeared them with blood before he had them tucked away again, breathing out a shaky prayer of thanksgiving. His right arm and hand were drenched in scarlet.

Finally he looked at the wound, or what could be seen of it through the torn, blood-soaked sleeve of his shirt. The ball had passed through his upper arm. He saw no bone protruding, but it was bad. Broken this time, he was certain.

His heart gave a ragged thump against the wall of his chest, and another wave of dizziness had him clenching Seamus's sides with his knees. He looped the reins high on the saddle and kept the horse moving at a walk while he struggled out of his shirt and got the garment tied around his upper arm, as snug as he could make it.

By the end of it, he was shuddering with chills and fighting to stay in the saddle, but he thought he'd slowed the bleeding some. Enough to make it to German Flats? It was miles still. But maybe he needn't make it that far. There were outlying farms, taverns, smaller settlements, but the sun was down and dusk falling, and it would soon be dark. He couldn't stop because Crane could be coming behind him still, hoping he'd wounded him badly enough that he might not make it far.

Lord, I've come so far. And she's tried so hard. Please...just a little farther.

Pain burst through the bones of his brow and cheek, and he dropped the reins to trail on the road. He'd fainted forward into the hard arch of Seamus's neck. The horse's gait lurched. Neil tried to straighten again, but settled for dropping his good arm around the roan's neck. A good horse, Seamus, kicking Crane like that...more than made up for leaving him months ago when he'd fallen from the stone on Willa's land...

He was falling again now, falling with his coat still clutched to his chest. His last glimpse before he hit the earth was a feeble glow of light, as of a door in the distance opening onto the dusk.

He tried to shout, lying on his back in the road, or was he in the laurels? He couldn't remember. He didn't know if he'd managed the shout either.

There was a faint sound as if from far away. A voice?

God Almighty, dinna let it be Crane...

It was his last thought before a roaring like the crash of waves came down, and he half-believed he was in the sea again, with the cold and dark closing over him.

"Dr. MacGregor was *wrong*," Samantha Keppler pronounced, leaning against the bed frame as Willa severed the second newborn's cord and laid him on the quilt beside his brother, older of the two by five minutes. She caught a glimpse of Anni's expression—as if she didn't know whether to laugh or cry—before turning to greet the arrival of Goodenough, behind her a flushed and anxious Charles, back from his trip down creek.

Goodenough's gaze fastened on the babies nestled against Anni's side, and her smile came full and gleaming. "Lord help us. Mister Neil was wrong."

"We know." Samantha's small face pulled into a pout. "I have two more brothers, when all I wanted was one sister."

"Brothers?" a voice whooped, and a disheveled, sweaty Sam squeezed into the room.

Charles and Goodenough crowded with the children around the bed. Anni's brow was kissed, the babies' fingers and toes counted, a flurry of questions asked and answered. Willa dropped the afterbirth the twins had shared into a bucket, cleaned her knife and returned it to its sheath at her neck.

Her words cut through the happy chatter. "I left the children. I must go now."

All through the birthing, dread had kept its hold on Willa. Even now, it was all she could do to stand there and take her leave with civility. She took in their faces—Charles's relief; contentment beginning to beam through Anni's stunned fatigue; Goodenough with her brows starting to pucker.

"There something wrong, Miss Willa?"

"Maybe not," she said, though her heart jumped with foreboding. "But I should get back."

Goodenough was already in motion, reaching for the bucket with the afterbirth. "You go, then. See to your own. I'll be staying the night."

She was almost to the door when Anni called, "Willa? *Thank* you."

Willa looked back at Anni's face framed by sweat-dampened hair, husband and children safe and accounted for around her bed. Anni had called her a fool while in the grip of labor. Even though clearly Anni regretted that utterance, words more true couldn't have been spoken.

She tried to smile to show all was well between them. Then she was in the yard, Anni's travail shoved from her thoughts, her entire being focused on the boy and girl she'd told to stay inside the cabin no matter what. And on Francis, who'd told her Anni sent for her when she hadn't.

The sun was nearly set, but there was light enough to see her home if she hurried. Before she reached the path her feet had worn in another life, she was running.

She smelled the smoke before the trees thinned to show the lurid dance of firelight in the yard, and the dread that had smoldered during Anni's labor burst into a conflagration of terror. She'd left her carrying basket at Anni's cabin and so ran unhindered through the falling dusk to burst from the woods into the yard, mouth open in a silent scream, no breath to give it voice. Half the cabin was engulfed in hungry flames.

THIRTY-FIVE

L ight in the distance, more tongues of leaping orange, revealed to Willa the field beginning to burn, the dry corn standing on its hill-ocks going up as fast as the cabin. Above her in the sky, twilight was fading to purple, but around the cabin, the ground was bathed in fiery light, as were the two men in the yard. Two men matched in height and build, locked together in battle: Richard Waring and Joseph Tames-His-Horse, frozen eye to eye, lips peeled back from gritted teeth, a tomahawk poised above them. Joseph clutched the weapon. Richard clutched at Joseph's raised arm, but if they made any sound at all, Willa couldn't hear them. She heard nothing above the fire's terrible roar and crackle.

"Matthew... Maggie!" Screaming their names, she raced around the cabin, choking on smoke, seeking a way within unbarred by fire, calling to the children, stopping to listen for their screams in reply.

There was no sound save the flames devouring the last remnant of her father's hand upon the earth. The last remnant of the life she'd hoped to reclaim. *But not the children. Please, not the children.*

Searing heat and burning debris scorched her skin. Rounding the porch on the far side of the cabin, she saw three figures, men, running up from the field. One still held aloft a burning torch. Closer by, Richard and Joseph were exchanging blows with their fists. The tomahawk lay dis-carded in the grass, its blade catching a gleam from the burning cabin. She wanted to scream Joseph's name, to plead with him to help her find the children, but knew he was helping in the only way possible.

The porch was already engulfed, the fire more advanced at the cabin's front. She wouldn't get in that way. She was bathed in heat and light, but neither Joseph nor Richard seemed aware of her presence. The three men— she recognized them from Keegan's store that first day in the village—

raced into the yard, armed with muskets, all their attention on the fighters. Joseph had gotten the upper hand in the fight, but two of the men piled onto him now, dragging him off Richard. One clubbed him over the head with a musket, and he dropped to his knees. The third snatched the hunting knife from his sash, disarming him.

Richard wiped blood from his nose and spotted the tomahawk lying in the grass. The murderous intent on his face made the rage in Willa flare hotter than the fire. She drew the knife from its sheath at her breast.

The flame's dry roaring covered the noise of her feet, but at the last moment, her throat opened and she screamed, shrill and ululating. The men holding Joseph captive, perhaps too startled, made no move to hinder her as she passed them.

Richard heard her as he bent for the hatchet. He straightened in time to keep his throat from being slashed, taking the blade instead down the length of his forearm. Bellowing in surprise and pain, he struck her a blow to the head that knocked her to the ground.

Grass was in her mouth, the grit of dirt between her teeth. White sheeted her vision.

"Fool woman!" Richard's boot struck her side. "Didn't I say burning's what you'd come to?"

A weight fell on her, shoving the air from her lungs. Knees sought to push apart her thighs. There was a reek of male sweat, the metallic smell of blood—the drip of both onto her face—Richard cursing, wrenching at her skirts.

"I gave you every chance, offered you everything," he said, bleeding, panting, fighting with her petticoat. "I'll have one thing from you at least—"

For an instant, she looked straight into Richard's face, into his eyes pale and fire lit, frenzied with hate…and excitement. And she knew. He had done this before. Somewhere in a village while crops and lodges burned, he had raped women who were her sisters, her mothers. And when he was done with her, he would throw her to the other men. She heard their hoots and shouts and knew this would happen, all while the children burned and Joseph was made to watch, if he still lived. She had heard these stories. Now they were her own.

Only she still held her knife. She felt it now across her open palm. Richard in his lust to take her had not taken *it*.

Resolve flowed through her limbs, and with it, feeling. Her fingers clenched the knife's hilt. She raised her arm to plunge the blade into the broad back pinning her down.

The knife was jerked from her grasp.

Richard's weight lifted. She lay stunned for a second, then rolled onto her knees, heard men shouting—a different sort of shouting, enraged, alarmed—sensed a mill of confusion and bodies near her, expected all the while another blow, a slash to her throat. But these things didn't come.

Willa blinked and cleared her vision. Richard had his back to her and was in a fighting crouch, blood streaming from the gash she'd opened in his arm.

Joseph, free of the men who had held him—one of whom was on his knees—brandished the knife with which she'd meant to kill Richard. It was Joseph's hand that had snatched it from her. Blood coursed from a cut on his brow, streaking his face like war paint, but through that mask she saw it in his eyes. He was saving her from killing Richard, by killing him for her.

"No!" The scream came from her throat as a musket fired. She felt the breath of the ball as it passed.

"Hold your fire—this Indian's mine. Then *her*." Richard raised a hand, signaling the man holding Joseph's hunting knife, and caught the weapon as it was tossed.

The knife Joseph had taken from her was half the size of the one Richard now wielded, but it was Joseph who made the first rush. Richard lowered his shoulder and hurtled forward to meet it.

For the smoke and tears that stung her eyes, Willa didn't see clearly what happened next. It seemed Richard meant to feint to the side and deliver a slash to Joseph's belly, but something happened—Willa thought he must have tripped—for he fell hard into Joseph. There was a brief struggle, the two of them grappling on their feet. Then Richard slumped to the ground and lay face down.

The long blade he'd welded protruded from his lower back, driven straight through his own belly. Joseph sprang away, looking ready still, his face fierce and expectant, as if he did not realize what had happened.

Richard didn't move.

Had Joseph got his knife away and thrust him through with it, or had Richard in falling into Joseph somehow impaled himself on the blade? It had happened too fast. She didn't know. Nor did she know what Richard's men had seen. She scrambled to Joseph's side as they rushed forward, shock on their faces. One turned Richard over, grasped the blade, and yanked it free. Blood came gushing.

"Idiot!" another shouted. "Now he's like to bleed to death."

"Get the Indian! He's knifed a white man!"

"He's *murdered* a white man."

"Maybe not. Get him anyway. I'll gather the horses."

They left Richard lying in his blood, big hands clamped over his belly, red snaking through his fingers. One man ran for the horse shed. The others came at Joseph, faces white and savage in the fire's light.

Joseph turned to her with eyes of sorrow. "Run," he said, pressing the small knife into her hand and giving her a shove that nearly sent her sprawling.

But she kept her feet, and her head. She sprinted toward the woods on the far side of the burning cabin, ignoring the screaming pain in her side where Richard's boot had landed, the throbbing of her cheek and temple where his fist had struck. Sobbing as she ran.

No one pursued her.

At the woods' edge, she stopped. Two men had fallen on Joseph as if to kill him on the spot, but after several blows they bound him unresisting. They tied him to a horse's saddle when the animals were brought up, while the third man tore Richard's shirt and wrapped his torso tight with it. Even Willa could see the dark bloom that stained the bindings.

It wasn't murder, but it might yet be. Or made to seem so. There was no hope for Joseph if Richard died. Scant hope if he lived.

One man swung onto Richard's big mare. The other two between them lifted Richard to the saddle.

"I...can...ride," he ground out and somehow stayed upright.

The second man slid off the horse, mounted his own, and in seconds they were riding out of the yard at a trot that must have jarred Richard unmercifully. Down the track past her burning crop they went, Joseph running hard to keep from stumbling and being dragged.

Willa screamed after them. "Where are they? Where are my children?"

If they heard her, they paid her no mind. Eyes stung with smoke and despair, voice all but spent, she turned back to the cabin, her heart tearing out of her chest with the need to find the children, to do something for Joseph. She could not do both.

She could not do either.

She fell to the ground in a tangle of skirts, coughing and choking. Like the billowing smoke, the faces of her lost ones rose before her. Kingfisher. Goes-Singing and Sweet Rain.

Papa, who had built the cabin. Mama, who'd made it their home. Oma, who thought her beloved books a waste of time, who didn't even have a grave.

Neil MacGregor, who saw past her fear into her soul and wanted to give her what it craved. The children she hadn't wanted but had grown to love in spite of herself. Maggie... Matthew.

The Almighty had fashioned for her another family, had placed them in her path so she must step over them in order to leave them behind. In fear she'd done just that. She'd spurned His gift, thinking she could keep the world at a distance, protect herself from its pain. But the world had pushed its way in regardless, both the good and the evil of it. She'd refused the good. Now she had nothing but the ashes the evil had left her.

"Forgive me," she whispered to the children who were dead, to the man who was gone, to the God she had mistrusted.

The cabin roof fell in with a crack of timbers. Sparks columned upward. Ashes and debris blew outward in a blackening cloud, but she didn't move to safety. On her knees, arms wrapped about her belly, the woman who had been Burning Sky rocked herself and wept.

When she heard them, Willa thought the voices were only memories taunting, for they were children's voices, calling to her. Calling her *Istah*. Mother.

Her dead children. Was the grief and regret not enough to crush her, but their ghosts must come to haunt her in this moment? She buried her face in sooty hands, as the ashes rained down.

"Istah!"

"Get back! Away from the fire!"

Ghosts did not rush with bruising force into the arms of the living. They did not grasp and tug with the urgency of flesh. Willa dropped her hands to look at those pulling at her now. Children's hands, very much of this heartbreaking world.

"Please, Istah, get back from the fire!"

She had no will to resist them. In a wondering, aching daze, she let them lift her up and tug her toward the trees. Stars glittered through the haze of smoke that billowed above the clearing. The firelight was beginning to dim, but it was enough to show her the faces of Matthew and Margaret Kershaw, filthy, tear streaked, singed around the edges, but whole.

Her voice was a thread, constricted by smoke and heat and tears. "How? Where...?"

Before they could answer, she had them in her arms, laughing for the joy rising in her. Because she laughed, so did they, and while the collie she hadn't even noticed until now licked and nudged and wriggled over them all, in tumbled snatches they told her everything—how Richard Waring had come riding up with his men, forcing Francis to leave and shoving them inside the cabin, where he tied them and left them to burn as the cabin was put to the torch.

How Francis had come back after they were shut within, breaking in through the door that used to open into another room.

How Joseph had come as well, but they didn't know from where, and fought with Richard while Francis got them out of the fire and up the slope into the trees and told them to hide and not come out.

How they saw Willa running from the trees right after that but were too frightened to come down and did they do wrong, should they have come down before now?

"No. Oh no," Willa told them, stroking small sturdy backs, kissing sweaty brows and smearing soot all over. "I am happy now that you didn't come down."

Matthew was the first to pull from their embrace. "We're sorry we let your cabin burn."

"And the corn!" Maggie cried, a wail of anger in the words as she gazed toward the still-burning field.

"Corn?" Willa said, shaking her head. "What do I care for corn when you are both safe?"

The cabin was still falling in, the blackened timbers crumbling onto themselves. Willa's heart ached at the sight, but that which was truly irreplaceable wasn't lost. Later she would make sense of the rest, especially Francis's role in it all—Francis, who had lied to her and saved her children, then vanished like the smoke still curling thick into the night sky.

Right now it was Joseph who needed her.

THIRTY-SIX

S he took up the tomahawk left in the yard and led the children by the path to Anni's cabin, across the foot log over Black Kettle Creek. Struck mute by their sudden and bedraggled appearance, Charles and Goodenough, the only two still awake, listened in disbelief, then horror, as Willa told her tale of fire and blood.

"Richard's taken hurt bad?" Goodenough, arrested in the act of lifting a kettle at their arrival, set it on the hearth and ran from the cabin without another word.

"Richard?" Charles echoed, standing from the chair he'd occupied in peace moments ago. "And who's this Indian—Joseph? What's he to do with…" His glance fell to Matthew and Maggie.

"He is not the father of these children," Willa said. "He's my brother. He's come and gone this summer long, hunting for us."

"Richard said he shot an Indian." Charles sounded stunned. "Weeks ago. Over by—"

"That was Joseph. But there is no time to explain." Willa gave Matthew and Maggie a gentle push forward. "Will you see to these children so I can go to him?"

"Of course, but—"

"I'll go with you!" Matthew protested.

"You will not." Willa turned on him with unassailable resolve. "Stay here where I know you will be safe."

Lanterns burned around a log house near the smithy and farther on at Keegan's store. Willa saw them from the crest of the path before she plunged down the slope and crossed the footbridge used when the mill was shut for the night. As she raced down the track, she saw figures, silhouetted in the light, moving about both structures. One of those figures outside the log house was as tall as most of the men, but skirted—Goodenough, who had bolted from Anni's cabin moments before Willa.

Goodenough paused to speak to someone outside, then pushed past to go within. That would be where they had taken Richard. Joseph must be at the trading store. A prisoner.

Someone would have ridden for the Colonel. Would Joseph be spared long enough for Elias Waring to hear the truth of how his son was injured—burning her out of her home, trying to kill her children?

But what was the truth of those last vital seconds? Only Joseph could tell her that.

Willa raced past the smithy to the store, ignored the shadowy faces of men loitering on the porch, pushed open the door, and collided with Jack Keegan standing just inside. Jack steadied her as she staggered.

"What have they done with him?" She craned to see past the stacked goods cluttering the store. Others were within but hidden from her sight. She could hear their voices. She could hear the thud of fists on flesh.

"Joseph!" She yanked free of Jack's grasp.

Two men, bloodstained and disheveled, came from the back of the store and stood in front of Willa—two who had ridden with Richard. A third joined them. The fists of the third man were cracked and bleeding.

"They brought the Indian here for keeping," Jack explained, "till the Colonel's seen to Richard."

"He's done nothing wrong. It was Richard Waring and those three." Willa flung an arm at the men blocking her way, her voice hoarse as she said, "They set fire to my cabin. They tried to burn my children inside it."

"She's lying," the man with the bleeding knuckles growled. "That Mohawk did the burning. Like they always do."

Willa had run from Anni's cabin with Joseph's tomahawk in hand, hidden in the folds of her skirt. She raised it now, pulling back her teeth in a snarl. Only Jack Keegan's long reach kept her from hurling its blade into the smirking face of the man with Joseph's blood on his hands.

"Willa, calm yourself! Colonel Waring will—"

"Do not tell me to calm myself!" She wrenched loose from him a second time. "Ask Francis Waring. He saw everything. He knows. Richard forced him to help."

This only amused the other men. One laughed. "Waring's half-wit? Can that boy even talk?"

"Francis speaks! He was there. He will tell you…"

The words died on Willa's tongue. Someone had entered the store behind her. She knew it by the looks of the men fronting her. By those looks, she knew who it was before he spoke.

"What will Francis tell us, Wilhelmina?"

Elias Waring looked as if he'd aged a decade in the months since Willa last saw him. In the glow of the store lanterns, his hair looked gray. His shoulders stooped as he leaned on his stick. Fresh grief scored his face.

"Richard?" she asked him.

"I left him living. Goodenough is with him." The Colonel's eyes, distant with the shock of his son's injury, said what his words did not. Richard's life hung by a thread.

Willa felt ready to collapse from the exhaustion of this terrible day, but her battle was far from over. Words she must say to this man clogged her mind like logs jammed in a mill race. While she scrambled for the right ones to begin, the Colonel's gaze fell on the three men blocking the maze of trade goods. "The rope is ready. Where is he?"

A stunned second passed while Willa digested that. *Rope.* They were going to hang Joseph, without even hearing her side of the story. The blood rushed from her face.

"Colonel…no." She stepped in front of him, raising soot-smeared palms. "Look at my face, my hands. These men burned my cabin and my fields this night. They tried to burn my children. Richard was with them, leading them. Richard did these things!"

There was a flicker in the distant eyes, a flinch of the fixed mouth, but she could not be sure her words had penetrated what surely must be shock.

"Don't listen to her nonsense," one of the men behind her began, but Willa pressed on, desperate, fighting down panic.

"Joseph only fought with Richard to save my children and me. I don't know if Joseph even gave him that wound, or if Richard fell on the knife he wielded. Do you hear me, Colonel? Joseph will tell the truth."

The men had lingered to hear the outcome of this talk, but one of them snorted at that. "Get the Indian. Now."

Colonel Waring, staring hard at Willa's face, held up a hand. "Wait."

For the first time, it seemed he took in her sooty clothes, her hair tangled down her back. He lifted a hand to turn her chin toward the light of the nearest lantern. His fingers brushed the throbbing place between her cheekbone and temple, where Richard struck her.

"My son did this?"

"That is the least of it, Colonel. While I was catching Anni's babies, Richard was trying to kill my children."

"Your children?" The Colonel's face lost what little color it held. "Where are they now?"

Willa hadn't known she was crying until she took a breath and heard in it a sob. "Francis got them out of the burning cabin where Richard left them bound. They're with Charles and Anni."

"She's lying. Ain't a word of that true." Whichever man spoke behind her, his voice sounded less belligerent than desperate now.

The Colonel snapped a look past her. "Would you have me believe she burned her own crop, her own cabin?" He put a hand on her shoulder, where her gown was scorched through, the skin beneath showing raw and blistered. "That she did *this* to herself?"

"Naw, we ain't—"

"Shut your gobs," Jack Keegan snapped. "Let 'em get this straight between them."

The Colonel's eyes widened as more of what Willa had said sank in. "Anni's delivered? You attended her?"

"Yes. Goodenough didn't make it in time, but I was there. It is twins again. Boys."

Instead of the joy this news should have brought, something like anguish broke over the Colonel's face. His skin turned an alarming gray.

"Please, Colonel," Willa pressed. "Let Joseph go. He will return to his people at Niagara, I promise you. He only tried to help me—he has always been kind to me. He was my strength and comfort all the years I lived with his people. He has harmed no one who didn't harm me first."

That brought an uproar of protest. "A buck like him? Think he wasn't up against us at Oriskany?"

"He might've been the one to kill your boys, Colonel—or your wife and—"

"No!" Voices stilled at the Colonel's thundering reply. It appeared to take a monumental effort, but Elias Waring, county magistrate and colonel of militia, surfaced fully from the visage of the devastated father, and focused his mind on the matter in question. "The Indian is accused of no crime but the one witnessed this night. And no, Wilhelmina, I will not release him. Not until Richard is able to speak for himself. But neither will I see him hanged outright. He stays where he is."

Willa was at least permitted to see Joseph. She dodged to the rear of the store, but halted in astonishment at what she found behind the barrels and shelves. Joseph sat on the floor, knees drawn, head pillowed on his arms, black hair shining in the lantern light. Standing over him like a tiny guardian angel was Maeve Keegan, blue eyes snapping, lopsided mouth set in a lipless pucker, wisps of hair floating above her head like milkweed down.

"I'll not be havin' beatings in my store!" Maeve punctuated the pronouncement with a crack of her cane on the floorboards. "There'll be no more hittin'. No more blood. Where's that boy o' mine that's gone and let this happen?"

"Ma?" Jack came hurrying back, pushing past Willa. "Come away, Ma. This is no place for you to be."

Maeve glowered up at her son. With startling speed her cane shot out and jabbed him in the gut. "I'll not come away, Jacky. I'm after guardin' this poor young man from harm. T'ree against one...'tis cowardly!"

Maeve's temper was up, though whether she understood what was happening, or exactly who she was defending, was anyone's guess.

"Get back now." She brandished her cane but spared Willa a nod. "She can stay for she's a woman and may be of some use. The rest of ye— and ye, Jacky—back!"

Joseph's tomahawk was plucked from Willa's hands before they let her near him, still she had the absurd impulse to laugh as she knelt. Joseph had lifted his head at this unexpected championing of his person, and there was an answering flash of humor in the one eye not swollen shut. Pain doused it quickly. And sorrow.

"How badly are you hurt?" Willa looked him over. A battered face. Shallow gashes on his arms, his hands. That seemed to be all. Had he not been bound, he might have fought his way free without aid. "You will have a chance to speak in your defense. I will speak for you..."

She'd tried to keep her voice steady, strong, infused with a confidence she didn't feel, but something in Joseph's expression made her falter. He looked at her through the snakes of blood congealing on his skin, and she knew something was changed.

"I heard how you spoke to those men," he said, "and to the one you call the Colonel. You spoke of the Kanien'kehá:ka, but you called them *his* people. 'He will go back to his people at Niagara,' you said."

"Joseph…" The floorboards pressed hard against Willa's knees, but she didn't shift a muscle. The pain pressing her heart was far worse.

Joseph lifted his hand as if he would touch her face, but let it fall back. She knew then what was changed about him. It was the absence of something that had been there from the day they met, in that distant cornfield. He no longer hoped for a future with her. Even as his sister.

"Once," he said, "they were *our* people."

It was as if a curtain had swung between them, cutting them off from each other. He from her world. She from his. A pit of sorrow opened in her belly, deep enough to match that in his eyes.

She had long known in some part of her soul that this moment would come. She'd thought when it did there would be some measure of relief in it, for both of them. There was none. A grief and loss she'd never expected washed over her, while old Maeve Keegan stood by with her scowl and her cane.

There were no words to express this grief. Had there been words, there would have been no time to speak them; someone else had come into the store, someone in the throes of their own anguish and loss. A woman's keening wail sent a coldness racing up Willa's spine. She was on her feet and moving to where she could see the front of the store before the sound of it died.

Goodenough stood in the doorway, the front of her stained with blood from breasts to thighs.

"He's dead!" she said, voice still high with wailing, and though she faced them all, it was to one person she spoke. Elias Waring. "Our Richard is dead."

Thirty-Seven

They came for Joseph, the three who aided Richard to his last violent deed. Before Willa emerged from shock, they were hauling him toward the door, Maeve Keegan's cane unavailing. Colonel Waring and Goodenough—one dazed, the other inconsolable—were gone. Willa alone was left to protest the men dragging Joseph out into the night.

"The Colonel said he is not to be hanged!"

Two of the men kept their hold on Joseph, while the one holding a lantern dealt her a shove with a meaty hand. "It wasn't murder before."

Willa staggered off the porch but didn't fall. Looking wildly around for an ally, she glimpsed Goodenough and the Colonel moving away toward the smithy, leaning into each other as if neither could stand alone.

"Colonel! Wait! Will you permit this?"

As one, the pair swiveled back to view the scene: Joseph pinioned between his captors, the rope dangling from the oak that overspread the store yard, the gathering onlookers, many starting to raise taunts, demands, a few protests—all faceless to Willa. All save one. A face starkly white beneath soot smears, hovering at the edge of the shifting light cast by lanterns in the milling crowd.

"Francis!"

The name carried above the escalating voices, silencing many but alarming the one Willa meant to draw in as an ally.

Francis backed toward the cloaking shadows beyond the oak. By a sheer act of will, she didn't pursue him, which would have hastened his retreat. Instead, she held out a hand and as calmly as she could said, "Francis, please. Twice you have warned Joseph and kept him from being discovered. Will you help him now? Will you help me?"

That raised more murmurs from all sides; Willa paid them no heed.

On the edge of darkness, Francis teetered, as the gazes of those gathered, including his father's, turned their weight upon him.

"You saved my children—" Willa fought to steady her voice, which rasped with the smoke she had breathed. "You saved them, Francis. Whatever Richard forced you to do, I'm not angry with you. You didn't want to lie to me so that I would leave the cabin, did you?"

Francis was looking only at her now. Slowly, he shook his head. Around them, voices rose again, but no one interrupted, not even the men holding Joseph between them.

"It turned out that Anni did need me—you have two new nephews now. You did a good thing for your sister, Francis. But it was Richard who made you tell me what you thought was a lie, was it not?"

Francis had begun to grin at her news of nephews, but now his bony face stiffened, and his eyes, enormous and afraid, scanned the crowd staring at him. Seeking his brother's towering figure somewhere among their ranks, bearing down on him with fists clenched?

Willa dared a step toward him. "Richard cannot hurt you now. Never again."

Goodenough, the Colonel close behind her, had come forward into the ring of lantern light, those nearest making way. Face wet with tears and voice thick, she said, "Francis, honey, you got something to say 'bout this terrible thing, go on and say it."

Francis opened his mouth, but no sound came out. It was too much— the stares, the faces. They were confusing him, frightening him.

"Francis," Willa said. "Look at me, just me, and tell me what Richard did."

Later she would wonder how the rest of her life—how all their lives— might have unfolded had she worded that last request some other way.

"He b-burned down your father's b-barn," Francis said.

The unexpected words hovered in the night air, suspended by Willa's indrawn breath—and that of every soul within hearing. A murmur was borne back through the crowd to those who hadn't heard.

"What's he saying? Does he mean Dieter Obenchain's barn?"

"Back during the war? 'Twas Indians burned that barn, wasn't it?"

Willa heard their voices, sensed the confusion sweeping out from the center of this drama, and struggled with her own. She stood blinking stupidly, knowing she must say something.

"Papa's barn?" She could barely feel her lips moving or her feet on the ground or the hands limp at her sides. Only the hammering against her ribs was solid and strong, a beat so slow it didn't seem like it could be her heart. "That barn burned long ago. There is nothing left of it but ashes."

Francis nodded, refuting none of this. "Your p-parents were inside when Richard b-b-burned it. They screamed..."

The night and the lanterns and the staring faces tilted around Willa. She felt hands on her, steadying, and looked into Jack Keegan's constricted face. His mouth moved, but Willa heard no words. There was a roaring in her head.

The Colonel stepped forward, pulling away from Goodenough, staring at his son alone in the lantern light. "Are you telling us *Richard* killed Willa's parents? That he burned them—alive—in their barn?"

"He started the f-fire," Francis said. "They went in to g-get the animals, and they never came out. I saw him—Richard—after. He was afraid. He buried their b-bones."

Willa saw the horror of it on Elias Waring's face. "At the lake," she said to Francis, fearing she would be sick, "where you didn't want me to see their graves."

Francis locked his eyes with hers. "Richard didn't want you to f-find them. He was angry that I m-made them pretty."

"With the stones," Willa said. "And the crosses."

"It wasn't right, no c-crosses."

Those around them pressed closer, not wanting to miss a word. Francis's shoulders drew in tighter. His hand dropped to his thigh, stiff fingers tapping. At any moment, Willa knew, he would bolt into the darkness.

His father spoke in a voice so broken it held no threat. "Son, if there's more to tell, say it now."

Willa waited. The Colonel waited. All of Shiloh waited.

Francis closed his eyes and stood his ground. "Then you came b-back and Richard was afraid you'd know, so he got Mr. Crane to shoot the arrow in your door to scare you off—and steal your spade and k-kill your goat and b-burn your cornfield when it was green. You wouldn't leave or m-marry him, so he m-made me help him b-because you trusted me, and if I didn't, he'd hurt me w-w-worse than b-before."

There was a groan from somewhere in the crowd, but Willa didn't take her eyes off Francis, who gasped in a great breath and plunged on before anyone could stop him.

"Richard said, 'Burn the cabin and leave the half breeds inside,' b-but I couldn't. Then Richard made me leave so he could do it, but I only went into the woods, and I saw what he did, what they did—" Francis swung toward the men still clustered around Joseph. There were only two now; one had slipped into the darkness unnoticed. "*Him...*and *him.* They tied the children in the c-cabin, and Richard threw in torches. Then Joseph c-came from somewhere and tried to save the children, b-but Richard fought him. Someone had to get them out, so...I did. I didn't want them burning up to b-bones."

It was the single longest speech Willa had ever heard out of Francis Waring's mouth, one she would never have thought him capable of making. One she would never, in all her days, forget. But for the present, the horror of it overshadowed all else, dulling her awareness of a shifting in the crowd, making her slow to realize that while Francis had been speaking his chilling revelations, a quieter drama had been taking place a few paces away.

The Colonel had slumped against Goodenough, who was struggling now to hold him upright, arms locked around his chest. His head was fallen limp against her bloodstained breasts.

"Elias! Someone help!" Goodenough's cry held the same panic Willa had known while her cabin burned and her children were nowhere to be found.

Jack Keegan was the first to reach them. Bodies moved in and out of the swinging light, blocking Willa's view of the Colonel and Goodenough. Then she remembered Joseph and turned dazed eyes to find him. Having become the accused, his guards had fled.

Still bound but free, Joseph was backing into the shadows beneath the oak where the empty rope still swayed. She'd turned in time to glimpse his face, still readable despite his swollen, bloodied features. For an instant his regret and loss seemed to fill the night. Then he took another step back and vanished into the darkness, as though he simply ceased to be.

Willa turned her back on the spot where he'd been, lest others be drawn to look thence, and with a heart too heavy to feel relief, she crossed to the knot of people hovering around the Colonel.

THIRTY-EIGHT

E lias Waring insisted on going home, though any number of cabins nearby would have opened their doors to him in need. He rode under his own power, but with a man at either stirrup prepared to catch him should he fall.

Willa followed on foot, entering the big stone house only after Goodenough had seen the Colonel to a bed and changed out of her bloodied garments. At some point a basin was brought, and Willa washed her face and hands until the water blackened, and fingered her snarled hair into a braid.

Though other shadowed figures lined the hall that ran the center of the house, waiting for word of the Colonel, Willa stood alone, her back against the paneled wall. She spoke to no one, though she felt their stares— sympathetic, curious, a few wary with suspicion. She supposed it would always be so, no matter if she lived among them twice as long as she'd lived with the Mohawks. Just now she didn't care. The tumults of the day and night had left her raw as broken eggshells, all her pieces scattered.

She thought of Joseph and prayed fervently, wordlessly, for his safety. She thought of the children, safe at Anni's, and thanked God for them. She tried with all her heart not to think of Neil MacGregor, wherever he had gone.

Oma, she thought at some point, as people came and went around her, talking softly to one another, waiting. *Francis did not speak of Oma.* Where into all that tale of fire and death and betrayal had her grandmother fallen and been lost?

She closed her eyes at last, too weary to think at all, just as Goodenough emerged from the parlor, closing the door behind her and jerking Willa wide awake. The housemaid set a lighted candle on a nearby sideboard. "You're still here. Good. He's wantin' to see you."

Willa looked into the face nearly level with her own, brown and handsome, but terrible in its composure. The candlelight picked out the grief in Goodenough's eyes.

"It's his heart, but he says we're not to fret. You ever hear such foolishness? I wish that Mister Neil…"

"So do I." Willa couldn't swallow back the longing she felt for Neil's calming presence. His gentleness. His care. The longing went deeper every time she let it in, but she knew it was shared with half the settlement on this night of death and birth. If she could go back and not send him away, if she could undo that one thing—say yes instead of no—would everything else have turned out differently? better?

Goodenough was watching her in the candlelight. "There's something I need to say to you, too, so things can be right between us."

Willa waited, numb with exhaustion and regret.

"I told you how Richard was kind to me the day the Colonel bought me and we started upriver for this place. You mind that?"

She had to think a moment. "When we did the wash at Anni's." The day she mailed her second letter to Tilda Fruehauf, under Richard's nose. "I remember."

"Listen, then, and hear me on this." Goodenough's lips trembled as she spoke. "A bit ago, the Colonel and me, we was alone with Francis, and he talked some more. We know now. That poor boy, he's carried all these things he seen his brother do. And Richard did do a heap of wickedness leadin' up to this night, and saw evil done, and had whatever there was left of that boy I met crushed out of his soul. We didn't see it clear…and now I reckon you think me a fool."

Willa shook her head. "There was a part of me, a very small part, that wanted to believe…" She couldn't finish the thought aloud.

"Well," Goodenough said. "He was that boy once, and when you see me grieving, just know that's who it is I'm crying over."

She was weeping now, though she made no sound. Willa touched her sturdy arm, then squeezed it. "I have not forgotten who Richard was. I will grieve too."

Lips pressed tight, Goodenough gave a sharp nod. "You go on in to the Colonel. He got some things to settle with you, I reckon."

Elias Waring was abed, propped against a bank of pillows. Francis, scrubbed and clean shirted, crouched before the hearth across the room. Lem was there, in a straight-backed chair beside the bed, looking bewildered by what had transpired this night. It might be some time before he understood. Willa remembered how long Goes-Singing had taken to grasp that her father had fallen in battle, fighting men like Elias Waring and his sons. Sam. Nick. Edward. Richard. All dead now. So many dead.

She halted in the center of the room, undone by the eyes of the man in the bed, suffering eyes sunken in a face so bloodless it was gray. What was there left to say between them?

The Colonel's voice was weak but steady. "Does the Indian live?"

It wasn't a thing she'd expected him to be thinking about. Her heart constricted with worry, even as it grasped at hope. "Those men who meant to hang him fled when Francis spoke against them. Joseph slipped away into the dark. That is what I saw and all I know."

Let him fly from this place—even if I never see him again in this life— with the wings of a swift high hawk, let him fly.

"Let him stay away," the Colonel said from his bed, uncannily close to echoing her thoughts, "and he will live. At least his death will not be my doing."

Another chair stood at the bed's foot. Willa sank into it, her knees unable to support her any longer. The Colonel seemed to weaken as well, sinking back into the bedding with a soft groan. At once, Goodenough was there, tugging at a blanket, fussing that he needed his rest else something worse befall.

"Sally," the Colonel said, "I'm tired and grief-sick but not about to pass. Leave off your fretting."

The small remonstrance only served to further agitate Goodenough. "You ain't dying tonight, that's certain truth. There's living to be done yet. I aim to see you do your share."

Even as she fussed, her hand was stroking the Colonel's face with a tenderness so intimate Willa felt she ought to look away. Had he called her *Sally*? Perhaps her ears had played her false. Perhaps in another second, she would drop onto the carpet and lie there unconscious for a week.

"Mama?" Lem said from his bedside perch, worried by their talk of dying. Goodenough's skirts didn't conceal the hand that reached from beneath the bed covers and patted the boy's knee.

"It's all right, Lem." Elias Waring shot Willa a look and drew his hand away. She could tell he had more to say to her, but he waited for Goodenough to cross to a table by the door, where a tray of tea things rested. "My stableman, Crane... He's been a part of your troubles?"

"So it would seem." If what Francis said was true, and she had no reason now not to believe him, it had been Aram Crane who'd watched her farm for Richard, who'd done the small things to vex and frighten them.

Francis. Having unburdened himself of his secrets, he'd retreated back into his own world, happily lining pieces of kindling on the hearth bricks. It would need some thinking, but she would find some way of rewarding him for saving her children and Joseph. It would take a lifetime to reward Francis Waring.

"I understand why Francis kept that knowledge to himself," the Colonel said after a heavy silence. "But why did you not come to me with it? I would have dealt with Crane."

"I only had suspicions, Colonel. No proof of who was bothering us. But..." She hesitated, having second thoughts about telling him what else she knew about Aram Crane, who had once faced men like Colonel Waring across the line of battle. She studied the Colonel's stricken face, debating whether she should add one more thing to burden his mind. "Where is Aram Crane? Do you know?"

"That is a very good question. I haven't seen the man for days."

Willa looked at her hands in her lap.

"You said you didn't know whether he was harassing you, but there's something you know about—or against—the man." When she didn't raise her head, the Colonel added, "I am stronger than I must look, Wilhelmina. I can bear it. Tell me."

She raised her head. "He is an army deserter. From the fort at Niagara."

From across the room, Goodenough turned to stare at her. Lem looked from face to face, his expression puzzled, his little legs swinging.

Elias Waring's face had fallen blank. "Fort Niagara? That's still in British hands." Understanding made ripples through the blankness, drawing lines ever deeper across his brow, beside his mouth.

"Joseph was sent from Niagara to find him," she said, "and take him back to his regiment—the Eighth I think it is. That is what my brother does. He's tracks deserters for the British."

Anni's father absorbed all this with remarkable composure, yet Willa could see what it cost him, could see the look of sickness in his eyes, knowing he'd sheltered the man for so many months. "Do you think he—your brother—has Crane in custody now?"

"That is what I thought, until I saw him trying to save my children while my fields and cabin burned. Now...I do not know."

She hadn't meant to further distress him, but at her words, the Colonel winced.

"Yesterday I questioned Richard—" His voice caught on the name; a glint of tears came into his eyes, and his chin quivered. "He claimed to have no knowledge of Crane's whereabouts." He drew a breath and clenched his jaw. "If ever I lay eyes on the man again, your Mohawk brother will have no further need of seeking him—unless it be to collect his scalp."

Willa was beyond even shuddering at such words. *As long as Joseph is safe. And Neil is safe…somewhere. And the children…*

Desire to see Matthew and Maggie Kershaw welled up, overwhelming all other needs. It pulled at her with such urgency she thought she might just make it as far as Anni's before she collapsed to sleep on a rug by the hearth, with their small bodies curled warm against hers. Without a word she stood from the chair and started toward the parlor door.

"Willa. Bide a moment." At the Colonel's voice, she paused, finding it hard to focus her eyes on him, much less her mind on what he was saying. "I'll have someone send to Anni and Charles, have the children brought here, if you'll agree to stay."

"Stay?"

"For as long as you need."

Beside the bed, Lem kicked his feet. "Matthew and Maggie? They're comin' here?"

"If Miss Willa says," his mother told him. "Now hush."

But Lem jumped off the chair, bouncing with excitement. "Please, Miss Willa?"

"Miss Willa don't need your help makin' up her mind." Goodenough grabbed her son as he tried to scoot past her. "Francis? Take this boy down to the kitchen and his bed."

There were groans. There was pleading. Finally there was quiet as Francis led Lem from the parlor.

For an instant, before Francis's blond head—combed into order now—passed from view, Willa thought it could have been Richard ushering out a younger sibling. The Richard of long ago, not yet twisted and hardened by the violence he'd seen and done, by hate and grief and greed.

Perhaps Richard hadn't meant to kill her parents, only to raze their farm and drive them off, as others whose loyalties were suspect had been driven out along the frontier all the years of the war. Not an admirable thing, but something many men had done to one another, men who now reaped in their fields or minded their shops and trades, no one thinking the worst of them. But he *had* meant to kill Matthew and Maggie. Could she spend even one night in that house, seeing the ghost of the boy, as well as the man, in every corner?

"I won't insist, but I hope you'll consider it." Elias Waring's face was grave as he turned to Goodenough. "In my desk, Sally…the papers?"

Goodenough sighed. "I'll get 'em. But then you finish this and get some sleep."

"Yes ma'am." The Colonel's mouth slanted with amusement. On any other night, it might have been a smile.

Goodenough crossed to a large, finely crafted desk and opened a drawer. "This the one you want, on top?"

At his nod she withdrew an official-looking paper with a broken seal and brought it to the bed. The Colonel beckoned Willa, who drew near to take it. "It came over a week ago, but I hadn't the heart to bring it to you."

The notice of her eviction and the time of the auction where her land was to be sold, to be held at German Flats in a matter of days. While it would never be Richard who owned it, someone, most likely a stranger, soon would.

She was almost too numb to feel defeat. Almost. "I see it would be wise to accept your offer of a roof."

"It's the very least I hope to do. Francis has related all he saw this night, including"—the Colonel's lips clenched as his gaze went to her bruised cheek and temple—"including Richard's attack upon your person. Wilhelmina, can you forgive the sins of my family against yours?"

Willa opened her mouth, on the verge of saying words born of the rawness of her grief, when something like light shot through her, giving understanding in the midst of weariness and shattering loss. This thing that was asked of her was not impossible, however much it felt so. Moreover, it was a thing she must do now, right now, while she was too numb for the tumult of emotion sure to come in the days ahead to cloud her mind and dim that sudden light. And that light was telling her that though she had twice lost all that was dear to her by no choice of her own, to forgive or not was her choice to make.

"I can forgive them, Colonel," she said. "And I do. Please send for the children to come to me here. For tonight at least, we will stay."

Later, when they were all safe beneath one roof—even the collie—and she had touched them, seen the children's dark heads side by side on a pallet in the room where she would sleep, and Goodenough had laid out one of her own clean shifts for her to wear, Willa caught the housemaid's sleeve as she started to take her leave.

"Goodenough," she said, low so as not to wake the children. "Did I hear the Colonel call you Sally?"

"You did." Goodenough's face bore the marks of weeping, but into it came a light undimmed by the heartbreak of the past hours, brighter than the candle she carried to light her way through the darkened house. "I made a gift of it to him—my name from before—the day Lem was born. Only thing I had to give was truly mine. I'm named Sarah, same as was my mistress."

The crop wasn't an utter loss, though it might as well have been. Half an acre stood, somehow spared by the flames. Not enough to feed one person through a winter, let alone three—one of them a boy who'd grown a hand's breadth over the summer and was eating to make up for it. And it began to look as though there would be three of them, at least for a while.

It was two days since the fire, one since they buried Richard.

Willa walked among the cornstalks, bending now and then to brush her fingertips against a pumpkin's cold rind. The acrid smell of burning suffused the damp autumn air. A smoke pall hung over the blackened field and clearing, awaiting a breeze to bear it away.

Another kind of pall hung over her spirit.

Neil MacGregor was lost to her, and she hadn't seen Joseph since the night he was almost hanged. She wondered in her heart about the children and whether Joseph—if he was safe—would come for them, whether they would want to leave her now that she had nothing.

Weariness dragged at her as if stones had been sewn into the hem of the petticoat Goodenough had lent her. Though pieced from modest homespun, likely it was Goodenough's best, and here she went trailing it through the sooty remains of her field.

They hadn't wanted her to come there, Goodenough or the Colonel. But she'd had to come, had to see the devastation by the unforgiving light of day. She'd brought the children with her, unwilling to let them out of her sight again so soon. The horse borrowed from the Warings' stable was tethered between the field and the cabin's remains. The children's voices and sometimes the collie's carried across the blackened ground from the yard, where they poked about the rubble for anything that might be salvaged.

She doubted they would find anything. The cabin and all it held was lost. The drying beans. The rings of dried squash and pumpkins in the loft. Clothing, cooking pans, cups, plates. The small cherished things brought from the north to remind her of Goes-Singing and Sweet Rain and her years with the Kanien'kehá:ka. As if the Almighty had chosen to wipe away both her former lives with one searing stroke.

Leaving her with what? Not the solitary life she once thought to lead, free of the terrible pain of loving. But she couldn't yet see the shape of a new life rising from these ashes, though she supposed there would be one, since she still drew breath and must live it.

"Burning Sky."

Willa caught that breath at the sound of her name, but the voice that spoke it sent relief washing over her.

She was smiling when she turned.

THIRTY-NINE

At the edge of what remained of her cornfield, looping the reins of his spotted mare around a beech sapling, was Joseph Tames-His-Horse, still whole, though marred by the fresh scars from his fight. Willa all but ran to him.

She hadn't yet shed tears for Joseph. They came now as his arms went around her. His chest was strong and warm beneath his bloodstained shirt. Her heart opened to him, her brother. "I feared I wouldn't see you again."

Joseph pulled her tight against him, almost crushing. She was glad, for it told her he wasn't badly hurt. Too soon he put his hands on her shoulders and put her from him so he could look into her face. "I would not leave you without a word."

"Even if half of Shiloh was after your neck?"

Joseph raised a brow—the one that didn't have a cut slicing through it. "Are they?"

Willa grimaced through her smile, hurting to see him wounded. His eye at least was open again, the swelling subsided, though under it the skin was dark with bruising. "You won't be hunted. Not by Colonel Waring. But he says you must never return."

Joseph stared beyond her to the ravaged field. "I will go for now because I must. I make no promise about never returning."

His gaze fell to her face, sorrowed, and she knew that it would be a long time before she saw him again.

The column of his throat convulsed as he touched her face. "We met in a cornfield. Now we part in one."

Willa's throat was too tight to speak. There was a second horse, saddled, tied to Joseph's mare. With a small jolt of surprise, she found her voice. "Aram Crane—did you find him? Is that his horse?"

"I found him, and that is his horse. I plan to keep it for my troubles. But him, I let go."

"You let him go? Why? Will you go after him again?"

Instead of explaining immediately, Joseph unlaced a bag behind his mare's saddle and withdrew a letter, battered and creased. "If I am to hunt meat for my family before the winter, then I must return to them. There is no more time for tracking men. But here is a thing I found among that man's belongings. It was meant for you."

Frowning, she took the letter from Joseph's hand. "Aram Crane had a letter for me?"

The corner of Joseph's bruised mouth drew in. "He was not meant to have it. I think it was given to the smith to bring to you, and maybe it was that man who also penned it, but the words are—"

"Neil MacGregor's?" she interrupted, having already made out the name of the sender. Fingers trembling, she unfolded the single page. It wasn't a long missive—far too brief, when her heart craved a book of his words—but she devoured it with an eagerness she was helpless to conceal.

> *My Dear Willa,*
>
> *And now abideth Faith, Hope, Love, these three; but the greatest of these is Love. If there is also Pain, that is Love's mirrored side. Even the love the Almighty Lord gives to us, His Children, brought Him a Pain and Loss immeasurable and yet… He that spared not His own Son, but delivered Him up for us All, how shall He not with Him also freely give us all Things? Trust in His Goodness, Beloved, and the path He has prepared for you, and do not be too angry when you learn of the Doings of your Devoted Servant…*
>
> *Neil MacGregor*

She read the words again, grateful for them, comforted by them yet pierced with regret that she had denied such a man her love. Her heart underscored what were surely his last words to her with a silent and belated amen, though she puzzled over that last line. What *doings* did he mean? His leaving? She couldn't be angry with him over that. She'd been so certain she wanted to walk her path alone, had bent all her will toward making Neil believe it.

But the heart is more courageous than the mind, and sometimes wiser.

When at last she looked up, Joseph's strong brown face swam in her tears. She blinked them away and saw the hurting in his eyes too.

"You love him," he said.

"Not well enough. Not soon enough. He is gone away." Gone, and expecting her to be angry with him. "And now you must go," she said, looking into her brother's eyes and suddenly remembering something that had taken place beyond the confines of her own troubles. "The council at Fort Stanwix. I never yet heard about it. Did you go there?"

"I did not, but I spoke with some who did." Joseph told her briefly about the peace treaty, how nothing much had been settled and that there was to be another soon, this time with the chiefs of the Continental Congress. "Much will be decided then, I think, about where all the Longhouse nations will be allowed to live, here or in a new place. As for me, I will take my mother and sister and go where Thayendanegea sees fit to settle us. Perhaps," he added with a faint wryness, "I will make tables for all my Wolf Clan sisters who do not think to bring them on the journey."

Willa tried to smile. She would need another table now. And a cabin to put it in. But Joseph would not be the one to make it.

He seemed to have the same thought as she. "You have a village now, hen'en? They will care for you, if you let them."

"I know. Colonel Waring will let me stay under his roof as long as I have need." Which might be a long time, since in a matter of days she would lose even the dirt beneath her feet.

Joseph drew breath to speak, just as somewhere in the still-standing corn behind Willa came a giggle, a shushing, then a volley of whispers. Willa glanced behind her. Matthew and Maggie Kershaw peered from the golden stalks.

"I am ready to take them now." Joseph nodded toward their poorly concealed audience, then to his extra horse. "If that is still what you wish."

"It's not what *we* wish!" The boy came first out of hiding, face set in a familiar, stubborn firmness. His sister followed on his heels, fleet and graceful as a fawn, her face hopeful, open to every sling and arrow the world—or Willa—might yet fling at her.

The sight of them made something warm and full press up against her heart; it nudged against the emptiness Neil MacGregor should have filled, taking up a little of its room, and because all she could do was stand there and let herself feel it—so glad for it, so glad—it was left to Joseph to speak.

"What is this you are saying, young brother? As I remember it, you spoke different words the day I met you and your sister."

"Hen'en," the boy said. "That is true. But we didn't know *your* sister then. You said we would like her, and we do."

Maggie pulled her lower lip between her teeth, nodding agreement.

Willa put a hand on both their heads and laughed, mostly so she wouldn't cry. "That is good, for I like you. Both of you."

A smile tugged the girl's lip free of her teeth. "We want to adopt you."

Willa blinked and her lips parted, but she didn't speak, uncertain she'd heard what she thought she had.

The boy turned on his sister, annoyed. "That's not how we were going to say it."

"It is! We want her for our mother."

"I know." Matthew sighed, and with color mounting in his face addressed Willa. "We know how it's done, adopting, and there's the creek for the washing—but we thought maybe that part isn't needed because we're all Wolf Clan already. We don't have to go to Niagara to find our people. We don't *want* to go. We want to stay and be your children."

When Willa was again struck speechless—this time by the emotion swelling in her throat—Joseph inserted gently, "Perhaps you should have begun by asking this woman if she wishes to be your mother."

Had it not been so touching, the boy's surprise and chagrin would have made Willa laugh again. He might have been flustered by this turn, but his sister leaped the gap in their plan as nimbly as the deer she resembled.

"Will you?" she asked, twining small fingers with Willa's. "Be our mother?"

Willa's knees hit the ground, and she gathered them into her arms. "I would be honored to be the mother of such brave and good children." As she knew she had been in her heart, even before the night of the fire.

Blinking back tears, she let them go and rose, catching Joseph's eye. He was happy for her, but this was hurting him as well; leaving was in his eyes.

"Say your farewells to Joseph," she told her children. "Then you may take my knife and go cut those last pumpkins. We will take them to Goodenough, who might be persuaded to let us make a mess of her kitchen—and a few pies."

Pies from the last pumpkins she would ever grow on her papa's land.

With joy and grief she watched Joseph and the children embrace, before they hurried off to do as she asked, already arguing about who would do the cutting.

"It is good, my sister," Joseph said. "It is part of what my heart hoped for you."

But not the whole. As she turned back to him, the enormity of what she had agreed to fell on Willa with crushing weight.

"How will I provide for them with no land?"

She told him then how she was to lose her farm, with no way found to stop it even though Richard wouldn't be the one to own it. But Joseph only smiled.

"Remember what the Scotsman wrote to you, about trust? He speaks wisdom."

Willa touched the bodice of her jacket where she had tucked Neil's letter. Joseph pretended not to see that and moved away from her to untie the reins of his horse.

She followed, saying quickly, "I haven't thanked you for saving me and the children, the night of the fire."

He paused with the reins in his hands and looked at her, his eyes deep with love. "What sort of man would I be, if I did not do such a thing for my sister?"

"Not the man I know you to be," she said, and the tears came again, without shame. "I will always be thanking you, Joseph, in my thoughts, in my heart. Remember that." She took his hand in hers. With her other she traced a fingertip across his jutting cheekbone, where the tight bronze skin had been broken by Richard's fist.

Joseph took both her hands in his. "And you remember this: you will not be alone, Burning Sky...Willa," he amended. "'A bruised reed...'"

"'Shall he not break,'" she finished, though it hurt to say the words. "I know. I am never truly alone."

Joseph started to shake his head, as if she'd misunderstood him. Instead he put his hand on her shoulder, leaned close and kissed her mouth. "I go," he said. Then he turned the horses and walked away from her without looking back.

Joseph Tames-His-Horse did not look back until he'd climbed the ridge north of Willa's land and paused below the crest in a stand of yellowing poplar. Smoke still hovered thin over the clearing where the cabin had stood. The wind had been strangely calm since the night of the fire, as if the earth itself held its breath, waiting.

It was a hard thing, perhaps the hardest he'd ever done, sitting his horse beneath the poplars and watching his sister's tiny figure moving far below, poking through the ashes of her home, looking lost and forsaken, though in truth she was neither. There was nothing left to do or say, and he knew that he must go, yet he struggled with himself. Something still held him motionless too, watching, waiting.

It was some moments before movement on the track that led to Shiloh drew his gaze, and the breath went out of him in a sigh like the breeze that finally stirred, quivering the yellow leaves above his head, ruffling the mare's long mane, stirring the clearing's pall.

There were three of them coming up the track, all on horseback. Joseph knew them for men who carry news of import. It was clear in the set of their shoulders as they rode, and though the distance was far, he had seen one of them often enough to put a name to him now.

He touched the place at his side that still sometimes pained him and thought, *So be it.* And then, reluctantly, *Awiyo.*

It is good.

Even so, Joseph Tames-His-Horse did not wish to see more. He looked a last time on the distant figure among the ashes, unaware of the future bearing down on her, and sent his voice to her softly on the wind. "Do not be afraid of what is coming, my sister."

With the press of a knee, he turned the mare along a game trail that threaded up to the crest of the ridge, the deserter's horse following, and there he paused. He didn't look behind him again but forward, over many trails to where a new land beckoned, where the People waited, in need of all their warriors to sustain them.

He clicked his tongue to the mare and rode down to meet them.

FORTY

W ith the children busy among the pumpkins, the collie at their heels, Willa had wandered up to the yard, though there was no use in sifting yet again through the cabin's remains. Not a charred beam was left unturned or drift of ash unstirred, perchance it hid some small salvageable thing. She simply wasn't ready to turn her back on her past yet again and return homeless to Shiloh.

Soon the auction would be held in German Flats. Soon a stranger would put his name to her land.

She straightened from the rubble, stopping herself in time from wiping more soot on Goodenough's petticoat. Instead she strode toward the slope behind where the cabin had stood and bent to clean her hands in the browning grass.

As she did so, something near the tree line caught her eye. She climbed to it and, in utter disbelief, bent to pick up Neil MacGregor's Bible.

A few paces into the trees, half-buried in last year's leaves, lay her musket. She stood there, caught in wonder and bewilderment, until it came into her mind that Matthew must have brought them out of the fire, only to lose them in the chaos of that night.

Willa sat on the grass with her heart swelling within her, laid the musket beside her, and held the Bible across her knees. Some of its pages were rippled from the damp, its cover spotted with scorch marks, but it could be saved—not like poor *Pamela,* too long abandoned on the islet in the lake. She couldn't bear to open it, however, and see the tiny words written in the margins of so many of its pages, or those on the slips of paper scattered throughout. Not yet. They would be for later, for many laters to come, to remember the man she might have spent her life loving.

She held the Bible to her nose, cherishing the weight of it, the smell of the leather, and thought with a bleakness that her life thus far amounted to a trail of small things pulled from ashes: keepsakes brought on journeys, miraculous survivors of tragedy.

Or now, things not so small. She had Matthew and Maggie. She had her children. Willa closed her eyes, half-formed prayers for Neil flitting through her mind. Prayers for herself and the children she would do her best to raise. Prayers for Joseph.

She drew her knees up, letting the Bible slide down her thighs into her lap, and rested her head on folded arms. Her bottom was getting cold. Damp. She was thinking how the children would tease her when they saw it, but that wasn't what made her lift her head sharply and look for them. It was the collie's barking and the sound of horses coming up the track.

It was habit to check the musket's powder, though after lying in the woods, what was left in the pan would be useless. Still she came out to meet whoever approached with musket gripped in one hand, Bible in the other.

Escorted by the frisking collie, the horsemen had reached the yard. There were three of them. One was Elias Waring.

Relief flooded Willa. Hot on its heels came concern. The Colonel had only risen from his bed yesterday, for Richard's burial. He shouldn't have ridden all this way, and it amazed her that Goodenough allowed it. And the man riding beside him… She squinted, casting back in her mind to that day on the road above the mill, with the Colonel's mule, and Richard come with that man to assess her land.

It was the same man. Wendell Stoltz, the assessor who'd come in the spring at Richard's fetching. Was that what this was about? Were they come to forcibly remove her? Then who—?

The third rider had been fishing inside his coat, as if to assure himself something put there was safely there still. His head was bent, an unfamiliar, broad-brimmed hat blocking his face. Now he raised his head.

She barely registered Maggie sliding down from behind his saddle or

Matthew from behind the Colonel's. The children ran to her, chattering. The collie circled them, barking. Willa stood like a woman chiseled out of oak, unable to move or speak, seeing nothing beyond Neil MacGregor, who had dismounted and stood now with his horse's reins in hand, staring at her as he had that day inside the mill, as if nothing else in the world was worth his notice.

Time did a strange thing then. It tangled and twisted, looping back on itself like a cord tied in knots. She didn't remember Neil closing the distance between them. Of a sudden he stood before her, drinking her in with great swallows as though he'd thirsted long for the sight of her. Then he was talking about her land, and her father, about Albany and—

"You have been to Albany?" She cut into his tumbling words, her voice harsh in its abruptness. It made his eyes widen. She'd forgotten how beautiful they were, bluer than the bits of sky showing now in breaks between gray clouds. She'd forgotten how pleasing was the shape of his mouth that had smiled at her so often when she hadn't deserved a smile.

His mouth wanted to smile now, she could tell, but something cautious in his eyes wouldn't quite let it. "Aye. To Albany. I went to find Tilda Fruehauf, after I learned her letter to ye was stolen." He glanced at the Colonel. "I kent 'twas the only way to get at the truth in time, to have it straight from the woman herself."

"A letter to me? But who...?" She was having trouble taking it in, with her heart beating loud in her ears, and the children tugging at her and asking questions, and the dog letting the world know its happiness at this reunion.

Neil MacGregor raised a hand. "Wheest!" he said to one and all. Though he laughed as he said it, the noise and tugging ceased.

Willa set the musket on the ground, next to it the Bible, then straightened with her eyes on his, determined to understand. "You went to Albany...for me?"

"Of course," he said, frowning a little. Then the frown went away, and he said, "Aye, I was forgetting. Gavan never made it to you with my letter. He's all right, though, on the mend. I've seen him. Seems the same hand did us both harm, he and me."

"I... He..." And then she understood; he spoke of the letter Joseph had only just given her. She pressed a hand to the place where the missive was tucked into her bodice and began quietly to cry. It did not make half the sense it probably should, but it didn't matter. Neil MacGregor was here. Not just his words on a paper or in his Bible, but himself standing in front of her, telling her he left Shiloh not *because* of her, but *for* her.

She wiped a palm across her cheek to stem the tears, then saw the state of her hand. "I am all over soot!" she exclaimed, embarrassed for what she must look like after sifting through the fire's devastation.

"Willa." Neil's voice was thick with feeling. She thought his arm was about to come around her, but he stopped himself. It was then she saw; only one of his arms was inside a coat sleeve. The other, the same that was wounded when she found him, hung once again in a sling, snug against his shirt.

"You are hurt?"

"'Tis nothing. A bit of trouble on the road back, is all."

"More than a bit," said Wendell Stoltz, inserting himself into the conversation. "I found him at a tavern a few miles shy of German Flats, shot through the arm."

Neil had been waylaid on the road, Stoltz went on to explain, and ridden injured for miles before falling from his horse practically in the tavern yard. After having his arm set and a night's sleep, Neil—in company by then with Stoltz—had pressed on, determined to reach her.

The children listened to this account with wide-eyed admiration, but a flush had risen from Neil's neck, and in his eyes was contrition. "I didna ken then what was happening here," he told her, with a glance at the Colonel.

"But who was it waylaid you? A highwayman?" Willa asked, unable to quell a jolt of fear, belated though it came.

"That's what I thought at first," Neil said. "But no. 'Twas Aram Crane shot me. And got away with the deed."

"Neil..." Though gripped by concern, his name on her tongue was a sweetness she savored. "We were right about Aram Crane. He wasn't what he pretended to be. He..."

But Neil was nodding. He already knew. Of course, the Colonel would have told him all.

"I'm sorry, Willa," he said. "So sorry about the cabin, but I thank the Almighty Lord with every breath that you're safe, you and the children. And...Joseph?"

"Gone back to his people," she said. "I only wish he'd got that man and saved you this hurt." She reached to touch his bound arm, tenderness for him nearly overpowering, but drew back in uncertainty before her fingers brushed him. "But what is this about Albany? And my mother's cousin? You have *seen* her?"

"I have," Neil said, eyes shining.

"It seems," the Colonel interjected, "your Albany relation is a meticulous hoarder of correspondence."

Willa drew in her breath. "Papa's letters?"

The Colonel looked on her dawning comprehension with a pleasure that almost chased the grief of the past days from his face. "Dr. MacGregor has acquired a dozen letters written by your father in the early years of the war, but there's one of particular significance...if I may?"

The Colonel looked to Neil, who drew a thick bundle of letters from his coat and, seeming to know which was wanted, handed one to the Colonel. Elias Waring scanned the creased, yellowed page while they waited in silence—even the children—then cleared his throat. "This was written by Dieter Obenchain in spring of 1778:

Though you may think otherwise, I have given long Consideration to
many of the Persuasions for this Rebellion against the Crown you have

presented in your letters, weighing them against what Holy Scripture
tells us: "If it be possible, as much as lieth in you, live peaceably with all
men." But what is to follow when, despite all Effort to the Contrary, a
man sees around him another Scripture coming to pass: "for they speak
not peace: but they devise deceitful matters against them that are quiet
in the land."

The words transported Willa to her childhood, to evenings on the cabin porch with mending in her lap and a novel tucked half out of sight, to snatches of half-heard conversation flying above her head while she stitched and stole glances at the more absorbing world between the book's pages.

I grieve it should come to this, but am content that I have waited as
long as a man can do so, praying without ceasing that this War would
not force a Stand upon me, who came into this land to live in Peace.
But it has done so, and here I declare it. I am for Liberty. I am for
Independence. Though it has taken me long to come to it, I hope not
too long, for the sake of dear Rebecca, all that is left to me on this earth,
lest a day come when our beloved Willa returns to live among us—a
Day such as I pray for, also without ceasing. If it proves too late, then
may God forgive me, and protect those He placed in my earthly care.
"This thou hast seen, O LORD: keep not silence: O Lord, be not far
from me. Stir up thyself, and awake to my judgment, even unto my
cause, my God and my Lord."

It was a moment before Willa realized the Colonel had stopped reading. Looking into the faces of the three men waiting for her to speak, she saw in them the satisfaction they had been suppressing all this while. "And this is unmitigated proof?"

Stoltz chuckled at the recollection of his words. "It means," he said, "there will be no auction of your land, not with such proof of your father's loyalties to the Patriot cause. I matched your father's signature to that on the land deed, and earlier this morning Colonel Waring—myself and Dr. MacGregor witnessing—made over the deed to the sole surviving heir of Dieter Obenchain."

They meant her, Willa realized. *She* was the sole surviving heir. The land wouldn't be auctioned. It was hers.

Stoltz rounded up the letters and handed them to her. Willa wiped her shaking hands on her skirt—forgetting it wasn't her own—and held them as she would a fragile glass. The letter on top was streaked and spotted with brownish stains.

She raised her eyes to Neil, whose mouth tilted in apology. "I bled a bit on them. Sorry."

Dear man. She wanted to throw her arms around him, to tell him she loved him, that she had been a fool, that she never wanted him to go away again. But all she could say was, "Oh..."

If she was speechless, Matthew Kershaw wasn't.

"We don't have to leave?" he asked, looking from face to face for confirmation.

"We don't have to leave," Willa echoed, but for her it wasn't a question. She simply needed to hear the words spoken to make them finally, irrevocably, real.

"Not unless you wish to." Neil stepped close and finally—oh, finally—touched her. His hand cupped her shoulder, then, as if he couldn't help himself, her face. "I'm sorry, Willa, for all you faced alone. I didna want to leave ye, but there was no time to be lost."

Lost. Willa closed her eyes, caught between all she had lost and all she had gained, and the fact of this man now standing there touching her. "Cabins can be rebuilt. Crops planted again. But this..." Opening her eyes, she raised the letters. "None of that could happen without this."

Something in the way Neil was touching her must have communicated to the Colonel and Stoltz, even the children, for when Willa glanced around again, the assessor was showing Matthew something out of his saddlebag, the collie trailing after them, and the Colonel had taken Maggie's hand and the two were walking toward the horse shed, which had survived the fire.

She and Neil stood alone in the yard, his hand warm against her cheek. She wanted to keep looking into his eyes forever but lowered hers in shame.

"Willa." Neil took his hand from her face, leaving her wishing for its warmth. "I thought you'd determined to be alone, to give your heart to no one. You made that clear enough to me. But the children...they tell me they've proposed to adopt ye."

She risked a glance at his face, saw in his eyes the mingling of amusement, warmth, and aching question.

"Is it just their notion," he went on, "or did you accept their proposal?"

She swallowed and said, "I sent Joseph away without them. They are my children. I accepted."

Both happiness and hurt crossed his eyes, much as it had Joseph's. She knew he was remembering his proposal by the spring, after the first crop fire. The one she had spurned.

"I accepted," she said again. "But I made them ask me twice."

Neil searched her face, dark brows drawn, and she saw he didn't yet understand.

"You have only asked me once."

She was looking into his eyes the moment hope dealt his hurt a stunning blow. Then it came, the smile that made her heart melt.

"Wilhelmina Obenchain, as I stand here breathing, you're the most headstrong, stubborn-minded—"

"Sooty?"

"Aye, that too, but I've seen how ye clean up." He breathed out through his nose, shaking his head. "Now dinna interrupt me. Where was I?"

"I am stubborn?" she prompted.

"That you are. You're also the most fearless woman I've ever kent, and I love ye full well. Now will you marry me and let me leastwise pretend to take care of ye?"

Fearless. Did he truly think her so? She had never been that, not in the ways that mattered, but because of him and the children, she was learning to be. By God's grace, she was learning.

It bloomed in her throat, the great love and need she had for this man. At first she couldn't speak around it, could only nod her head. Finally she lifted the letters, stained with his blood. "If this is how you pretend, Neil MacGregor, then I cannot wait to see what you do when you are in earnest."

His eyes searched hers, the smile frozen on his face. "Then that's... *aye*?"

"Oh, aye," she said. "I love you. And I mean to be Willa MacGregor before the first snow falls."

For a moment, Neil looked at her, breath coming deep, as though he'd held it too long. Then he took her soot-stained face between his hands. Never minding the two men and two children who'd stopped pretending not to watch them—he kissed her, and in it Willa felt a fierceness of possession that startled and thrilled her. It entwined like a fiery thread with the tenderness he'd always shown her, weaving of the two a rich new cloth, strong and beautiful and whole.

He drew in his breath then, breaking off the kiss to hold her away from him. "I canna believe I nearly forgot. I've more to tell ye."

Willa's heart was overflowing, but she laughed at his eager expression. He looked like one of the children bursting with a secret to share. "What more can there be?"

Something in his eyes made her heart skip, even before he said, "I've another letter for ye."

"Another of Papa's letters?"

"No." He reached again into his coat. "This one's from your grandmother."

"Oma?" When had her grandmother written any letters? Then Willa looked at what Neil held out to her. Not an old letter like Papa's, faded with age or worn with much reading. Its seal was unbroken.

She took it then, stunned, sat down on the ground, placed her papa's yellowed letters beside her, and said, weakly for someone moments ago called fearless, "Oma is alive?"

Neil lowered himself to sit beside her, careful of his wounded arm. "And sends her love, from Albany."

"She has all this time been in Albany? Why did no one know?"

Warmth spread from her shoulder as Neil MacGregor leaned against her and kissed her temple. "Open it. She'll speak for herself."

Willa glanced up to see the children and the collie coming across the yard to them. She broke the seal and, when her family was gathered around her, read to them of a miracle.

6 September 1784
To Wilhelmina Obenchain
Shiloh, New York State

Dearest Granddaughter,

This is a Letter I have composed many times in the past twelve years, often in the darkness on the edge of sleep, always with Tears. But never in all my wishing and composing did I expect the Almighty to grant me Opportunity of writing it in Truth. That will show an Old Woman she still has much to learn about her God.

Your young Scotsman tells me with Gravest Certainty and Regret that Rebecca and Dieter are no more. This I did not know for Fact, though I was all but certain of it. Let me explain why this is so.

I left Shiloh in the autumn of 1777, sent away by your parents to

Albany, where they believed I would be safe from the escalating Dissen-
tion and Violence on the frontier. I went by night, escorted by a trusted
friend of Maeve and John Keegan—the only souls in Shiloh to whom
I confided my intentions. Here with my niece, Tilda, I have remained,
with no sure Word of my vanished daughter and her husband until
your young Man's arrival yesterday.

I have seen those drawings of his, the ones he sent on to that
Society in Philadelphia that had the Temerity to imply he is on the
brink of losing his Privilege of fulfilling the Commission they sent him
to undertake. The more fools them, if they let him slip away. He seems
not to mind one way or the other, and has told me an Astonishing
Thing—that his Reason for venturing into the Frontier was but a
Means, not an End. A Means to bring him into your Path. I hope you
will not think badly of him for his telling me of you, how you met,
what you did for him, and how he learned to know you as a woman
returned from Captivity—though I am made to understand that
what began as Bondage you through Resiliency transformed into a Life,
one encompassing a husband, children, and, I am certain, much Joy.
Though the ones who took you from us have been the cause of my Loss,
I grieve with you for those you loved who are no more. No Mother
should have to see her Children pass before her. How my heart yearns
for that Day all Tears will be wiped away! When we both shall see our
Precious Ones again.

Mr. MacGregor tells me your Ordeals have not broken your spirit,
but on the contrary have made you Strong. Never, he confesses, has he
met a Woman such as yourself, unmatched in Courage and Conviction
(Granddaughter, I believe this Scotsman is more than a little in love
with you). Through his eyes I see you now, tall and shining and clean
of Heart. Soon, I pray, I will behold you with my own eyes, which are
still clear-seeing—not a Boast every woman having reached the age of
seventy-and-eight may make. In the spring, he promises, he shall fetch

me back to Shiloh, and to you, Granddaughter, if you wish to see this
foolish Old Woman again.

Oh, my dear, if I could turn back the years…but we are not given
such Powers in this life. Rather, having repented of old Works, we are
left to walk forward in the New. But there is one memory I must
stir—that book you went off to read that Terrible Day we lost you.
Are you surprised I remember it? Would it Surprise you more to learn
I obtained a copy years ago and have read every page of it—twice?
When I come to you in the Spring—if you permit me—you will have
it for your own. I will forbear spoiling the ending, only to say it is well
worth the Effort and I promise you, Wilhelmina, that I will let you
finish it—and any other book you desire to read—in Peace. I have
come to see the Merit in books, and in Granddaughters reading them,
and nothing will please me more, after I have seen your Face again,
than to place this copy of Richardson's Pamela *into your hands, then*
spend my evenings watching you sit by the Hearth (without need of a
pile of mending to hide behind), and discover for yourself how the
Story ends. And after you have done so, there is here by my chair a
Trunk full of books set aside for you by Your Loving Oma,
Dagna Fruehauf Mehler

"Oma…" Willa breathed out the word, tears streaming as she finished reading. She looked up to see Neil watching her with shining eyes.

"I dinna think I need ask whether you want me to fetch her from Albany," he said.

Willa wiped away a tear, then felt a slender arm come around her waist.

"Why are you crying, Istah?" Maggie asked her, looking up with worried eyes that longed to comfort. "Who is Oma?"

Matthew, hunkered beside his sister, was frowning in an effort to understand. "Don't you want her to come here?"

Willa hugged her daughter, then brushed the tousled hair from her son's face. "Oma is my grandmother," she said, and smiled through the last of her tears. "Your great-grandmother. And I want very much for her to come here, to see my beautiful family."

"We have a great-grandmother?" Maggie asked, clearly fascinated by the notion.

"She's coming here to live with us?" Matthew asked, excitement mounting in his voice. "With books?"

Neil and Willa both laughed, catching gazes across the children's heads. "Yes," Willa told them. "She's bringing books. She's coming home."

Home. It was the land beneath them, yes, but so much more than that. Home was in the eyes of Neil MacGregor, looking at her with love. Home was in the faces of these children she would cherish, for as long as the Almighty lent them to her—and forever in her heart. In them the two rivers of her soul had met and now flowed on together, clear and sure.

In them she was home.

Author's Notes
and Acknowledgments

In the course of researching the historical backdrop of this novel, I read dozens of books written about the eighteenth century, but there's only so much factual detail a writer can insert into a novel before she stops her story in its tracks to give a history lesson. For readers interested in learning more about the time period and events that influenced the story and shaped the characters found in the pages of *Burning Sky*, I offer the following notes.

The American Revolutionary War (1775–1783) proved extremely devastating to the New York frontier, in part because of its northern border shared with Canada, to which many Loyalists and pro-British Iroquois retreated, and from which they staged regular raids. These were part of the overall British campaign against the colonies, but on a smaller scale they consisted of personally motivated reprisals against Patriots for their attacks on Iroquois towns and Loyalist settlers. These reprisal raids, such as the attack upon Cherry Valley that Neil MacGregor found himself caught in, continued until the war's generally accepted ending—and beyond. General Lord Cornwallis surrendered to Patriot troops after his defeat at the Battle of Yorktown in October 1781, yet pro-British war parties were still roaming the Mohawk Valley during the summer of 1782, destroying property and taking prisoners. The New York frontier Willa Obenchain returned to in the spring of 1784 was a landscape of blackened homesteads and razed settlements, few of which had been reclaimed.

The *Haudenosaunee* (People of the Longhouse), also called the Six Nations of the Iroquois, are a league of independent nations that, centuries before the Revolutionary War, were united under a set of laws called the

Great Law of Peace. These nations are, from east to west as they were situated across the Mohawk Valley and western New York: Mohawks, Oneidas, Onondagas, Cayugas, and Senecas. The Tuscaroras joined the League in the early eighteenth century and dwelled primarily on Oneida land.

Toward the end of the 1600s, long before the war between the Colonies and the Crown, some members of the Six Nations immigrated north to Canada due to the influence of French Jesuit missionaries. While they continued to consider themselves close kin to the Mohawks and other nations of the Haudenosaunee, they remained apart. (It is among these Mohawks that Willa Obenchain lived for twelve years, and from there that she returned to her home in New York.) In 1710, four Mohawk men from the Haudenosaunee in the Mohawk Valley traveled to England to meet Queen Anne. While there, they asked for Anglican missionaries to come among them, in part as a safeguard against the French Jesuits leading more of the people away to Canada, thus weakening their nation. Queen Anne sent the missionaries, and soon Anglican Christianity took hold among the Mohawks, and to varying degrees the western Longhouse nations.

In the 1740s the spiritual revival called the Great Awakening led to New Light, or personal-conversion-oriented missionaries, coming among the Iroquois. Prominent among these missionaries was Samuel Kirkland, who by the late 1760s had settled among the Oneidas at one of their primary towns, Kanowalohale. There he dedicated himself to preaching the gospel, education, and the procuring of material needs for a people grown dependent on European goods as their lands became overhunted by their own involvement in the fur trade, and by encroaching white settlers. It was a clash between Kirkland's conversion-oriented Christian beliefs and those of the Church of England, longer established among the Six Nations, that caused fissures to form among the Iroquois. It took a war to reveal the extent of these cracks in the fabric of the centuries-old League. While most of the Iroquois nations chose to fight for the British, most of the Oneidas and Tuscaroras, in part because of their loyalty to Kirkland, chose to fight for the Patriots. For the Iroquois, as much as for European colonists, the Revolutionary War was no less than a civil war.

As early as 1772, free white citizens of the Mohawk Valley had been pressed to sign an oath of allegiance to King George, but in the years to follow, loyalty to the king crumbled under the weight of taxation and other restrictive acts of Parliament, an ocean away. By 1775, the lines between Patriot and Loyalist were already being drawn in New York so swiftly that some colonials were slow to realize the peril of not choosing sides. Neighbor pressured neighbor to sign oaths of allegiance to the new Continental Congress, and to declare their partisanship publicly. To refuse, even to dither, was tantamount to admitting oneself a British sympathizer. Homes, land, businesses, and lives were lost to fence-sitting, as Loyalists' property was seized and held, and many Loyalists jailed, abused, or driven from the colony. While the Treaty of Paris, signed by the United States and Britain in September of 1783, gave Loyalists the right to reclaim and dispose of their property within a year's time, resentment against these former neighbors was so strong in New York that the state ignored this provision and continued to confiscate and sell Loyalist property until 1788.

Negotiations for the Treaty of Fort Stanwix (the second council that Neil, Joseph, and Willa anticipate happening soon after the end of *Burning Sky*), held between American Congressional Commissioners and representatives of the Six Nations, took place during October 1784. The Six Nations came to this treaty still divided in their loyalties and worried about their future. The distressing terms of peace between the United States and Great Britain were made known—terms in which the Iroquois were excluded and the lands they claimed as sovereign nations relinquished by the British to the Americans. Because the war had left thousands of pro-British Iroquois huddled in makeshift, disease-ridden camps outside Fort Niagara in the west, their attendance at Fort Stanwix for this vital treaty was thin. Negotiations stretched for days, at the close of which, despite Iroquois efforts to stress their status as free and independent nations, the Six Nations were compelled to relinquish any claim to lands in the Ohio country and a huge tract of territory comprising the northwestern sector of the present state of Pennsylvania. News of the land cession was met with widespread resentment and bitterness. Led by Joseph Brant (Thayendanegea), many of the Six Nations refugees settled in southern Ontario along the Grand River, assisted by the Canadian government. Though the nations were scattered across the US/Canada border, the Haudenosaunee would eventually reestablish the Iroquois League according to the old pattern, and see their nations-within-a-nation status acknowledged by the federal government.

My heartfelt thanks to the following authors for the books I found most indispensable during the writing of *Burning Sky*. Without their scholarship and expertise, my desire to write stories set on the eighteenth century American frontier would have gone unfulfilled.

Barbara Graymont, *The Iroquois in the American Revolution*

Timothy J. Shannon, *Iroquois Diplomacy on the Early American Frontier*

Isabel Thompson Kelsay, *Joseph Brant, Man of Two Worlds*

Alan Taylor, *The Divided Ground*

Joseph T. Glatthaar and James Kirby Martin, *Forgotten Allies, The Oneida Indians and the American Revolution*

Samuel Kirkland Lothrop, *Life of Samuel Kirkland, Missionary to the Indians*

Richard Berleth, *Bloody Mohawk: the French and Indian War & American Revolution on New York's Frontier*

James E. Seaver, *A Narrative of the Life of Mrs. Mary Jemison*

E. Wilder Spaulding, *New York in the Critical Period 1783–1789*

In addition to the above titles, for help with Kanien'keha, the language of the Mohawk people, I'm indebted to the works of David Kanatawakhon Maracle, *Kanyen'keha Tewatati* and *One Thousand Useful Mohawk Words,* as well as to Kelly DeLisle Johnson, who graciously fielded my questions about her language and provided many more resources besides. I'm grateful to Catherine MacGregor, Catherine-Ann MacPhee, and Iain MacKinnon for their translation of the passage of Gaelic that appears in the story. In the case of both of these beautiful languages, neither of which I speak, any mistakes in their rendering on these pages are mine alone.

It was my mother, Jeanette Puryear Johnson, who related to me the story of my great aunt, who loved to read books as a girl, and my great-grandmother, who hid them. Thanks for passing down that bit of family history, Mom.

My thanks to Pat Iacuzzi, Lynn Leissler, and Debbie Sitter for their feedback about the Mohawk Valley and southern Adirondack setting of the story, and to Pat Iacuzzi as well for reading an early chapter of the work in progress. My other gracious readers of the early chapters were Jim Sitter, Laura Frantz, and J. M. Hochstetler. Thank you all.

And to the writers who frequent the Books and Writers Community online, especially Diana Gabaldon, I couldn't have asked for more gracious mentors over the past fifteen years than you have been. *Thank you* doesn't cover it!

My gratitude to my agent, Wendy Lawton, for her enthusiasm and skill in helping books find homes, and to my editor, Shannon Marchese, who made this a stronger story in so many ways, as did Nicci Hubert and Laura Wright. My appreciation belongs as well to Kendall Davis, Amy Haddock, Lynette Kittle, and the whole WaterBrook Multnomah staff. Kristopher Orr and Mike Heath, I want to hug you both for finding Willa. You made this writer very happy.

Lastly, especially, thank you, Brian, for supporting me and believing in me for…well, we probably shouldn't count how many years it's been. God knows. He also knows that anything I've accomplished as a writer is because of you.

Readers Guide

Heroes and heroic characters abound in _Burning Sky_…

1. Describe Willa Obenchain. How did her years with the Mohawks prepare her for the challenges she faced upon her return to Shiloh? How does she change over the course of the novel?

2. Neil MacGregor and Joseph Tames-His-Horse are very different men, each with their own brand of heroism. Each helps Willa in her time of greatest need. Compare their actions and their heroism. How might the story have unfolded had either man not followed that still small voice in the end?

3. Neil sees himself as one of the "weak things of the world," yet knows he serves a mighty God. Have you ever faced a challenge in which you let God be strong in your weakness?

4. Had Francis Waring lived today, he would undoubtedly be diagnosed based on "his odd ways," as one character describes him. What do you think that diagnosis would be? What was your reaction to this unlikely hero?

5. Anni Keppler is the first to welcome Willa back to Shiloh—a brave act, considering how most frontier settlers viewed anyone suspected of British or Indian sympathy—though at times the person Willa has become is hard for even Anni to accept. What do you think of Anni? Is she a good friend to Willa in the end?

War, and the damage it inflicts upon the soul, is a theme that permeates _Burning Sky_.

1. In the early chapters, Willa is a woman on the brink of giving up, feeling crushed beneath the weight of her losses. What was it about

finding Neil MacGregor that helped her summon the strength to keep living? What does she recognize in him?

2. Contrast Neil's response to brutality with that of Richard Waring or Aram Crane. Do the differences in these men's wartime experiences give clues as to why each became the man we meet in *Burning Sky*? In what ways?

3. Do you think Willa is correct in surmising Colonel Waring is too close to Richard to be objective about the psychological damage his son has suffered? Have you ever failed to see someone clearly because they were close to you?

4. Were you previously aware of the hostility endured by those who didn't declare themselves Patriots during the Revolutionary War? What was the most interesting or surprising thing about this time period you learned from reading this story?

Loss is an inescapable reality of war, as each character in *Burning Sky* experienced.

1. Examine the different types of loss the characters suffered. Do you identify with one character's loss more than others? In what way?

2. Neil's injury-induced dyslexia is crippling to his desire to become a noted botanist, yet God doesn't take away that desire. Looking back on the story, is God's strengthening hand upon Neil visible as he steps out in faith? In what ways? In times of testing, from where do you draw your strength?

3. Willa suffers tremendous loss, including her identity—twice. Much of her journey centers on discovering who she is after these losses. Is she successful in this? Have you ever been forced to redefine yourself after a significant loss?

4. Joseph enters this story nursing a hope but is eventually forced to relinquish it. Have you had to give up a dream or a hope when it

was clearly not part of God's plan for you? What did that teach you about trust? about God's nature?

Home and family, and how one defines them, is another theme of *Burning Sky.*

1. After losing two families, Willa fought hard against accepting Neil and the children into her heart. What is the turning point for her regarding each of them? Can you find a specific scene or moment?

2. Many impediments stood in the way of Joseph's heart's desire, including the traditions of his Iroquois clan and family. Have you had to choose between a cultural or family tradition and pursuing a personal desire?

Glossary

Scots words and dialect

forby — besides, as well

canna — cannot

blethering — blathering

kent — knew

dinna — do not

ken — know

havena — have not

didna — did not

isna — is not

willna — will not

bautie — rabbit

wouldna — would not

verra — very

doesna — does not

hadna — had not

couldna — could not

gomeral — fool, simpleton

braw — brave

bairns — small children, babies

wasna —was not

fash — to fret or make a fuss

wame — stomach

Mohawk words

Onerahtókha — the budding time, April

tohske' wahi — it is so

Kanien'kehá:ka — (Ga-nyen-gay-ha-ga) People of the Flint; the Mohawk, one of the Six Nations of the Iroquois

hen'en — yes

hahnio — come on

Kanien'keha — the Mohawk language

Sekoh — a greeting (say-go)

Onyota'a:ka — People of the Standing Stone; the Oneidas, one of the Six Nations of the Iroquois

Okwhaho — wolf/Wolf Clan, one of the three Mohawk clans, Turtle, Wolf, and Bear

nia:wen — thank you

wa'kenhaten' — I am sorry

yah — No

se'nikònrarak — be careful

aki — ouch!

satahonhsatat — listen

tha'tesato:tat — behave

awiyo — good

Onerahtohko:wa — time of big leaf, May

Ohiari:ha — the time of ripening, June

istah — mother

Ohiarihko:wa — time of much ripening, July

Seskeha — time of freshness, August

Seskehko:wa — time of much freshness, September

About the Author

LORI BENTON was born and raised east of
the Appalachian Mountains, surrounded
by early American and family history
going back to the 1600s. Her novels trans-
port readers to the eighteenth century,
where she brings to life the Colonial and
early Federal periods of American history,
creating a melting pot of characters drawn
from both sides of a turbulent and shifting
frontier, brought together in the bonds of
God's transforming grace.

When Lori isn't writing, reading, or researching eighteenth-century
history, she enjoys exploring the mountains of Oregon with her husband
and their dog.